Policy and Politics in Six Nations

A Comparative Perspective on Policy Making

Stella Z. Theodoulou

California State University, Northridge

Prentice
Hall

Upper Saddle River, NJ 07458

Library of Congress Cataloging-in-Publication Data
Theodoulou, Stella Z.
    Policy and politics in six nations: a comparative perspective on policy making / Stella
Z. Theodoulou.
        p. cm.
    Includes index.
    ISBN 0-13-086603-2
        1. Policy sciences—Case studies.   2. Political planning—Case studies.   3. Comparative
government—Case studies.   I. Title.

H97 .T4 73 2001
320'.6—dc21

2001016310

For Alex
My sunshine and reason for being.

Editorial Director: Laura Pearson
Senior Acquisitions Editor: Heather Shelstad
Assistant Editor: Bryan Prybella
Editorial Assistant: Jessica Drew
Executive Managing Editor: Ann Marie McCarthy
Production Liaison: Fran Russello
Project Manager: Karen Berry/Pine Tree Composition
Prepress and Manufacturing Buyer: Ben Smith
Art Director: Jayne Conte
Cover Designer: Bruce Kenselaar
Director of Marketing: Beth Gillett Mejia

This book was set in 10/12 Berkeley Book by Pine Tree Composition, Inc., and was
printed and bound by Courier Companies, Inc. The cover was printed by Phoenix Color Corp.

 © 2002 by Pearson Education, Inc.
Upper Saddle River, New Jersey 07458

Printed in the United States of America
10 9 8 7 6 5 4 3 2 1

ISBN: 0-13-086603-2

Prentice-Hall International (UK) Limited, *London*
Prentice-Hall of Australia Pty. Limited, *Sydney*
Prentice-Hall Canada Inc., *Toronto*
Prentice-Hall Hispanoamericana, S.A., *Mexico*
Prentice-Hall of India Private Limited, *New Delhi*
Prentice-Hall of Japan, Inc., *Tokyo*
Pearson Education Asia Pte. Ltd., *Singapore*
Editora Prentice-Hall do Brasil, Ltda., *Rio de Janeiro*

Contents

Preface

The study of comparative public policy is relatively new, but in the era of the global economy and the interdependence and connectedness of nations, it is valuable to study policy from a comparative perspective. The problems and issues that face one industrialized nation will eventually materialize in some form or shape in other nations. Thus questions such as why one nation finds it easier than another to pursue a consistent environmental policy or to provide health care through private provision rather than collective are important for students to ponder. The benefit of studying policy comparatively is that it affords students the opportunity of understanding policy issues and concerns through the use of generalizations. The purpose of this text is to provide students with the opportunity for cross-national policy learning. For example, they can learn from the British and Japanese experiences with national health care provision when debating the future direction of health care provision in the United States. Beyond this practical objective of the cross-national learning experience, *Policy and Politics in Six Nations* also seeks to integrate public policy with mainstream comparative politics. Such a perspective attempts to provide the reader with an insight into policy making, which is grounded in a solid appreciation of how nation-state political processes are related and connected to the public policy process.

Policy and Politics in Six Nations emerges from courses that I have developed and taught over the years and from my many discussions with colleagues and students about the problems of understanding public policy in different national settings. Based upon my experience, I strongly believe there is a need for a text that blends an introductory perspective to public policy with a traditional treatment of comparative government and politics.

Finally, I would like to express my thanks and appreciation to the following individuals. To my research assistant, David Goodman, thank you for your extensive work on health and welfare policy. To my editors, thank you for your determination to see this in print. To my office staff, in particular, Cynthia Harris for your tenacity in typing this manuscript, thank you. Elizabeth, thanks for the use of the guest house so I could shut myself away from the world. To Amy and Ed, I can only do what I do because of your support. And finally, but not least, to Marti, thanks for allowing me to be me and you to be you.

Stella Z. Theodoulou
Los Angeles

List of Boxes,
Tables, and Figures

PART I

STUDYING PUBLIC
POLICY FROM
A COMPARATIVE
PERSPECTIVE

Chapter One
The Value and Art of Comparative Public Policy

Although studying policy comparatively is a relatively new endeavor, comparison of social and political phenomenons is not a modern practice; indeed, it is one of the most common human exercises and can be dated back to ancient Greece. One of the first political philosophers to compare and contrast was Aristotle in the fifth century B.C.[1] Aristotle classified Athenian city states according to their form of political rule. The basic tenet of comparison is that others could be different. Two types of comparisons can be undertaken. First, there is descriptive comparison, which attempts to identify differences and similarities between two or more units. The second, analytical comparison, tries to answer why differences and similarities occur between two or more units.

What Is Comparative Public Policy?

How, why, and to what extent different nations pursue particular policies is both interesting and useful in the era of the global economy and the interdependence and connectedness of nations. Comparative public policy is the study of why two or more political systems or governing bodies adopt the public policies they do. Studying policy comparatively provides models and examples that can be used to deal with similar problems and issues in different settings. Those who study policy comparatively are not just interested in the type of policy passed but how the policy is made, how it is delivered and what it achieves. The scope of comparative policy can be cross-national or within one geographical unit or it can look at policy sectors. It has been argued that comparative public policy is, in fact, a method. That is to say, it is a particular way of studying policy.[2]

Comparison may be made between different nations, agencies, and governments with regard to a policy or policies, or comparison can be within one geographical setting over time, for example the American government's environmental policy in 1990 compared to its environmental policy in the year 2000.

The Benefits of Comparison

The main benefit of studying policy comparatively is through assessing one situation against another, one's own situation can be better understood, including constraints and possible options that might be available. Studying how one nation makes policy expands the policy options available to us. Many would argue that it is good to learn from the experiences (negative or positive) of others. Indeed, Martin Harrop argues comparison of different nations' adopted policies allows us to identify the conditions under which certain policies fail or succeed.[3] Comparative public policy has practical benefits. It allows us to see why a particular policy may work in one nation and why not in another or the conditions that are necessary for policy success. Harrop emphasizes this does not mean we ignore that nations may differ from each other, but we should be able to judge which policies are adaptable from setting to setting.[4]

Today the growing interdependence of nations often forces upon us a comparative framework. Certain problems cross over physical borders, so how one nation deals with a "shared" problem provides examples to other nations when it comes time for them to adopt policy strategies to deal with the same problem. Next, studying policy comparatively also helps us understand how similar institutions and political processes operate in different settings; it provides information to answer Harold Lasswell's "who gets what, when and how?" question.

The study of comparative public policy can improve classification schemes of different governments and policy outcomes. And as all social scientists know, classification is a stepping stone to explanation which, in turn, allows us to build theories that then lead to prediction. Essentially, comparison is a fundamental tool of analysis that hones our descriptive abilities. It is through the identification of differences and similarities of cases that better concept formation and operationalization can be achieved. Comparison is intrinsic to explanation and that's what policy researchers and political scientists hope to achieve.

No grand theory prevails in comparative public policy. Most authors agree that diverse perspectives should be integrated into research on policy development and that single-factor deterministic theories should not be solely relied upon. Additionally most comparative policy authors would acknowledge that there are methodological problems very similar to those encountered in the general field of comparative politics. Such problems should be kept in mind when analysis is conducted. Przeworski and Teune refer to such problems as the five major issues of

---

Box 1.1   The Issues of Comparative Methodology

---

1. Is it possible to discover timely comparable measurements of the same phenomena in different nations?
2. Are there appropriate indicators that can serve as usable representatives of general policy concepts?
3. Do the available facts fit more than one theory?
4. Can similar outcomes be achieved through a range of policy instruments, while seemingly similar policies may be associated with quite different results?
5. The context in which action is taken is important to understand, but contexts differ from each other.

---

comparative methodology.[5] The issues which should be acknowledged before any study is undertaken are shown in Box 1.1.

The Art of Comparison

In the following section, the main methods and approaches used over the last forty years to study policy from a systematic comparative perspective will be discussed. The approaches and methods are not mutually exclusive or exhaustive. Indeed several of them can be used in conjunction with each other. It should also be acknowledged that there is much debate over which is the "best" approach or method. Basically, authors select a method and within that method they then take a particular approach.

What Method?

The majority of comparative policy studies fall into one of three categories: case studies, statistical studies, or focused comparisons. It is common for proponents of one method to criticize and negate the other methods. However, in truth, each has its advantages and disadvantages. Often choice is determined by the researcher's interests, resources, and data availability.

The Case Study: Such studies focus upon a single case (an individual policy of one nation) for a stated period. For example, we may look at education policy in Sweden from 1967 to 1997. A case study is of a particular sector in a specific country. When a number of individual case studies are taken together, then comparative analysis can be undertaken. The objective being for authors to use the conclusions reached independently in several nations on the same policy sector so as to be able to derive generalizations that allow explanation elsewhere to be made.

The benefit of utilizing case studies is they provide researchers with a detailed description of generally what is going on and what relationships exist. They tell us how policy is made. Case studies allow us to test deviant cases against a theory built on the study of a number of different cases. The overall benefit of case studies is they provide cross-sectional perspectives on the same policy sector in a number of nations. The main critique of the case study method is that it is too descriptive and not good at answering why something might occur. As Harrop argues case studies are problematic because they accumulate knowledge rather then cumulate it.[6]

The Statistical Study: In this method, researchers use statistical variables to determine whether patterns can be identified as explanations for why and how policy strategies are adopted and policy outcomes achieved. In such studies, data is gathered on social, economic, and political factors. The main advantage to such a study is it usually looks at a large number of nations so as to be statistically significant. Next, it allows for policy outcomes to be categorized and policy styles to be classified.

The problems of such studies are fairly apparent. First, researchers are drawing conclusions based upon numbers and operationalized variables. This negates other nonquantifiable factors, such as culture, that might affect the policy context. The claim has been made that statistical studies are too mechanical. Finally, statistical manipulation of data can lead to unwarranted conclusions and is subject to interpretation that can be questionable.

The Focused Comparison: Such studies fall between the other two discussed methods. Basically, focused comparisons compare a small number of nations or specific policy sectors, for example, environmental policy in Japan and Germany. The strength of such a study is it does not ignore the particulars of each context in which policy is adopted. The major weakness is that if the sample of nations is too small then the explanations can be limited. However, having acknowledged this, sometimes such studies are the most revealing in terms of knowledge and information.

The Approaches

Once a researcher has decided upon the method to be utilized, an approach will be taken. When looking at policy comparatively, it is important to comprehend how the different governments making policy work. Nations' individual institutional arrangements and policy-making processes must be understood. Additionally, the context in which each government makes policy must be looked at. This all necessitates that individual nation's history, culture, and political environment be acknowledged. Keeping this in mind, the literature on comparative public policy shows five major approaches utilized by researchers. Each approach tries to analyze why nations vary in their policy outcomes. Which approach can be judged the "best" depends on the individual researcher's needs, objectives, and values. However, each approach does provide a clear and separate focus.

The Cultural Values Approach: Authors such as Rimlinger use this approach to argue that if we want to understand why particular nations adopt certain policy strategies we should look at a nation's distinctive historical experience.[7] The assumption driving this particular approach is that nations derive specific values which become embodied in their cultures and this then shapes societal attitudes which in turn lend support or opposition to certain kinds of policy. A clear example of this is the value of rugged individualism entrenched in American political culture. Rugged individualism as a cultural value has clearly affected American policy makers' choice of policy in the domestic sphere in areas such as welfare.

The Neo-corporatist Approach: This approach emphasizes that interest representation and its linkages to government through institutionalized bargaining should be looked at in each nation where policy is being analyzed. The assumption behind such an approach is that formulation, adoption, and implementation of policy depend upon the intersection between government and organized power bases behind each issue area. In each policy issue area, there is a continual process of bargaining and negotiation between organized interest blocks and the government. It assumes lines between the public and private sectors are blurred which results in a system of shared responsibilities among major societal actors.[8] Simply put, the state works in close cooperation with major business corporations, labor unions, and other nongovernmental bodies representing groups in society when policy is made. Necessary partnerships are being formed between the state and organized interests and if one wants to understand environmental policy in the countries under analysis then such partnerships should be identified and studied.

The Institutional Approach: Authors such as Weir and Skocpol argue that the nature of the state in each nation under study must be understood if policy strategies are to be understood.[9] Central to this approach is the belief that the state is at the center of the policy process. Policy is the product of those who control the state. The relationship among state, economy, and society takes significantly different forms in different nations, and this affects policy making. The state is an active element in the policy process and only after understanding the nature of each specified state can policy outcomes be understood. Certain states will produce certain policy outcomes because of the way in which state structures and capacities intersect with key societal actors to facilitate the key operating features of the policy making environment.

The Socioeconomic Approach: This approach relies heavily on convergence theory. Such a theory posits all industrial societies are fundamentally similar. They all share a marked decline in political conflict. Public policy is not a consequence of political factors. Eventually, it is the nature of all advanced industrial societies to respond to similar problems with similar policy choices. Essentially all or most advanced industrial societies develop common features. This approach is used by some authors to explain welfare state development in advanced industrial nations.[10] Such authors argue the exigencies of modern technology and advanced economics produce standardized effects upon social structures. In turn, these give uniformity which overrides other factors which may make for policy diversity, such as culture or the structure of the political system. As nations become advanced industrially, they tend to become increasingly comparable in their major institutional arrangements and their social systems generally. It is economic mechanisms rather than political arrangements which determine the role of the state and therefore policy outcomes. Policy outcomes are explained by the primacy of economic factors, such as the need to stabilize wages and prices, and the need for a continual supply of skilled workers, and not political factors.

Convergence theory is a deterministic perspective that emphasizes an end of ideology. Lipset argues that since the 1950s, ideological conflict in advanced democratic societies has declined in intensity.[11] This decline is directly the product of the changing economic structure. As the economic structure changed, it led the working class, who were becoming more affluent, to abandon "left"-wing ideology and become integrated into the mainstream capitalist value system. Also as the problems inherited from the industrial revolution faded or were solved there became no need for ideological cleavage around what was to be done in society. Lipset calls this a post-politics phase.[12] Other authors point to the similarity of programs adopted by political parties in various nations as empirical confirmation of the decline of ideology.[13] What occurred was an absence of policy differences. When changes in government occur through electoral mechanics, it is unlikely to result in substantially different policy outcomes. Marcuse states it is better to argue that what has occurred is not an end of ideology but a transformation of ideology so as to create a false consciousness amongst the working class.[14] It is this which leads them to support policies that cater not to their own but to other classes' well-being.

To sum up this approach it is socioeconomic rather than political factors determining policy outcomes in the modern state. As economies develop and industrialization advances, new economic, social and environmental dislocations are created and government is provided with greater financial resources. The net result is a convergence of national policies and a decline of ideological conflict. As Wilensky posits, it is the level of affluence of a nation which determines its policy choices.[15] As nations develop similar economic growth patterns, they develop similar solutions to policy problems.

The Politics Matters Approach: This approach came about from direct criticism of the socioeconomic approach and its inability to explain why some nations develop certain types of policy earlier than others and why sometimes less advanced nations have more generous spending levels on certain policies then advanced nations do. In short because the socioeconomic approach did not explain adequately why significant policy differences occur. The chief proponent of the politics matters approach is Francis Castles.[16] Castles and his supporters argue that there are distinct differences between affluent liberal democracies, and this is clearly seen in the political choices made by such nations and the policy outcomes that occur. Political factors such as the level of centralization or the dominant ideological position favored by the voters will affect the type of policy strategy chosen by a government. Hibbs argues policies vary with shifts in partisan control of government.[17] Ian Gough argues policies emerge from the competition between business and their need for capital accumulation and workers.[18] Thus, the strength of labor and business will shape the policy agenda.

Basically the authors utilizing this approach took the studies of those advocating the socioeconomic approach and showed that their data did show variations within certain policy areas. In essence, they argue that there are similar policies overall but there are different levels of expenditure and different choices within the policy of where resources are spent. Such authors do not argue economic factors are unimportant, rather they posit that both political and economic factors are complementary explanations of policy outcomes.

The discussion so far has shown there are different methods and approaches used when studying policy from a comparative perspective. However, a common underlying assumption to all the discussed methods and approaches is the belief that we can only learn by assessing different situations against one another. The question remaining is who should be studied and what policies should be compared?

Chapter Two
What Nations and What Policies to Study?

Adam Przeworski and Henry Teune argue there are two general designs that yield different answers to the question of what nation and what policy to study.[1] They discuss studying systems that are either very similar to each other (the most similar design) or very different to each other (the most different design). The most similar design is the most commonly used. Briefly, authors utilizing this design select two or more political systems which for the most part are very similar in respect of the widest possible range of attributes and they attempt to identify whether any differences exist. For example, two nations on the surface may appear to have similar political historical structures and cultures but in fact could have very different policy processes. In this case researchers would be interested in analyzing why the differences occur. In the most different design, two or more nations are selected on their fundamental dissimilarity in as many respects as possible. The objective is to be able to identify any similarities in policy making between essentially different nations. The differences are taken as givens and analysis focuses not on the differences but rather on whether there are similarities. Much of the reasoning behind both of these designs is to avoid what Sartori calls the comparing of stones and rabbits.[2]

Which Nations to Study?

Political scientists may differ in their interests and in which methods and approaches they utilize, but what they do seem to have in common with each other is the belief that their own approach is the most useful. If a survey was conducted asking political scientists to identify which individual nations should be compared, there would be no real consensus. However, there might be some agreement when it came to policy areas to be compared.

It is my contention that which nations and which policies are most worthy for inclusion is a debate that cannot be overcome. The purpose of this text is to introduce readers to the most essential elements of policy making, while allowing for meaningful comparison across countries. The key is to expose readers to different political systems and the context in which public policy is made. Thus, the United States, Great Britain, Sweden, Brazil, Japan, and Germany will be compared across four areas of topical social policy. The objective is to sensitize readers to the specific nation's institutional arrangements and policy outcomes while at the same time allowing some insight into whether differences and similarities do occur.

I am sure some political scientists will argue studying policy areas because they are topical is not sound theoretically. I would agree, but I would also point out that because a problem is topical it does not mean it is any less important or worthy of investigation. It is my hope this text enhances the reader's understanding of inevitably similar social policy problems and the range of possible solutions to them. The problems and issues that face one industrialized nation, for example, in the area of education will eventually materialize in some form or shape in other modern nations. Questions such as why one nation finds it easier than another to pursue a consistent environmental policy or provide extensive health and welfare benefits from public sources are important for us all to ponder. This text's goal is to provide readers with a cross-national policy-learning experience. It is important to understand how some nations have dealt with problems that might be future problems for other nations. Beyond this goal, the text also attempts to integrate mainstream comparative politics with public policy. It is vital that readers understand the institutional and political arrangements of a nation if they want to understand that nation's policy-making process and its policy outcomes. Thus, this text will look at each nation's political development and processes.

Keeping in mind the question of do you look at the most similar or the most different nations, the inclusion of Brazil in this text will be problematic for many political scientists. The question for them will be whether the United States, Great Britain, Sweden, Japan, and Germany are really comparable to Brazil. Those who question the inclusion of Brazil do so on the grounds that it does not qualify as an advanced nation and that its democratic status remains more then somewhat precarious. They argue Brazil has only become affluent recently and has experienced more years of non-democratic rule than democratic rule in the post–World-War-II period. It has a weak record of public sector intervention, an absence of economic development on a scale comparable to other advanced industrial nations, and finally a lack of democratic institutions. Basically some argue that Brazil is an emerging market that is a transitional democracy rather than an advanced industrialized democratic nation.[3] I would not disagree with this characterization of Brazil; however, I do disagree with the notion Brazil cannot be compared to the other nations in the text. My contention is that there is enough in common to make comparison possible while at the same time sufficient differences exist to make the comparison interesting and worthwhile.

The six nations were chosen because they do represent degrees of industrialization and democratization. I am interested in seeing if differences occur between durable market democracies and transitional market democracies. A durable market democracy is an industrialized nation that has had at least forty years of uninterrupted democratic practice and where conflicts within society are played out within democratic institutions and according to the rules of the democratic political game. The United States, Great Britain, Germany, Japan, and Sweden qualify as durable democracies. The rules of democracy have been achieved, refined, tested, and strengthened through years of practice. A transitional democracy is a nation whose democratic institutions are fragile and unreliable. Societal conflicts are likely to involve disputes about existing democratic institutions and also the desirability of the institutions themselves. It is less certain that groups will play by the democratic rules or accept decisions arrived at under the rules. Finally, civil society is less developed. Brazil qualifies as a transitional democracy.

In addition to being characterized as varieties of democracies, all six nations are industrialized and relatively affluent. The World Bank categorizes all of the nations with the exception of Brazil as high-income nations. Brazil is classified as an upper-middle income nation. Currently Brazil is ranked as the world's eighth-largest economy. Brazil can be compared because it has basic attributes in common.[4] Francis Castles notes that similar arguments as those that can be used against Brazil's inclusion were used twenty years ago when some authors included the new democracies of Greece, Portugal, and Spain in comparative policy studies.[5] However, recent studies of such nations have focused upon how policy outcomes are comparable with those of other advanced Western nations.

Basically this text presents multiple policy case studies with the majority of analysis focused upon the individual cases and then on comparisons between them. It is a comparative case study of four policy sectors. The policy sectors were chosen because they are typical of the range of activities performed by modern democratic states in the social policy area. The policy sectors discussed in the text are all high profile and rapidly evolving. They are of import to policy making in industrialized democracies.

The objective is to account for policy development in each national setting. Actual policy will be traced historically and its structure and organization focused upon. Given the vast size and complexity of the four policy sectors and the amount of activity of different levels of government over the last fifty years, obviously a study like this one cannot pretend to give the complete picture of policy activity in the six nations. Rather this study is confined to the main features, laws, and regulations in the four policy sectors in Brazil, Germany, Great Britain, Japan, Sweden, and the United States.

Industrial policy is not discussed and many will lament its omission as it is a traditional area that has motivated so many scholars to study policy comparatively. However, the choice of policy areas in the text is driven by the desire to convey to readers how different industrialized nations deal with common social issues and problems.

The Plan of the Text

In this section, the comparative method and its approaches have been introduced. In the next section, each nation's political development, governmental setting and policy processes will be discussed. The objective in this section is to provide readers with the knowledge that it is essential to understand institutional and political processes and arrangements so as to comprehend specific policies in a given nation. Part Three of the text deals with the four specific policy sectors. Each chapter will discuss not only the theoretical discourse surrounding the area, but also the evolution of policy, the level of state intervention, the policy agenda, the actors, and the policy outcomes within each nation. The final section of the text will attempt to slow the linkage between politics and policy through discussion of the differences and similarities in the six nations.

Suggested Further Readings

F. Castles, *Comparative Public Policies* (Cheltenham: Edward Elgar, 1998).

M. Harrop (ed.), *Power and Policy in Liberal Democracies* (Cambridge: Cambridge University Press 1993).

A.J. Heidenheimer, H. Heclo, C.T. Adams, *Comparative Public Policy* (New York: St. Martin's, 1990).

M. McCool, *Public Policy Theories, Models, and Concepts* (Englewood Cliffs: Prentice Hall, 1995).

D. Stone, *Policy Paradox: The Art of Political Decision Making* (New York: Norton Co., 1997).

S.Z. Theodoulou and M. Cahn, *Public Policy, The Essential Readings* (Englewood Cliffs: Prentice Hall, 1995).

PART II

THE NATIONS

National Profiles

	Brazil	Germany	GB	Japan	Sweden	US
Population						
Population (millions)	171,853,126	82,087,361	59,113,439	126,182,077	8,911,296	272,878,000
Population Growth (%)	1.5	0.01	0.24	0.24	0.12	0.85
Urban Population (as % of total pop)	80	87	89	79	83	77
Population aged 65 and above (as % of total)	5	16	16	17	17	12
Economy						
GDP (U.S. $ trillions)	1.04	1.74	1.242	3.08	176.2 (billion)	8.083
Real Growth Rate (%)	3	2.4	3.5	0.9	2.1	3.8
GDP per capita (U.S. $)	6,300	20,800	21,200	24,500	19,700	30,200
GDP-Composition by Sector (%)						
Agriculture	14	1.1	1.5	2	2.2	2
Industry	36	33.1	31.5	38	30.5	23
Services	50	65.8	67.0	60	67.3	78
Exports (as % of GDP)	7.4	26.8*	28.7*	11.1*	43.8*	12.1*
Imports (as % of GDP)	10.1	25.3*	29.2*	9.9*	36.8*	13.5*
Central Governments Revenues (billions)	151	977	487.7	407	109.4	1.722 (trillions)
Central Government Expenditures (billions)	149	1.024 (trillions)	492.6	771	146.1	1.653 (trillions)
Debt (billions)	258.1	N/A	N/A	N/A	66.5	802
Budget Deficit (as % of GDP)	-6.1	-0.9	0.6	2.0	-1.6	0.9
Inflation rate (%)	5	1.8	3.1	1.7	2	2
Industrial production growth rate ($)	4.5 (1997)	5	1.0	-5	4.4	3.6

Society

Death Rate (per 1,000 people)	8.79	10.76	10.64	8.12	10.77	8.8
Life expectancy (years)	64.06	77.17	77.37	80.11	79.29	79.67
Birth rate (per 1,000 people)	20.4	8.7	11.9	10.5	12.0	14.3
Fertility rate (births per women)	2	1.26	1.71	1.48	1.83	2.03
Infant mortality rate (per 1,000 live births)	35.4	5.11	5.8	4.1	3.9	6.3
Under 5 mortality rate (per 1,000 children)	40	6	7	5	5	9
Child malnutrition (% of children under 5)	6	N/A	N/A	3	N/A	1*
Adult literacy (as % of total pop)	84	99	99	99	99	95
Unemployment rate (%)	7	12	5.5	3.4	6.6	4
Labor force (millions)	59.1	38.7	28.2	67.23	4.5	136.3
Population below poverty line (as % of total pop)	20	N/A	17	N/A	N/A	13
Personal computers (per 1,000 people)	30	305	263	237	361	459
World Bank Income Ranking	Upper Middle	High	High	High	High	High
Human Development Index Ranking (out of 174 nations)	74 Medium	14 High	10 High	9 High	6 High	3 High

All data for 1999 except * which is for 1997/98.

Chapter Three
Brazil

Twenty-first-century Brazil is a transitional democracy facing multiple challenges in its drive to consolidate its relatively new political structure. The nation is one of the world's largest countries and also one of the most populous. These factors in combination with the weakness of its democratic institutions and its decentralized and highly fragmented political order pose serious problems for politicians and have far-reaching ramifications for the policy-making process.

The population of Brazil is not only very large but also extremely diverse. Brazil is a society of racial and ethnic complexity with social conditions stemming from the country's early years as a plantation society. In spite of government-initiated changes boosting industrialization and economic diversification, there are despairing inequalities in the distribution of wealth and power. However, Brazil enters the twenty-first century as the most industrialized nation in South America. The economy is rapidly modernizing and its population is largely urban. Indeed 80 percent of its citizens live in the major urban centers of the country.[1] Urbanization is a relatively new phenomenon. Until the 1960s, the majority of Brazilians lived in rural areas. Most of the country's land and resources are still controlled by a small wealthy elite while the majority of the population lives in poverty.[2] One of the consequences of this rapid urbanization is the extensive slums and shanty towns on the outskirts of each of the larger cities. Such areas are inhabited by rural migrants who have been enticed to the city by the promise of employment.

The Political Setting

Brazilian politics is shaped by its quest for economic and social development. Many authors view the country as a model for state-led development.[3] Since the 1930s, the Brazilian state has felt compelled to intervene in the domestic economy, because of the effect of external economic crises. Mechanisms such as protection, subsidies, and import substitution have been commonly utilized by the Brazilian state. Brazil's early economic development was based on export-led growth of agricultural products and minerals. The world depression of the 1930s led the Brazilian state to diversify its economy through industrialization with the state heavily participating in key sectors of the economy. By 1990, the Brazilian state was the major participant in some of the country's largest industries.[4] During the 1990s, because of external economic crises such as the instability of Asian stock markets, the Brazilian government reduced the level of direct intervention in the economy. By 1995, Brazil ranked among the World Bank's upper-middle-income countries.[5] However, at the same time Brazil's foreign debt was more than $159 billion, one of the highest in the world.[6] Inflation, by 1990, was 5,000 percent, falling to around 20 percent in 1996.[7] Today inflation hovers at around 5 percent.[8]

Modern Brazilian Political Development

Politically, Brazil has seen cycles of democratic suspension. Achieving independence in 1822 in a relatively peaceful process, the monarchy was established and lasted until the creation of the republic in 1889. Wealthy landowners in the southeast dominated the republic until the revolution of 1930, which eventually established a military-backed dictatorship. The 1930 revolution came on the heels of plummeting coffee prices and put into power Getúlio Vargas, whom many credit with changing the shape of Brazilian politics for the rest of the century.[9] Vargas's provisional revolutionary government launched a massive industrialization program and centralized all political power in the national government, placing strict controls on the regional governments.

Under Vargas in the early 1930s, a state corporatist model of government was implemented. All groups were organized in state-sponsored associations, and demands upon the state by societal actors were answered in a controlled manner by the government. Citizen participation was limited to mobilization within state-created and state-regulated unions and professional associations. State corporatism rejects the notion of competition amongst groups. For example, if steel workers demanded a wage increase, it was a state agency that would determine the level of increase and how the employers would pay it.[10] In 1937, as elections were to be held, a coup led by Vargas took power and established his dictatorial rule. Through a series of "reforms" and mandates the Estado Novo (New State) was established. Basically, the reforms were a consolidation of the state corporatist model. Vargas ruled with the backing of the land-owning elite, the military, the urban working and middle classes, and politicians who had been excluded from power under the old republic. The industrialization policy of the early 1930s continued in conjunction with protectionist policies, and Vargas passed a series of social policy reforms aimed at keeping his urban workers' support base. The Estado Novo was, without doubt, authoritarian and Vargas a dictator who squashed all representative bodies.[11]

As the Second World War took hold, more and more of the working and middle classes mobilized to place pressure on Vargas to democratize. He scheduled elections for 1943 but postponed them on the condition that presidential elections be held in 1945 in which he would be ineligible to run. Fearing that Vargas would once again postpone the election, a group of military officers staged a coup in October 1945 and forced Vargas to resign. This ushered in a new era of mass politics and the creation of a new government under Enrico Dutra. President Dutra did not make any major changes in the political system but did withdraw government support for industrialization. Vargas returned to power in the election of 1950. He interpreted his victory as a mandate to return to his past policies. The country soon came to a political impasse, and there was government deadlock. Fearing defeat, Vargas committed suicide in 1954. The next ten years saw political and economic instability with the nation's economic and social problems building.

By 1961, Brazil had descended into political chaos and was under the leadership of President João Goulart. Goulart was perceived by many Brazilians, including the military, as a Communist sympathizer who was determined to take Brazil too far to the left. The fear of communism and the gradual disintegration of the economy led to the military coup in 1964.[12] The military took power with two primary objectives. First, they wanted to eradicate the left; and second, they wanted to rebuild the collapsed economy. Gullermo O'Donnell labels the type of government installed in Brazil in 1964 as bureaucratic authoritarian.[13] Such a regime emerges in response to an economic breakdown or severe crisis and is led by the military and key civilian allies, such as economists, engineers, and bureaucrats. The military remained in power until 1985 and ruled with repressive methods. At certain times, they were more repressive in their methods than at others, although at all times all opposition or criticism of the regime was silenced.[14]

Coinciding with repression was a period of economic growth, which has come to be known as the Brazilian Miracle. Brazil grew faster than any other economy in the world and moved away from coffee as its main export to the manufacture and export of other goods. Billions of foreign dollars poured into the country and were invested in those sectors considered critical for development. By 1974 increased criticism of the military and the political order they had established led to gradual reforms allowing limited political organization and electoral participation.[15] It was minor reform not a radical liberalization.[16] Over the next ten years, the opposition led by the Brazilian Democratic Movement (MDB) began to force more and more liberalization (*abertura*) through electoral victories. At the same time that the political system was transitioning to democracy, the economy started to falter. The net result was the removal of the liberalization process from the military's hands and its capture by organizations within civil society.

By the 1980s, the economy was in severe recession. Brazilian foreign debt was more than $100 billion, the largest in the world, and inflation was out of control. The failure of the so-called Brazilian Miracle intensified societal criticism of the military regime and widespread street demonstrations demanded a direct popular election for a new president. In 1984, the widespread social disorder led to the election of Brazil's first civilian president since 1964, Trancredo Neves. Neves died unexpectedly before he took office and his vice president, José Sarney, was sworn in as president.[17]

The newly elected Sarney civilian government faced two immediate challenges: the recessed economy and consolidation of the new democratic regime. Sarney was not particularly favored by many liberals. He was distrusted because of his close ties to the old military rulers. His government was weak and involved in conflicts with the church, the unions, businesses, and overseas investors. Inflation in 1985 was approximately 300 percent, and foreign debt was mounting. In a last-ditch effort to stabilize the economy, Sarney introduced the Cruzado Plan in February 1986. All prices and wages were frozen and in a short space of time inflation ground to a standstill. This allowed Sarney's government a short period of popularity, which soon came to an end when prices and wages were unfrozen in December 1986. The year 1987 saw inflation explode and foreign debt payments drain the country of all capital. The government had no choice but to implement an economic austerity program. Additionally many Brazilians were dissatisfied with what they perceived to be their government's failure to dismantle authoritarian models of policy making, corporatist institutions, and military influence. In order to halt the growing lack of confidence in the new democratic regime, the legislature drafted a new constitution that went into effect in October 1988. The new constitution remedied previous institutional arrangements through reconstructing the republic.

In 1989, the first election after the new constitution's drafting, 80 million Brazilians voted Fernando Collor de Mello President. Collor immediately implemented an economic program with the objective of decreasing inflation. The program failed to contain inflation which reached 1,500 percent in 1991. Under Collor the Brazilian state also started to cut back its role in the economy and protectionist trade policies were dismantled. Collor's presidency was brought to an abrupt end by charges of influence peddling and corruption. He was impeached in September 1992 and was succeeded by his vice president Itamar Franco, who served out the last two years of Collor's term with little impact.

In the 1990s, Brazil worked hard at reestablishing its democratic institutions. The move to democracy was consolidated by the election of one of Latin America's most prominent intellectuals, Fernando Henrique Cardoso, as president in 1994. Cardoso's victory was the largest victory in forty years of Brazilian electoral politics. The first two years of his government witnessed fundamental legislative reforms. Such reforms resulted in massive reduction of the state's involvement in the economy. Cardoso introduced a privatization program which sold off many of the state's enterprises. For example, the government telecommunications monopoly was broken up. Cardoso also eliminated restrictions on foreign corporate investment in Brazil. Additionally, government expenditure was cut across the board and land reform and redistribution was initiated. By 1997, revitalization of the economy had slowed once again because of external economic crises such as the collapse of the Asian stock markets and Russia's default of its foreign debts. Cardoso had no alternative but to introduce an austerity program.

In spite of a faltering economy, Cardoso won reelection in 1998 for a second four-year presidential term. Cardoso immediately set about reviving the economy by securing a $41.5 billion loan package from the International Monetary Fund (IMF). In return for the loan, Cardoso introduced legislation to cut government spending, and restrict the taxation and social security systems. Currently Cardoso pursues stringent economic measures, such as devaluation of Brazilian currency against the U.S. dollar. His objective is to lower the cost of Brazilian goods in overseas markets, thereby making Brazilian exports attractive. Such policy should result in an increased flow of foreign cash into Brazil.

Brazil in the year 2000 is a society with marked inequities. Such inequities exist between the urban and rural areas, between regions, and between socioeconomic classes. There are inequalities in access to wealth, education, health care, and basic services such as water, sewage, and electricity. In 1998, the wealthiest 20 percent of the population received 63 percent of the country's income, while the poorest 50 percent earned 12 percent.[18] The gap between rich and poor is among the most substantial in the world. Policy makers face a whole army of pressing social problems. Despite the size of the economy, growth of almost four percent in 2000 and the level of economic development, poverty, hunger, disease, and general inadequacy of modern services prevail. Urbanization has compounded such problems with overcrowding and lack of suitable housing. The numbers migrating to the cities outpace the growth of the job market and the level of urban services needed to survive. Brazilian cities are characterized by slums, shanty towns, and homelessness, especially among children and teens. Rurally, the population fares no better and indeed many of the problems discussed earlier are even more acute in the countryside.

The Governmental Setting

A republic since 1889 that has always been categorized as a federal system, the Brazilian state has seen substantial changes in its governmental institutions and their functioning over the years. The discussion earlier showed how democratic government was suspended for periods of time and military rule under a series of presidents was established.

Before the distinct elements of Brazil's government are detailed, we should first acknowledge some basic generalizations about the state's organization. First, Brazil is a presidential system of government. Next, the church and state are officially separated. Third, the federal structure is decentralized. The twenty-six states, created by the 1988 constitution are divided into five thousand municipalities. This allows for substantial patronage systems of considerable influence. Such decentralization has led to fragmentation. The president and congress may have the authority to legislate on matters, but state and local governments have total authority over how legislation is implemented.

The Constitution

Since its founding as a republic, five constitutions have been implemented. The constitution of 1988 is currently in operation and breaks with certain legacies from the past. It is responsible for shaping Brazilian politics as we enter the new millennium. It was the 1988 constitution framers' hope that the new constitution would bring about a more democratic state where exercise of state power and authority would be restrained. To this end, they decreased the executive's influence, strengthened the fiscal base of regional governments through increased tax revenues, extended the powers of the national legislature, and tightened civil and political rights. From 1988 on, the republic comprises twenty-six federated states and one federal district. The constitution shifted substantial responsibility to state and local governments, especially in the area of funding. Today regional governments have considerable authority over their internal affairs. Under the 1988 constitution, equality for all citizens under the law is guaranteed. The constitution gave the national legislature (the National Congress) considerable powers to counter those of the executive (president). Finally, it eliminated the indirect mechanism for election of the president and established universal suffrage. All citizens sixteen years or older can vote by secret ballot in elections for president, congress, state governors, and state legislators. Voting is compulsory for eighteen- to seventy-year-old individuals who are literate, and voting is optional for those who are illiterate, over seventy, or sixteen to eighteen years of age.

In recent years, many argue that the 1988 constitution, although attempting to consolidate democracy, has hindered institutional performance and political and economic reform.[19] Rather than creating a coherent system of checks and balances based on a clear and strict separation of powers, such as utilized by the United States, the constitution created an ill-defined separation of powers and unclear lines of authority between the institutions and levels of government.

The Executive

The Brazilian president is both head of state and head of government. In order to be elected, a candidate must receive an absolute majority of the popular vote. If no candidate does so on the first ballot, then a second ballot is conducted and the candidate with the majority is elected.[20] Presidential terms are four years. A 1997 constitutional amendment allows the president to run for a successive second term. Brazilian presidents appoint their own cabinet and are advised by a presidential council. The council consists of fourteen members, including the vice president, the minister of justice, the presidents of the two chambers of the National Congress, the majority and minority leaders of both congressional chambers, two individuals elected by the senate, two individuals elected by the chamber of deputies, and two appointed by the president.

The Brazilian president is, for many Brazilians, the supreme authority. Indeed how citizens view and rate the overall effectiveness of government is based upon their perception of the individual president. With the 1997 constitutional amendment allowing presidents to run for a successive second term, in the new century popular elections will be a test of presidential performance.

In keeping with the desire to democratize, the 1988 constitution refines presidential power. Thus, presidential appointments are now subject to congressional approval, the presidential budget may be reviewed by the National Congress and executive decrees no longer exist. Presidents do have emergency powers, which allow them to pass thirty-day emergency measures (*medidas provisórios*). At the end of the thirty days, the congress can pass or reject the measures. In reality, emergency measures have not been a constraint on presidential exercise of power; rather, presidents from Collor on have used them extensively. Each time such powers were assumed, presidents used economic crisis as the prevailing reason for their exercise. One author cites Collor as using such presidential discretionary powers almost every forty-eight hours.[21] Indeed Collor passed more than 150 emergency laws in his first year of office. Rather than being a restraint, presidential emergency powers have led to more than 80 percent of all legislation originating in the executive branch.[22]

Brazilian presidents also have immense power over the bureaucracy, especially at the higher levels. Presidents can hire and fire at their own initiative. The one area where presidential appointment power is restrained is the appointment of cabinet officers responsible for economic policy. In this case, the president must consult with congress, the trade unions, and business associations before an appointment can be made.

In addition to the presidential council, the minister of economy and planning holds considerable influence over the president. This is partly because of the nation's economic condition but also because of the authority that the position embodies. The ministry of economy is the most powerful executive agency outside of the presidency and has control of the federal budget and responsibility for economic policy making. In many ways, the minister of economy is the equivalent to a prime minister in a parliamentary system of government. Many would argue Cardoso's success electorally is largely because of the performance of Havre Franco as the minister of economy.[23] Finally a national defense council advises the president on defense and sovereignty issues.

The Legislature

Brazil's legislature, the National Congress (*Congresso Nacional*) is a "balanced bicameral" national legislature. That is to say, one house does not clearly dominate the other. The National Congress consists of the Federal Senate (*Senado Federal*) and the Chamber of Deputies (*Camara do Deputados*). Elections to both houses take place simultaneously. The senate comprises eighty-one members: three from each of Brazil's twenty-six states and three from the federal District of Brazil. Each senator is elected by majority rule to serve eight-year terms: one-third are elected after a four-year period, two-thirds elected after the next four-year period. The Chamber of Deputies' 513 members are elected for four-year terms by a system of proportional representation. The size of each state's delegation is related to its population size; however, the constitution establishes a minimum of eight deputies and a maximum of seventy deputies for each of the twenty-six states. In reality this has led to over-representation of certain states. In 1998, the nine least-populated states elected 72 deputies even though they represented approximately 6.5 percent of the population. This was roughly equal to the same number as São Paulo State, where 20 percent of the population lives. This has become a major point of criticism leveled at Brazil's system of representation.

Today congress is responsible for all matters within the twenty-six states and the federal district of Brasilia, and the municipalities. This includes initiation of fiscal and budgetary matters, international treaties, national, regional, and local planning, and matters dealing with the armed forces and territorial limits. Additionally, congress can review the presidential budget, approve or reject emergency measures and override presidential vetoes. It also has considerable oversight powers, and thus, can initiate investigations, public hearings, and summon ministers of government to report before them at any given time.

The Judiciary

The Brazilian legal system is based upon Roman law. The structure of the Brazilian judiciary is that of a network of state courts and a system of federal courts. The states administer their own judicial systems whereby municipal judges and justices of the peace deals with minor criminal matters. The principal judicial institution is the Supreme Federal Tribunal, which is located in Brasilia and consists of eleven judges appointed for life terms by the president and confirmed by the senate. All appointments to the Supreme Federal Tribunal are made by the president and are subject to senate approval. Each state and the federal district of Brasilia have a Regional Federal Tribunal consisting of seven judges appointed for life. Labor, the military, and the electoral system also have their own specialized tribunals. The Supreme Federal Tribunal is equivalent to the U.S. Supreme Court and is the final appellate court. The state courts are headed by the Regional Federal Tribunals. Penal codes govern the powers of judges, and this inhibits the courts from making broad interpretations of the law.

In theory, the judiciary is independent of the executive; however, in reality this has not always been the case. Indeed, in times of authoritarianism, the Brazilian judiciary has been dictated to by the executive. Judicial review of presidential emergency measures has been something that is used rarely to challenge presidential initiatives.

In recent years, the judiciary has been heavily criticized for being corrupt and negligent of its responsibilities. The charge is particularly made of the rural court system that many see as the instrument of the powerful landowning class. The urban courts have also been heavily criticized for their reluctance to defend the nation's children. As evidence for this charge, critics cite the low prosecution rates for child prostitution, child pornography, and the killing of street children. All attempts to reform the judiciary have met with little governmental support. Compounding the judicial system's problems is the high level of police corruption and involvement in crime.

The Bureaucracy

As in so many other industrialized nations, in the post-1945 period, the Brazilian bureaucracy has grown tremendously in size and power. This has led to serious questioning of its role in Brazilian society. Even the military grew quite wary of the bureaucracy's size and power. The last military president, Figuerido, in the mid-1980s created a specific ministry to reduce the size of the bureaucracy.[24] Where the bureaucracy's power has grown is through the key role it has taken in economic and political development. The bureaucracy operates and controls both state firms and semi-public ones, often incurring financial debt and projects without authority from central government.

Much of the way in which the Brazilian bureaucracy operates is based on clientalism. Thus, bureaucrats often advance and protect the interests of their particular sectors rather then society's interest as a whole. With privatization some of the bureaucratization of politics in Brazil has grown weak. However, the Brazilian bureaucracy's size has not been dramatically reduced.

State and Local Government

There are twenty-six state governments and the federal district of Brasilia. Each state has a governor and a legislature. Governors are elected for four-year terms for a maximum of two successive terms. Each state is then divided into municipalities (*municipios*), which have an urban seat and a rural region. There are five thousand such municipalities with great variations in population size and geographical mass. For example, nearly two-thirds of municipalities have twenty thousand or smaller populations, while the municipalities of São Paulo have more than nine million people. Each municipality is administered by a mayor and a council who deal with local taxation, planning, and all basic services. The federal government is heavily responsible for the areas of education, health, and infrastructure.

Political Parties

Parties in Brazil are generally weak because of their inability to develop clear ideological positions. Their individual bases of support are incoherent and fluid. This will prove problematic for democratic consolidation because political parties are a crucial agent of representation and interest aggregation. Party identification is practically non-existent among the voting public. Rather Brazilian parties represent regional or sectional interests or serve as personal instruments of political leaders. Data show that nearly 60 percent of the electorate expresses no party identification.[25] Party membership is even weaker with very few Brazilians being card-carrying members of political parties.[26]

In the early 1980s, Brazil moved to a multi-party system. Such a system allows for parties to be formed and reorganized relatively simply. This system replaced the 1965 military-established two-party system.[27] Most of the parties that emerged in the 1980s had their roots in political parties of the pre-1964 military regime. Today the major parties are the Brazilian Social Democratic Party, the Liberal Front Party, and the Brazilian Labor Party. Additionally seventeen other parties hold seats in the Chamber of Deputies. In congress, party discipline hardly exists and congresspersons follow their own dictates. It is also very common for elected representatives of one party to switch parties often. Indeed, during some periods large numbers of elected officials change parties at the same time.[28]

Interest Groups

Until the end of military rule, interest groups were controlled or coordinated by the Brazilian government. This was an endemic feature of the corporatist model installed by Vargas. Starting with liberalization and now during the consolidation of democracy, interest groups have regained a certain level of autonomy. Interest groups such as the left wing of the Catholic church, business lobbies, agrarian groups, and trade unions are all critical to the government's social and economic policies. Today an impressive number of groups are active in Brazilian civil society because the basic functions and policies of government simply do not reach the majority of Brazilians. It is common to see Brazilians taking to the streets led by their particular group leadership to protest. Interest groups are an integral actor in policy making and as such will be discussed in the next section.

The Policy-Making Process

Over the years, there has been considerable change in the way policy is made and implemented in Brazil. These changes range from shifts in power and authority to limits on what government, at both the national and state levels, can and cannot do. The 1988 constitution attempts to control the tendency of the Brazilian state to centralize power and authority, and this has had an effect on the policy process in terms of where policy is formulated, adopted, and then implemented. The increased fiscal base of state and local governments in the late 1980s and early 1990s has removed many of the constraints on state government in terms of formulating and implementing policy. In 1998, Brazil's state and local governments received more than 60 percent of the country's main tax revenues.[29] This compares to just over 50 percent in 1992 and 20 percent in 1980.[30]

Congress is no longer a passive actor in the policy process. Today it initiates legislation, rejects or approves of presidential emergency measures, and through its fiscal power of review can ultimately impose itself on the policy choices of the president. This does not mean that the president is constrained in terms of policy initiation. Rather the president still has wide-ranging powers with which to frame policy and influence the policy-making process, but now he is subject to investigation and review. The invoking of emergency measures is rarely challenged, although congressional approval is required, and has been a major way for presidents to bypass congressional consent for a policy. In a seven-year period (1988 to 1999) only eighteen presidential emergency measures were rejected by congress.[31]

The major characteristic of the policy process in Brazil is clientelism. From agenda setting to implementation undue influence is asserted by societal and political actors. This is perhaps an inevitable legacy of the days of bureaucratic corporatism. Extensive and overlapping networks linking the executive, key senators and deputies, bureaucratic agencies and sectional interests dominate the Brazilian policy process. Cardoso refers to these networks as bureaucratic rings. He argues that because of the highly fragmented and permeable nature of the Brazilian state, special sectional interests align themselves to bureaucrats and shape public policy so as to benefit themselves. Bureaucrats enter into these alliances not only to safeguard their own agency survival but also for what rewards it may bring them when they are no longer employed by the state. Cardoso concludes that few policies can be successfully implemented without the resources and support of these bureaucratic rings. One only has to look at many of the large development projects initiated in the last two decades as evidence of the role of bureaucratic rings. Such projects brought lucrative rewards and benefits to government officials who controlled their jurisdiction, to private contractors who built them, and to politicians and bureaucrats who received kick backs of both a financial and political nature.[32]

Organized business as opposed to labor has consistent access to and influence on the policy process. Brazilian business associations are separate from political parties and have no close ties to the state. Business lobbies are regularly responsible for electing candidates into office. They also clearly patronize certain bureaucrats extensively. In this manner they are clearly also participants in the bureaucratic rings. Their influence is most clearly seen in economic policy making, where no policy is passed without sufficient input and in many cases backing of business groups, such as the Federation of São Paulo Industries. Labor has failed to become part of the formal policy negotiation process with the state and business interests. There is little reconciliation between the interests of labor and business and thus collective bargaining with state mediation is unfamiliar to Brazilian policy making.

Once policy has been implemented in Brazil, the process of compromise and bargaining, which is so evident at other stages of the policy process elsewhere, intensifies. There is constant negotiation over how policies can be sidelined or interpreted. There is also little oversight of implementation, and policy evaluation is really not conducted. Thus, policy implementation is highly politicized and policies are constantly being molded once they are put into practice.

Some authors describe the policy-making process in Brazil as fluid and ambiguous with clear policy domain demarcation.[33] It may be difficult to pinpoint who mobilizes issues, or how agendas are set, or how policy is formulated, but it is possible to see whose domain a particular policy area falls under. Without a doubt, the executive branch controls foreign and military policy, while the bureaucracy is heavily in command in social and economic policy making.

Chapter Four
Federal Republic of Germany

Early in the twenty-first century, "new" Germany is coming to terms with the consequences of reunification and its implications for policymaking. Since unification in October 1990, Germany has suffered inevitable social and economic disruption. The immediate years following unification were about the process of reuniting West Germany and East Germany and dealing with its immediate aftermath. A decade later, the problems are somewhat different. Economic prosperity has not been extended from the Western to the Eastern states. Indeed some authors would argue living standards in the Eastern states are far below the Western states and actually not much above the levels of the East's previous communist regime.[1] Many Germans would contend reunification has not brought what it initially promised. Thus, frustration is common; some East Germans loudly complain about being shut out of the "new" Germany's economic and political leadership while their West German counterparts argue how the Eastern states are a heavy economic burden upon the West. However, evidence suggests that over time, differences in political and social attitudes are disappearing.[2] Still tensions persist today, and they affect both politics and policy making. How these tensions and the problems they produce are handled will be the principal challenge facing the German polity in the next decade. Before we look at the new reunified Germany, it is beneficial to understand the divided Germany of 1945 to 1990.

The Political Setting

In February 1945, at the Potsdam Conference, the Allied Powers divided the soon-to-be defeated Nazi Germany into four military occupation zones.[3] The city of Berlin was also divided into four zones. Remaining territory was administered and later absorbed by either Poland, France, or the Soviet Union.[4] In the immediate years following the division, tensions between the Allied Powers grew, and it soon became obvious that a common occupation policy was impossible. France, the United States, and Britain objected to what they perceived as a communist state and society in the Eastern zone.[5] The three Western Allies moved in 1948 to ensure that communism be isolated to the Eastern zone and combined their three zones of occupation into one.[6] It was also an attempt to establish the start of German self-government in the Western zone.[7] On May 23, 1949, the Federal Republic of Germany (FRG), known as West Germany, was established. In October of the same year, the Soviets officially transformed the Eastern zone into communist East Germany or the German Democratic Republic (GDR).[8] Theoretically both the FRG and GDR were nation-states; however, in reality neither was fully sovereign. The FRG deferred in foreign policy and international relations to the United States, while the GDR adhered to the Soviet Union's dictates.

The FRG was to be a capitalist liberal democracy, while the GDR was to have a Soviet-style communist socioeconomic and political order with a dominant communist party loyal to Moscow. Germany was clearly divided into two very different political systems. Neither was indigenously created, rather they were installed by the two "superpowers." Neither nation demonstrated complete support for the newly established regime. However, most people in each of the Germanies accommodated themselves to the "new" system.[9] The two Germanies were not equal to each other in respect to land mass, population size, or resources. The GDR suffered in every respect. This disparity was exacerbated by the FRG's receipt of Marshall Plan funds. (The Marshall Plan was responsible for large-scale economic investment in the reconstruction of Western European economies after the Second World War.) Both the FRG and the GDR went through distinct stages of development leading up to the events of reunification in 1990.

Modern German Political Development: The FRG 1949 to 1990

Unification was preceded by three distinct stages. The first stage, from 1949 to 1969, took place under the leadership of Chancellors Konrad Adenauer (1949 to 1963), Ludwig Erhard (1963 to 1966) and Kurt Georg Kiesinger (1966 to 1969). All three were members of the Christian Democratic Union (CDU).[10] In this stage, the following arrangements were introduced and established: a parliamentary system of government, a welfare state, government regulation of the economy, and decentralization of governmental responsibilities establishing strong regional governments.

Under Adenauer, the FRG was politically stable and economically prosperous. There was a period of rapid industrial expansion and the resulting prosperity became known as the Wirtschaftswonder (economic miracle). Funded by its industrial wealth, the government expanded the social welfare system. By 1963, the FRG was a leading political and economic force in Europe. From 1963 to 1968, the FRG government pursued a policy (*ostpolitik*) of improving political and trade relations with its neighbor GDR. However, after a new constitution was ratified in the GDR in 1968, ostpolitik was abandoned. The new constitution declared the GDR to be a separate socialist state of German nationality and unification was only possible if the FRG became a socialist state.

With the defeat of the CDU by the Social Democrats in 1969, the FRG moved into its second stage of development, from 1969 to 1982. The leaders in the second stage were Social Democratic Chancellors Willy Brandt (1969 to 1974) and Helmut Schmidt (1974 to 1982).[11] Brandt renewed ostopolitik, and in 1970 signed a treaty with the Soviet Union reorganizing Europe's post-war boundaries. Two years later, the FRG and the GDR recognize each other's sovereignty. This allowed for both nations to be admitted into the United Nations in 1973. Brandt, although popular, was forced to resign when an East German spy was discovered on his personal staff. Under Brandt the economy grew, there was full employment, and the state extensively increased social services and benefits. With the mid-seventies recession, the Schmidt administration ushered in cutbacks and witnessed increases in unemployment. The levels of cutbacks and unemployment were less severe than in the rest of Western Europe; however, they did weaken Schmidt's base of support.

In the third stage of development preceding unification (1982 to 1990), the CDU was returned to power under the leadership of Chancellor Helmut Kohl.[12] A new fourth party, the Greens, came to prominence in the parliament on an environmentalist and pacifist platform. Kohl articulated the politics of reunification. As the 1980s progressed, the FRG solidified its status as a leading economic power and became more prominent in the international arena through its public articulation of support of the new democracies emerging in Eastern Europe. Kohl's political power was solidified by victories in the 1983 and 1987 general elections. From 1984 to 1987, the FRG and the GDR moved closer through new accords on financial and border matters. The new closer relationship was solidified by an official state visit to the FRG by GDR president Erich Honecker in 1987.

GDR 1949 to 1990

Four distinct stages in the GDR's development led up to reunification. The first stage, 1949 to 1961, saw the building of socialism. In this period, a socialist state modeled on the Soviet system was installed. Thus, the GDR became a one-party state under the control of the *Sozialistische Einheits Partei* (Socialist Unity Party—SED). Full employment, housing, health care, education, and other social services were all provided to citizens directly by the state. Economic and political life was tightly controlled by the SED and the state. This stage culminated with the building of the Berlin Wall. With Soviet approval, the GDR government sealed all borders between East and West. In Berlin, they did it initially with a barbed wire fence and then they constructed the actual wall. Soon after construction, all borders were fortified with mines and troops. The GDR government ordered border troops to shoot to kill any East German smuggling across the border. The Allies made no real attempt, except for diplomatic protests, to stop the building of the wall. It seemed clear that as long as the GDR stayed within their own borders, the West would not move against them.[13]

The years 1961 to 1970 marked the second stage of the GDR's political development. In this stage, socialism was consolidated, and the government attempted to bring greater material benefits to its citizens. In spite of gains in living standards, the East still lagged far behind the West in this period.[14] In 1968, with ratification of a new constitution, the GDR was declared a socialist state. As discussed earlier, this made unification possible only if the FRG became a socialist state. Additionally, the constitution outlined new rights and protections of civil liberties for citizens. David P. Conradt argues that in this period many East Germans made peace with the nature of their political system.[15] Simply put, they reconciled themselves to the regime's social contract. Such reconciliation was made possible by their perception of having general freedom in their personal and private lives, while having a tolerable standard of living and availability of goods, especially in comparison to other Eastern European Communist states. They had guaranteed incomes, affordable housing, free health care and pensions if they were disabled or elderly, and finally there was some social mobility. In return Conradt argues the regime asked its citizens for system support, to work hard, and to accept state authority.[16]

The 1970 border treaty between the Soviet Union and the FRG forced the Soviets to enter into the 1971 Berlin Quadripartite Agreement. This agreement between the Soviet Union, the United States, Britain, and the FRG guaranteed Western access to Berlin through the GDR. Feeling betrayed, the GDR attempted to sabotage the accord. This led Moscow to replace East German President Walter Ulgricht in 1971. Ulgricht's successor Erich Honecker led the GDR into its third stage of political development, from 1971 to 1985. Defacto recognition of the FRG by the GDR took place in 1972 with the treaty of basic relations between the two nations. During the Honecker period, liberalizing concessions were made. For example, freedom of worship became easier and travel visas and immigration petition restrictions were eased.

Throughout the 1970s and 1980s, the GDR became more reliant upon the FRG, particularly economically. At the same time, the economy entered a period of recession and there was stagnant industrial output because of prior short-term industrial planning. In return for economic aid and support for GDR exports with the European union, the GDR government opened up its political structure a little more.

The final stage of political development prior to reunification was from 1985 to 1989. Pressurized by the Soviet's Perestroika policy, the GDR, like other European communist states, was forced to introduce a series of liberalization reforms.[17] Initially, President Honecker argued Perestroika threatened his regime's ability to survive as a nation-state. The only thing separating East and West Germany was socialism, and if it no longer existed there would be no reason for reunification not to occur. However, as Perestroika took hold in the Soviet Union, the GDR economy showed increasing signs of strain, and fueled by growing public dissent, Honecker introduced a series of wide-ranging political reforms. Travel restrictions to the West were further eased, allowing several thousand East Germans to immigrate to the West through visas to enter other former East European socialist states.[18] Symbolic of the liberalization was Honecker's visit to West Germany in 1987. Two years later, the GDR was in a state of crisis, Honecker resigned, and his successor, Egon Krenz, promised even more reform. On November 9, 1989, the GDR government announced they saw no function being served by the Berlin Wall and borders with the West were opened up.

Reunification and the New Germany 1990 to Today

The opening of borders led to thousands of East Germans and West Germans attacking the Berlin Wall and demolishing it. More than a quarter of a million East Germans poured into West Germany. In order to stop the wholesale exodus of its population, the GDR government conceded more and more to demands for democratization. At the same time, the FRG government welcomed East German visitors and provided extensive aid packages to East German immigrants. The FRG also invested a large amount of capital in the East German economy. The cry for union became stronger and stronger as East Germans demanded greater economic prosperity and freedom. At the end of November, FRG's Chancellor Kohl announced a ten-point unification plan. Krenz resigned as his party's leader and interim prime minister Hans Modrow was sworn in.

In March 1990, the first free elections were held in East Germany. More than 75 percent of voters voted for parties committed to unification. One month later, the new prime minister, Lothar de Maiziére, announced his government's intention of unifying with West Germany. Many argued it was the only way to stabilize East Germany's economic and social structures. In July 1990, West Germany and East Germany entered into a monetary, economic, and social union. Thus, the West German mark was introduced into East Germany. Authors such as Peter Merkl argue that the process of unification was one of an imbalance.[19] Every time a choice was made on whether it should be done the West German or the East German way, the West German way was chosen. This led many East Germans to feel their nation was not only defeated but was being systematically dismantled by her sister nation. It eventually led to growing cleavages and tensions, both during and after reunification.

Reunification was achieved on October 3, 1990 with the official dissolution of the GDR.[20] Immediately all East Germans became citizens of the FRG. In December, the first all-German elections were held.[21] Helmut Kohl's coalition scored a decisive victory. Six months later, the newly elected German parliament, representing both Eastern and Western states, named Berlin the new capital of Germany. Reunification was achieved peacefully and quickly thanks to lack of resistance by the Russians, political flexibility by the West Germans, and cooperation from other Western industrialized nations, in particular the United States.[22]

The new Germany has had to deal with numerous economic and social problems. For example, housing shortages, strikes, unemployment, budget deficits, xenophobia, soaring crime rates, and public demonstrations. Additionally reunification brought with it complex and practical problems of integrating two different political systems. The Kohl administration met the challenge of integration by imposing West German practices onto the Eastern states. As a result of Kohl's failure to meet the complexities of integration with innovative policy making, two problems surfaced in the nineties. First, the cost of unity. Providing goods and services to the less developed Eastern states placed a major strain on the Germany economy. Budget deficits increased dramatically by the government's transfer of capital from the West to the East. Then economic recession hit. Kohl introduced austerity programs cutting back on services, increasing taxes, and reducing government subsidies. Additionally, East German industry was paralyzed. West Germans felt worse off, and East Germans did not feel that much better. There was economic disparity between the two halves of the country. Industry in the Eastern states was also weak and could not compete in Western European markets. Thus, the government had to invest large amounts of capital and time in East-German-based industry so as to make it competitive. This slowed the overall German economy and weakened the strength and competitiveness of German goods in foreign markets.

The second problem was East German disaffection. Many East Germans had lost their jobs because of industrial reorganization; others had lost their homes under a law that allowed repossession of land and property if it proved to be illegally confiscated previously by Nazi or Communist governments. Finally, a large number of East Germans simply felt lost as to whom they were. They felt a sense of cultural rejection. To compound all of this, the Eastern states did not initially experience gains in standards of living. In the immediate years following unification, unemployment was much higher in the East than West; East German salaries were lower for exactly the same jobs; and state pensions were not brought into a condition of parity. For many East Germans, reunification had not brought a significantly better life.

Xenophobia and right-wing physical aggression against foreigners became prevalent. Immigrants competed with Germans for fewer resources.[23] 1992 saw xenophobia reach its peak when media attention, both internally and externally, focused upon it as a possible sign of a Nazi renewal. Such attention led to massive counter-demonstrations by millions of Germans opposed to fascism and its racist and anti-foreigner sentiments. The government responded with a strict crackdown on right-wing groups who articulated xenophobic platforms. In 1993, to defuel xenophobia, the government revised its asylum policy, whereby foreign political refugees were admitted to the country. Many Germans felt the previous policy was too liberal.

In the 1994 national elections, Kohl retained power, although with a reduced majority. The problems facing Germany in the mid- and late-1990s were the same as those immediately following reunification. By 1997, unemployment was at its highest since World War II, at 12.2 percent. There was a general economic recession, a growing budget deficit, and inflation. Kohl introduced a series of austerity measures cutting billions of dollars from the welfare system.[24] The cuts were met with protest from both the unions and the opposition parties. As time passed and unemployment and inflation still rose, the protest intensified.

Kohl also pushed for a single European market and currency, which also met with opposition. One year after austerity measures were introduced, unemployment rose to 21.2 percent in the Eastern states and overall to 12.6 percent. Labor took to the streets demanding Kohl's resignation. In spite of the political turmoil, Germany joined with ten other members of the European union and adopted the Euro as the single European currency.[25]

As 1998 progressed, and as Kohl continued to lose popularity and unemployment rose, it was inevitable that he and the CDU would lose the election in September of the same year. Indeed the Social Democratic Party (SDP) swept into office. Under the leadership of Gerhard Schroder, the SDP formed a coalition with the Green Party.[26] Schroder, in his first two years as chancellor, introduced tax cuts for low-income families, restructured the military, eased the process for immigrants to become citizens, closed nuclear power plants, and attacked unemployment.

Today Germany is firmly committed to parliamentary government and provision of social services to its citizens and a fair distribution of income. The achievements of reunification have been significant. The social and economic disruption caused by reunification was inevitable given the rapid process of integration. Today the Eastern states still do not have economic or political parity with the Western states. West German democratic institutions have been installed in the East. However, the early setbacks of deinstitutionalization and mass unemployment in the East, and the resentment and protest it created, has stabilized. Both East and West Germans exhibit more stable attitudes and economic expectations as Germany continues into the new century. Both populations have had to readjust their expectations of what unification would bring them. However, the nation's economic performance and competitiveness internationally are still not stable and the German government still faces the challenge of paying for welfare benefits and social services at acceptable levels to both West and East Germans. How the German polity responds to these challenges and pressure will be crucial in terms of Germany retaining its position as one of Europe's leaders.

The Governmental Setting

The FRG was established as a parliamentary democracy and a federation of states under the Basic Law in 1949. The Basic Law was initially to be a temporal document that would be replaced by a constitution once reunification had taken place. However, as time passed, it has become accepted as the German constitution. Since 1949, the Basic Law has been amended several times, most recently in the 1990s so as to allow the integration of West and East Germany. The unification amendments reconstituted the five original Eastern states and admitted them, one by one, into the federal union without changing the basic West German state infrastructure.[27] The union treaty of 1990 allowed East Germany to retain a number of laws that conflicted with FRG statutes until a new all-German parliament brought about a uniform agreement governing both Western and Eastern states.

The Constitution: The Basic Law (*Grundgesetz*)

Although the Basic Law was to be replaced once reunification occurred, it has been retained as the constitution of the new Germany. This is mainly because of the general perception by both political leadership and the general public that it works very well, and thus, there is no need to replace it. Constitutional order exists and the Basic Law is recognized as a constitution. Within the Basic Law, three principles are reflected. First, Germany is a Republic based on federal structures.[28] Next, Germany is a state based on the rule of law (*Rechtsstaat*).[29] Third, the state guarantees the social welfare of its citizens.[30]

German federalism concentrates legislative powers at the federal level and administrative and judicial powers at the state level. With the exception of formulating some educational and cultural policies and the maintenance of the police, the state assemblies legislate very little. However, the administration of all laws, including federal laws, is almost exclusively in the states' hands. The federal administration, with the exception of foreign services, border protection, and defense, is limited to the personnel of federal cabinet ministers and institutions. Such bodies collect information to draft legislative bills. Even taxation is federally legislated and state administered.[31] Taxes are shared by the state and federal governments and, in part, are redistributed from the richer to the poorer states.

Each state has a chief executive (minister-president or first mayor) chosen by a popularly elected legislature. The key federal institution is the *Bundesrat* (Federal Council) which is representative of all state governments. The Bundesrat is the final arbitrator if disputes between the states and federal government occur. It is also the upper house of parliament; however, it is not an elected body. Bundesrat members are civil servants and are appointed by state governments. The four largest Western states tend to dominate federal politics while the five Eastern states play a much lesser role.

The Rechtsstaat (rule of law) essentially guarantees German citizens the right to due process, the preeminence of the constitution over all other legal norms, and the commitment of all states' authorities to the law and the separation of powers. In essence the basic idea of German constitutionalism as stipulated in the Basic Law is limited government based on a system of checks and balances with decision making authority dispersed through federalism.

The principle of social welfare provision or of the "social state" is so entrenched within the Basic Law, it cannot be amended.[32] The general adherence to a welfare state was vital to many Germans and with reunification has increased in importance because, although East Germans rejected a communist state in terms of distribution of income, they did not reject the idea of social welfare being a natural service provided for by the state.

The Executive

The chancellor is the parliamentary head of government and is chosen by a majority of the popularly elected lower house of parliament, the *Bundestag* (Federal Assembly), usually by a coalition of parties for a four-year term of office. Head of state is the president of the republic who is elected for a five-year term with a two-term limit by the *Bundesversammling* (Federal Convention). The federal convention consists of Bundestag members and an equal number of members from the state legislatures. The Basic Law clearly distinguishes responsibilities and obligations of the president from the chancellor. Of the two offices, the president is clearly the weaker. The president's functions are ceremonial and nonpartisan. The German president stands above the political fray much like the British and Swedish monarchs. It is the president's responsibility to sign treaties, preside at state functions, receive foreign ambassadors, promulgate laws and oversee Bundestag protocols. The president has no authority to make policy. Presidents are usually chosen because they are moderates. In times of crisis when no candidate can command the support of an absolute majority of Bundestag members, the president decides whether there is to be a new election or whether a minority government is formed under a chancellor who is elected by a plurality in the Bundestag. This has not occurred in the post-1945 period.

Similar to other parliamentary democracies, the chancellor as head of government is very strong and his power is established by a series of articles in the Basic Law. The chancellor determines the guidelines of government policy and selects and dismisses ministers. The chancellor selects all cabinet members (approximately twenty) from among the parties forming his backing coalition. They are then appointed by the president. The cabinet meets weekly with the chancellor, although it is not for the purposes of ministerial input into the decision-making process. Rather, the meetings are for coordination of policy arrived at through negotiations between individual ministers and the chancellor. Thus, collective responsibility is not developed.

The only way to remove a chancellor is by electoral defeat in the Bundestag election or in a constructive vote of no confidence. In essence, what this means is a majority in the Bundestag simultaneously elects a new chancellor as they vote no confidence in the existing chancellor. However, this is very rare and Bundestag members are inclined not to do so because it would mean not only splitting their own party but also coalition partnering parties.[33] Chancellors tend to stay in office for long periods of time because of the existence of strong disciplined parties, which keep their voting coalitions and thus governing coalitions together.

Chancellors are very powerful but are subject to constraints. The major constraint, because of the makeup of the electoral system, is that it is very hard for any party to win an absolute majority in the Bundestag. Every chancellor needs coalition partners. It is the responsibility of chancellors to ensure they keep their partners "happy" so as not to lose them and push them to the opposition side. The Bundesrat may have a different political makeup. Therefore, the chancellor also has to keep in mind what the states want. The split between legislative power and administrative power between federal and state government also constrains the chancellor. Next, all government decisions are subject to the constitutional court's (*Bundesuerfassungsgericht*) authority. Its decisions are binding, and thus it determines whether an action is compatible with the Basic Law. Finally, monetary-policy decision making comes under the jurisdiction of the central bank (*Bundesbank*) and this can conflict with a chancellor's economic policy decision making.

The Legislature

The legislature is a bicameral federal parliament currently consisting of the 669-member (although it is usually 656 seats) federal assembly or Bundestag (lower house) and the 69-member federal council or Bundesrat (upper house). The former is popularly elected under a system combining direct and proportional representation at intervals of no more than four years while the latter consists of state-appointed civil servants. Thus the Bundesrat has no elections. Composition is determined by the composition of the state-led governments. The Bundesrat has the potential to change any time one of the sixteen states holds an election. In Bundestag elections, voters choose both individual district representatives and the political parties that represent their interests. Fifty percent of seats are elected by pluralities from single-member districts while the remaining 50 percent are elected by a proportional system, in which only parties are named, no individual candidates' names appear on the ballot. A party must receive at least five percent of the national popular vote for representation. The final distribution of each party's seats is adjusted in proportion to the total popular vote. Regional or minority parties that win pluralities in at least three electoral districts are exempt from the five-percent rule. Bundesrat representation is determined by population, with each state having no less than three and no more than six seats. This favors the smaller states because it gives them a veto over any action that requires a two-third majority, such as constitutional amendments. Each state delegation must vote as a block and according to its state government's instructions. Both houses hold significant and wide-ranging powers.

As in other parliamentary systems, the German executive branch derives power directly from the legislative branch. In short, there is not a sharply defined separation of powers between cabinet and legislature. According to the Basic Law, all federal budget and tax legislation is initiated by the executive. However, because the chancellor is the leader of the majority coalition in the legislature no sharp division between the two branches exists; thus, although the majority of bills are initiated in the cabinet there is usually a strong consensus from the Bundestag around the legislation. Chancellors and the cabinet propose legislation and then send it to the relevant Bundestag committee. The committees have substantial power to shape the legislation according to what they see best meets national interests. Committees generally consult with a wide range of societal groups, both for and against the legislation. This leads to a more consensual-oriented outcome. The bill emerges from committee to the Bundestag floor where it has three readings. It then goes to the Bundesrat, which integrates implementation procedures into all legislation. Finally it is given to the president for his signature.

In its legislative role, the Bundesrat has only a suspensive veto over most legislation. It can only delay and not prevent passage of bills approved by the Bundestag. The exception to this rule is legislation dealing with state governments' administrative responsibilities. Here the Bundesrat has a veto, which cannot be overridden. Many authors consider these bills to be the most important ones before parliament.[34]

The dominant characteristic of the Bundestag is strong party unity and discipline. The Bundesrat's key characteristic is its strong administrative role. Overall the dominant characteristic of the German legislature is coalition government. There is not only continuity of political leaders but also stability of government coalitions. Reunification has not altered this. Two major parties (CDU and SDP) form coalitions with various other parties to provide government. However, recent events in the late 1990s point to changes in the party system and voting behavior and the effect on future coalition formation is uncertain.[35]

The Judiciary

Unlike Britain and America that follow common law, Germany, as Brazil does, follows civil law or Roman law procedures and organizations. Civil law differs substantially from common law, which is based on precedents. The major characteristic of the German judicial system is activist judges. The Germany judiciary is an independent institution and rulings are consistent with accepted constitutional law. German judges are thus not arbitrators. Rather, they actively safeguard the implementation of societal goals set by the state. Theda Sckopol refers to this as the judicial system relying on the capacity of the state.[36] In defining the meaning of laws and implementing their administration, German courts play a significant role in shaping policy. This affords them a major role in German government. With reunification the judiciary has come under considerable pressure and thus scrutiny to resolve the policy issues that unification brought about.

All judges are appointed by federal or state governments, depending on the court, and are drawn from practicing lawyers. Structurally the German judiciary consists of three branches. The first branch is the criminal civil system and deals with cases in all sixteen states. Cases may be appealed to the federal high court.[37] This court of appeal may also hear disputes among the states. The second judicial branch is the constitutional courts which interpret their respective state constitutions and the Basic Law. The most important of these courts is the federal constitutional court (Bundesuerfassungsgericht) which is the authoritative interpreter of the Basic Law, and thus, the final arbitrator of constitutional disputes. This is the power of judicial review. Such a power gives the court vital political importance because the size and volume of constitutional regulations mean political, economic and social conditions are strongly affected and determined by constitutional law.[38] The federal constitutional court has a total of sixteen judges; half are selected by the Bundestag and half by the Bundesrat and the court is split into two panels. One panel deals with the Bill of Rights (Articles 1 to 20 of the Basic Law). The other panel judges disputes among federal bodies, among states, and between levels of government. The third branch of the judiciary is the administrative court system. Consisting of the social insurance/security court, the finance court and the labor court. Each deals with citizen challenges to bureaucratic decisions in their respective jurisdiction and is headed by a federal court of appeal.

The Bureaucracy

Protected by civil service provisions, the German bureaucracy is extremely powerful; the vast majority of civil servants are employed by state and local government with only a small percentage being federal employees. Bureaucrats are primarily careerists who work with ministers and their respective legislatures. Structurally the bureaucracy can be seen as a series of overlapping layers consisting of national, regional and local agencies. Such a network makes it hard to demark specifically the responsibilities of each layer. Generally the German bureaucracy is perceived as efficient but rigid and officious.

To ensure fair representation of partisan perspectives all top officials are appointed on the basis of party affiliation so as to ensure all major societal groups representation. The remainder of bureaucrats are chosen on the basis of merits, with an elaborate system of examinations and licencing.

State and Local Government

The federal republic is composed of sixteen states, eleven of which made up the old FRG and five the former GDR. State government is relatively autonomous and enjoys independent powers. Each state has a regional assembly (*Landtag*) and a governor (minister-president or mayor). Elections for each of the states are held in independent, staggered four-year cycles, which generally do not coincide with elections in other states. State governments implement much of the federal government's legislation. Autonomy is guaranteed by each regional governments ability to raise revenues through ownership of their own enterprises, such as museums, television networks, recreational facilities, and housing complexes.

Political Parties

The German party system is a multi-party one. Thus, several parties are represented in the Bundestag. However, government has been the domain of three parties, two of which dominate and a third, a small pragmatic party, which until 1998 would join a coalition with either of the other two. The two major parties are the CDU and the SDP. The former is a moderate right-wing party while the latter a moderate left-wing party. The smaller pragmatic party is the Free Democratic Party (FDP).

During the 1980s and 1990s, new parties have emerged to challenge the other three parties. The Greens and the Party of Democratic Socialism (PDS) which is the former communist party of the GDR have won legislative seats. Two other smaller parties on the extreme right have also emerged. The Republicans and the German People's Union (Deutsche Volksunion or DVU) are nationalist parties emphasizing aggression toward immigrants and ethnic minorities. As of yet these two have not managed to win seats in the Bundestag but they are visible electorally because both have exceeded the five percent rule in regional elections and have won seats in state legislatures.

German parties cannot really rely on stable electoral support. Party identification levels are declining and there is greater electoral volatility. The emergence of new parties in the 1980s and 1990s is the product of increased issue voting and falling electoral turnouts. Generally, disillusionment with past politics is growing as the electorate becomes more heterogenous. However, party membership remains high and parties still remain the main vehicles for political leadership to emerge from. To this extent German parties are firmly rooted in civil society. Katz and Mair argue that German parties have changed from being catch-all parties to cartel parties.[39] Such parties operate as agents of the state and ensure their own collective survival. Thus, they are closely linked with the state and have weaker links with the electorate, and act less as representatives of civil society.

Interest Groups

Interest group membership is prevalent in Germany, and surveys have found Germans to have a higher propensity to join an interest group than individuals in nations such as Britain.[40] German society is composed of a number of organized groups. Such groups work not only to bring about overall material gains to their members but also to bring about overall societal gains. Thus, German interest groups fulfill public functions and are part of the nation's permanent institutional arrangements. This has led one author to describe the German state as a series of "para-public institutions."[41] In essence, the state maintains relationships with organized interests through institutions such as the labor court. In such institutions, interest groups are seen as collaborators rather than adversaries, and they work together to bring about consensual outcomes.

The range of groups is wide, with business and labor enjoying considerable prominence. Some groups are more cohesive than others and thus wield more influence. Over the years German interest groups have become less dependent upon political parties and thus now promote goals that further their own interest rather than that of a particular party. For example, business works with the SDP as much as they do with the CDU. The weakness of organized interests in Germany is that, as they have become part of the fabric of society, they have failed to articulate the interests of a number of new sectors, such as foreign workers, consumers and working women.

The Policy-Making Process

Authors such as Richardson call the German policy making style a consensual one.[42] The German policy-making process is very complex with a high number of participants. Reunification has only added to this complexity of process and actions. Constitutionally, the chancellor is charged with defining general policy guidelines. The chancellor is responsible for developing a list of topics that will be addressed by policy makers. In reality, policy is formulated in a collaboration between specific ministers, the chancellor and Bundesrat members. The chancellor's party governs in a coalition with other parties present in the Bundesrat. Thus, political parties are an important actor in the policy process. Each party making up the governing coalition is constantly attempting to influence the governmental policy agenda. The prevailing characteristic of policy formulation and adoption in Germany is compromise. Compounding this is the multi-levels of government. There are clearly established areas where the states are the major policy-making actors. For example, culture, the media, education, and the police are state-dominated policy arenas. In other areas joint policy making and coordination of decisions between the states and the federal government takes place. There is a wide range of areas that are jointly financed.

Also participating in policy formulation are public institutions, such as the Bundesbank, and interest groups. Such actors lobby for their interests to be articulated in policy and provide expert advice and information to policy makers. Interest groups have a strong informal role in formulation and adoption. At times interest groups are the initial authors of a piece of legislation. This is particularly true if it is of low public visibility and pertains to matters that require specialist input. In all other instances, before any legislation reaches parliament for adoption, interest groups will have had an opportunity to present their views and perhaps propose alternatives to the policy being proposed. Conradt argues ministerial/bureaucratic policy design is extremely influenced by organized interests.[43] Additionally, the appointment of group representatives to ministerial commissions and councils gives interest groups further input into the policy making process.[44] Finally, the federal constitutional court is a key actor in policy formulation and adoption. Through the power of judicial review the court can decide on whether a policy is constitutional and thus allowable. Additionally through its decisions the court dictates guidelines for future policy. In short, the constitutional court can determine formulation and adoption of policy by saying what government can and cannot do.

The involvement of all these actors of course depends on the context of time, the economic and social costs, the issue and level of controversy. What is always a given is the need for an adopted policy to be the one that gets the most consensus. If political compromises are not final then conflicts are resolved through the courts. What is possible in German policy formulation and adoption is the product of what can and cannot be allowed by the courts.

Reunification brings with it a special set of problems for policy formulation. There are real differences between the Eastern and Western states. Such differences are exacerbated by laws creating the notion of winners and losers, which of course leads to a competitive rather then consensual policy making arena. Changes have been made to the Basic Law that allow for unequal burden sharing. One example is the 1994 change in article 72.2 of the Basic Law. Prior to 1994, the article called on the government to provide uniform living conditions. Now the article has been rewritten so as to require the federal government to initiate laws that bring about comparable living conditions. Thus, East and West Germans can receive different levels of benefits.

Consensual policy formulation is also under strain from the end of the economic miracle. Under high growth rates policy making was distributive; with the slowing of the economy, policy making has to be more redistributive. However, at the same time, there has been a general erosion of both elite and mass consensus on the role of the public sector and the level of state interest in the economy. Germany as other nations has increasingly found the need to cut back on what it can provide from public revenues to its citizens. As in other European welfare states, the German government has sold off some public enterprises and made cuts in levels of governmental expenditure on social services.

Germany employs a marble-cake style of federalism very similar to that of the United States from the 1960s on. In such federalism, the powers and responsibilities of the federal government (national) and the state governments (regional) are fused; simply, there is considerable overlap, and it is hard to differentiate where federal powers and responsibilities end and state governments begin. Because of marble-cake federalism, policy implementation is carried out mainly by state government bureaucracies. State governments essentially implement many of the federal government's policies. However, because of the relative autonomy of regional government there isn't uniform implementation of policies and this leads to disparity of outcomes. Just as there are a multitude of actors exerting influence over formulation and adoption there is also a number of groups and institutions participating in implementation at the state level through the exertion of influence. Reunification has added to the diversity of implementation in the states. This is partly because of the federal government's inability to meet the financial demands of coordinating policy implementation in the expanded Germany and also because increased regional flexibility is needed to meet the demands of unification.

Policy evaluation is not actively conducted in Germany. Review of policy output is left to interest groups and bureaucrats who look at the costs and benefits of implementation. The assessment that takes place is at a societal level through public debate. Increasingly Germans are asking for less intrusive policy.

Post-reunification Germany faces new challenges in terms of its policy making. The biggest challenge will be to formulate and adopt policy that reflects German policy makers' desire for consensual outcomes. The ability to avoid the notion that some people win and some lose out is becoming increasingly difficult. In short, the ability of policy to meet the common good through the cooperation of multiple interests and thus compromise is becoming harder and harder for German policy makers to accomplish. The reason for this shift is the increasing pressure placed on government resources for integrating two systems that have different levels of economic, political, and social development.

Chapter Five
The United Kingdom of Great Britain and Northern Ireland

The Britain that enters the twenty-first century is very different from the Britain that emerged in the post–Second-World-War era. Indeed the last years of the twentieth century witnessed dramatic changes in the British political landscape. The emerging political agenda of the twenty-first century has constitutional and institutional reform on it, as well as continuities and changes in public policy.

The Political Setting

To understand British politics in the late 1990s and in the early years of the new century, one has to first grasp the country's post-war history. Britain's post-war political development is clearly composed of four overlapping stages: 1940 to 1955 comprised the post-war consensus; 1955 to 1979 comprised the consensus under strain; 1979 to 1997 comprised the ending of the consensus; and 1997 to today is the post-Thatcherite consensus under New Labour.

Modern British Political Development

1940 to 1955: The Post-War Consensus: There was broad agreement between the parties that held government in this period on the fundamentals of the British polity. The coalition government of 1940 to 1945 under Winston Churchill, the successor 1945 caretaker government (mostly Conservative party) also under Churchill, the Attlee Labour governments of 1945 to 1951, and Churchill's Conservative government of 1951 to 1955 all adhered to the same guiding policy principles for Britain. This does not mean there were not differences in emphasis or rhetoric or that there was total agreement between the major parties on all facets of policy. Rather, there was general agreement on broad policy arrangements. The post-war consensus involved three fundamental planks.[1] First, Britain was to play a major role in world affairs;[2] second, Britain was to be a welfare state; and third, it was to be a mixed economy.

Britain, in 1945, saw itself and was perceived by others as a great power. Although it was outmatched in population size, industrial production, and military capacity by both the United States and the U.S.S.R., it was far in advance of Germany, Italy, France, and Japan. Its position was guaranteed, first, because it was one of the three major powers at Yalta and Potsdam, which both constituted the post-war settlement. Next, it possessed a large empire. And third, it had a "special" relationship with the United States through the strong historical, cultural, and linguistic links between the two nations.

British foreign policy was based on the special relationship with the United States, its leadership of a multiracial commonwealth, and possession of nuclear weapons and a large conventional military force. All three combined to give British decision makers what they believed to be a high-profile world role. Led first by Labour's foreign secretary, Ernest Bevin and then Conservative's Anthony Eden, Britain perceived its foreign policy to be vital to world peace, and that it was a nation with important global interests that had to be protected. In this light, Britain developed a series of treaties aimed at containing communism. It implemented an imperial policy combining the development of an empire, the creation of the commonwealth, and a system of global bases and strong points.[3] And finally, it backed the development of a British atomic bomb.

The post-war consensus on the welfare state was the accepted notion that there should be a wide range of publicly provided benefits and universal services available to all on demonstration of need and, in the case of services, free at the point of receipt. In short, social policy was to provide "cradle to grave" benefits and services for all citizens. The keystones of the welfare state were health care to all regardless of income, a comprehensive social security system and pensions based on national insurance contributions, and a state educational service mandatory to age fifteen and exempt from student fees. A welfare state consensus was built by many factors. First, the Labour party played a prominent part in wartime governments; Labour was firmly committed to social democracy and pressed its views. Next, wartime expansion of the role of government in the economy was expected. Third, two documents were created that acted as blueprints for the new modern Britain. These documents were the Beveridge Report (1942) and the White Paper on Employment Policy (1944) authored by John Maynard Keynes. Both advocated sweeping change of what government provided its citizens and were evidence of the government's commitment to postwar social construction. Finally the welfare state's establishment was supported by a leftward ideological shift in both elite opinion and public opinion about the nature and role of government in a modern society. Main welfare state measures were introduced first by the wartime coalition and then the Labour government (1945 to 1951). However, they were also broadly continued by Conservative governments in the remainder of the 1950s.[4]

Economic policy in the period established a mixed economy. In such an economy, four-fifths was to be private sector owned and one-fifth public sector. The economy was to be run on Keynesian lines in such a way as to maintain full employment. Simply, the economy was to be largely private with a significant public sector composed of nationalized industries. The British government was accepting the responsibility of managing the economy at a level of demand sufficient to maintaining a high and stable rate of employment. In order to do so, they were prepared to employ Keynesian methods, such as manipulation of fiscal and monetary mechanisms. The goal was to create and operate a corporatist partnership with business and labor which would curb inflationary pressures and industrial conflict. It was felt the smoothest way to change the wartime economy to a peacetime economy was through the introduction of a mixed economy.

The post-war consensus established in the years 1940 to 1955 provided the framework of Britain's foreign, social, and economic policy until the 1970s. Whether it was successful in achieving its desired ends is another matter. Indeed, the Suez crisis of 1956 attacked Britain's role as an independent world power. When both Churchill and Attlee resigned in 1955, two of the post-war consensus architects were removed from political power and thus the post-war consensus lost important political leadership.[5]

1955 to 1970: Post-War Consensus Under Strain: By 1955 the post-war consensus was under pressure caused by a decline in the comparative position of the British economy and Britain's international status. Both Conservative governments (1955 to 1964 and 1970 to 1976) and Labour governments (1964 to 1970 and 1974 to 1979) adhered to the policies of the post-war consensus but faced mounting criticism and were constantly under attack. By 1974 there was rapid decolonization; Britain's empire existed in name only. The commonwealth had been eroded as a political entity and trading bloc. The special relationship with the United States had weakened.[6] Also, Britain had to reorient its policy toward Europe when it was admitted into the European Community (now known as the European Union).[7] In domestic affairs, successive governments faced unforeseen problems. Compared to other advanced industrial economies, Britain was experiencing slow growth, mounting inflation, and persistent balance of payment crises. This was compounded by rising public expectations regarding welfare and increasing public discontentment at the levels of taxation required to sustain the British welfare state.

Basically the 1970s saw the erosion of the post-war consensus because of a credibility loss in its intellectual foundation and the government's loss of political authority.[8] There was a basic decline in the ideological persuasiveness of the post-1945 consensus. This decline is evident in the mounting influence of anti-consensual ideas in the Labour and Conservative parties. Such ideas paved the way for the overthrow of the post-war consensus by Margaret Thatcher and her Conservative government in 1979.[9] Anti-consensual ideas were responsible for policies such as non-interventionism practiced by the Heath government (1970 to 1972), the Labour government's setting of monetary targets after 1976, and the emergence in the 1970s of both right- and left-wing intellectual alternatives to Keynesian economics. Up until Thatcher, successive governments lost political authority because they were perceived as incapable of reversing national decline and dealing with the unions. The post-war consensus finally broke when Callaghan's Labour government's five percent pay norm was broken by striking Ford automobile workers, truck drivers, and public sector unions. Labeled by the media the "1978 Winter of Discontent," Conservative party electoral victory soon followed in 1979.[10]

1979 to 1997: The Ending of Consensus: This period clearly sees the end of the consensus and the pursuit by Conservative party leader Margaret Thatcher and her successor, John Major, of New Right Policies.[11] Margaret Thatcher and the Conservative party held office in three successive administrations from 1979 to 1990. Her policy agenda has been labeled Thatcherism and was based on two objectives. The first was to restore British prestige and aggressively reassert the country's international interests, and second, to "roll back" the frontiers of the state in economic and welfare policy. Simply, the wholesale retrenchment of the welfare state. The full range of policies aimed at the second objective was not implemented until her second administration (1983 to 1987).

Essentially Thatcherism represented an ideological reversal of the post-war consensus and a return to the primacy of the private sector. John Major's Conservative government (1990 to 1997) continued Thatcherism by arguing low inflation was the key to economic renewal and strength, and privatization and "internal market" reform in the health and education areas were needed to contain inflationary conditions.

In foreign policy, the Conservative governments from 1979 to 1997 tried to reassert Britain globally by a number of policy items. There was an aggressive pursuit of British interests in the European community. Thatcher fought hard at achieving a balance between what Britain paid in contributions and received in receipts from the community.[12] She stopped Britain's participation in the common Euro currency. Major eventually adopted a "wait and see" policy on a single currency. Next, the "special relationship" with the United States was renewed. Thatcher's fervent anti-communism made her a close ally to Ronald Reagan. The relationship cooled during the Major years with Bill Clinton's election. Third, in the early 1980s Thatcher took a strong anti-Soviet stance. Successive Conservative governments also emphasized strong national defense based on nuclear weapons. Finally, Britain showed a willingness to use armed force in pursuit of national objectives. This was seen in the Falklands war under Thatcher and Britain's participation in the Gulf War during the Major administration.

In domestic policy, successive Conservative governments departed from the post-war consensus by following economic policies that reduced the rate of inflation by maintaining high rates of unemployment.[13] This was a rejection of Keynesian economic management in favor of monetarism, which emphasized control of the nation's money supply. Next, tax cuts were implemented across the board but in particular at the high end so as to encourage individual enterprise. Third, large-scale privatization of public sector industries and services was carried out.[14] Additionally, a series of legislative curbs on trade union activity was implemented.

The centerpiece of the domestic policy reform agenda was reform of the welfare state. Reforms were based on the introduction of "quasi markets," the emphasis on selective rather than universal welfare, and encouragement of private pensions, education, and health care. Three goals lay behind the reforms: (1) the containment of costs and promotion of greater efficiency and value for money in welfare provision; (2) needs-based provision to only the most needy; and (3) enhancing the private sector to provide social services rather than the state.

The years from 1979 to 1987 represented a sharp ideological difference between the Labour and Conservative parties in the areas of social, economic, and foreign policies. However, from 1987 the two parties started to converge once again. This convergence was largely because of the actions of successive Labour party leaders in the period, who saw that the Labour party had little chance of electoral success and capturing government unless they moved to the center or even right of center.[15] Labour leaders such as Neil Kinnock, John Smith, and Tony Blair realized that Labour's image as a staunch left social democratic party had to be changed to one of a neo-liberal party. This meant a rejection by Labour of a Keynesian-Beveridgean welfare state. Thus, in the general election of May 1997, Labour, under Tony Blair, fought a campaign emphasizing their commitment to a free market rather than mixed economy, which would be based on the state acting as a regulator and facilitator of the provision of services rather than a direct provider. This represented a clear departure from traditional Labour party values and a move closer to the Conservative party platform. This produced a new consensus. Blair proved right and Labour was elected to government for the first time in eighteen years.

From 1997 On: Post-Thatcherite Consensus Under New Labour: The Blair government's first policy statements indicated that they meant to keep their neo-liberal right of center policy agenda. Blair publically announced that his government would continue the previous Conservative governments' spending limits for the first two years of his administration, that there would be no tax increases for at least five years, and that monetary policy would be controlled by the Independent Bank of England. The new consensus that emerged in 1997 was thus based on the acceptance by the "new" Labour party of the main social and economic changes made by the Conservatives in the previous eighteen years. Under Blair's new Labour party government, Britain has pursued a modest role within the European Union, there has been tight control of public spending and more targeted and efficient value for money provision of welfare services through support for quasi-markets and other means.

Britain today is a free-market economy with the state's role limited to the supply side of the economy and whereby priority is given to maintenance of a low inflation rate. This policy agenda has manifested itself in a distinct set of policies that emphasize the new consensus. For example, Britain sees itself as a middle-ranking European state with cultural, diplomatic, and military resources allowing it to be part of the global politics consultative process. Britain's EU role is more positive, thus leading to the acceptance of and participation in the single currency. Blair also maintained good relations with U.S. president Bill Clinton and closely cooperates with U.S. foreign policy, such as in Iraq in 1998.

In domestic policy, Britain entered the twenty-first century as a low-tax regime with tight controls over public spending; the state is non-interventionist in the industrial sector and has not restored union powers and privileges. Additionally privatization is a generally accepted principle, although now with tighter regulation of privatized utilities. The Blair government is also committed to the notion of "welfare to work," thus discouraging social dependence. And finally the government supports education, health, and housing being provided at real cost rather than through subsidized or complete state funding to citizens. For example, the abandonment of state funding of university fees was replaced with the introduction of student loans. Britain today under Tony Blair has adopted much of the Thatcherite social and economic agenda but combined it with more compassionate implementation.

The Governmental Setting

Great Britain is a constitutional monarchy whose whole system of government is based on the principle of parliamentary sovereignty. Traditionally, it has served as a model for many "newer" nations attempting to construct democratic political systems. It is a system of government that has gradually and peacefully evolved into a democracy, unlike many others where the democratic transition has been turbulent, inconsistent and uncertain.

The Constitution

Many texts on comparative politics cite the British constitution as a prime example of an unwritten constitution.[16] In other words, no single document is in existence that encapsulates British constitutional law. However, the term unwritten constitution is misleading, for much of the British constitution is indeed written down; it's just not codified in one document. Indeed, the British constitution comprises multiple documents as well as a set of rules, customs, laws, and general understandings that have been adopted over the years.[17] The written part of the constitution, the historical document, comprises the Magna Carta written in 1215, the 1628 Petition of Rights, and the 1689 Bill of Rights. The unwritten parts are the entire body of laws enacted by Parliament, precedents established in judicial courts, and European Union Law. Part of having an unwritten constitution is that it allows for a degree of flexibility. The British constitution, unlike the American constitution, can be amended by the same process as the ordinary law.

The main characteristics or guiding organizational principles of the constitution are that it establishes a unitary state, based on parliamentary sovereignty, that enshrines the rule of law within a system of fusion of powers organized as a constitutional monarchy. The United Kingdom is a political union of several countries, each with a different constitutional status, with all power emanating from the Westminster Parliament.[18] Regional governments are all subordinate to central government which is located in the Houses of Parliament in Westminster. No powers are constitutionally reserved for the regional governments. However, in the 1990s each region was granted its own regional assemblies. As each assembly evolves, this will more than likely change. In formal terms, parliamentary sovereignty is where all legitimate authority resides in the national legislature. Parliament is the supreme law-making body today and all parliamentary laws override all other sources of law.[19] Parliamentary sovereignty is recognized by the courts.[20] The prime minister as head of government is answerable to the elected chamber of parliament (the House of Commons) and may be dismissed by it.

The rule of law simply assumes all powers exercised by elected representatives and bureaucrats have a legitimate foundation and are exercised in accordance with authorized procedures. Also, the rule of law allows for citizen redress. That is to say, all citizens have available to them a legal remedy for wrongs committed against them by other citizens or officers of the state. Fusion of power takes place at the national level. Parliament is the supreme legislative, executive, and judiciary authority and includes the monarch and both houses of parliament. The fusion of executive and legislature is also seen in the operation of the cabinet. The British cabinet is a selective decision-making body and shapes, directs, and takes responsibility, under the prime minister's leadership, for government. This is a central feature of Britain's governmental system. The British monarch is head of state but fulfills a purely ceremonial function. All powers of the crown are exercised by the government or state officials.

In the last twenty years, pressures for constitutional changes have increased and the constitution is clearly on the public agenda.[21] Constitutional reform became a central topic of debate in the late 1980s. Demands for reform came from across the political spectrum. It culminated in 1991 with the formation of Charter 88, a constitutional reform movement putting forward a series of proposals to reform the constitution. An agreement between the Labour party and the Liberal Democrats in March 1997 went further in establishing a list of proposals for constitutional reform. Among the suggestions is abolition of hereditary titles and the integration of the European Convention of Human Rights into law. By 1999 the Labour government had started to implement some reforms, but it is unlikely they will transform the British Constitution into a radically different document changing any of its dominant organizing principles.

The Executive

The British executive branch can be viewed as a core executive with key institutions placed at the center of government. Such institutions are the prime minister, the cabinet and its committees, the prime minister's office and the cabinet office, and the departments of government headed by ministers. The British prime minister

(PM) enjoys considerable power. The PM is the leader of the political party that gains a majority in parliamentary elections and is head of government. The job of the PM is to form the government; this includes appointing both cabinet members and non-cabinet members. The PM is also responsible for directing and coordinating the work of government and for general supervision of the civil service. This gives the PM authority to direct and coordinate policy and governmental strategy. Often PMs dictate to the cabinet what the government's agenda will be. In recent years, the PM takes special interest in economic, defense, and foreign policy areas. However, the PM may intervene in any department of government that he or she so chooses. The British PM is also responsible for requesting dissolution of parliament from the monarch. This is a significant power, enabling the PM (within certain time limits) to call general elections at times that prove fortuitous or advantageous to his or her political party. Additionally the House of Commons is controlled by the PM through his or her leadership of the majority party, and for the most part its disciplined voting allows the PM to dominate. The British PM is a high-profile office and is perceived by all sectors as the political leader of Britain.[22]

The cabinet plays a significant role in the political system through its role as the nation's top executive committee. It usually consists of twenty to twenty-two ministers, all of whom must be members of parliament from the majority party in the House of Commons and sometimes from the House of Lords (the non-elected chamber of parliament). Some cabinet members carry more weight than others. This usually depends on the ministry to which they are appointed. Thus, the Chancellorship of the Exchanger (budget responsibility) and the Foreign and Home Secretaries are the most important cabinet positions. The British cabinet serves several functions as seen in Box 5.1.[23]

British cabinet government operates on collective responsibility. This ensures that even when cabinet ministers do not all agree on a subject they act unanimously publicly. If a decision is unacceptable to a particular cabinet member, it's expected that he or she will resign. British ministers of government are also subject to ministerial responsibility. All ministers are responsible for their department and answer to Parliament. If a department fails in terms of administration or policy, then it's expected

---

Box 5.1   Functions of the British Cabinet

1. Formally approves decisions made by PM.
2. Is the final court of appeal for disagreements that occur in cabinet committees or departments of government.
3. Manages crisis situations and issues of major political controversy.
4. Blocks, slow downs, amends, and qualifies government policy and legislation.
5. Acts as a sounding board for general debate amongst ministers.
6. Legitimizes all government decisions.
7. Is the symbol of collective government and responsibility; all ministers publicly support cabinet decisions.[24]

the individual minister will take responsibility rather than the government as a whole, and tend his or her resignation. The PM and the cabinet may be removed through their automatic resignation if defeated on a Commons vote of confidence.

There are some authors who argue Britain is no longer a cabinet government but rather a prime-ministerial form of government.[25] Thus, the PM dominates governmental decision making, deciding what the policy will be in consultation with whoever he or she thinks is necessary. The PM sets the policy agenda and ideological framework of the government. This is very different from a cabinet government in which the collective executive (the cabinet) shares in the making of all decisions and is equally accountable for them. Evidence seems to point to Britain still being a cabinet system of government that is now driven and organized by the PM. The PM is very much more than first among equals in relation to the rest of the cabinet.[26]

The Legislature

Britain's legislature is known as parliament and comprises the monarch, the House of Lords, and the House of Commons. It is sometimes technically described as The Queen in Parliament. In actuality, the legislature is bicameral. The House of Lords is the older of the two houses and has undergone considerable reform since its first inception in Anglo-Saxon times. Much of the reform has reduced the lords' power. The twelve-hundred-member House of Lords is the upper house and is non-elected.[27] Four-fifths of its members are hereditary peers; the rest are appointed. It is considered, despite its loss of power over the years, as an essential part of the legislative process. The functions of the house are fourfold: it deliberates matters of current interest to the nation; it legislates through revision of House of Commons bills and initiation of non-controversial bills; it scrutinizes government policy and administration; and it acts as final court of appeal.[28] Although not elected, a number of the members declare party allegiance publicly. Part of New Labour's 1997 election manifesto was reform of the House of Lords. Some of the reforms they have suggested deal with member composition and determination of how they sit in the house. Public opinion supports abolition of the House of Lords or replacement of it with some form of elected second chamber.

The lower house of Parliament is the House of Commons. The Commons comprises 659 representatives (MPs) democratically elected by popular vote and is a source of real political power.[29] In 1998, elections were held for a Northern Ireland Parliament and in 1999 for the Scottish Parliament and Welsh Assembly. MPs are elected as party representatives rather than individuals, and this allegiance underpins their parliamentary activity. The strength of party discipline in the Commons is such that the government usually employs its majority to enact its legislative agenda.[30] The House of Commons has five main functions, representation, legislation, scrutiny of governmental and civil service actions, a national debate forum, and recruitment of government. The true role of the Commons is legitimation through its authorization of governmental activity. As discussed earlier, the PM is the leader of the party with the majority in the Commons, and all government ministers are chosen from the majority party. Political opposition to the government is formally recognized within the Commons with roles assigned to the leader of the opposition and his "shadow" cabinet.[31] The main Commons committees are: standing committees, which examine and amend legislation; select committees, which scrutinize government expenditure; and the main government departments and committees of the whole House, which consider in part finance bills and all constitutional legislation. There is also a whole array of party committees. The Commons has undergone change over the years with the most important being the formation of departmental select committees to scrutinize the departments.

Compared to parliaments in other Western democracies, the British parliament does not carry as many powers or influences; however, it is still an important institution.[32] The reason for it carrying less influence and power lies in the fusion of executive and legislature. British parliament is controlled by the government through its majority in the Commons. In spite of the provision that allows parliament to force a government to resign through a vote of no confidence, it rarely does this.

The Judiciary

The British judicial and legal system has been emulated by many other political systems. Indeed, many of its key principles and rights have been incorporated within the U.S. legal system.[33] It is based upon common law tradition with early Roman and modern continental influences. Britain has several layers of courts and two kinds of legal proceedings, criminal and civil. The final court of appeal for both types of cases is the House of Lords, where law lords hear the appeals.

The British judiciary is far more limited in function than the German or U.S. judiciaries because of the principle of parliamentary sovereignty. Thus, there is no judicial review in Britain whereby the courts have the power to judge the constitutionality of legislative acts. Rather, the British courts determine whether policy directives or administrative acts violate common law or a parliamentary act. The judiciary in Britain does not play any role in policy making. Add this to its inability to rule on matters of constitutionality, and it is easy to see why it is generally rendered less politicized and influential than judiciaries in the United States or Germany. However, in recent years the courts have been called upon to adjudicate political battles over the rights of local government, police activities in urban riot situations, and the role of unions and the police in industrial disputes.[34]

The Bureaucracy: The British Civil Service

Ministers of government are in charge of departments of government that deal with particular substantive areas. Ministers come from the majority party in parliament and are elected as individual members of parliament first. As such, ministers are responsible to parliament and ultimately the voters because they are elected by the people. British civil servants or bureaucrats are responsible to ministers; they are not elected, and they are responsible for advising ministers on policy and implementing government decisions. In Britain, civil servants are career officials who serve government regardless of which party is in office. This requires that they be politically impartial and carry out decisions regardless of whether or not they agree with them.

Each department is assigned a senior civil servant, the permanent secretary who has chief administrative responsibility for running the department. They are assisted by a whole hierarchy of other civil servants, including deputy secretaries and under secretaries. The job of all of these civil servants is to help their individual ministers develop policy and then oversee the day-to-day implementation of adopted legislation.

In spite of a reputation of being efficient and free of partisanship, the civil service has been attacked and reformed in recent years.[35] In the 1980s and again in the 1990s, the civil service was restructured through a series of far-reaching managerial reforms. The civil service today is considerably downsized and organized along corporate lines. Many top civil service managerial positions are no longer awarded on the basis of service but are opened to national searches and filled by individuals who might never have had senior civil service experience. This change has led some authors to argue that the civil service of the future will no longer be depoliticized and that its key features are under attack.[36]

The bureaucracy also comprises two other distinct sets of agencies that are sanctioned by the state but that are not directly democratically accountable. Such agencies can be referred to as semi-public agencies. The first of them are nationalized industries, which are dwindling in number and influence. The second are nondepartmental public bodies. These are quasi-non-governmental organizations and are known as quangos. There are three types of quangos in existence in Britain: executive bodies, tribunals, and advisory bodies or agencies. All quangos over the years have increased influence and enjoyed considerable administrative and political advantages.[37] Each quango takes responsibility for a specific area or function and can combine governmental and private-sector individuals.

During the Thatcher years, attempts were made to reduce the size and number of quangos; however, there has in reality been an explosion in their numbers. This is partly because of the pursuit of privatization. Many individuals are concerned with the power of quangos and the fact that they are not democratically accountable to the public. It has led many critics to claim that they protect the interests of their particular clients rather than society as a whole.

State and Local Government

According to the constitution, there is no constitutional division of powers between the central government and regional government (local governments) in Britain. Local governments can be either councils or authorities at the county, borough, or district level. All local government bodies are controlled by central government policies and laws. This is particularly true in terms of budget and spending. Local government is basically responsible for police and fire services, roads, traffic, housing, building regulations, libraries, environmental issues, and schools paid for by central-authority-direct grants. Many authors note that since the 1950s, local government has become increasingly an item on the public agenda and that the parties clearly differ ideologically on its role.[38]

Reform of local government structure was carried out during the 1970s and 1980s. During the 1980s the British new right started redefining local government's purpose. Thatcher's government placed strict controls over local government in 1984 so as to curtail local government spending. They also, in 1990, changed the method by which local governments could tax their populations. Basically the Conservatives took local government's ability to tax property away and replaced it with the annual community charge tax. Dubbed the poll tax, this new charge set a fixed amount to be paid per person. Basically the poll tax shifted the burden of local taxes from property owners and businesses to individuals, and taxed rich and poor alike. The poll tax was unfair to lower-income families, because rather than paying a tax on the value of their property, every individual living in a home (rental or self-owned) would pay a personal tax. Opposition to the tax was strong and led to rioting in the streets of London. It also signaled the end of Margaret Thatcher's reign. She was removed by her own party as leader in 1990. The poll tax was repealed in 1992 and replaced with a local government-based tax on property value, with discounts for certain types of properties and low-income individuals. Basically what Thatcher and her government were attempting to achieve was to change local government from being a direct provider of services to a facilitator of service provision through changing its revenue base. This can clearly be seen with the introduction of quasi markets and privatization of utility services. Under the Conservatives, all local authorities had to engage in compulsory competitive tendering.

Tony Blair's Labour government is far more favorably disposed toward local government.[39] However, New Labour has kept much of the restructuring of local government achieved by their Conservative predecessors. Local government today is only one provider of services at the local level. However, the Local Government Act, which came into force on April 1, 2000, replaced compulsory tendering with a duty on local authorities to achieve best value. The legislation also introduced new reserve powers.

Political Parties

The British political party system is traditionally described as a distinct two-party system. That is to say two major parties regularly contest and hold office and operate in a disciplined manner within the legislature. However, recent events have complicated the party picture. It is true that government has been the sole province of the Labour and Conservative parties in the post–Second-World-War era; however, other parties have surfaced in recent years to challenge their dominance. Minor parties have had increasing success since the 1970s; in 1997, fifty-six parliamentary seats were won by such parties in the general election. Thus, it is more accurate to describe the British system as a two-plus party system.

Some authors have described the post-1945 period as a two-party system that evolved into a dominant party system.[40] That is to say a system where several parties compete electorally and gain legislative representation, but one party regularly holds office and another party regularly forms the largest opposition. Such authors use the electoral dominance of the Conservative party as proof.[41] However, Labour's sweeping victory in 1997 and their relative popularity today makes this a thesis that might not be tenable in the twenty-first century.

In terms of structure, British political parties are centralized, disciplined, and cohesive. They are also more or less permanent. That is to say they do not disappear once the election is over, and they do not allow elected officials to act as individuals rather than party representatives in the legislature. Thus, British parties are ideologically based and programmatic, particularly if compared to American parties.

The ideological cleavage between the two major parties has narrowed since the election of Blair's New Labour. New Labour is the result of a thorough reform of ideology, structure, and policies by the Labour leadership. Labour has clearly moved into the center ground and appropriated a lot of the conservatives' neo-liberal agenda. The break with the past is symbolized by the replacement of the language of clause four in the Labour party manifesto. The old clause-four language specified the party's commitment to socialism. The new language pays homage to democracy.

In response to defeat after eighteen years in office, the Conservative party has made changes in their organization. Their objective is to make the party more democratic, to allow more minority membership, and to centralize national party headquarters' influence over candidate selection.[42] In short, they are moving to the center or near right of the center.

At the constituency level and in local government, the two major parties no longer have dominance and are being challenged by minor parties such as Liberal Democrats and the Greens. Overall in Britain, in the twenty-first century, the parties have moved to the center rather than offering voters distinct choices on the left-right spectrum. The debate is no longer on what is to be done but on how it is to be done. That is to say, the parties no longer have different ideological agendas, they just disagree on how to achieve their shared visions of how Britain should progress.

Interest Groups

Throughout the post-war period until Margaret Thatcher's election as PM in 1979, the most influential interest groups in Britain's political system were class-based, that is to say, those representing business interests and trade unions.[43] Such groups constantly vied to influence economic and social policy. Successive governments attempted to gain such groups' cooperation when they formulated and implemented policy. However, in the majority of instances, it was with very little success. The consequence was that by the mid-1970s much of the British public felt the country was being held hostage by such interests generally and, in particular, by unions. Hence, the Thatcher government imposed a series of bills that were aimed at curbing union power and influence.[44] The Blair government has done little, if anything, to restore union influence. Business interests have also been forced to change the way they operate and have developed closer ties with parliament rather than the executive. Over the years, lobbying has increased generally across the board from all types of groups. Some authors describe the changes as the institutionalization of consultation between government and sectional groups. Such a process is a systematic dismantling by government of corporatist-style consultation with traditional sectional groups such as the unions and business.[45]

The major development since the 1960s has been the development of new social movements, such as the women's peace movement and various groups representing the various growing ethnic and racial communities. Such groups are organized around the promotion of nonmaterial benefits for their members. They focus much of their attention on societal values and how they affect their interests. Such groups can be labeled cause groups because they are formed to promote some particular attitude, belief, or principle affecting their members.[46] Such groups have been prominent in the United States for many years.

The Policy-Making Process

At the center of the British policy-making process are the prime minister, cabinet, and the cabinet committee system. Considerable concentration of power has been placed in the prime minister's office and the PM's control of the cabinet will often tell much about a particular PM's role in policy making. The PM has a direct relationship with all ministers and is informed of all new policy initiatives. This allows the PM to dominate policy making, for he or she can use the powers of their office to decide which policy should proceed and which should be dropped. The PM also has the power to decide key issues and sets the ideological framework for the government's policies. Traditionally PMs have been more closely involved in defense, foreign affairs, and economic policy than in other sectors, such as transportation. Ministers rely heavily on their civil servants in helping them formulate policy to be placed before parliament and the PM. One cannot underestimate the influence of the civil service on policy formation and implementation, in particular, the power of the treasury through its control of departmental spending. Such control essentially means the treasury can and does influence every other ministry's policy proposals. Parliament has little direct participation in policy formulation. Their role is to adopt after scrutinizing policy details and possibly amending new legislation.

Policy making in Britain has been characterized as incrementalist.[47] Policy emerges either through close cooperation in a client or corporate relationship, between sectional interest groups and government departments, or policy emerges through a central-local dependency relationship. British policy making is closely influenced by policy communities or sub-governments.[48] British public policy is normally then worked out through a process that emphasizes consensus and consultation with affected interests. Civil servants, ministers, and representatives of special sectional interests cooperate with each other when policy is formulated. It is often argued that the result is the promotion of the interests of the department or the interests of the client rather than those of society as a whole.

British policy makers act as if they are guardians of the public interest; they understand what is best for the public but refer very little to the public itself. Most political activity is bargained behind closed doors by special interests and interested specialists. Secrecy is a key trait of British policy making; the government limits public access to information, believing a passive public accepts what its government feels is in the public interest. The result is a closed policy-making process based on selective consultation with special interests. However, the system of party competition encourages policy innovation and the attempt to impose a consensus. Parties have a vital interest in ensuring that when each is not in government the new government does not repeal its old policies.

To summarize: British policy making is corporatist with an incremental decision-making process. Consultation regularly takes place between government, civil service, and special sectional interests. This will eventually even be true of those issues that spill over into the general public arena and involve media attention and non-ministerial members of the government.

Chapter Six
Japan

Japan is a nation everyone knows of but seems to know little about. Its culture and political system are mysteries to many of us even though it's one of the world's major industrial powers.[1] Although considered a stable democracy, it is a relatively new one. Only after 1945 with Japan's defeat and the American occupation after World War II did democracy become fully accepted ideologically and institutionally.[2] Today, Japan is considered a liberal democracy that is modernized but not culturally Western.[3] Thus, when comparing Japan with other nations, its non-Western culture must always be kept in mind.

The Political Setting

One hundred and fifty years ago, Japan was a traditional feudal society based on Max Weber's ideal type of traditional authority.[4] A ruling elite was given legitimacy through the emperor and was protected by the military. Real power lay with the military clans ruling in the name of the emperor.[5] With the forced opening up of Japan by American gun boats in 1853 came modernization and rapid economic development. In the following three decades until the end of World War II, Japan developed into an autocratic state that flirted unsuccessfully from time to time with democracy. With American occupation after World War II, Japan was transformed into a democratic state.

Modern Japanese Political Development

Democracy came through the American written constitution that was forced upon the Japanese in 1947.[6] It is basically still the constitution that Japan has today, and many refer to it as the MacArthur Constitution after General MacArthur, who was head of the American occupation forces.[7]

The new constitution heralded a period of political decentralization and sweeping reforms such as land reform that allowed farmers to purchase the land they had been farming as tenants. The business and labor sectors also underwent change. Unions were encouraged and economic deconcentration occurred.[8] Family-controlled conglomerates (*Zaibatsu*) were broken up. These changes were, for the most part, welcomed by the Japanese and led to greater freedom than most Japanese had ever experienced. Free public debate and wide-ranging ideological groupings emerged. Party politics was revived, and parties of the right and left were encouraged by the occupation forces.[9] It soon became clear that a general societal consensus was in favor of rebuilding the economy and strengthening Japan's international position. Parties with agendas supporting such goals were awarded electorally in the immediate post-war years. In 1946, the ideologically conservative Liberal party (LDP) led by Yoshida Shigeru was elected to govern, though their reign was short-lived because of divisiveness within their ranks. In elections held in 1947, the Japan Socialist Party (JSP) won a narrow victory and formed a coalition government that lasted approximately eighteen months. The LDP returned to power in 1948 under Yoshida, who continued to be prime minister until 1955.

In the late 1940s, America's desire to reform Japan was replaced with the objective of turning her into a strong ally. Some authors refer to this change in occupation policy as the "reverse course."[10] American decision makers chose to achieve this through the promotion of Japanese economic development. The last years of the 1940s saw the beginning of the rebuilding of the Japanese economy. The program of economic deconcentration was reversed, and big business was encouraged to reorganize. The Yoshida government was encouraged to adopt anti-inflation policies and to implement austerity programs. Additionally the activities of labor unions considered radical were curbed and the communist movement was tightly monitored and penalized. To ensure Japan's defense and security, the United States and Japan entered into a security treaty that allowed American military bases and forces to be stationed in Japan. This treaty, in conjunction with the 1952 San Francisco Peace Treaty and its collateral agreements, aligned Japan firmly with the West. With the peace treaty ratification, full sovereignty was restored to Japan.

The 1950s political debate was dominated by the subject of Japan's post-war international role. Right and left were clearly divided over the issue. In 1955, the LDP merged with the Democratic Party to form the major conservative opposition. The conservatives favored close ties with the United States, limited rearmament, and revision of the mutual security treaty so as to bring about greater parity between the United States and Japan. The left, led by the socialist and communist parties, opposed the mutual security treaty and wanted Japan to be non-aligned, thus ruling out close ties with either the United States or the Soviet Union. As the 1960s approached, Japan faced its first post-war democratic crisis. The crisis culminated in 1960 with large-scale public demonstrations and riots in Tokyo and other major cities over ratification of a revised security treaty. Opposition to the treaty was based on the belief, by many, that the treaty would make Japan a permanent military ally of the United States and an enemy of the Soviet Union and China.[11] The crisis led to the resignation of Prime Minister Kishi Nobusuke but not to the rejection of the revised treaty.[12] By September, the legislature had ratified the treaty and political calm was restored. This established the LDP's supremacy over Japanese politics and for the next three decades until 1993, the LDP managed to win every general election, though not always by a majority, establishing a stable predominant-party regime, which pursued a policy of cooperation with the United States overseas and a domestic policy of economic development.[13] LDP hegemony was helped by the cleavage that developed in the Socialist party. A moderate group of socialist legislators split from the main party to form the Democratic Socialist Party (DSP). The split caused long-term damage to the opposition and thus helped solidify LDP monopolistic control of government.

With the desire to avoid another crisis of the nature of the 1960 events, the LDP chose to follow a non-controversial policy agenda by concentrating on economic issues. Nobusuke's replacement, Prime Minister Ikeda Itayota promised to double household incomes in ten years. This plan was welcomed by all sectors of Japanese society, and it ushered in an era of political stability and rapid economic growth. The economy had started to recover during the Korean War years (1950 to 1953) with the utilization of Japan as a logistical base.[14] Subsequently, Japan witnessed a series of growth spurts. From 1955 to 1973 GNP grew at an annual average rate of nine percent. This was much faster than any other industrial economy's growth rate. By 1970, Japan was the third-largest economy in the world. Japan's success was quickly labeled an "economic miracle."

The reasons for the "miracle" are many. First, it can be credited to the presence of a strong economic bureaucracy that had expansive administrative powers to promote industrial growth and plan development. Next, corporate leaders followed the strategy of long-term gains over short-term profits, thus reinvesting constantly to improve and update technology. Additionally big business realized that "happy" and "contented" workers were crucial, so Japanese corporations provided guarantees and benefits that elsewhere were provided by the public sector.[15] Third, the Japanese work force was educated and skilled, with a strong work ethic that dictated against strikes and stoppages. Fourth, the Japanese became eager consumers of all the newly available goods. And finally, resources did not have to be spent on security and the military because of American provision of basic national defense. In spite of the Vietnam War, the Japanese public's attention was focused on the economy and so when renewal of the national security treaty occurred in 1970, the 1960 political crisis was not repeated.

Rapid economic growth ended in the 1970s with, first, the abandonment of a fixed foreign exchange rate by the United States, and second, the increase in crude oil prices.[16] The first event caused the value of the Japanese yen to rise and the cost of exports to increase, making them less attractive. The effect of the second event was recession. Through a drive to expand Japanese exports and other policies, the Japanese economy did start to grow again, but it was at a much slower rate of about four to five percent annually.

Economic growth brought with it several problems. For example, a shrinking rural population engaged in agricultural production, and rapid urbanization occurred with resulting overcrowding, air and water pollution, and an overloaded transportation system. However, by the end of the 1970s Japan was a middle-class society with a relatively equal distribution of income and few areas of extreme poverty.

The LDP's control of government throughout the 1970s was accompanied by frequent change in cabinet membership because of factional infighting. From 1972 to 1982, Japan had six prime ministers, all from the LDP. The period also witnessed a growing number of political scandals. A large number of elected officials, including a former prime minister, were charged with influence-peddling.[17] The scandals affected politics. National voting rates declined, and public opinion polls showed increasing indifference amongst voters. Additionally the LDP lost electoral support, although not enough to lose control of government. During the mid-1980s the LDP's fortunes were revived by their new leader Nakasone.[18] Prime Minister Nakasone was a conservative who supported rearmament and a more active role internationally for Japan. However, the LDP's dominance came to an end in 1993 when a coalition of eight opposition parties formed a cabinet under Prime Minister Hosokawa Moriho.[19] The LDP's reign of supremacy ended because Japan was hit by another economic recession in the early 1990s. Unlike the economic crisis of the 1970s, this time around voters blamed the government and its policies for the recession.[20] The scandals of the 1970s and 1980s also took their toll, and the 1990s saw new corruption allegations against LDP politicians.

The 1993 defeat brought an end to the one-party rule of the LDP and the party system in which the LDP ruled with the JSP being the opposition. The defeat also brought instability, which is still prevalent today. Hosokawa resigned in 1994 amidst allegations that he had accepted an illegal gift in 1982. He was replaced by Hata, who soon afterwards was left without a majority in the lower house of parliament when the largest party in the coalition withdrew from it. Hata was forced to resign. His government was replaced by a coalition cabinet of LDP and Socialist Party members that came to power under Murayama Tomiichi, the leader of the Socialists. However, factionalism increased and political parties continued to split and reformulate. This led to the political demise of Murayama who resigned in January 1996 to be replaced by LDP member Hashimoto Ryutaro. Hashimoto formed a new coalition government with the Socialists and Sakigake, a progressive conservative party. Political and economic problems continued to contribute to instability and social uncertainty and led to the defeat of the LDP in upper-house elections in July 1998. Hashimoto accepted responsibility for the defeat and resigned as prime minister. His successor was fellow LDP member Keizo Obuchi, who formed a new coalition in 1999 with the Liberal party, a new party formed by former LDP members.

Japanese politics in the first year of the new century is in a state of flux. Democracy does not appear at risk, but as voters remain disillusioned the current organizational structure does appear to be. The breakdown of the party system is the first indicator of this disillusionment. Recent electoral reforms are expected in the immediate years ahead to accelerate the party realignment process.[21] Globally Japan has also faced shifting pressures to take international responsibility commensurate with its economic power. The public remains skeptical of such a role for their nation. Without doubt, Japan is standing at a political crossroads. However, it still remains one of the world's healthiest and most highly educated, affluent, and productive nations.

The Governmental Setting

Japan is classified as a constitutional monarchy that is unitary in structure. It is generally acknowledged to have a strong state where there is limited public discussion of controversial issues. This does appear to be changing. Numerous scholars have noted recently a shift toward party-centered politics and an increasing focus on global politics.[22]

The Constitution

As discussed earlier, the constitution governing Japan today is the 1947 MacArthur Constitution. The constitution states Japan is a constitutional monarchy that operates as a parliamentary democracy with the emperor acting as the symbolic head of state. This is very similar to Great Britain and Sweden. According to the constitution, the Japanese people are sovereign and exercise their sovereignty through elected representatives in the sole law-making body of the nation, the National Diet.

Featured prominently in the postwar constitution are "the rights and duties of the people." Thirty-one of the constitution's 103 articles are devoted to such rights and duties. Fundamental human rights, such as freedoms of speech, writing, publication, public meetings, and associations are delineated in the constitution. Additionally, the constitution guarantees freedom of thought and conscience; academic freedom; the prohibition of discrimination based on race, creed, social status, or family origin; and a number of welfare rights such as the right to "minimum standards of wholesome and cultured living"; the right to "equal education"; the "right and obligation to work" according to fixed standards of labor and wages; and the right of workers to organize. Limitations are placed on personal freedoms only insofar as they are not abused or interfere with public welfare. The Supreme Court is bestowed the power of judicial review. This is, in part, meant to serve as a means of defending individual rights from infringement by public authorities. The Japanese constitution in many way goes further in enumerating rights than either the United States Constitution or many other Western constitutions.[23]

The role of the emperor was relegated under the MacArthur Constitution to mere figurehead, and the Japanese royal family plays no role in politics and are hidden from public view, unlike their British or Swedish counterparts. The change in the emperor's status was designed to preclude the possibility of military or bureaucratic cliques exercising broad and irresponsible powers "in the emperor's name"— a prominent feature of 1930s extremism. The constitution defines the Diet as the "highest organ of state power" (Article 41), accountable not to the monarch but to the people who elected its members. Laws relating to the imperial house must be approved by the Diet.

The emperor's constitutional status became a focus of renewed public attention following news of Emperor Hirohito's serious illness in late 1988. Crown Prince Akihito became the first person to ascend the throne under the post-war system. As the new emperor, Akihito, in an attempt to modernize the Japanese monarchy, publically articulated, in 1989, his determination to respect the constitution and promote international understanding.

Another interesting feature of the constitution is Article 9, the "No War" clause. This clause states two important premises. First, that the Japanese people "forever renounce war as a sovereign right of the nation and the threat or use of force as a means of settling international disputes"; second, the constitution states that "land, sea, and air forces, as well as other war potential will never be maintained." Article 9 has had broad implications for foreign policy. However, it has not prevented the Japanese government from building its military capacity. During the late 1980s, increases in government appropriations for the self-defense forces averaged more than five percent per year. By 1990 Japan was ranked third, behind the then-Soviet Union and the United States, in total defense expenditures, and the United States urged Japan to assume a larger share of the burden of defense of the western Pacific. Given these circumstances, Article 9's continued relevance can be questioned. However, it remains an important brake on the growth of Japan's military capabilities. The general public, according to opinion polls, continues to show strong support for Article 9.

The Executive

Despite constitutional provision, the executive branch and not the legislative branch has been the source of most legislative initiatives in Japan. Also, with LDP hegemony of the Diet the executive branch has been strengthened beyond what the constitutional framers envisioned. As in all other standard parliamentary systems of government, the Japanese prime minister is elected by the members of the lower house of parliament. Thus, the political party with the most members sitting in the Diet elect the prime minister. If one party does not have a clear majority, it must form coalitions with other parties so as to form the government, that is to say elect a prime minister. The process of coalition forming can be time-consuming and complex, and often parties of different ideological persuasions will form governing coalitions. Of course this makes the longevity of such governments somewhat tenuous.

The prime minister is head of government, while the emperor is head of state. As head of government, the prime minister has the constitutional authority to appoint and dismiss the cabinet. Additionally the prime minister may submit bills to the Diet in the name of the cabinet. Also, the prime minister is commander-in-chief of the self-defense forces and can declare a state of emergency. The prime minister's other duties are to report to the Diet on the state of the nation and its foreign affairs, supervise the civil service, and approve or disapprove legislation and cabinet orders. If a prime minister resigns or ceases to hold office, the whole cabinet must also resign. Prime ministers can be removed by votes of no confidence. If such a vote is passed the prime minister either resigns or dissolves the lower house of the Diet and calls a general election in the hope of winning majority support in the legislature.

The post-war political system vests executive power in the cabinet. Cabinet ministers include those appointed to head the twelve ministries of government and the ministers of state placed in charge of the agencies and commissions of the office of the prime minister. At least 50 percent of the cabinet must be sitting in the Diet, although in practice very few cabinet members are chosen outside the ranks of the ruling party in the Diet. In practice, ministers have little supervisory power and responsibility, often because they are chosen on the basis of their seniority in the ruling party. Thus, many cabinet members are inexperienced in the policy areas they are assigned to.

The powers and responsibility of the cabinet are wide-ranging and similar to other cabinets in Western democracies. The Japanese cabinet advises and takes responsibility for any action by the emperor.[24] They name the supreme court's chief justice, who is then formally appointed by the emperor, and all other supreme court justices and those of lower courts too. The cabinet can also call the Diet into extraordinary session and the upper house into an emergency session. Finally, they can approve expenditure of the state's reserve funds. However, the cabinet is constitutionally subordinate and collectively responsible to the Diet.

The Legislature

Japan's legislature, the Diet (*Kokkai*), is an elected bicameral body comprising the upper house, the House of Councillors (*Sangi-in*), and the lower house, the House of Representatives (*Shugi-in*). Both chambers are elected by universal adult suffrage. The representative's term of office is four years and the chamber has approximately five hundred members, two hundred of which are elected from eleven regional blocks on a proportional representation basis, and the remainder of which are elected from single-seat districts. The House of Councillors consists of 252 seats and members are elected to six-year terms in staggered elections, one-half being reelected every three years. The Diet is covered in Article 41 of the Constitution and is deemed "the highest organ of state power" and "the sole law making organ of the State." The function of the Diet is to enact laws, which the executive branch, led by the cabinet and operating through the national civil service, implements. The Diet primarily, then, is responsible for making laws, approving the government's annual national budget, and ratifying treaties. It can also initiate and draft constitutional amendments, which, if approved, must be presented to the people in a referendum. The Diet may conduct "investigations in relation to government." The election of the prime minister by Diet resolution establishes the principle of legislative supremacy over executive government agencies. As stated earlier, the government can also be dissolved by the Diet if it passes a motion of no confidence. Such a motion has to be introduced by fifty members of the House of Representatives. All government officials, including the prime minister and cabinet members are required to appear before Diet investigative committees and answer inquiries. The Diet also has the power to impeach judges convicted of criminal or irregular conduct.

Of the two legislative chambers, the House of Representatives has the greater power. This is in sharp contrast to the pre-war system in which the two houses had equal status. One example of the representatives' greater power is seen in Article 59 of the constitution. According to Article 59, the House of Representatives can pass a bill that the House of Councillors has rejected. In order to do this, there has to be a two-thirds vote. Three exceptions to this principle exist: the approval of the budget, adoption of treaties with foreign countries, and the selection of the prime minister. In all three instances, if both houses have a disagreement that is not resolved by a joint committee of the two houses, after thirty days pass the decision of the House of Representatives will be the decision of the Diet. The Diet is responsible for budgeting, setting both taxes and the allowable expenditures of all segments of the central government. In this area, the House of Councillors is extremely important.

The Judiciary

The Japanese system is modeled after European civil law and is strongly influenced by the British and American legal systems. The constitution guarantees the independence of all judges, who are bound only by the constitution and the laws of the land. Judges cannot be removed from the bench unless declared mentally or physically incompetent to perform official duties, and executive agencies cannot discipline them. A supreme court justice, however, may be removed by a majority of voters in a referendum that occurs at the first general election following the justice's appointment and every ten years thereafter. Up until now, this has not occurred.

The supreme court is Japan's highest court and is the final court of appeal in all civil and criminal cases. The chief supreme justice is appointed by the emperor after designation by the cabinet. All lower court judges are nominated by the supreme court. The supreme court has the power of judicial review and also determines judicial procedures, oversees the judicial system (including the activities of public prosecutors), and disciplines judges and other judicial personnel. Decisions are rendered by either a bench of fifteen justices or a bench of five. The large bench is required for cases involving constitutionality.

Japan's judicial system is unitary, thus, there is no independent system of prefectural level courts equivalent to the U.S. state courts. Below the supreme court are eight high courts, fifty district courts, and fifty family courts. Summary courts, located in approximately 575 cities and towns, perform the functions of small courts and justices of the peace in the United States. They have jurisdiction over minor offenses and civil cases. The supreme court is generally reluctant to exercise its power of judicial review. This is mostly because the court wishes to avoid becoming involved in politically sensitive issues.[25]

T.J. Pempel argues the supreme court "has been an important, if frequently unrecognized, vehicle for preserving the status quo in Japan and for reducing the capacity of the courts to reverse executive actions."[26] There have been exceptions to this conservative trend, such as the rulings on the unconstitutionality of the electoral district apportionment system.

The Bureaucracy

Several authors have described the Japanese bureaucracy as an elite bureaucracy with tremendous power and decision-making authority.[27] Their power is compounded by their insulation from direct political pressure because there are very few political appointments to the civil service. Cabinet ministers are usually career politicians who are moved quite frequently from post to post, often staying in one position less than a year. There is little opportunity for cabinet members to develop a power base within a ministry or force their subordinates to follow their dictates.

Authors such as Chalmers Johnson discuss extensively the power of the Japanese bureaucracy in recent years.[28] Johnson argues that in recent years it has become apparent that there are limits to the bureaucracy's power. For example, the LDP has taken on an extensive role in policy formation eroding the bureaucracy's power in this area. B. C. Koh argues the reason this may have occurred is that in many cases LDP members are far more policy-oriented than bureaucrats and have developed more policy expertise.[29]

Another constraint upon bureaucratic power is the emergence of an affluent society that has challenged the control of the Ministry of Finance's influence over the economy. Such affluence has placed incredible resources, and with it power, in the hands of corporate Japan. Japanese companies have a certain autonomy, which challenges administrative guidance over them.[30] For example, the ministry could not restrain aggressive and often politically controversial purchases by Japanese corporate investors in the United States, such as the Sony Corporation's acquisition of Columbia Pictures in 1989.

This whole issue as well as foreign pressure has tended to politicize the bureaucracy, and the net result was divisiveness in the late 1980s and early 1990s.[31] Many bureaucrats have complained that their market-opening reforms, designed to placate United States demands, have been sabotaged by business interests.[32]

State and Local Government

Japan is divided into forty-seven administrative divisions known as prefectures. Each has a governor and a unicameral assembly, both elected by popular vote every four years. The administrative divisions are then subdivided into smaller units. Each administrative unit is required by law to maintain departments of general affairs, finance, welfare, health, and labor. Departments of agriculture, fisheries, forestry, commerce, and industry are optional, depending on local needs. The governor is responsible for all activities supported through local taxation or the national government.

Cities (*shi*) are self-governing units administered independently of the larger jurisdictions within which they are located; in order to attain city status, a jurisdiction must have at least thirty thousand inhabitants, 60 percent of whom are engaged in urban occupations. City government is headed by a mayor elected for four years by popular vote. There are also popularly elected city assemblies. Larger cities are divided into wards (*ku*) that also elect their own assemblies, which, in turn, select ward superintendents.

Outside of the main urban centers are self-governing towns (*Machi* and *Cho*). These all have their own elected mayors and assemblies. Villages (*son* or *mura*) are the smallest self-governing entities in rural areas. They often consist of a number of rural hamlets (*buraku*) containing several thousand people connected to one another through the formally imposed framework of village administration. Villages have mayors and councils elected to four-years terms.

Japan's unitary system of government means local jurisdictions mostly depend on national government both administratively and financially. There is a high level of organizational and policy standardization among the different local governments because of the power of ministries to intervene in regional and local government. Local tax revenues are insufficient to support prefectural and city governments, thus, such governments depend on the national government for subsidies. The amount of revenues derived from local taxation is 30 percent. The term "30 percent autonomy" is often used to describe Japanese local government.[33] However, local governments are not entirely passive. Citizens have a strong sense of local community, are suspicious of the national government, and identify strongly with their own city or town. Some of the more progressive jurisdictions, such as Tokyo and Kyoto, have introduced policies in areas such as social welfare and environmental policy that the national government has later adopted.[34]

Political Parties

As discussed earlier, up until 1993 Japan had a predominant party regime dominated by the LDP. LDP hegemony was solidified by a generally disorganized opposition, a booming economy, and a generally satisfied electorate. Once recession hit and scandals took their toll, LDP dominance and the party system were shaken. Japanese party politics is marked by constant formation of new parties. Today the party system is multiparty but under increasing pressure from disillusioned voters. Voting turnout and party membership are both declining, and a growing "no party" movement supports candidates who run as independents. For example, the governors of both Tokyo and Osaka in 1995 were former TV personalities who had no political backing when they ran for office. Today there are five major parties, which face an uphill battle as they struggle with developing agendas that deal with the Japan of today rather than the Japan of yesterday.[35]

Interest Groups

The role of interest groups in policy making demonstrates the emphasis on consensus in Japanese politics. Sectional interests are wide-ranging, from economic, such as occupational and professional associations, to ideological groups representing minorities. Research shows that the great majority of Japanese are connected, either directly or indirectly, to one or more interest groups.[36]

The post-war period is marked by extremely close relationships between major interest groups, political parties, and the bureaucracy. Many groups identified so closely with the ruling LDP that it was often difficult to discern the boundaries between the party and the various groups. Many LDP legislators in the Diet were officers of leading interest groups. Groups of LDP legislators formed *zoku* (tribes), which represented the interests of occupational constituencies, such as farmers or construction workers. Areas such as agriculture saw close working relationships between *zoku,* interest groups, and bureaucrats. Other parties such as the Socialist Democratic Party of Japan also have close links with interest groups. Many leaders as well as Diet members of both the Japanese Socialist Party and Democratic Socialist Party have been at one time trade union officers. All Japanese political parties rely heavily on interest groups electorally.[37] Interest groups provide funding, blocks of loyal voters, and local organizational networks. For such support over the years, the government has implemented policies that have distributed the rewards of economic growth among the population at large. The result has been political stability. Perhaps a reflection of this distribution of economic rewards is seen in repeated public opinion polls, where 90 percent of respondents view themselves as "middle class."[38]

Japanese interest groups are powerful because of what they can contribute to legislative campaigns. Similar to the U.S. electoral process, it takes a lot of money to run for office in Japan and authors such as Woronoft, Curtis, and Kishimoto all argue that money has corrupted democracy in Japan more than in any other major industrial nation with the possible exception of Italy.[39] Additionally Japanese interest groups draw power from what they contribute to "pork barrel" politics. Thus, Japanese voters are conditioned to think of what politicians can do for their local needs and what they can deliver.

The Policy-Making Process

Politics and policy making in Japan is pragmatic and limited by particularistic loyalties. That pragmatism has led to a consensus-building policy process. Policy makers undertake extensive and elaborate consensus building, usually involving all of the concerned parties. Everyone must be consulted informally and everyone must be heard. Policy making has to be done in such a way that opposition does not develop. Once preliminary agreement is reached by all those involved, a formal meeting is held in which the agreed-upon policy will be proposed and adopted. This process is called *nemawashi* (root trimming or binding) and suggests how change in policy takes place. Decisions are "the sum of the contributions of all." Although consensus building is, for leaders, time-consuming, it is necessary. It not only promotes group goals but also protects individual autonomy. In the Japanese political system, most groups, with the exception of minority groups, play some role in the *nemawashi* process.

The post-1945 policy-making pattern is for close collaboration between the ruling party, the elite bureaucracy, and important interest groups. It is often difficult to say who is exactly responsible for specific policy decisions. An important factor in the policy making process is the homogeneity of the political and business elites. Most elite members tend to be graduates of the top-ranked universities. Regardless of these individuals' regional or class origins, their similar educational backgrounds encourage their feeling of community. Early homogeneity is also fostered when top bureaucrats retire early. It is common for such bureaucrats to retire in their fifties and then assume top positions in public corporations and private enterprise. They also become politicians. By the late 1980s, most post-war prime ministers had civil service backgrounds.

This homogeneity facilitates the free flow of ideas among members of the elite in informal settings. The concentration of political and economic power in Tokyo—particularly the small geographic area of its central wards—makes it easy for leaders, who are almost without exception denizens of the capital, to have repeated personal contact. Another often-overlooked factor is the tendency of members of the business and bureaucratic elites to sacrifice their private lives for the national good.

A largely informal process takes place within elite circles where ideas are discussed and developed prior to more formal policy development. This process often takes place in approximately two hundred deliberation councils (*shingikai*), each of which is attached to a ministry. Membership of these councils is composed of officials and prominent private individuals in business, education, and other fields. The deliberation councils represent a more advanced stage in policy formulation where consensus and compromise can be arrived at over minor differences. The decision arrived at is usually one that is acceptable to the majority. These bodies are legally formed but have no authority to force governments to adopt their recommendations. A further policy-making institution of some significance in the early 1990s was the LDP's policy research council. As discussed earlier, the council advances constituents' requests to legislators. It is an effective means through which interest groups state their case to the bureaucracy through the channel of the ruling party.

At the heart of the policy process, because it drafts the national budget each year, is the Budget Bureau of the Ministry of Finance. This responsibility makes it the ultimate focus of interest groups and other ministries that compete for limited funds. In spite of the constant search for harmony and consensus, every sector/interest in Japan is in strong competition for resources. Great skill is needed by politicians and budget bureaucrats so that mutually acceptable compromises are reached. The policy process is one of intense rivalry. How long the system can continue to minimize antagonisms and maintain an acceptable balance of power among sectional groups is unclear. This is particularly true as Japan enters the new century with growing social inequality, an aging society, and the "internationalization" of its society and economy.

The majority of legislation passed by the Diet originates in the civil service. When the LDP is in power, drafts of bills are reviewed and approved by the policy research council. Within the Diet legislative bosses form *zoku* (tribes) to work through informal policy making networks with their bureaucratic and business allies. Such groups dominate policy making in all major policy areas. Most bills originate in a *zoku,* as do many administrative measures implemented by a government ministry or agency.

Policy is made then by subgovernments with special interests being promoted by politicians and bureaucrats. This allows both politicians and bureaucrats to benefit. Bureaucrats protect their turf and politicians receive campaign funding. As a result, most policies are conservative and protectionist, thereby promoting the interests of well-organized, well-connected, and wealthy sectional interests. Each sectional interest is represented by its own *zoku* which protects it against anyone threatening its interests. When reform of the administrative apparatus is broached, such as in 1997, it is quickly killed or gutted of its substantive content.

A policy-making process that revolves around subgovernments in the manner of the Japanese system is disjointed and incoherent. Decisions in one area are seldom coordinated with decisions in other areas. Legislation is passed but there are not comprehensive, coherent long-term patterns of policies. Attempts at reform have been made. For example, the eight-party coalition of 1993 challenged the policy tribes and subgovernment networks and imposed a more centralized system. A council of representatives of the coalition parties took control of decision making, leaving little influence for *zokus.* However, the system lasted less than a year. Now eighteen project teams made up of Diet members of the three leading coalition partners is given the task of policy making. Additionally a policy board of three members (one from each party) was created to identify policy priorities. At the start of the new century, it can safely be concluded that the old system is back.

Chapter Seven
Sweden

Sweden enters the twenty-first century as the model for social democratic societal development. It is a developed modern industrial nation that, although small in population, has a fairly large land mass.[1] Today Sweden can be characterized as an urban industrial economy attempting to answer a question that all democratic societies at one time or another will have to answer. In spite of the nation having one of the world's highest standards of living, since 1991 it has experienced serious economic recession that has led to demands for government retrenchment. More than 90 percent of Swedish industry is privately owned; however, the government over the years has exercised great control over the economy so as to moderate economic fluctuations.[2] Sweden, as one of the most extensive providers of public services to citizens, has been forced to reassess its traditional commitment to full employment and an advanced welfare state.

The national budget in 1996 included revenues of $104.8 billion and expenditures of $116.1 billion.[3] In order to meet such a deficit, the Swedish government had no choice in the late 1990s but to continue the austerity measures it introduced in the early 1990s. Both the early 1990s and late 1990s saw cuts in the number of bureaucrats and social welfare programs. Additionally, the tax system has been reformed so as to reduce income tax for all but the highest earners. Sweden for many years prior to this had the highest income tax thresholds of any Western liberal democratic nation. Finally, taxes on goods and services have been increased.

The question facing Swedish policy makers today and others tomorrow is: How can the deficit and unemployment be controlled without cutting back even further on social policy benefits? Indeed many Swedes now favor restoring the welfare benefits that were cut in the 1990s to combat recession.[4] Conservative politicians argue that what is needed is more investment, and that can only be achieved through more cuts in taxes. The problem is, in order to have the system of high government-subsidized benefits, it requires a high level of governmental revenues that can only be generated by a high taxation level.

The Political Setting

The Social Democratic Party has held power alone or in coalitions for much of the time since 1932.[5] Indeed no other Western political party has enjoyed such dominance in government where free and competitive elections are held. The consequence of this domination by the Social Democrats has been that labor has had incredible influence over political, social, and economic developments. This has led to debate over how to reconcile the interests of workers and business in modern Sweden.

Modern Swedish Political Development

Social reforms that made Sweden a leader in public sector provision were enacted in the 1920s, and a high level of unionization was solidly established by the 1930s. The Swedish Social Democrats of the late-nineteenth and early-twentieth century were ideologically committed to public ownership of the economy and thus nationalization of industry. However, by the 1930s they had to abandon this position because of the alliance they formed with the Agrarian Party. The Agrarians were strongly opposed to nationalization and believed in a partnership with business. The Social Democrats moved to accommodate the interests of business and talked of their commitment to democratic control of the economy so as to secure full employment and decent living standards and wages for labor. This did not mean they totally eliminated the possibility of public ownership. Rather, they stressed there would be certain areas and times when it was not desirable, and other areas and times it might be appropriate. This compromise was sufficient for both labor and business, and it provided a basic framework for agreement and thus the resolving of political conflicts when they occurred. It was generally agreed that Sweden would remain a capitalist society where private individuals and institutions owned and controlled industry. Next, government should be committed to full employment and the promotion of economic growth without extensive intervention in corporate management. Third, the benefits of economic growth should be equally distributed and the state should provide welfare benefits at a level that was necessary to ensure equal distribution of wealth. Finally, industrial relations were not to be the province of government but would be regulated by labor unions and employees together.

This agreement laid the foundations for the expansion of the welfare state in Sweden in the 1940s and 1950s. The result was the creation of an advanced welfare state that was more comprehensive than any other.[6] Underlying this comprehensiveness is the belief that the provision of welfare benefits is part of a citizen's rights.

This is a very different attitude than in the United States, where welfare benefits and their provision are seen to be solely for the alleviation of dire living conditions for the poor and most needy.

In the 1960s and early 1970s, the Social Democrats concentrated upon improving the benefits and services being provided. They achieved this through public investment in the social infrastructure and the expansion of public sector employment. Sweden in the 1960s saw the building of many new hospitals and schools and in the early 1970s a government-employed workforce that doubled in size.[7] In order to finance such expansion, income taxes across the board were increased. All sectors of Swedish society, including the lower income segment, were asked to shoulder a much larger tax burden.

The objective of the Swedish welfare state is the redistribution of income through universal provision of benefits and services, ensuring that all citizens enjoy basic social needs regardless of their income. Social services are directly provided, and there is less emphasis on cash benefits. In order to do this there has to be a thriving economy capable of sustaining full employment and growth. Real wage increases have to occur on a regular basis, which in turn extends the revenue base of the state so it can continue public provision of benefits. Welfare state expansion requires economic growth, and sustained growth requires wage stabilization or restraint by the unions so as to keep inflation down.

From the above discussion, it is possible to see some of the challenges faced by the Swedish state in the 1960s and 1970s. Further challenges were promoted by the growth of immigration and the granting of full eligibility for welfare benefits to all immigrants. Immigrants were to be equal in all respects to native Swedes. The entry of women into the labor force in mass numbers in the 1960s provided further challenges.[8] The Swedish state actively promoted the entry of women into the workforce through a series of policies that ensured not only equality but the conditions necessary for many women to be able to work. Maternity leave and subsidized public day care were offered to all working women.

The general political climate started to change in the early 1970s. Sweden emerged from the world economic slump of 1974 and 1975 with high inflation, growing foreign debt, and large budget deficits. In elections held in September 1976, the Social Democrats, after forty-four years in office, lost to a coalition of the Center, Conservative, and Liberal parties. Behind this defeat was not only the economic condition but also mobilization of three distinct groups against the Social Democrats. The first group was the neo-left who were concerned with the consequences of post-war economic growth. The Social Democrats were blamed for the problems resulting from urbanization, industrial damage to the environment, the neglect of local communities, and unequal gender relations. The second group who mobilized against the Social Democratic government was labor. The unions initiated a series of challenges, including strikes, aimed at employers' power and rights. They went as far as challenging the accepted principle of private ownership. Employers were the third group to mobilize against the Social Democrats. By the 1970s, many businesspeople were complaining that the public sector was too big and that the state was intruding too much in labor negotiations. Particularly frustrating to employers was the centralized system of wage bargaining.

The new coalition government elected in 1976 quickly introduced austerity measures to contain inflation and improve Swedish exports. The measures were met with resistance, and in May 1980 a general strike was held that brought the country to a standstill for ten days. Six months later, the government survived, by one vote, a motion of no confidence. In May 1981, a massive strike of white-collar workers coincided with the split of the coalition government. A second general strike was averted, and a central-liberal minority government was formed. In the 1982 parliamentary elections, the Social Democrats were returned to power and managed to hold government until 1991 through a series of elections, deaths, and resignations.[9] In the September 1991 elections, although the Social Democrats were the largest individual party in parliament with 138 seats, they did not have a majority to govern. Thus, a coalition of the Moderates, Center, Liberal, and Christian Democrat parties was formed under the leader of the Moderate party, Carl Bildt. Bildt's government quickly enacted an austerity program that accelerated the deregulation of the economy, made large cuts in government spending, and removed restrictions on foreign-majority-owned enterprises in Sweden. Within two years, thirty-five state-owned companies were privatized and there were reductions in welfare payments.

The new coalition government's tenure in office lasted until the 1996 September election, when the Social Democrats were returned to power with 45 percent of the popular vote. The party won 161 of the 349 seats in parliament. The former Social Democrat Prime Minister, Inguar Carlsson, was asked to form a new coalition government. Rather than do this, Carlsson formed a minority government.[10] Carlsson resigned in March 1996 as both prime minister and chair of the Social Democratic Party. He was succeeded by a moderate Social Democrat, Göran Persson, who had served as finance minister in the Carlsson government from 1994 to 1996.

In elections called in 1998, Persson's Social Democratic Party maintained its hold on power. Although their percentage of the vote and number of seats was down from 1994, alliances with the Left Party and the Green Party allowed them to maintain control of the government. The relationship has proved to be rocky as the parties disagree on issues such as Sweden's relationship with the European union.[11] The alliance with the Left Party and the Green Party is a shift toward the left by the Social Democrats, whereas the 1994 to 1998 alliance by the Social Democrats with the Center Party was more toward the right. Some analysts in the Swedish press suggest the move to the left came about because many voters abandoned the Social Democrats due to the cuts in welfare programs and benefits between 1991 and 1998.

Swedish politics today is shaped by the continuing dilemma of how does the state provide social services and benefits at a rate that is acceptable to its citizens and in line with state revenues? The question facing the Swedish state is the following: In light of recession and lackluster economic growth and the rapid increase of the immigrant population, can the Swedish welfare state be as advanced and comprehensive in nature as it has in the past? Part of this discussion also involves a reconciliation of labor and business once again. Is Social Democracy in crisis or is it in a state of adaptation . . . that is what faces Sweden in the immediate years of the twenty-first century.

The Governmental Setting

Sweden is a constitutional monarchy with a parliamentary form of government. Over time there have been political and constitutional changes. Such changes are responsible for shaping Sweden's institutional arrangements today. The constitutional monarchy is governed under the 1975 constitution, which eliminated the constitution of 1809 and the Parliament Act of 1866.

The Constitution

With the ratification of the new constitution in 1975, the last vestiges of the monarchy's power and authority were removed. The monarch is still head of state but is not head of government. The king can no longer preside over cabinet meetings. He is also no longer supreme commander of the armed forces. All power is defined as emanating from the people. The new constitution includes an extensive bill of rights. The monarchy today occupies a symbolic role and performs ceremonial functions.[12] For example, under the new constitution the king no longer invites party leaders to form the cabinet. From 1975 on, the speaker of parliament nominates the new prime minister, who then appoints cabinet members. Further, laws no longer have to be promulgated by the cabinet in the presence of the king. Finally, parliament can require the cabinet or individual ministers to resign if a formal vote of no confidence is taken.

Sweden is a unitary state; thus, the majority of political functions are exercised by national and local institutions that are subordinate to parliament and the central government. The Constitution of 1975 merely formalized the practices of government as they had existed in Sweden since the first world war.

The Executive

In Sweden, executive power is vested in the cabinet, which is responsible to the national legislature, the *Riksdag*. The head of the cabinet is the prime minister, who is either the chairman of the largest party in parliament or the largest party within a coalition of parties in parliament. The discussion earlier indicated since 1932 this has been either the Social Democrats or a non-socialist coalition of political parties. The job of the prime minister is to be head of government, while the head of state is the Swedish monarch. The prime minister chairs cabinet sessions and is also responsible for defining government policy. The prime minister is chief spokesman for cabinet policy within and outside of the legislature. A deputy prime minister is appointed from the cabinet to coordinate government activities. The royal chancery assists the prime minister. The chancery is made up of a staff of political advisors and civil servants.

All cabinet members are appointed and selected by the prime minister. They will be either department ministers or ministers without portfolios.[13] The number of each varies from prime minister to prime minister. Ministers may be removed from office by either the prime minister or the parliament through a vote of no confidence. The ministerial positions usually correspond to the Riksdag's standing committees. For example, there are ministers of industry, defense, foreign policy, and agriculture. The cabinet performs a series of basic functions outlined in Box 7.1. Although the cabinet meets formally and informally on a regular basis, all decisions are not made collectively but rather individually outside of the cabinet. Ministers will make decisions in consultation with senior civil servants in their ministries and the prime minister. The collective body is then informed. Unlike other European nations, each ministry is small in size in terms of the numbers of civil servants employed.

In addition to the cabinet, the executive is made up of fifty central agencies which administer government-operated services. All such agencies are headed by government-appointed directors (who retain civil services status) subordinate to cabinet ministers. However, they do function autonomously from their respective ministers. They are accountable to the collective rather than the individual ministers. There are two types of state agencies: administrative agencies (*ämbetsverk*) and commercial agencies (*affärverk*).[14] Both types of agencies are accountable to the cabinet, and citizens have the right to appeal their decisions in administrative courts, to the cabinet, and in the final court of appeal.[15]

The Legislature (Riksdag)

The Riksdag operates as a parliament and is a unicameral legislature with 349 members elected by popular vote on a proportional representation basis to serve four-year terms.[16] Allocation of 310 seats is on the basis of the nation's 28 constituencies; the remaining 39 seats are allocated according to each party's share of the national vote. Such a system was put into place to ensure first a system of representation responsive to the general populace and second to eliminate small parties. In order to win a parliamentary seat, a political party must win at least four percent of the national vote or 12 percent of the vote in a single constituency.

The Riksdag is Sweden's principle law-making body. It also provides the legislative basis for cabinet formation and tenure as discussed earlier. After each general

---

Box 7.1   Swedish Cabinet Functions

1. It submits legislation to parliament.
2. It promulgates laws passed by parliament.
3. It issues ordinances specifying how laws should be enforced.
4. It guides the activities of local authorities and central administrative agencies.
5. It hears appeals against state administration decisions.
6. It appoints top-level civil service posts.

election, the speaker of the Riksdag consults with the party leadership and nominates a prime ministerial candidate whom the whole body then elects. The prime minister is elected if no more than half of the Riksdag membership vote against him. It is possible for minority governments to be formed in the absence of a single-party majority or a coalition of parties with a majority. The Riksdag can vote no confidence in the case of either the prime minister or an individual cabinet minister. In order to do so, thirty-five Riksdag members must sign the motion of no confidence and an absolute majority must approve it.[17]

The Swedish parliamentary system is similar to other parliaments in its responsibility for government accountability. Ministers on a daily basis will be questioned orally and in written form by Riksdag members. Often question time evolves into general debate. The Riksdag's legislative powers include the right to tax and appropriate, the right to propose a constitutional amendment, the right to initiate changes in civil and criminal laws, and the right to schedule national referenda.[18]

Riksdag officers include a speaker and three vice speakers, all elected by majority vote.[19] Their job is to preside over debate and, after consultation with committee chairmen, to determine the order in which bills and committee reports will be heard on the Riksdag floor. Like other legislatures, all work is done in committees. The Riksdag is divided into sixteen standing committees with approximately the same powers of scrutiny and amendment as U.S. congressional committees. However, unlike U.S. congressional committees, bills cannot be killed in committee; all bills must be reported back to the full parliament with recommendations from the committee for action.

The Judiciary

The Swedish legal system is a civil law system influenced by customary law. The judiciary in Sweden is organized as a structural hierarchy with three tiers: the supreme court *(Hogsta Domstolen)*, six courts of appeal, and one hundred district and city courts. It is entirely independent of the executive and legislature. The supreme court is the final court of appeal in all cases and may consider new evidence. The courts of appeal, in addition to being appellate courts, administer the court system in their individual areas and train judges. District and city courts are courts of first instance and hear the largest number of cases. They are presided over by judges who are assisted by a popularly elected panel of three to five citizens. Jury trials exist only in libel cases.

In addition to the civil and criminal justice system discussed above, there is also a separate administrative justice system organized also on three tiers. The first tier is the county administrative courts, which hear appeals against public authorities' decisions. These decisions can range from tax assessment to business license revocation. The county administrative courts' decisions can be appealed to one of four administrative courts of appeal and ultimately to the supreme administrative court, which exercises authority on behalf of the cabinet. Additionally, labor courts and market courts govern labor disputes and business practices. All judges are appointed by the prime minister and cabinet and are theoretically apolitical, that is to say, they operate much like other high-ranking civil servants.

A special feature of the Swedish judicial system is the office of the ombudsman. It was created as another check on the abuse of authority by government officials. Any citizen who feels he or she has been mistreated or dealt with in an unfair manner by a government authority may lodge a complaint with the ombudsman. The office of the ombudsman then launches an investigation and can bring any evidence of error or wrongdoing before the courts or issue a public reprimand. Ombudsmen are appointed by the Riksdag for four-year terms. The function of the ombudsman is twofold. First, the offfice oversees how the courts and civil servants observe and apply the law. And next, it protects citizens' rights and freedoms. There are four ombudsman offices, each dealing with different areas of jurisdiction.[20]

The Bureaucracy

Much of the bureaucratic structure has been discussed earlier in terms of the ministries of government and the state agencies. The Swedish bureaucracy can be characterized as a decentralized network of boards and agencies that operate on county and municipal levels. They operate autonomously from the cabinet and parliament so as to allow implementation of government policy to be free from political interference. However, they are constrained by government through budgetary constraints on their day-to-day operation and policy directives. Since the 1980s, the Swedish bureaucracy has been significantly reorganized and downsized.

Such changes came with the introduction of privatization, government cutbacks caused by the recession, and the general desire to shift lines of authority and responsibilities. In this area, significant developments have occurred. First, the government now sets goals that it wishes to see achieved and allows its agencies to identify for themselves how they will achieve the goals. Next, administrative responsibilities have been shifted from the state agencies to local government authorities. This allows for more creativity and initiative from local government. Third, state agencies have been decentralized. Thus, each agency has created subdivisions or autonomous units within it. Two objectives are behind these changes. First is the desire to cut costs through the promotion of more efficient public administration. And second is the desire to make the bureaucracy more responsive to citizens' needs and demands.

State and Local Government

Sweden is divided into twenty-one counties, and each is governed by an administrative board appointed by the central government. The county administrative boards govern in conjunction with county councils, which are popularly elected. Each county is divided into municipalities governed by popularly elected councils. Each county is led by a governor appointed by, and responsible to, the cabinet. Local government is responsible for implementing medical and health care; social welfare programs; education; housing policy; land use; ambulance and fire service; and cultural, youth, and athletic programs. The central government helps finance local government implementation activities through program-specific grants and general grants created to offset differences in individual local authorities' tax laws. Each county has authority to levy income tax on its citizens.

Political Parties

Sweden has a multiparty system because of its electoral system of proportional representation. The Social Democratic party is the dominant party electorally as the discussion earlier stated. There are four other major parties: the Left party, the Liberals, the Center party, and the Moderates. Additionally since the late 1980s and early 1990s, there are three minor parties: the Environmentalists (Greens), Christian Democrats, and New Democracy. The multiparty system has.not led to parliamentary instability or political stalemate, unlike in Italy. In Sweden, stable government has been sustained, and the parties have adapted to changing economic and social conditions. The main explanation for this stability lies in the nature of the voting blocs that support the parties. The blocs are loosely organized as either socialist or nonsocialist. Such a clear demarcation allows for parties and voters to line up behind the socialist coalition or the non-socialist coalition, thereby allowing political fragmentation to be avoided. The Social Democrats, the Left party, and the Greens usually vote together on legislative matters and are generally perceived to be the socialist coalition. The remaining parties vote together as the non-socialist bloc. Majority-backed governments have been easy to form because of the existence of these blocs. Swedish political parties have played a major role in helping to initiate systemic reforms and policy outcomes.

Interest Groups

The range of interest groups active in Swedish politics is very similar to that of Great Britain and Germany. Organized interests can be identified as economic interest groups, employer groups (business), agrarian groups, and organized labor (the unions). Each of these interests aligns itself with political parties. Sweden has a highly institutionalized system of democratic corporatism.[21] Such a system is one in which there is institutional openness and broad group participation in the political system and consequently the policy process.

The Policy-Making Process

Authors have described policy making in Sweden as consensual.[22] In short, the policy-making process in Sweden is one which can be characterized as pragmatic and open to bargaining. What facilitates such openness and willingness to compromise is democratic corporatism. Bargaining between the government and a small number of well-organized interest groups in large part determines policy. This is very different from pluralism, where interest groups exert influence on policy makers from the outside. In corporatism, organized interests are ever-present participants in the policy-making process and are involved at every stage from formulation and adoption through implementation. Thus, organized interests participate in the formation and implementation of policy. Organized interests have been integrated into the policy-making process in the post-war period by a variety of mechanisms.[23] For example, there are regular ad hoc tripartite consultations between government, labor, and business representatives. Next, organized interests are included on all public commissions of inquiry. Third, organized interests are part of the Remiss procedure. Under this procedure, interest groups and administrative agencies are invited by ministerial departments to comment on legislation that is pending. Finally, organized interests are represented on ministerial advisory committees and on the state agencies' boards.

Keeping in mind how corporatism works, other factors germane to how policy is made in Sweden can be distinguished. First, the principal sites of policy initiation and ratification are the cabinet and the Riksdag. Depending on the strength of the government, the relative significance of the two institutions in the policy-making process will vary. However, because of the cabinet's centrality vis à vis the state's administrative structures and organized interest groups, it remains the main source of policy initiation and coordination.

While the cabinet plays the central role in the formal policy-making process in Sweden, the bureaucracy at various levels of government, state-owned enterprises, the judiciary, and the four ombudsmen control implementation and enforcement of policy. Such groups can be referred to as administrative elites. These elites also help refine policy once it is enacted. Theoretically, the ministries of government formulate policy and the state agencies implement it. However, in practice this distinction is blurred and there will be times when the state agencies make discretionary decisions that in many ways formulate policy. Political parties through the cabinet and parliament are crucial to formulation and adoption.

Chapter Eight
The United States of America

Since 1945 the most distinctive feature of American government is that significant change in the nation's political institutions has not been accompanied by significant changes in political culture. Americans today view politics very similarly to Americans in 1945. This does not mean that there have not been periods of mass discontent. Rather it means that such discontent has led to the altering of governing institutions and not a transformation of the American polity's political culture.

To understand U.S. modern political development is to comprehend a dichotomy of social expectations. On the one hand, a defining point of American political culture is the belief that limited government is good government. On the other hand, Americans have high expectations of what government is expected to do. Since the 1930s, government has expanded tremendously its intervention in people's everyday lives. The traditional distrust of political authority and government still remains and is probably even higher because of the increase in governmental daily involvement in citizens' lives. The dichotomy is one of push-pull: Government is not to be trusted and it should not be all-pervasive, yet on the other hand government should protect, regulate, provide, and govern.

The Political Setting

America's modern political development has been shaped by struggles, both within the nation—between various ethnic, religious, political, and economic groups—and externally with other nations. As the Second World War ended in 1945, America faced a very different world than when it entered the war. America left the war as the world's leading military and economic force. The war effort had been expensive and American lives had been lost; however, the war ended the Great Depression, provided social and economic mobility, and vastly expanded the role of the federal government.[1] The use of the atomic bomb and the growth of nuclear power led to a forty-years' arms race between the United States and the U.S.S.R. with the two powers becoming rivals for global hegemony. In the decade following the end of World War II, the United States became the wealthiest nation in the world. Government spending both at home and abroad plus consumer demand led to an era of widespread prosperity, improved living standards, and increased social mobility.

Modern American Political Development

The first post-war administration was headed by President Harry S Truman. Truman was a New Deal Democrat struggling to change America's social conventions. However, in his first term in office he faced a Republican-dominated Congress that was determined to protect the status quo.[2] For example, in 1947, over Truman's presidential veto, Congress passed the Taft-Hartley Act. This act was a restrictive labor law, which regulated labor and increased employer power though limiting the power of unions. Truman also found himself battling Congress over civil rights reforms. Legislation aimed at preventing lynching and abolishing the poll tax was rejected. Truman, however, was successful in integrating the armed forces and ending discrimination in the federal hiring process. In spite of opposition from Southern Democrats, Truman won reelection in 1948. His second term saw much of the same from Congress regarding his social and economic proposals. A presidential proposal for national health insurance legislation was soundly defeated by Congress. However, the administration had some successes. In this period, the minimum wage was increased, social security coverage was extended, and funds were appropriated for low-income housing projects.

Truman's successor in 1952, Republican Dwight D. Eisenhower, made it clear to the American public that he wished to see a return to smaller government and fiscally conservative economic policies. However, there was some continuance of New Deal policies during both his terms in office. Social security was expanded, the minimum wage was increased, and funds were spent on a public workers' program.[3] Eisenhower's eight years in office also saw cuts in defense spending. Generally, the period is one of peace and prosperity. GNP rose significantly; with six percent of the world's population, America produced half of the world's goods. Productivity rose and with it came changes in the labor market. Additionally income rose. Between 1945 and 1960, the median family income, adjusted for inflation, almost doubled. This increased the size of the middle class to two-thirds of all Americans. This growth of middle-class America reflected full employment, new opportunities, and increased federal spending. Prosperity led to the growth of suburbia, a baby boom, and more and more women entering the job market. Middle-class families were buying homes, cars, TVs, and increased education.[4] To facilitate educational opportunities, the government enacted the 1958 National Defense Education Act, which provided loans to college students and funds for teacher training. Prosperity, however, did not reach everyone. Michael Harrington, in his text, *The Other America: Poverty in the United States*, revealed an economic underworld of forty million to fifty million Americans, who were excluded from the prosperity.[5] Nearly one-fifth of the population lived below the poverty line. The poor were included in many groups, but especially among minority groups and inner-city dwellers.

The most notable political development of the Eisenhower period was the judicial activism of the U.S. Supreme Court ushered in under new Chief Justice Earl Warren. Warren, who was appointed in 1953, transformed the American legal system by expanding civil rights and civil liberties. The centerpiece of the court's decisions was the 1954 *Brown v. Board of Education of Topeka*. In this decision, the Warren court declared that school segregation violated the equal protection clause of the Fourteenth Amendment. In short, segregation of all educational establishments was unconstitutional. This began a new era in civil rights, which Eisenhower reluctantly supported with federal resources.[6] The remainder of the 1950s saw race discrimination and the struggle for civil rights for African Americans rise on the public agenda. By the end of the decade, there was clearly a simmering of dissent in American society.

The 1960s witnessed reform generated by presidential initiatives, judicial rulings, and social protest from the civil rights movement, the women's movement, the youth movement, and the environmental movement. John F. Kennedy's election in 1960 promised much; however, little was delivered. Kennedy's actions were cautious and pragmatic. The Kennedy presidency saw a continuation of Cold War policies through expanded involvement in southeast Asia, an arms buildup, and increased defense spending. Civil rights were not high on Kennedy's agenda, possibly because he knew the only way to get Congressional Southern Democrats to back his foreign policy initiatives was to be quiet on civil rights. However, he did propose a comprehensive civil rights bill to Congress, which had still not been passed by his assassination in November 1963.

Lyndon B. Johnson, Kennedy's successor, surprised many by his dedication to domestic reform. In July 1964, he proposed the Civil Rights Act, in memory of Kennedy. This act asked Congress to prohibit segregation in public accommodations and end discrimination in education and employment. Johnson also declared a "war on poverty" so as to end poverty and social injustices in America. In response, Congress established the Office of Economic Opportunity in August 1964 to direct the war on poverty programs.[7] After Johnson's landslide victory in the 1964 presidential election, he unveiled an ambitious series of reforms, which he labeled the "Great Society." The reforms were mostly an extension of Democratic New Deal philosophy. The late 1960s saw the introduction of Medicare, Medicaid, and urban development funding. Congress also passed the 1965 Voting Rights Act, which protected the rights of minorities to register and vote. Two further noteworthy policy changes under Johnson are the 1965 Immigration and Nationality Act and Executive Order 11246, which required groups engaged in business with the federal government to take affirmative action to remedy past discrimination against

African Americans. Both of these actions have had far-reaching and unexpected impacts on American politics.

Johnson's domestic policy agenda was truly ambitious, costly, and contentious. And it soon ran into problems. Additionally much of the Great Society's goals were undercut by the Vietnam War. Vietnam was proof of America's commitment to Cold War goals and the containment of communism. Continuing its policy of containment, as the 1960s passed, the United States committed more and more troops to Vietnam. It became a long and costly war. On the civil rights front, unprecedented gains were made.

Vietnam's impact on American politics is extensive. Many policy changes were generated by American involvement in Vietnam. For example, the United States saw the end of conscription and introduced other laws, such as the War Powers Resolution of 1973, which attempted to regulate presidential power. More importantly, Vietnam changed the way many Americans felt about the nation's involvement in foreign affairs. It produced a desire to return to the isolation of the past. Also, many Americans felt their mistrust in government and politicians grow as a result of America's war effort. The near-impeachment of President Richard Nixon confirmed what many Americans felt—they already suspected that government leaders were not credible or honest. Republican Richard Nixon, elected first in 1968 and then again in 1972, exercised more power than any peacetime president. The growth in the abuse of power by presidents led to what Arthur Schlesinger Jr. called the Imperial Presidency.[8] Such a presidency is one that pays little attention to the constitution and sees the presidency as all-powerful. Two of the reasons given for such growth were, first, congressional willingness to allow the president great latitude in foreign policy and, second, congressional willingness to give presidents increased authority.

Nixon was elected by a coalition of voters who were dissatisfied with what they perceived to be liberal policies. He promised voters a restoration of law and order and an end to Vietnam. Nixon's presidency was plagued by inflation, stock market decline, and the United States' first overall trade deficit since the nineteenth century. Nixon imposed wage and price controls and minor welfare reforms. The success of Nixon's administration was foreign policy. His Vietnamization program reduced American casualties and cut back America's involvement in the war. Under the Nixon doctrine, relations were opened with China and a Strategic Arms Limitation Treaty (SALT 1) was signed with the U.S.S.R. in 1972. However, many of Nixon's achievements were dismissed by his abuses of power and the Watergate scandal, which led to his resignation under the threat of impeachment in August 1974. Watergate left a legacy of increased citizen fear of excessive state power. Nixon was succeeded by Vice President Gerald Ford, who pardoned his predecessor upon taking office.

From Gerald Ford on, domestic politics in the post-Watergate era has focused on economic issues. Ford's administration, 1974 through 1976, saw America facing a mix of inflation and recession.[9] Under such conditions unemployment and prices rose. Just as in other nations discussed in this text, the Arab oil embargo affected the economy. Ford was defeated in 1976 by the Democratic candidate Jimmy Carter. Carter ran as a Washington outsider, which served him well electorally but added to his problems once elected. Although admired internationally for his advocacy of human rights, Carter failed to turn the economy around. He grappled unsuccessfully with rising inflation, an energy crisis, and unemployment. More importantly, he was at odds with Congress, and many of his initiatives were foiled by the institution in spite of it being controlled by his own party, the Democrats.

Ronald Reagan was elected to office in 1980 on the tide of growing conservatism. Reagan promised to restore America to its rightful place in the world pecking order, to cut government, and to stimulate the economy though supply-side economics.[10] He also renewed Cold War antagonisms. In 1981, Congress cut taxes and social programs and increased defense spending. Reagan advocated a huge military buildup and supported plans for the Strategic Defense Initiative (Star Wars). This was a multi-billion-dollar missile defense system. Over his next seven years in office, although many Americans became personally wealthy, many more slipped into economic hardship, military spending rose, government revenues failed to increase, and an extremely large budget deficit developed. When Ronald Reagan was elected President in 1980, the United States was a creditor nation. In 1988 when he left office, the United States was the world's largest debtor nation. Reagan left office a popular president in spite of scandals such as Iran-Contra. His record shows decreases in unemployment, inflation holding steady, a large deficit and more individuals living in poverty.

George Bush, Reagan's Vice President, was elected President in 1988. Most of his agenda was Reagan's, and so he continued much of the previous administration's policies. The collapse of the Soviet Union had transformed world politics. There was no longer a Cold War. Successful in foreign policy and lauded for his management of the Persian Gulf War in 1991, Bush's economic policy was heavily criticized. The war caused prices to rise, and war costs put pressure on federal revenues. Also, Bush had promised "no new taxes"—only to then raise taxes. His tenure saw the deficit grow, and he seemed to have no answer to combat the problem.

In 1992, America elected Bill Clinton, a "New Democrat," who supported efficient government, economic growth, a balanced budget, and health care reform. Clinton gave America a centrist policy agenda that successfully eliminated the deficit. On the negative side, when the Democrats lost control of Congress in 1994, significant health care reforms pursued by Clinton failed. However, he delivered a resurgent economy that is still booming as he prepares to leave office in the winter of 2000. So successful in terms of his economic policy, he is the first Democratic president in the post-1945 period to be able to pose the question "Are you better off today than you were eight years ago?" He did so at the party convention in Los Angeles in August 2000.

The centerpiece of Clinton's centrist measures was the 1996 Personal Responsibility and Work Opportunity Reconciliation Act, which reformed welfare policy. The legislation basically ended the safety net for the needy and less well-off Americans. It upset many liberal Democrats, but it solidified Clinton's hold on the center in American politics. Unfortunately Clinton's legacy will not be his obliteration of the deficit or economic recovery but that he was impeached by the House of Representatives in December 1998 on charges of lying under oath and obstructing justice in a civil case brought against him. He was acquitted by the Senate in February 1999.[11]

At the start of the twenty-first century, although the United States confronts a world order very different from the one it faced in 1945, it remains a major player in the global system. A further change facing the nation is that it is a post-industrial economy, based more on services and information processing than on manufacturing. This can be credited to the development of a global economy, where capital and business relationships cross national and regional borders. Today, millions and millions of American jobs depend on world markets. Expansion of American corporations has led to reduction in labor costs, access to foreign markets, and loss of American jobs. At the same time, foreign investment in the United States has significantly grown. Events in markets around the world affect American financial markets. To attract investment, increase trade, and regulate the global economy, the United States joined regional trade organizations, such as the Asia-Pacific Economic Corporation (APEC), and entered into treaties, such as the North American Free Trade Agreement (NAFTA).

Accompanying economic change has been social change. America in the year 2000 was more diverse than it ever was in 1945. This new diversity reflects rising immigration rates, which is the legacy of Johnson's 1965 immigration legislation, and increases in illegal immigration. By 1998, according to census data, immigrants accounted for 9.8 percent of the American population compared with 4.8 percent in 1970. Legislation has been passed to toughen immigration policy; however, America today is a multi-cultural nation. This will undoubtedly affect the policy agenda in the new millennium.

The Governmental Setting

American governing institutions are based on enduring operating principles. The operation of democracy is based on six democratic ideals (see Box 8.1). These ideals form the basis of the democratic system in the United States, which seeks to create a union of diverse peoples, places, and interests. Almost every author stresses the in-

---

Box 8.1   American Democracy's Operating Ideals

1. People must accept the principle of majority rule.
2. The political rights of minorities must be protected.
3. Citizens must agree to a system of rule by law.
4. The free exchange of opinions and ideas must not be restricted.
5. All citizens must be equal before the law.
6. Government exists to serve the people, because it derives its power from the people.

stitutionally fragmented nature of the American political system. Such fragmentation makes the possibility of winning coalitions at the federal level very difficult. Such a situation has led to what some describe as gridlock or ungovernability. This is indeed a tension that one must comprehend when looking at the American political system.

The Constitution

According to the U.S. Constitution, the American political system is a "republican form" of government. The constitution is the governing document of the United States. It is a written document that is the oldest such document in continuous use in the world today. Drafted in 1787 and ratified in 1788, it replaced the Articles of Confederation, which had created a weak national government and strong state governments. The framers of the constitution wished to create a stronger national government that derived power from the people and not the states.[12] Thus, the constitution established a national government independent of the states; however, state governments are reserved certain powers, such as police powers and public safety.

To understand the American constitution it is necessary to see that it reflects four basic organizing principles: federalism, separation of powers, checks and balances, and the supremacy clause. Federalism (Article IV) divides governmental power between the national government (federal) and subnational governments (states). Separation of powers constitutionally divides governmental powers among the three branches of government. Legislative power is vested in the U.S. Congress (Article I), executive power in the president (Article II), and judicial power in the federal courts, headed by the U.S. Supreme Court (Article III). This is perhaps the most significant difference between the American system and the other systems discussed in this text. Checks and balances are a device that ensures the separation of powers. Under checks and balances, each branch can keep the other two branches from encroaching on its constitutional powers. Finally, the supremacy clause (Article IV) specifies that the laws of the constitution and the nation are supreme in regard to the laws of each state.

Each principle was a necessary component of securing limited representative government, and, more importantly, they guaranteed ratification. The framers designed a system that asserted government as a necessary evil that should be limited in its ability to control citizens' lives. They were so wary of the potential for inevitable tyranny that they designed an institutional structure that (a) required several diverse constituencies to agree before a bill was passed and (b) where each part of the structure was against all the other parts. This, of course, has become problematic and made policy making difficult, for no single institution dominates the policy-making process as in other nations. Over time, there have been changes in the way the constitutional principles operate. For example, many powers reserved for the states have shifted to the federal government. Article V deals with how to change the constitution through the amendment process. Indeed, since its ratification the constitution has been amended twenty-seven times.[13] The first ten amendments provide citizens with legal protection from a potentially intrusive national government. Thus, collectively, the first ten are known as the Bill of Rights.

The Executive

Of the three branches of government, the American presidency has changed the most over the last two hundred years. Indeed, presidential power has grown tremendously since the first days of the nation's inception. The president and vice president are elected to office on the same ticket by the electoral college, which is elected directly from each state. Presidents serve fixed four-year terms.[14] Since 1951 and the Twenty-second Amendment, presidents have been limited to two terms in office.

Constitutionally the president has not been granted vast powers, and yet over the years American presidents have been very powerful and assumed powers that they were never granted under the constitution. Earlier it was seen that Schlesinger refers to this as the development of the Imperial Presidency.[15] Under the constitution the president is commander-in-chief of the armed forces, the conductor of U.S. foreign relations, chief executive, the administrator in legislative affairs, and head of state.

Presidents have expanded their actual power because the constitution loosely defines presidential power. Theoretically presidents are merely to stimulate the legislative function, and congress's job is to make laws. Over the years the public has come to expect a policy agenda from its presidents; thus, presidents do have policy agendas and many times congress passes it, although, of course, congress may refine it. The president is the chief legislator. As commander-in-chief, the president has the ability to commit troops to foreign soil. Since 1932 this has come to mean presidents can do it in such a manner as to engage in hostilities. Under the constitution, congress is the institution that possesses the war declaration function. As part of the Watergate fallout, congress did pass a series of laws that were aimed at regulating presidential power. None of the laws erode presidential power; they simply try to place restrictions on its expansiveness.

Presidential power is limited by the constitution, congress, the supreme court, the media, and public opinion. Congress may check presidential power through the appropriations process, the confirmation process, the impeachment process, and through limiting and passing laws that presidents are constitutionally obligated to implement. Whether congress chooses to limit presidential power depends on its inclination to. The latter part of the twentieth century witnessed strained relations between the two branches. This strain is partly caused by the separation of powers provision which allows for separate election for the two branches. There is always a possibility of divided government, where one political party controls one institution and the other institution is controlled by the other party. Up until 1945, most presidents worked with a congress controlled by their own political party. But since 1952 presidents often confront a congress where the opposing party has a majority in at least one of the houses. It is inevitable that strain will occur and that the effectiveness of presidential leadership will be limited. A further constraint since the late 1970s is the appointment of an independent counsel. Such counsel may be appointed by congress to investigate any case of alleged wrongdoing involving the president, vice president, or other major administrative officials. The impeachment of Bill Clinton led many to argue against the independent counsel's office. They argue that the office is not accessible, and there is little oversight of it. It has unlimited resources, including money, and this can lead to abuse of power. It can also be argued that the appointment and investigation processes can both be partisan-biased.

American presidents are crucial policy makers and initiate agendas they were elected around. More and more they have to use public opinion to gain support for the agenda when they face an unfriendly congress. Additionally presidents have to deal more effectively with a large number of bureaucratic agencies that exert influence over policy making and implementation. Over the years a number of regulatory agencies have been given broad authority by congress over certain issues. These agencies make regulations that affect policy implementation, for they have the force of law. Often the regulating agency has a better relationship with congress than the president, and this diminishes the president's authority.

The cabinet is appointed by the president and approved by the senate. The president has at his disposal a cabinet that is made up of senior administrators who head key executive branch departments, of which there are currently fourteen. Each department head is known as a secretary, and they include the secretary of state, the attorney general, and secretary of defense. The president is free to extend cabinet membership to other senior-appointed officials. The number of cabinet members varies from president to president. The American cabinet has no legal standing, and it is used only as a symbolic tool of government. Each department head advises the president individually on matters of policy and government administration.

The Legislature

The legislative branch of the U.S. government is congress. It is a bicameral national legislature consisting of the house of representatives and the senate, the two houses being jointly assigned legislative powers in the national government. The constitution vests congress with significant powers so that it can be the dominant branch of government. As the discussion of the presidency demonstrates, this was not the case in the twentieth century when presidential power expanded. That is not to say congress cannot act to limit presidential powers. As we have seen, this has also been the case in the last forty years. However, what has occurred is that congress has chosen not to assert its role as policy initiator. Congress finds it more effective to refine presidential legislative initiatives.

The house of representatives is made up of 435 members who are elected directly by popular vote to serve two-year terms.[16] The house's membership is allocated by population, and the number per state varies. The objective of the framers of the constitution was to make the house more responsive to popular will. The senate is made up of one hundred members—two from each of the fifty states—who serve six-year terms. Elections for the senate are by popular vote with one-third elected every two years. The senate was designed to be the deliberative national body. Until 1913 and the Seventeenth Amendment, senators were elected by state legislatures, rather than the people. Congress' structure is one of the most important compromises in the ratification of the constitution. To allay small states' fears that they would be disadvantaged, it was decided that one house of congress would have each state equally represented.

The two central powers of congress are legislation and oversight. Legislation, or law making, is a long and complicated process with only a small number of bills introduced to congress actually becoming laws. For a bill to become a law it must be passed in the same form by the house and the senate and then be signed by the president. If the president vetoes it, it can still become a law if the houses of congress pass it again with a two-third majority. Any bill that has not been passed by the end of each congressional session is considered dead and must be reintroduced in the next congress. In order for the legislative process to begin, a member of congress must introduce a bill (or proposed law) to the house or the senate. It is then forwarded to an appropriate legislative committee. The committee debates the bill and after considering it, may approve or amend it and pass it onto the full house or senate. If the committee fails to approve it or votes to take no action on it, the bill dies. The majority of introduced bills die in committees. If approved, it's placed on the calendar of the house where it was introduced and debated according to the rules of that house. During the debate, amendments may be voted on. After the debate, a vote is taken. If a majority votes for the bill, it goes to the other house of congress, where it's considered under the same basic procedures.

The legislative process is one huge obstacle course made up of successive hurdles. Often to get over each hurdle a coalition of support has to be built. The net result is a system of relationships and networks, where often support is determined by reciprocity amongst congresspersons rather than the merits of the legislation.

The oversight power is the ability of congress to monitor the implementation of laws that it passes. Included here is also the authority to investigate the executive branch through the holding of public hearings. There are numerous modern examples of such hearings from Watergate to the Iran-Contra affair to Whitewater. Because it controls the appropriation of funds for programs each year, congress can oversee programs being administered by the executive branch.[17] In doing so, they can shape implementation through either appropriating funds or rewriting the law. Many critics have argued that congress over the last fifty years has abdicated its law-making function for oversight.[18] They cite a number of reasons for this abdication. Among the reasons is the desire to win reelection (the incumbency effect) and the expansion of presidential power.

Congressional organization is structured so that discussion and debate take place in committees and subcommittees. Such a system allows members to specialize in a specific issue area. Committees are organized topically. Often members will serve on committees that deal with areas of constituency concern. Because of its centrality, the committee system affords committee chairs great power, such as controlling when bills will be taken up and the hiring of committee staff.[19]

The relationship of congress with the executive branch is critical to the workings of American government. Friction is common and over the last fifty years, as discussed earlier, there have been strained relations caused by divided government. In 1995, the relationship broke down completely with the president and congress unable to agree on a federal budget. This resulted in government shutdown. Congress has been criticized over the last decade for being no longer representative as a body.[20] Demographically, this is true. In the 1990s, approximately 9 percent of congress were African Americans, 4 percent Hispanics, 0.5 percent Asian, and 12 percent female. The most common profession of congresspersons was the law. In terms of abdicating their responsibilities, it does seem to be true that many of the laws not passed by congress are ones that would benefit the majority of people, for example, national health care reforms. So what laws pass? Many would say those that are backed by powerful and wealthy special interests. This leads many to argue congress is no longer representative of the people as a whole but representative of sectional interests who can contribute financially to a congressional campaign.

The Judiciary

The American legal system is based on English common law. Of the three branches, the judiciary is the most weakly defined in the constitution. In 1789, congress enacted the Judiciary Act, which established the federal courts' jurisdiction.[21] In 1803, the supreme court established the foundation for a more substantial judicial role in policy making. In *Marbury v. Madison,* the courts' right of judicial review was established. This is the power to declare any act or action unconstitutional. Judicial review is a power that gives the judiciary a central role in the checks and balances system. Judicial review does not, as many individuals think, belong solely to the supreme court; where appropriate, other courts may strike down laws that violate the constitution.

In spite of judicial review the judiciary for the most part is weaker than the other two branches of government. Their weakness is the result of a number of factors. First, congress has the ability to establish court jurisdiction in nonconstitutional cases. Next, justices are appointed by presidents (for life) and confirmed by the senate. Third, the courts rely on the executive to enforce their decisions. This is no easy matter when a decision flies against public opinion, as in the case of *Brown v. Topeka.*

Over the years the judicial branch, through the supreme court, has become a controversial actor within the policy-making process. It is argued that by passing judgment on what is constitutional, it sets policy agendas. The desegregation issue is a prime example of this. The U.S. Supreme Court in the mid-1950s set the civil rights agenda by telling the federal government that desegregation was a violation of rights. Another way in which the judiciary is involved in the policy-making arena is through providing a vehicle for individuals and groups whose interests have been ignored by other policy-making institutions.

The Federal Bureaucracy

The bureaucracy comes under the auspices of the executive branch and carries out the executive functions of the government. The bureaucracy comprises fourteen executive departments (cabinet departments) that are responsible for the major federal programs. Their chiefs (secretaries) are directly responsible to the president or to agencies within the executive office of the president, such as the Office of Management and Budget. There are also some 2000 executive agencies designed to deal with specific tasks. Examples would be the Environmental Protection Agency, the Securities and Exchange Commission, and the National Labor Relations Board. Most executive agencies are contained within departments. For example, the Internal Revenue Service is an agency within the Department of Treasury. However, a few agencies, such as the Central Intelligence Agency, are independent.

The twentieth century witnessed a large expansion of executive agencies. This has come about as society has changed and its needs have grown. The senior officers of the executive branch agencies manage a workforce of approximately 1.8 million civil servants.[22] Although part of the executive branch, the bureaucracy answers to congress because of congress' control of the budgetary process. This can sometimes influence bureaucratic action.

In recent years the bureaucracy's size has been criticized. Many believe that it is unwieldy and thus hard to control. More critical, though, is the ability of bureaucrats to influence policy or to make it. They can influence policy in a number of ways. Bureaucrats possess information that is often needed by policy makers, and they influence implementation of policy by actually being the day-to-day administrators of programs. Bureaucrats make policy through their ability to make regulations that have the force of law. Why should there be concern over increasing bureaucratic influence in the policy-making process? Because bureaucrats are not accountable to the general public. They are not elected but appointed, and once appointed it is hard to remove them. American bureaucrats, like their fellow bureaucrats elsewhere, are not passive in the policy-making process.

State and Local Government

As the American government is a federal one, authority and jurisdiction are divided up amongst the national, state, and local governments. Such decentralization causes unwieldiness, redundancy, and often a slow-moving response to issues and problems. However, it is also a way to represent the diversity of such a large nation as the United States. State governments play an important role in the governing of America. They plan and pay for most roads, run public schools, provide water, organize police services, licence professionals, and arrange elections. However, state and local governments are not separate entities, because they cooperate in administering services. While states are part of the federal system, local governments are part of the state system and, thus, they have no independent constitutional standing and are not a form of federalism.

The constitution establishes the relationship between state governments and congress. Basically everything that has not already been delegated to national government is the province of state governments. In those situations where there is a dispute over jurisdiction, the federal courts decide whose claim is valid. In the twentieth century, the courts tended to favor policies that gave more powers to the national government at the expense of state governments. Also, because of a fiscal mismatch, the national government is in a superior position to the state governments. This is still true even with the enactment of the 1972 General Revenue Sharing Act, where state and local governments receive a portion of federal income tax paid by the citizens. Lack of parity is especially true since the introduction of New Deal programs in the 1930s. Since then, the national government became involved in areas, related mainly to the economy, that had previously been the states' responsibilities. As a result, a cooperative form of federalism emerged in which the national government had the upper hand. Through federal grant allocations state governments must pursue goals defined by the national government.

State government can help in contemporary policy making apart from implementing broad national policy objectives. At the state and local level, experimentation may take place. The cost of failure at the local level is much less than if a national policy was implemented. In the early 1990s, welfare reform was experimented with in Wisconsin before the national government implemented national change in 1996. Today, federalism resembles a marble cake, where functions and financing are shared between national, state, and local governments.

Political Parties

For most of America's history it has had an indistinct two-party system. Many individuals vote into office the candidate of one of the two major parties, who then votes as he or she thinks best. That is to say not always as the party position dictates. The party system is the result of the electoral system, which is a winner-takes-all, plurality system. This has negated the vote of third parties. A vote for a third party is a lost vote because losers get nothing. This is unlike proportional representation where seats in legislatures are proportioned out to votes.

Many argue that the Republican and Democratic parties are less important than they were fifty years ago. Slightly more than a third of all Americans identify as independents and thus elections are now up for grabs. Also, voting in presidential elections has declined to around 50 percent. In terms of influence on policy, the two parties appear very similar to each other. They propose policy agendas that are vague and centrist. They do so in order to appeal to the largest number of voters. Many have said this is the reason why voters have lost interest and are no longer affiliating with the parties.

The debate in America between the parties is not on what is to be done, but on how it is to be achieved. They believe in much of the same policy outcomes, but they disagree on how to achieve the outcomes. In 1996, both parties agreed on welfare reform; it was only in some of the details they disagreed. Often the disagreement is so minute that it does not affect the type of reform or policy being formulated. Each party does present a platform which can be summarized as a series of comprehensive policy proposals. Theoretically these platforms are the product of parties balancing the needs of various interests in society. Finally, both parties' candidates often fight for the same campaign contributions, thus allowing themselves to be influenced as policy makers by the same interests. For these reasons, many Americans' confidence in their party system has eroded.

Interest Groups

Interest groups in America have grown in numbers and in influence over policy making since the 1950s. Their prominence is partly caused by the increase in distributive and redistributive policies by the American government. The decline of parties has also led to the saliency of American interest groups. The types of interest groups that exist are extremely diverse and include mass organizations as well as local groups interested in a sole local issue. There are, of course, the traditional groups representing business and labor.

Interest groups influence policy making in the United States through a variety of ways. Mainly they influence policy by being funders of policy makers. That is to say, their ability to contribute financially to campaigns may influence elected officials to formulate and implement certain types of policy. The nature of the electoral system with its emphasis on the need for financial resources in order to run for office facilitates this role for interest groups. Many have pinpointed the failure of health care reform in the early 1990s to the amount of money spent by groups such as the American Medical Association and health insurance companies on lobbying against it. Additionally, there are times when individuals who have lacked access to the policy-making process have been able to utilize interest groups to articulate their position and thus gain broad public opinion around their interests and a successful policy outcome. The case of African Americans in the 1950s and 1960s demonstrates this argument. However, this is not the norm. Those groups with little resources have little access, and thus their influence in policy is minimal.

A further effect of interest groups on policy making according to Antony Downs is the "iron law of political dispersion."[23] Downs argues that with such open access to multiple policy decision makers as in the United States, that as one group profits from a federal program so do all others. It is inevitable that benefits are distributed across the board. In essence, American government has ended up handing out too much to all the various interests, and this has led to inefficiency and excessive government. The only problem with this view is it assumes that all groups are equal or that there is not bias for certain groups at the expense of others. Certain groups such as American business are advantaged while others who speak for the poor or minorities are disadvantaged. There is no doubt that business is advantaged because of its access to large sums of money that can be "poured" into the policy-making system to make it more "friendly." To counter this argument, authors such as Salisbury argue that the proliferation of groups has actually led to a weakening of groups' influence on the policy-making process.[24] Every issue attracts multiple supporters and opponents; this makes the policy-making environment more open and allows decision makers more freedom because they are not tied to any one group or cause. Also, as constituencies become more complex, more interest groups prevail, thereby reducing the influence of any one group. Finally, the explosion of interest groups actually could be leading to cross-pressurized legislators. Thus, legislators might have ties with one group, but because of the pressure they face from the multitude of other salient groups, they cannot make a choice because of conflicting pressures and information and the possibility of alienating too many constituents. They tend to stay away from making decisions that actually make policy. Rather, they continue to make incremental policy choices.

The Policy-Making Process

The American policy process can be characterized as a decentralized one with multiple points of access. The structure of institutional arrangements as dictated by the constitution facilitates this type of policy-making process. B. Guy Peters argues that American government has a number of policy-making structures but no real organization, for there is an absence of effective coordination and control.[25] For example, organized interests have the ability to enter into the policy-making process at a variety of levels and can also dispute any outcome in a variety of venues. Peters goes on to argue that over time individual policy domains have been able to gain autonomy from central coordination.[26] The one area where centralization does seem to occur most often is defense policy, and this is probably because there is the most consensus amongst national leaders. The fact that the United States has less extensive policy in many policy sectors compared to other industrialized democracies reflects the ideological consensus that exists around the role of the state in the intervention of the economy.

Multiple points of access can also mean multiple points of blockage. The process is one of push-pull. Getting a policy formulated does not necessarily mean that the policy will be implemented as it was adopted. For example, a law will be passed by congress, yet executive agencies must issue regulations to explain how the law will be implemented. The choice of implementation strategy and directions can change subtly the actual goals of the law. Also, once a policy is in place, it can be contested or undermined by the adoption of another competing policy. This is possible because of the lack of centralization in the policy-making process.

Not only is the process decentralized, but it is also fragmented and there are few mechanisms that can control the impact of such fragmentation. There are both advantages and disadvantages to such a system. The involvement of multiple actors means policy can be fully deliberated before agreement is reached, and some sort of consensus is reached. Next, the presence of multiple decision makers in the process should ensure a greater measure of innovation. Third, the decentralization of the process allows for the protection of individual rights and socioeconomic groups; no one institution can encroach or violate such interests and rights. The multiple points of access allow for a system of checks. The disadvantage of such a process is sometimes it is impossible to get a policy outcome. The multiple decision points in the process ensure that it is often difficult to get a policy through each of the stages of the process successfully. This is the gridlock often referred to in the 1980s and early 1990s. A lack of centralization in the policy process often produces policies that conflict with one another. This is especially true at the state level. A number of individuals will point to anti-smoking policies and government subsidization of tobacco growers to argue this point.[27] Second, the more actions and interests represented the more incoherent the policy. Often one policy has to please many, and it attempts to do too much without actually doing anything.

From an institutional perspective, presidents propose policies and implement them, while congress has the ability to deliberate policy. The courts are often seen to be influential in the policy process. However, courts mostly block or shape policies and do not initiate policy. The whole process is open to input from various sources through campaign contributions and other types of influence that support a candidate who supports their interests.

Suggested Further Readings

Brazil

T. G. Goertzel, *Fernando Henriquez Cardoso: Reinventing Democracy in Brazil* (Boulder: Lynne Reinner, 1999).

W. Hunter, *Eroding Military Independencies in Brazil: Politicians Against Soldiers* (Chapel Hill: University of West Carolina Press, 1997).

S. Mainwaring, *Rethinking Party Systems in the Third World of Democratization* (Stanford: Stanford University Press, 1999).

R. Roett, *Brazil: Politics in a Patrimonial Society* (New York: Praeger, 1984).

Germany

D. P. Conradt, *Germany's New Politics: Parties and Issues in the 1990s* (Berghahn, 2000).

D. P. Conradt, *Power Shift in Germany: The 1998 Election and the End of the Kohl Era* (Berghahn, 2000).

M. N. Hampton, C. Soe, and C. Soe (eds.), *Between Bonn and Berlin: German Politics Adrift* (National Book Network, 1999).

P. E. J. Pulzer, *German Politics, 1945–1995* (New York: Oxford University Press, 1996).

Great Britain

S. J. D. Green and R. C. Whiting (eds.), *The Boundaries of the State in Modern Britain* (Cambridge: Cambridge University Press, 1996).

S. Haseler, *The English Tribe: Identity, Nation and Europe* (New York: St. Martin's, 1996).

M. Perryman, *The Blair Agenda* (Lawrence & Wishart, 1998).

A. Wright, *British Political Process* (London: Routledge, 2000).

Japan

G. L. Curtis, *The Logic of Japanese Politics* (New York: Columbia University Press, 1999).

D. McCarjo, *Contemporary Japan* (New York: St. Martin's, 2000).

T. J. Pempel, *Regime Shift: Comparative Dynamics of the Japanese Political Economy* (Ithaca: Cornell University Press, 1998).

J. A. A. Stockwin, *Governing Japan: Divided Politics in a Major Economy* (London: Blackwell, 1998).

Sweden

D. Lachman, *Challenges to The Swedish State: The Myth of the Powerless State* (London: Routledge, 1995).

L. Miles, *Sweden and European Integration* (London: Ashgate, 1997).

H. Milner, *Sweden: Social Democracy in Practice* (New York: Oxford University Press, 1993).

A. Widfeldt, *Linking Parties With People* (London: Ashgate, 1999).

United States

W. C. Berman and S. T. Kalter, *America's Right Turn: From Nixon to Clinton* (Baltimore: Johns Hopkins University Press, 1998).

C. Bosso, J. Portz, and M. Jolley, *American Government: Conflict, Compromise and Citizenship* (Boulder: Westview, 1999).

J. Harman McElroy, *American Beliefs: What Keeps a Big Country and a Diverse People United* (Chicago: Ivan R. Dee, 1999).

PART III

POLICY SECTORS

Chapter Nine
Social Welfare Policy: A Safety Net or a Crutch?

Throughout the twentieth century, for many theorists and policy makers the provision of appropriate levels of well-being for citizens living in modernized societies has been an overriding concern. When we talk specifically of social welfare policy, we acknowledge a series of programs ostensibly designed to assist the poor and the working class in society. Social welfare policy attempts to redress the gaps or inequalities in society and is part of a government's overall social policy. Social policy covers a wide range of social and economic phenomena, from notions of self-esteem and individual rights and needs, to complex policy questions such as the relief of indigence and unemployment and the supply of goods and services, such as housing, education, and healthcare. The level of expenditure that a government allocates to social welfare policy is dictated by the extent to which a society believes its government should be responsible for providing for the social and economic security of its citizens through pensions and social security, in short the extent of its welfare state. Esping-Andersen argues that within market societies (i.e., capitalist economies), nations fall into one of three main types of welfare state regimes: conservative, social democratic, and liberal.[1] Classification depends on the extent to which the state seeks to work with or to counter the effects of the market on social inequalities. Esping-Andersen makes clear his regimes are ideal types. Indeed, many welfare states will have elements of all three types.

A number of authors have discussed why governments need to provide social welfare for their citizens. In many ways, examining why welfare should be provided allows us to discern the major goals of such policy. One perspective views welfare provision as a relief program that is an ancillary to economic arrangements.[2] Thus, governments provide services that absorb and control unemployment, disabilities, ill health, and aging. Such a perspective basically argues that social welfare policy is made necessary by the instability that is inherent in capitalist economies. A second

perspective argues that welfare policy regulates labor.[3] Provision of welfare is punitive and degrading and instills in the majority of individuals the fear of being on
government relief rolls. A further perspective put forward is that when democracies
collapse and are replaced by socialist regimes it is because of a "poison" that circu-
lates among citizens; the poison is the growth of the feeling that there are "haves"
and "have nots."[4] In short, societies cannot afford to have large numbers of individuals who are suffering obvious inequalities without relief. Welfare acts as a pacifier.
Welfare policy exists to help reintegrate disaffected groups back into the system.[5] In
its broadest sense, welfare policy provides security to those in need. Such security
can be temporary or permanent. A final perspective found in the literature is that
welfare policy should foster independence by encouraging citizens to be self-
supporting.

Different governments have different policy goals in mind when they formulate and implement welfare policy solutions. Generally welfare policy solutions can
be categorized into three broad types: rights, rules, and inducements. Rights are basically the provision of services and programs that individuals are entitled to by nature of their citizenry and their very being. Rules basically state who is eligible for
what services and programs. Finally, inducements, which can be positive or negative, are ways in which individuals are encouraged or discouraged to receive services and benefits.

The tools available to government for the provision of welfare fall under two
general categories. First, policies that benefit the poor. And second, policies that
help the general public. The first category includes general assistance programs that
give money, food, or clothing directly to qualifying individuals; work assistance
programs for the needy; and categorical assistance that targets aid for low-
income individuals. In terms of policies helping the general public, they can take
many forms. The most common is social insurance that covers income losses due to
illness, unemployment, and retirement. The second-most common are social regulation programs which protect individuals from the problems of industrialized society. Such programs would include consumer protection and worker protection
regulations.

Several approaches have been used by governments in the provision of social
welfare policy. The first is the preventive approach. This attempts to ensure that individuals do not become poor. The second approach is the alleviative approach.
This deals with those individuals who are already poor and attempts to provide
some kind of governmental assistance to alleviate their condition. The next approach used by government in its provision of welfare is the punitive. This is based
upon the assumption that if individuals are poor, it's because of their own moral
and character defects. In other words, it is their own fault. Therefore, government
should try to discourage them from being lazy by making it as difficult as possible
to obtain public assistance in the form of governmental benefits. And when government does have to provide assistance it should be minimal. The fourth approach is
the curative approach, which argues that causes of poverty, such as lack of education
and job training, should be cured. This approach emphasizes programs that attack
the causes of poverty. The curative approach is often used with a political strategy

of giving the poor some sort of control over the institutions that affect their communities. Community organization is encouraged. The last approach is the incomes approach. Individuals are encouraged to work while they receive government assistance. As their job-related income increases, their level of benefits decrease. The idea behind this is that an individual is better off working than not working. One way to achieve this is through a negative income tax.

All developed nations maintain a variety of social welfare programs as rights of citizenship. Welfare systems are established to provide safety nets to prevent individuals from suffering the effects of poverty. Welfare programs have always aroused heated debate because many critics claim welfare encourages its recipients to become dependent on government support and remain unemployed.

In all the nations discussed later in this chapter, the government decides how much welfare support to provide, and to whom, based on measures of economic well-being. Measures of economic well-being are based on national mean income figures. Mean income is the estimate of what a typical individual earns over a stated period of time, usually twelve months. Those individuals who earn less than a determined amount below the national mean are considered poor. Welfare programs targeted to people with relatively little income and few assets are categorized as *means-tested* welfare programs. Other forms of income support are referred to simply as *non-means-tested programs*. It is clear from the six nations that successive governments have utilized all of the above approaches at different periods of time.

In the majority of, if not all, cash welfare programs, benefits quickly decrease as recipients' incomes increase. Such programs are thus targeted, or restricted, to those with little or no income and minimal assets. Some programs further restrict benefits to those meeting additional, non-income requirements, known as categorical targets. For example, benefits might depend on a recipient being a single parent with dependent children.

Many welfare programs and benefits are solely for individuals belonging to identified groups. For example, the elderly or people with mental or physical disabilities receive several varieties of support that government provides specifically to them. Eligibility for social insurance programs depends upon individuals having made prior financial contributions to a fund, which can be drawn on later. Such programs provide support to workers and their families when they lose employment, retire, or become disabled.

Theoretically, welfare targets direct support to those most in need. However, many critics argue targeting creates problematic disincentives. For example, if a welfare recipient begins to earn money, or increases income, benefits may decrease and taxes increase. This can prove to be a disincentive for the recipient to continue to work. The system, thus, penalizes welfare recipients who find work; this is especially true for those in many of the low-wage jobs typically available to such individuals. Working at a minimal wage, minus taxes, is often less than income generated through welfare benefits. Targeting welfare benefits to certain groups can also create disincentives. People may opt for certain behavior patterns so as to remain eligible for welfare benefits. For example, a single woman may remain single or live with a partner rather than marry so that benefits are not decreased or lost.

The debate over welfare has often been defined by the need to promote socially approved behavior, on the one hand, while on the other hand society attempts to be compassionate to those less fortunate.

Brazil: Imitation of the Real Thing

Brazil has often been characterized as an "imitation" welfare state.[6] Strong beliefs in public assistance to those in need have never really existed in Brazil. As the nation moved from military rule to dictatorship to democracy, the welfare system has remained restricted and often the subject of political rhetoric rather than political action. For many Brazilians, the end of military rule was not only a victory for the forces of democracy but also for those who proposed welfare reforms. Such proponents argued the door was now open to expansion and a "new" commitment to public assistance. Since the 1980s, the Brazilian state has attempted to organize programs that would satisfy the demands of the "have nots" of Brazilian society. Progress was made toward universal coverage of social rights. That is to say that every individual, from birth, would have the right to a set of goods and services, which should be supplied either directly by the state, or indirectly, through regulation of civil society. In this vein, agencies such as the National Institute for Food and Nutrition (INAN) were created. However, all welfare policy solutions have been hindered by the weak cultural belief in public assistance and a lack of commitment to universality.[7] President Cardoso argues the resistance to expanding social welfare spending comes not from a lack of money but from a lack of justice.

Policy History and Evolution

Under military rule, little attention was paid to the people's social welfare, and they received little policy attention and public assistance. Indeed the military managed to steer much of the focus away from welfare policy and programs. This prevented the establishment of a "legitimate" public welfare system. Military rule, until its demise in 1985, was characterized by a lack of commitment on the part of the state to the needy. Public sector aid was minimal. Part of this was because of lack of funding. The Brazilian government gave priority to solidifying the authority and strength of the regime and economic expansion. Little was left to spend on social welfare policy. Benefits and services were limited and, for the most part, distributed disproportionately. The focus was on rapid growth and not on providing benefits such as payments to the unemployed. At the same time that the population was growing, so were social and cultural gaps. As the 1960s and 1970s passed, more and more Brazilians were living in poverty. The situation was exacerbated by the military regime's reliance on foreign aid and investment. Such monies had strict spending guidelines that required less spending on social welfare provision.

Change in governmental provision of welfare came about toward the end of civilian rule. A number of programs were initiated; however, they were limited and funded unequally. The welfare system that emerged was corruptly administered. By the late 1970s, a state-centered movement arose challenging bureaucratic adminis-tration of welfare programs. The movement was largely drawn from the middle-class and the industrial-working-class. Supported by the Catholic church and the entrepreneurial sector, widespread demands for changes in social welfare provision were articulated.

The end of military rule was seen by many as a victory for those proposing in-creased welfare provision. The door was open for radical expansion of policy. This "new" commitment to public assistance can be seen in the 1988 constitution. The new constitution contained the rhetoric of an ideology of universality of social poli-tics and was committed to solving Brazil's prevailing crisis. The constitution re-duced the workweek to forty-four hours maximum, established profit sharing for all workers, provided time and a half for overtime work and paid vacations to include a 30 percent base of an individual's salary; daycare facilities to be established for all children less than six, maternity leave of 120 days and paternity leave of five days. Additionally all workers were to be protected against arbitrary dismissal. All of this is stated in the constitution; however, the implementation of such provisions leaves much to be desired.

Welfare policy in Brazil, today, consists of a series of programs and services that provide the benefits of social security to the unemployed, the sick, the dis-abled, and the elderly. Such provision is under the Organic Social Security law of Brazil, enacted first in the 1930s and modified in the late 1970s and again in the late 1990s. The law covers urban workers, rural workers, and federal civil servants. The urban workers receive a wide range of benefits, including health insurance and old-age pensions. These benefits are funded by workers, employers, and the gov-ernment. Rural workers and federal civil servants receive lesser benefits. The pro-grams are limited, funded unequally, and coverage is sparse.

The economic development model chosen by civilian governments in the 1990s and the basis of state funding of social policies negate the universality prin-ciple. In practice, universality in Brazil is exclusion.[8] Brazilian social policy is not only inadequate (in quantity and quality) to cover the needs of the poor and low-income individuals, but it also deliberately excludes medium- to high-income in-dividuals from receiving benefits that in other welfare states are commonplace. Many middle-class Brazilians have no option but to utilize the private sector for pensions or educational services. In other nations, such as England, Sweden, and Germany, the option to remain within the public sector for provision of social benefits has always been available for middle- to high-income earners. In recent years, however, individuals in such nations have been encouraged to go outside of the public sector.

Part of the problem for the Brazilian state is that social inequality in the coun-try is enormous. It is impossible to maintain equal welfare policy for equals. In countries such as Sweden and Germany, the state has been able to achieve this "equal for equals" policy because of a long history of achieving low levels of social inequality through income and social policies developed since the 1940s.[9] What has been achieved through public-sector provision elsewhere is left mostly to the private sector in Brazil. Today, large numbers of Brazilians participate in voluntary associations that help the poor.

As discussed earlier, in the chapter on Brazilian politics and government, Brazilian society displays marked inequalities on all levels. The nation has major problems with poverty, hunger, disease, and providing adequate services, such as clean water and electricity. Data shows that approximately one-third of Brazilian families have a total income lower than two minimum wages.[10] The wealthiest 10 percent of Brazilians receive almost 50 percent of the nation's income while the poorest 50 percent of the population get little more than 10 percent.[11] Brazil has one of the widest income gaps in the world. An estimated one-fifth of the Brazilian population, about thirty-three million people, lives at the so-called "misery level."

Policy Structure and Organization

Much of the financing of social policy in other nations is raised largely through taxation and taxpayer contributions. However, in Brazil just under 50 percent of working individuals make no contributions to social insurance/security schemes.[12] Without a doubt, several fiscal gaps exist between what the government needs to spend on welfare and what it raises.

This is only one problem for the Brazilian state to grapple with in its provision of welfare benefits. The practices and problems created by lengthy military rule remain difficult to overcome. Additionally, the lackluster attention to public assistance and services to the poor, combined with an unwavering commitment to western economic practices in conjunction with the prevailing economic crisis have placed Brazil in a difficult position. Cardoso's second term has seen the implementation of drastic measures to cut government spending, increase taxes, and reduce indebtedness. In November 1998, Congress approved comprehensive social security reform. The reform was aimed at both general citizens' and government employee benefits.

The reform affects government employees in the following ways: (1) retirees are barred from returning to work in the public sector; (2) the financial and actuarial balance of the new system is enhanced through provisions to boost contributions of both active workers and retirees; and (3) pensions for certain classes of civil servants are capped, and retirees wishing to draw high pensions will have to now join private social insurance plans.

The most important change concerns the new criteria for retirement eligibility for all Brazilians, which require men to be sixty years old and have paid into the system for thirty-five years; women will have to be fifty-five and have paid into the system for thirty years. For those who have contributed less than the required number of years, the retirement age rises to sixty-five for men and sixty for women, and the amount of the pension becomes proportional to the years of contribution. Similar provisions (particularly as pertaining to retirement eligibility) were adopted for private-sector pensions. In January 1999, the Chamber of Deputies passed measures that converted the general provisions of the social security reform into specific laws by raising the contributions of government employees to their respective pension funds from 11 to 25 percent. Additionally a new tax ranging from 11 to 25 percent is levied on retired government employees. The law also sets a minimum monthly benefit equivalent to $1,010 for all individuals. Critics point out that the next bout of inflation could easily reduce this amount to a level insufficient to meet the minimal expenses of Brazil's retirees.

Cardoso's reform represents an ambitious agenda for restricting and reforming the public sector. The government estimates that the changes in social security laws will cut seventeen billion dollars from the federal budget over the upcoming eight years. The changes have not received widespread support. Opponents of the plan demanded that retirement be based strictly on the number of years worked. They argue the Brazilian working class is often forced to begin work at a very early age and that in the more impoverished areas of the country life expectancy is just fifty years. Keeping workers on the job longer is also expected to increase Brazil's unemployment rate, which is already at record levels.

Brazil faces a cycle which is hard to break. There is incredible need because of the inevitable by-products of economic recession; however, cuts in expenditure are one of the main ways governments attempt to meet recessions, thus creating more social inequalities. The fifth-most-populous nation in the world has 33 to 50 percent of its population living with no access to public services and benefits.[13] In addition, procedures developed to distribute funds and resources to the needy are heavily flawed and still plagued by corruption, waste, and inefficiency.[14] Consequently, the Brazilian government has reacted poorly to the constant need for assistance and services as well as to the temporal demands of national emergencies, such as droughts, famines, and diseases.

Future Outcomes and Policy Weakness

Many Brazilian social reformers, upset with the neglect of social welfare, argue social reform should be implemented top-down. They argue for a strong and paternalistic state. With the transition to democracy still not strongly consolidated, this could prove a dangerous road to take. The dominant conservative entrepreneurial political elite in Brazil claim the Western-dependent model will, in the next decade, boost the economy, spur growth, and solidify Brazilians socially. Privatization, an open economy through global financial liberalization and market expansion, foreign aid, and foreign investments will, according to the ruling elite, pull Brazil out of their economic troubles. In addition, the ruling elite believes that the public deficit is the root cause of Brazil's social problems. In fact, they promote reform of the already limited social welfare system to allow for more private control and limited public expenditure.

Unfortunately, the present policy strategy ignores the devastating consequences of continued devotion to Western economic models and reliance on foreign intervention. The austerity measures instituted under the Cardoso debt-restructuring plan have prevented an expansion of Brazil's welfare policies. This could be a problem given the huge disparities in income distribution.

Brazil's chosen model of economic development has created serious problems economically and socially. Economically, Brazil has allowed its national debt to escalate waiting for Brazil's dependency on foreign aid and investment to solidify its economy and spur growth. In addition, Brazil's decisions to privatize and deregulate industries has denationalized Brazil's assets and promoted de-industrialization that, in turn, further aggravates social inequality. Socially, the gap between the minority and majority, although enormous, is widening even further. At the same time, public services are being dismantled, federal expenditures are being cut, and despite the rise of privatization, taxes are rising and poverty and hunger are spreading rapidly. Politically, the limited amount of legitimacy that was gained at the end of authoritarian rule in 1985 is waning rapidly in the midst of continued corruption (vote buying, payoffs, and media manipulation), continued cuts in public spending and programs, and the unstable, dependent nature of the government. As a result, the Brazilian people distrust their government, and many individuals are pessimistic about change in the welfare system. However, the prosperity experienced under the Brazilian miracle and the democratization process since the late 1980s have led to a much deeper political engagement by the Brazilian populace, stronger trade unions, and a variety of grassroots organizations. Kenneth Maxwell argues that many Brazilians have found their political voice and are rethinking what it means to be Brazilian.

The future for Brazilian social welfare does not look good. The ruling elite in Brazil has devoted what little money they have and what limited resources they possess to making the Western model work in Brazil. They continue to attract foreign nations and companies to Brazil with lucrative contracts, reduced taxation, and limited liability in the hopes their capital will revitalize the Brazilian economy as well as fund programs and services aimed at protecting and securing their people. At the same time, the Brazilian government is so dependent on foreign investment that it is virtually impossible for them to make any changes to their system. Globalization has hurt Brazil's industrial capacity, stifled their economic markets and neglected to meet the needs of the population, in particular, the less-well-off. In 1999, the state government of Rio Grande do Sul suspended $257 million in corporate welfare benefits for American automakers Ford and General Motors. In their announcement, the state government targeted the cash to schools and hospitals. The state's development secretary justified the proposed cuts as "the government needing to invest in health, education, housing, and security." Ford and General Motors were given welfare benefits in the form of low-cost loans, infrastructure projects, and other "sweeteners" such as tax-code loopholes, direct grant payments, and contracts for unnecessary activities. It is uncertain if more state governments will follow suit and dictate to the national government social welfare policy innovation.

Germany: Status Maintenance with Minor Cutbacks

Kuhnle summarizes German social welfare in the 1990s as a confirmation of status quo with some minor modification and consolidation.[15] Prior to reunification, two distinct social welfare schemes were in existence. The West German system was characterized by pluralism, corporatism, and decentralization. There was high welfare provision within a hierarchical and ordered society. Esping-Andersen characterizes the FRG welfare state as conservative. When one looks at East Germany prior to re-union, welfare policy was centralized and universalistic. Central to welfare provision was equity of treatment and wide-scale coverage. However, it was also marked by deficiencies of quality.[16]

Post-unification the Western model prevails, as it has in so many other policy areas. Organizational uniformity in welfare policy was imposed on both Western and Eastern states. However, in reality, key elements of welfare provision remain separate.[17] For example, Western social insurance has been extended to the Eastern states with benefits converted at parity rate, with Eastern entitlements being calculated on the basis of Eastern income trends and not national income trends.

Policy History and Evolution

Under Bismarck, Germany introduced the first statutory social insurance system. In 1883, compulsory sickness insurance for certain industrial workers was introduced. The following year, workers were protected against work-related injuries through an accident insurance scheme. Provisions concerning old age and invalidity insurance were introduced by 1889. Such provisions provided the foundation for the steady expansion of social welfare in Germany until the Second World War.

Between the two world wars, Germany was committed to social welfare, and moves were made toward building a nascent welfare state. Social insurance was expanded through constitutional clauses that promoted a strong welfare ethos. In 1923, the Empowering Act (EA) was passed to replace the Poor Law of 1870. The Poor Law ensured assistance to those in need through payments administered by organizations representing the working class. Relief was administered to all in need and was not based on any specific type of employment. The 1923 legislation eliminated the Poor Law requirement of residency eligibility for benefits and promoted local responsibility for relief. The EA also incorporated employer/employee financing of the welfare system.

Under Adolf Hitler, the face of German welfare underwent change. Unemployment insurance was eliminated and replaced with a broad public works program, and the Second World War saw wholesale restriction of social welfare benefits. Restriction was continued under the Allied occupation until 1947. The period of 1945 to 1949 saw the German state struggling to reconstruct its social welfare system while integrating large numbers of refugees, war veterans, and war victims into German society.

It is with the enactment of the 1949 Basic Law that conditions were brought about that were conducive to social welfare legislation. As mentioned earlier in the discussion of the 1949 German constitution, the Basic Law guarantees a social state (*Soziale Reschtestat*). Such a state reproduced many of the features of the old Bismarckian welfare state.[18] Freeman and Clasen argue in essence that the 1949 constitution was a compromise between Christian Democratic beliefs about state responsibilities and Social Democratic notions of social justice.[19] Although the Basic Law ensures that the key elements of the German welfare state are uniformly applied throughout the nation, there were variations between the states in the ways in which social services were provided. Under the Basic Law guidelines, several social welfare framework laws were enacted.

From 1950 to 1969, Germany witnessed a period of economic growth and expansion of the social welfare system. A number of laws were enacted ranging from social security expansion (1957) to the construction of public housing to guaranteed minimum vacation. Legislation was also passed adjusting public pensions to periodic changes in wages and salaries. The 1970s was a period of welfare reform. Among the changes were social insurance expansion to cover more individuals, including the self-employed; rehabilitation payments and facilities were increased; and individuals were given wider choices in institutional providers and benefits. By the late 1970s increasing economic problems and mounting pressures from political parties, interest groups, and bureaucrats led to a slowdown in social welfare expenditure.

The 1980s saw further modifications and many benefits were cut back. The cuts, however, were not as severe as in other nations. Kept intact were family and parental allowances and tax payments that benefitted married couples. However, overall the era was one of cost containment by retrenching state social welfare provision, especially in the area of public pensions. Pension adjustment laws were enacted in 1982 and 1984. Under this legislation, pensioners were required to pay individual contributions (amounting to one percent) to sickness insurance, and the pension was tied to the development of gross wages earned in the year preceding the claim. Eligibility criteria for the disabled and older unemployed were also tightened. Further stringent reform was passed in 1989. Benefits were adjusted to the development of net wages, pension claims were lower, and the retirement age was raised to sixty-five (starting in 2001). Age-specific adjustment factors for those retiring earlier or later were also introduced. The net result of the changes was to diminish early-retirement incentives and stabilize the employer and employee's contributions to 20 percent, with the federal government picking up the remainder. Some critics also argue that the real value of pensions was significantly reduced.

Reunification has brought changes in Germany's economic and demographic conditions. As unemployment has increased so has economic inactivity, especially for those more than fifty-five years of age. Additionally, real-wage growth has declined. Millions of East Germans became eligible for social welfare benefits, without having ever really paid contributions. Also, rising unemployment and inactivity reduced the financial base of the social security scheme. The reach of social security was broadened in 1994 with the introduction of special insurance which subsidized care for the elderly and disabled. The government also attempted to cope with unemployment by encouraging older West German workers into early retirement schemes. This placed severe strain on public pension provision. In 1996, pension reform was adopted that changed the date for the sixty-five-age retirement from 2001 to 2004.

The year 2000 saw government proposals to alter funding of benefits and pensions. Real worth of pensions would decrease under such a proposal. The government has also attempted to stimulate private-funded pensions by making individual savings of four percentage points of the gross wage mandatory. Such proposals are a move toward private initiative and the introduction of market forces in social welfare provision.

Policy Structure and Organization

The principal characteristics of German welfare policy are social insurance, social assistance, social housing, and personal social services. Social insurance is a type of general assistance program that covers income losses caused by sickness, unemployment, old age, or disability. In Germany, social insurance functions as a semi-autonomous organization and is administered by social partners (employers and trade union representatives) and sponsored by the federal government. Box 9.1 shows the five areas covered under social insurance.

Social assistance includes benefits for those without access to social insurance. It is funded by local authorities through means-tested subsistence benefits for those

---

Box 9.1   German Social Insurance

Sickness:	Approximately one thousand funds exist. They range from locally based general schemes to occupational funds to contracted-out schemes (ERSATZ). Insurance pays for sickness benefits and health treatment. From 1993 on there can be cross-subsidization among schemes.
Unemployment:	Covered by a federally organized fund administered by the Federal Labor Office (FLO) and controlled by social partners and public authorities. Insurance-based benefits last for one year, although, under certain circumstances, they can last up to three years. Individuals are paid 63 percent of former income if they have children and 60 percent if they are childless. Thereafter, FLO administers a federally funded, means-tested unemployment assistance program. This amounts to 57 percent of former income for those individuals with children and 53 percent if childless.
Industrial Accidents:	Employers entirely fund benefits assigned under this program. Social partners administer the scheme.
Old Age, Survivors, and Invalidity:	Two schemes, one for blue-collar and one for white-collar workers. The funds pay for pensions to elderly, disabled, and their immediate survivors. Civil servants enjoy noncontributing benefits. In the late 1990s, the average old-age pension for a blue-collar worker was 40 percent of former income while for white-collar workers and low-wage earners it was 60 percent of former income.
Long-Term Care:	Administered by the sickness fund, in most states this is financed by employee and employer contributions with interim contributions from federal governments.

who do not have adequate contributions recorded to qualify for social security. All benefits paid are calculated according to needs rather than in relation to former earnings. The state governments fund care of those without other entitlements in residential or health institutions. The federal government assumes responsibilities for subsistence benefits for refugees.

Social housing is provided by a large number of voluntary and cooperative agencies. Local authorities reserve certain functions. Social services are organized into five national organizations under the German Red Cross, the Trade Union Worker's Agency (*Arbeiter Wohlfahrt*), the Lutheran Diaconate Services, the Roman Catholic Caritas Agency, and an association of small, locally based agencies (*Paritätische Wohlfahrt*).

German welfare policy is guided by the objectives of the social market economy. Germany tends toward a decentralized structure of institutions providing social welfare, with centralization in legislation and control. The federal government retains largely residual powers, except in the regulation of social security entitlements. Policy objectives are defined and articulated mainly by the federal bureaucracy. Social security and welfare legislation since the 1980s has increasingly been formulated and adopted on the federal level. States are mainly responsible for implementing, enforcing, and financing such laws. In personal social services, the states are the key policy-making actors. Generally welfare policy involves public authorities, social partners, service suppliers, funders, and other interested parties in corporatist consultative and decision-making structures.[20]

Social welfare financing is achieved through a combination of public and private contributions. Government funding is provided through the national treasury, state government, and federal government funds, each providing approximately one-third of the total government expenditure. Social assistance support comes mostly from sickness fund payments. Employers and employees pay equal amounts into sickness funds, which, in return, provide and monitor relief programs.

Future Outcomes and Policy Weakness

Relatively speaking, Germans enjoy entitlements with high replacement values in relation to former earnings. The system has come under increasing criticism in the 1990s for replicating social inequities of income derived from the labor market. Additionally, the system is criticized for discriminating against individuals and non-family units.

Reunification and economic recession in the 1990s have provided additional problems for the German social state. As the East German economy collapsed, it placed great demands on the German system of social assistance, social security, and work creation. On top of this, unemployment created incredible strain and brought the German welfare state to fiscal crisis. East Germany required massive subsidization. Personal dependency on state support has grown nationally and increased markedly in the Eastern states. With a large percentage of the East German workforce either unemployed or temporarily employed, the need for government relief is heavy.[21]

In other nations, recession and high levels of unemployment have led to a rolling back of the state. Wilson argues this solution was not available to German policy makers.[22] Although there has been welfare retrenchment in Germany, there has not been a significant change in what programs government provides its citizens—that is to say a rollback of what the state is responsible for providing socially and economically to its citizens.[23] Retrenchment has meant curbs on social assistance, reductions in levels of benefits, and stricter regulation to check for tax and social security fraud.

As in the case of other industrial nations, the distribution of assistance and relief has been greatly hindered because of costs as well as demands. The German welfare state enjoys strong political support at both the mass and elite levels; however, cleavages and welfare provision have become more evident in the late 1990s.[24] Unless sustained economic growth can be achieved in the upcoming first years of the new century, more expenditure cuts are inevitable. This will undoubtedly increase the polarization of Germans around the welfare issue.

Great Britain: Rolling Back the State

One of the central issues in British politics since the end of the nineteenth century has been social policy provision. In the last years of the twentieth century and the first years of the new millennium, serious questioning of the future of the British welfare state is taking place. Indeed, in May 1996 the front-page headline of a leading British newspaper was "The End of the Welfare State."[25] The article simply claimed that both the Conservative and Labour parties were ending the welfare state as it had been known in Britain for the preceding fifty years since its modern inception in the early 1940s. The new social welfare policy regime would be one that was less rigid and allowed for looser relationships between individuals and the government.

At the start of the new millennium, the welfare state still exists in Britain, although it is very different than the welfare state of the 1940s to 1970s. Government still provides its citizens with a vast array of services and benefits that combined makes up social welfare policy. The difference is that there are clearly changes in how social welfare is provided and to what level. The need for welfare provision by the British government is not in question. Today the gap between rich and poor is wider than at any time in the twentieth century; one in three children lives in poverty; social class determines life expectancy; and public services are severely underfunded.[26]

Policy History and Evolution

Similar to other European nations such as the German and Swedish welfare states, Great Britain's welfare state was developed on the traditions and values of collectivism. In all three nations, the welfare system has been built on the belief that every individual has the right to support in times of need and emergency. One of the oldest commitments to "support" came in the form of the British Poor Laws.

First introduced during the Elizabethan era in 1601, the Poor Laws were established to protect the poor in individual parishes as other avenues of protection began to dissolve. For the next two hundred years the Poor Laws became the basis for public assistance and the foundation for any subsequent welfare action.

The modern British welfare system was established after World War II in a series of reforms and evolved through three decades of expansion and modification. The baseline for the British welfare state was the 1942 Beveridge Report. The report was a product of a government-initiated commission and is seen by many as a radical departure in terms of what government provides its citizens.[27] It is not radical in terms of what it advocates. Rather it is radical because it represents an acceptance of the belief that the state's role is primary in the welfare field, instead of a stopgap when private initiatives fail. What is innovative about the Beveridge Report is the scale of the government's welfare endeavor and the implication that social welfare is a right conferred on the individual in virtue of citizenship.

Beveridge envisioned a society in which government provision of certain social welfare benefits and services would totally eliminate poverty caused by interruption or loss of an individual's earning power. The welfare policy which Beveridge advocated was one that attacked what was called the five giants of modern society: want, disease, ignorance, squalor, and idleness. Government would tackle such problems in a manner that would not stifle personal initiative and thus would not foster dependency. Social dependency is one of the major fears of all critics of the modern welfare state. Through a social insurance scheme government would provide its citizens with uniformly administered universal social security without means-testing.

From the end of the Second World War, British citizens paid a single weekly contribution out of their paychecks and in return they got cradle-to-grave provision of services covering the following: medical benefits, unemployment benefits, widow benefits, old-age benefits, maternity benefits, industrial injury benefits, and funeral benefits. Coverage was universal and provided subsistence benefits for all.

The success of the Beveridge Report can be attributed to a number of factors. First, it was attractive and simple. In reality, it was really a rationalization of existing insurance schemes that had gaps in coverage. Next, it was a practical expression of the desire to provide a national minimum for all. Third, it acknowledged that social policy had to be comprehensive and tackle all the inequalities of modern society. The Beveridge Report only dealt with want, but it laid the ground for legislation to cover the other giants. Simply, it expanded the notion of liberty from freedom to speak, write, and vote to freedom from want, from disease, from ignorance, from squalor, and from idleness. Finally it was an "all-in" insurance scheme. Rich or poor, you paid the same in and received the same benefits out. It consisted of flat-rate premiums and flat-rate subsistence benefits: Beveridge believed that "none should pay less because they are better situated or receive more because they are used to earning more."[28]

Until the early 1960s, the impact of the Beveridge Report was extensive in Great Britain. Thanks to liberal lawmakers in the Labour Party, coverage and eligibility for insurance and assistance was expanded, public programs and services were broadened and state intervention was increased. Arguably the most important legacy of the Beveridge Report was, however, the bulkanization of social policy. Prior to the Beveridge Report, social problems were tackled fragmentedly. Groups and interests were dealt with individually, and each had to compete for the same attention and resources. The Beveridge Report, however, created a national plan for the distribution of benefits and services that eliminated much of the competition and distributed funds and resources more fairly.[29] Unfortunately, as Great Britain approached the 1970s the funds for programs and services were difficult to find, resources were becoming scarce, and costs were rising rapidly. As a result, proponents of welfare policy were under tremendous pressure from a growing conservative opposition. To make matters worse, unemployment was still at dangerous levels, low-paid work was growing, public expenditures were escalating, and anti-welfare sentiment was on the rise.

Similar to many of the nations discussed in this text, the British welfare system was facing simultaneous pressures from rising demands, economic difficulty, and political change.[30] When the nation elected Margaret Thatcher in 1979 the British electorate gave the go-ahead to combative free-market, monetarist policy. Thatcher saw the mixed economy, state planning, full employment, and universal welfare as bulwarks against change and modernization. The next decade saw her presiding over an ideological revolution and a "rolling back of the state."[31]

Up until 1979/1980, British government social welfare services were grouped into five areas: cash benefits, health care, education, housing, and personal social services. Cash benefits consist of one of the following: national insurance, means-tested benefits and noncontributing benefits. National insurance covers retirement pensions, unemployment benefits, and invalidity and sickness benefits. Means-tested benefits include assistance benefits such as supplementary benefits and family income supplements. The principle noncontributory benefit was and is child benefits. Pre-1980s, the cash-benefit system was a complex mixture of low-rate insurance benefits with assistance support designed to provide a safety net for the most needy and vulnerable. There was some private and occupational welfare for the better off and a major noncontributory child benefit for all families. Cash benefits in 1980 accounted for approximately 10 percent of GDP, National Health Service and education about five percent each, housing approximately three percent, and personal social services less than one percent.[32] Approximately 70 percent of British households received at least one cash benefit, and health and education was available to everyone. It is clear to see the centrality of government welfare services in general public spending and in the everyday life of the British public.[33]

Thatcher's reform of the British welfare state was based on two clear objectives: expenditure cuts and denationalization of welfare. She argued that she wanted to reduce the dependency-creating effects of welfare through reduction of disincentives to be self-reliant. Thatcher attempted to create a more efficient benefit system by targeting benefits to the most needy. She encouraged a move away from the state as the primary agency of social insurance. The net result of her eleven years in office was large-scale expenditure cuts in welfare services, in particular in housing and education. Britain witnessed the erosion of much of what the state provided and made cuts in benefits that were as much as 15 percent. This was achieved by removing the indexation of cash benefits to wages. Benefits are now linked to price increases only. They fall in relative value as real living standards rise. Regulations were changed, affecting conditions of eligibility and payment, while "scroungers" were targeted. Scroungers were those who were considered to be getting state money for nothing. Thus, means-testing was introduced.

Despite such cuts and reforms, Thatcher failed to reduce overall spending significantly, so she moved to changing the way the state operated to provide welfare.[34] Basically, Thatcher restructured the welfare state so as to transfer state responsibilities in many areas to the private market. Privatization was responsible for the wholesale "selling off" of government responsibility in many areas of social and personal services.

Margaret Thatcher successfully reshaped social welfare policy in Britain because there was a general withering away of the consensus of social democracy. This consensus had protected the welfare state for many years. When the general perception within British society changed, and many citizens felt that social democracy had led to a politics of extremism with out-of-control labor unions, voters swung to Thatcher's radical message and supported her new welfare politics. When Thatcher started to tamper with the two areas of social policy provision that still commanded public support—health care and programs and benefits for the elderly—she ran into trouble. There was still general societal agreement around these two areas. With the pursuit of reform in these areas, she alienated much of the support within her own party and in the general public. It resulted in 1990 with her being overthrown by the party rank-and-file.

Her successor, John Major, maintained the new streamlined, oriented-to-the-most-needy British welfare state. However, he put a kinder, gentler face on it. When Tony Blair and "New Labour" were elected to office in 1997, they inherited social welfare policy that was very different from the welfare policy of Labour's last term in office.

Policy Structure and Organization

Blair's New Labour has basically kept much of the social welfare policy he inherited from his predecessors intact. There have, of course, been some modifications, but there has not been a move back to traditional Beveridgean programs and levels of provision. Since October 1996, only one main benefit has been available to people when they are out of work: the Jobseeker's Allowance (JSA). This replaced the contributory National Insurance Unemployment Benefit (NIUB) and, for unemployed people, the means-tested Income Support (IS). There are two forms of JSA, which are based on the two benefits it replaced: the contributing JSA and the Insurance-based JSA. To receive this benefit, individuals have to first demonstrate that they are "available for any work which they can reasonably be expected to do" and that they are "actively seeking work." Individuals are disqualified from the benefit for up to twenty-six weeks if (1) they leave a job voluntarily "without good cause" or are dismissed; and (2) if they refuse to accept a job offered by the Employment Service or fail to take up a "reasonable opportunity of employment." Unemployed school leavers are obliged to undertake some form of training in youth-training programs. If a youth is not registered in such a scheme, he or she receives no financial assistance from the state.

Public housing is now much closer to the American model than European-style public housing. It is a last-resort provision for poor people with problems. Sick pay has also been changed radically with stricter periods of eligibility. Provision now is an employer's responsibility for the first six weeks of sickness. State-earnings-related pensions have been cut back severely since 1987. Incentives are made for individuals to "opt out" and choose private pensions to top up their basic state pension. Supplementary benefit and family allowance income supplements have been replaced by income support and family income supplements, which are both means-tested.

Tony Blair inherited a social welfare policy that had more enhanced means-testing; a reduced role of national insurance benefits for old age, unemployment, and sickness; and reduced state spending commitments, particularly in the areas of pensions and public housing. New Labour under Blair is very similar to conservative criticism of the pre-Thatcher welfare state, hence their almost intact maintenance of the market-oriented economics of Thatcherism. They also claim the old welfare system encouraged dependency, was financially unfeasible, and damaging to society. Blair's Labour converges with their conservative predecessors' social welfare policy. Blair talks of a stakeholder economy.[35] Under such a system, he believes everyone deserves a fair chance, but at the same time, everyone is expected to exploit the opportunities which lawfully come their way. Collective provision in the form of government support should be designed to meet only those needs generally beyond the capacity of individuals, families, and communities to provide.

Blair has made stakeholders of everyone involved in the delivery and receipt of social policy. It is the replacement of Beveridge principles with a welfare-to-work approach.[36] Running up to the 1997 general election Labour promised reform of the welfare state without significant increases in public expenditure and, thus, high taxes. As Labour's 1997 election manifesto proclaimed: "The level of public spending is no longer the measure of effectiveness of government action in the public interest. It is what money is actually spent on that counts more than how much money is spent . . . New Labour will be wise spenders not big spenders."

Labour under Blair advocates a social welfare policy that creates more jobs by boosting long-term economic growth rates. Social security should support a better-educated and better-trained workforce by helping the unemployed get jobs and training. This is a practical departure from previous Labour party policy, for social policy had always been at the heart of Labour politics. Labour was the party of the expansive and caring welfare state. Indeed the creation of the welfare state in Britain was a defining moment for the party. Until the 1990s, they championed expansive social policy and extension of the scope and provision of the welfare state.

Now similar to the American social welfare model, Labour believes there should be reliance on voluntary organizations, private companies, and market forces to both support the welfare system and shoulder much of the burden. One of the first tasks of Blair's Labour Administration was the completion of a government green paper on what welfare policy should look like in the upcoming years. Green papers act as preliminary policy outlines and indicate how the government is to proceed. Under the proposal, Britain's new welfare system consists of three types of provisions: welfare as a channel for the pursuit of self-interest, welfare as the exercise of authority, and welfare as a mechanism for moral regeneration. Welfare as a channel for the pursuit of self-interest involves providing incentives to induce people to promote social well-being. Welfare as the exercise of authority involves the compulsion of people to act in ways to promote social well-being. Welfare as a mechanism for moral regeneration attempts to persuade people through moral arguments to promote social well-being. Ironically, the green paper took on much of the same arguments that the Poor Law did more than a hundred years ago. Labour attempted to implement some of the green paper's proposals in the last year of the twentieth century.

The modifications introduced under the Blair administration are really nothing more than fine-tuning of existing practices. The major modifications center around "welfare to work," which New Labour argues will act as a trampoline rather than safety net for the less well-off. This calls for the state to assist people to get back into the labor force through a variety of opportunities rather than providing them with a level of assistance that allows them to remain in unemployment and poverty. In July 1997, one of the first elements of the welfare-to-work policy was introduced for young unemployed Britains. Under this program, four options are available to the young unemployed: a private-sector job; work with a voluntary-sector employer; a job with a fifty-thousand-strong environmental work force; or full-time study on an approved course. Employers are encouraged to hire the young unemployed by government subsidies of approximately four hundred dollars per month for six months. If an individual refuses one of the four options, the person loses all benefits for the first two weeks (if without "just cause") and then receives benefits at 60 percent of the full rate. Those who refuse a second time lose benefits for four weeks. Additionally, Labour has reformed the tax and benefit system so as to reduce the disincentives against the unemployed taking work. Labour also has set up schemes to subsidize employers who take on unemployed individuals, and implemented job search and training measures to help people such as single parents find employment.

In April 2000, Labour unveiled an unprecedented assault on "benefit cheats," while they hoped at the same time to move more people into the ranks of the employed. The changes are to the Jobseekers allowance. Those receiving such a benefit will now be subjected to random calls from the local government job centers summoning them in for an interview within hours. Under the old system's rules, unemployed individuals obtaining benefits could only be summoned for a job center interview by letter. Now people will be phoned at variable hours during the day and given appointment times. Once at the job center, individuals are subject to a very intensive job matching. If an individual does not appear, then he or she will lose benefits. Next, any adult who has been unemployed for six months or more will be required to register for their job seekers allowance once a week instead of every two weeks. Those unemployed for less than six months will continue to register every two weeks. Labour's objective is twofold. First, to pressure long-term unemployed individuals into taking work at a time when the job market is booming. And second, to break the "black economy" where individuals work without reporting it and also receive state benefits. Part of the new rules is also a "two strikes and you're out" policy, which will leave a claimant who is convicted of two counts of benefit fraud stripped of any welfare payments. Around half a million people over twenty-five are covered by the new once-a-week signing-in system and telephone calls. Additionally, in areas designated special employment zones, long-term jobless will be given free cellular phones, beepers, and cash to help them find work within a given designated time.[37] Individuals will be expected to use the phones, beepers, and cash to maintain contact with specialists hired by the government to put them in touch with employers seeking to fill vacancies. At the same time, special squads are to be sent into the employment zones to connect the country's 1.1 million unemployed with the million-plus job vacancies.

Social welfare policy is managed indirectly by the national government. All laws are laid down by the government in Westminster. They also determine financing and expenditure limits. Responsibility for implementation is left to the civil service, while local government is left to actually deliver the services of the welfare state. Basically the civil service contracts with local government for the delivery of services. The central government pays for services, and all local government agencies are accountable for funds received.

Future Outcomes and Policy Weakness

The heart of the debate over welfare policy has changed dramatically over the last two decades. The debate is no longer about how much to expect and what should the British state provide to its citizens. The debate now is about how to make the choices concerning welfare services: choices about the range of services, about how they should be paid for, about how they should be delivered, and about who should benefit and how long benefits should be provided. In Britain, the debate is clearly shaped by the failure of the British economy to deliver the increased wealth needed to fund an expansive welfare state. Data shows the welfare state in Britain is not large by international standards.[38] However, the burden is still worrisome for policy makers.

The Conservatives and now Labour have restructured the welfare state by striking a balance between what programs are offered and the means of delivering them. Compared to other European nations discussed in this text, Britain's social welfare policy has undergone radical change over the last twenty years. Thatcherism managed to erode the culture of a welfare state based on universalism and consensus that the system should be for all and include coverage for all basic social conditions. Labour is now attempting to create a new culture in which the state is responsible for providing incentives and disincentives to shape citizens' behavior to be socially beneficial. It is an experiment that many are eager to see the results of. Will Britain's economic performance improve as it lightens its social welfare expenditure burden? Will social policy programs successfully become self-financing and profit-making for all? Or will Britain become clearly a society of winners and losers, of haves and have nots, where the have nots do not have a safety net and fall deeper into poverty and thus become disaffected?

Japan: Welfare Laggard or Responsible Compassionate Government?

Although many authors argue the Japanese welfare state emerged naturally from traditional patterns of social care, much evidence points to its construction being much more piecemeal. There is evidence that supports the notion that the development of Japanese modern social welfare was delayed because of the presence of traditional family, local, and corporate arrangements. Lee argues social welfare policy mostly came about in response to short-term political and economic exigencies.[39] The Allies occupation in the post-1945 period had undoubted influence on the welfare policy that emerged in the post–Second-World-War era and the notion that Japan was in many ways a welfare laggard.[40] Many fully expected Japan to adopt the Western model of social welfare. However, what emerged is an indigenous system, which is both unique and different in its welfare policy solutions than other industrialized democracies.

Policy History and Evolution

Prior to and during the Second World War, social welfare legislation was enacted. In 1938 the National Health Insurance scheme was introduced and in 1944 so was the Employees' Pension Insurance scheme. Both were expanded in the post-war period. In the immediate post-war occupation period, Western-style welfare reforms were introduced, but they were little more than symbolic. Many of the reforms came out of the Advisory Council on the Social Security System that was created in 1949 and led by the prime minister. The most significant of the reforms were the Daily Life Protection Law (1946), which provided universal public assistance to the needy, and the 1949 Unemployment Insurance scheme. Most of the other reforms were the restructuring and reordering of existing legislation such as the war-time pension programs.

The beginning of the 1960s saw economic growth, which gave rise to the conditions necessary for social welfare expansion. The national pension scheme that was introduced in 1959 started to operate by the early 1960s. It covered all those who had previously been excluded by the employer pension schemes. By the late 1960s, with continued economic growth and increased political party competition between the LDP and the JSP, Japan saw the emergence of a movement supporting the development of a Western-style welfare state. Roger Goodman argues 1973 was targeted as the "First Year of Welfare" (*Fukushi Fannen*).[41] From this time on, the notion that Japan was to be a welfare state was part of the public consciousness. Children's allowances were introduced in 1971 and pension benefit levels were significantly increased. The year 1973 saw the establishment of indexation to inflation for social security and other benefits. The net result of such improvements was a dramatic increase in Japanese social welfare expenditure in the 1970s. By 1980, Japan's assured benefits had reached levels similar to Germany and other European nations. However, as a proportion of Japanese GNP, social welfare expenditure was still lower than such nations.

Governmental support levels for social welfare expansion started to decline almost as quickly as they had developed because of lowered economic growth rates, increases in unemployment rates, and mounting governmental debt. By the mid-1980s the idea of a Japanese-style welfare state (*Nihongata Shakaifukushi*) started to be promoted heavily. Advocates pushed slogans such as "Reconsider Welfare," and "Welfare State Disease." Advocates of the Japanese-style welfare state pushed an idealized picture of Japan in which each community took care of its needy. In essence, this Japanese-style welfare society would fuse the welfare functions of government, business, the community, and the family to provide relief that would enhance benefits and lower public-sector costs. Hobsbawn and Ranger describe this as the "invention of tradition."[42] Reality was completely obscured, and historical evidence of lack of caring by citizens of each other was completely ignored.

When the economy started to grow once again in the late 1980s, there was widespread acceptance of the Japanese-style welfare state. Thus, there was a general perception that there was really no need for large-scale government aid for the poor and unemployed in Japan. Indeed data from the 1980s demonstrates that Japan had low levels of poverty while also having low levels of welfare spending per capita.[43] The economic strength of Japan allowed for such low poverty rates simply because of the high employment rate and average wages. In general in the 1980s, the Japanese disadvantaged were taken care of, but it was with little help from government agencies. Those less well-off or in need were taken care of by their families, or, if they were an employee of a corporation, by corporate benefits. The argument put forward by many was there simply was less need for government welfare policy in Japan.

In the mid-1990s the economic situation changed once again; recession hit, unemployment rates increased, and there was an aging population. Indeed Japan faces a population that is predicted to age faster than any other industrialized nation. In this context, government welfare provision is back on the public agenda.

Policy Structure and Organization

Social welfare in Japan is currently provided for through a complex system of provision of minimum standard of living for all citizens and protection from certain types of social and economic risks. Japan's social welfare policy has four main areas of provision: public assistance, social insurance, basic welfare, and public health. Health policy will be discussed in the next chapter. All current policy derives from arrangements located in the 1947 constitution. In Article 25, Section 2, the constitution refers to the maintenance of minimum standards of wholesome and cultured living and the responsibility of the state to promote and extend social welfare and security.

Public assistance programs are designed for those who require aid in maintaining themselves at a minimum level. Seventy-five percent of this program's benefits are provided by the national government, the remaining by local governments. Any individuals receiving public assistance must demonstrate that they are taking action to help themselves get off public assistance, and relatives must also provide mandatory, supplementary care.[44] Levels of care are decided by the Health and Welfare Ministry in cooperation with local welfare commissioners. In 1998, public assistance expenditure represented less than three percent of total welfare-related expenditures.[45]

Social insurance programs provide public pensions, unemployment insurance, worker compensation, and national health insurance. Public pensions are composed of two kinds: the employees' pension paid upon retirement at sixty and the national pension paid at sixty-five. Funding for both is from individual monthly contributions. Employee pension contributions are paid half by the employee and half by the employer, while national pension contributions are paid solely by individual. Those who are disabled are also provided pensions as are the survivors of individuals who either died or suffered injuries and made contributions. Benefits are designed to maintain standards equivalent to living standards prior to injury or death.

Unemployment benefits are paid for out of unemployment insurance funds, which come from employer and employee contributions.[46] The unemployed also receive counseling and assistance in job placement.[47] Basic welfare services are aid for the disabled, services for the elderly and services for children, which include aid for fatherless families. Government programs for the disabled include pensions, institutional care, rehabilitation programs, special education, and cash subsidies. Priority is given to services for the disabled outside of institutional settings, including medical counseling and "home helper" programs. The ministry of labor offers programs for vocational guidance and job opportunities.

Japan's rapidly aging population is making welfare services for the elderly a large social problem. The old-age welfare law of 1963 introduced various health benefits, a system of home helpers, and local welfare centers for the aged. Welfare services are also offered to needy families with children. The Child Welfare Law of 1947 established the government's responsibility to protect children in need. The 1964 law for the welfare of mothers, children, and widows provides financial assistance and services such as vocational counseling and homes for fatherless families.

Social welfare in Japan is based on a mixture of welfare-state principles, insurance, and individual responsibility. Financing of policy is based on member contributions and tax-based government subsidies. The central government bureaucracy is the main actor in formulation and implementation of social welfare policy. Much of this policy formulation is done by the Ministry of Health and Welfare.

However, because of the centrality of the budgetary process, the Ministry of Finance is a key actor in determining welfare expenditure. The Advisory Council on the Social Security system established in 1949 still plays an important role in developing policy alternatives. It is an independent body that regularly publishes recommendations and proposals on social welfare policy.

The role of local agencies in implementing social welfare policy has grown steadily since the 1960s. The municipalities, for example, handle the administration of the national pension scheme, while the central government oversees and subsidizes it. Finally, the important role of private corporations in social welfare provision up to the mid-1990s must be acknowledged. They participated through membership on various advisory councils and by paying approximately 50 percent of social insurance premiums for employees. Business is central to Japanese-style welfare, and it is expected to share more of the financial burdens of welfare provision than the state. Many corporations have their own private pension schemes and indeed are encouraged to keep workers on the payroll past the state retirement age of sixty.

Future Outcomes and Policy Weakness

Although Japan suffered heavily as a result of World War II, in the post-war period the state managed to successfully rebuild and develop social welfare policy. Welfare policy faces specific future problems. The first problem is an unnecessary shortage of resources caused by a decline in population growth rates and the slowing of the economy. Next are unclear procedures by which benefits for various groups can be determined. Third are organizational and operational problems within each of the areas of social welfare provision. And finally, cultural perceptions of the government's role in social welfare provision are a problem. Undoubtedly, Japan is undergoing rapid economic change, which is fostering new societal demands and expectations. Such change is forcing business to reassess its commitments. If business starts to put profits ahead of loyalties to workers, the government will be expected to promote new welfare measures. The Japanese-style welfare state will be tested. How it will react is uncertain; thus, the future direction of social welfare policy in Japan is uncertain. What is certain is economic recession has already forced cutbacks on social welfare services and programs in the immediate years of the new century.

Sweden: Still a Social Democratic Model?

Sweden is generally regarded as a prototype of a modern democratic society.[48] It is almost always portrayed as having the most developed and most extensive form of welfare state under capitalism. It is classified as a prime example of Esping-Andersen's social democratic model of a welfare regime.[49] However, like other industrialized nations, Sweden in the last few years has had to deal with a crisis of welfare expenditure. As economic growth declined and unemployment and public-sector debt increased, successive governments have had to face the challenge of reduction and reform in the face of continued expectations and interests from much of a population accustomed to a generous welfare system.

At the beginning of the 1990s, Sweden spent a greater proportion of its national income on welfare benefits and services than most other industrialized nations. Also, there was strong emphasis on direct provision of benefits and services that were universally accessible to all citizens. The Swedish welfare state was and is committed to mitigating class and gender inequalities and maintaining full employment. Consequently income inequalities and inequalities of living conditions are less than in most other industrialized nations, and there have been low levels of official unemployment.

Policy History and Evolution

The Swedish welfare system is based on the concepts of universalism and solidarity. Dating back to the eighteenth century, the Swedes have committed themselves to the public provision of income, goods, and services to all citizens without regard to previous contribution. More than a tradition, this commitment outdates the British Beveridge Report and Germany's Bismarckian legislation.

The origin of the Swedish welfare system is highly debated. Some historians believe that it developed as a result of the rising political power of the agrarian industry in the early 1900s.[50] Others believe its origin comes from the interests of the industrial working class in the 1930s, while another group attributes the welfare system's origin to the nature of the bureaucratically centered monarchical regime.[51] In reality, the Swedish welfare system was created as a result of all of these factors. In fact, the welfare state was born as Sweden began industrializing after a long agrarian tradition. Political instability and pressure to support industrialization caused the agrarian industry and growing working class to mobilize together. Urban elites and state bureaucrats utilized this fusion to gain support and pass legislation, as well as gain power in government. The extension of welfare benefits, therefore, became a tool to achieve these goals. Legislation such as the Poor Law of 1882, the Pension Act of 1913, and the National Unemployment Commission of 1914 began the process of extending social insurance and benefits, first to the working class and eventually to all Swedes. What can be concluded is that, like other policy areas, the development of social welfare in Sweden was the story of gradualism.

The consistent election of Social Democratic governments from 1932 to 1976 resulted in a welfare state in which social policy was a high priority. The 1930s represent a clear ideological shift toward the welfare state. Political alignments and labor market compromises were made, laying the foundation of the Swedish welfare model. However, in terms of policy outcomes, there were no real innovations. The Social Democratic government followed stimulative Keynesian policy. By 1936, the Social Democrats had increased welfare expenditure to 23 percent of total GNP.

In the immediate years following the Second World War, as Swedish industry continued to flourish, a whole host of major social welfare legislative initiatives were enacted. This resulted in the broadening of educational opportunities, expansion of pension benefits, collective bargaining agreements, and expansion of relief payments and insurance for the unemployed. By the early 1950s, all major social categories were covered by at least minimal social protection. The funding of programs and services was based on progressive taxation and employer contributions. Benefits were comprehensive, covering all core transfer and service programs. Some benefits, such as sick pay, were earnings-related, and replacement rates were not high. The service side of the welfare state had not yet been developed, even though transfer programs other than unemployment were state administered.

The remainder of the 1950s saw the establishment of earnings-related programs with high replacement rates. The 1960s and 1970s saw further expansion of social welfare. Additionally the service welfare state was established. As social welfare was expanded, Sweden also began to reorganize decision-making structures. In essence, decentralization of both administration and funding mechanisms took place. County councils were given increased authority to control and administer social welfare programs and services. This allowed for more locally responsive delivery of services. The major consequence of welfare expansion and a generous universal system was an extremely high tax burden. By the 1970s, Sweden had one of the highest-taxed populations in the capitalist world.

Throughout the 1970s, Swedes continued to experience high living standards and generous welfare benefits and services. The public sector employed more than 30 percent of the workforce and was spending 60 percent of the nation's GDP on welfare provisions.[52] There were substantial economic pressures to control social expenditure. The public-sector deficit was growing as was inflation, while productivity was lagging. However, there were no significant reductions or rollbacks of social protection, although several measures were adopted but never implemented because of change in government. From 1982 to 1991, the system remained largely intact; the governing Social Democrats did extend some social rights while also containing welfare spending in other areas. For example, the child allowance was increased and unemployment benefits extended. Cost-containment measures included reductions in the base amounts used to calculate social benefits such as pensions.

Authors such as Morris and Olsson felt that the outlook for the Swedish welfare state was extremely favorable and that Sweden was going to be an exception to the rule and escape national backlash, drastic cuts in public expenditure, deregulation, and privatization.[53] However, economic crisis in the early 1990s ended such expectations. By the early 1990s, it was evident that austerity programs were needed, and cuts in public expenditure would result. Consequently welfare reforms were enacted. The base amount of social benefits was trimmed once again, replacement rates were reduced, waiting periods for eligibility increased, residency requirements were introduced, and contribution periods lengthened. Finally, many new initiatives were taken to encourage the implementation of market-mechanisms in social service delivery and to foster the establishment of private providers to replace public provision. With the reelection of the Social Democrats in 1994, further cuts and modifications in social welfare provision have taken place. There are now less-generous benefits in many areas, stricter eligibility requirements, and movement toward a larger role for internal markets as well as social-insurance-based modes of funding. However, the Social Democratic model of social provision is still largely intact in Sweden, albeit under increasing pressure.

Policy Structure and Organization

Swedish social policy provides social security benefits such as social insurance, social assistance, and social services. All benefits are linked to the base amount by which the basic old-age pension is calculated. The old-age basic flat pension is annually indexed to prices. They are automatically inflation-proofed by the provision that the base is increased in direct relation to the consumer price index, and the increase is triggered off whenever that index rises by three percent. However, the base amount has been reduced by three percent between 1989 and 1991 and a further three percent in 1992. Social insurance schemes are universal in coverage, and there is no means-testing. Social insurance in Sweden covers sickness, unemployment, industrial disability, old age, and long-term care. Prior to the 1992 reforms the sickness benefit was 90 percent of a recipient's income. Post-1992, the first day of sickness is a waiting day where no benefits are paid, on days two and three 65 percent of income is paid, and thereafter up to twelve months, recipients receive 80 percent of income. If a recipient needs sickness benefits longer than twelve months, they are paid 70 percent of income. Employers are liable for the administration of sick pay for the first fourteen days of sickness. Employers are also responsible for investigating whether there's a need for rehabilitation after eight weeks of sickness.[54]

Basic old-age and disability pensions pre-1992 were calculated at 96 percent of the base amount. Post-1992 they have been reduced in value by six percent.[55] There are two statutory old-age pensions, a basic flat-rate payment, and an earnings-related scheme for high earners called ATP. Changes since 1994 mean the ATP is today calculated according to contributions throughout an individual's working life rather than its previous calculation of thirty years of contributions. Also, for both schemes' contributions, which had previously been paid by employer in the form of a percentage of their payroll, are now paid by both employers and employees. Employee contributions amount to 9.25 percent of their pay.

Unemployment benefits depend on whether an individual is a member of a trade union or not. Pre-1992, trade union members were part of a voluntary income-related scheme administered by the trade unions, with contributions paid for by employers. Non-union individuals claimed a flat-rate benefit administered by the labor market board. Post-1992, the income-related scheme has a five-waiting-days period for claims and a replacement rate of 80 percent of income rather than the previous 90 percent.[56] The flat-rate benefit has been reformed so that all employees pay two percent of their incomes into a new obligating scheme.[57] Limits have also been placed upon the length of time a claimant can register for unemployment benefits. It is now three hundred days for workers under fifty-five and 450 for workers aged fifty-five to sixty-four.

Social assistance benefits are means-tested and are known as social benefits. These are paid to individuals who qualify as low-income earners and are administered by local authorities. Recipients receive a benefit of three percent of the average gross wage. Additionally, recipients qualify for other benefits such as child and housing allowances. Housing supplements and child benefits are means-tested and provided to those who qualify. Supplementary assistance covers housing and child-rearing costs.

Although social security benefits have suffered cutbacks, social services have really not seen retrenchment of the same level, and in this area, Sweden still is a leader and a model to other nations. The centerpiece of such success is the parental benefits package, which goes far beyond any other industrialized nation. Parental benefits are provided by the parental insurance scheme that was introduced in 1974. Post-1992, parents are basically entitled to twelve months leave at 80 percent of gross earning. The time can be shared between parents, with at least one month taken by the father.[58] Parents have to have worked for six months for the same employer of twelve months of the preceding twenty-four months. If parents decide to share the time, they cannot take it at the same time. Parents are also entitled to a further 180 days of parental benefit to be taken at any time beginning with the delivery and ending with the child's first year in school. This is shared by both parents equally. Other circumstances, such as a child's illness, births of further children, visits to daycare, and doctor visits for children less than twelve entitle parents to a further parental benefit of up to sixty days per annum. This is groundbreaking in that it deals with one of the great problems of contemporary industrial society: How do women combine work and child rearing? It also ensures one-parent families the same degree of financial security.

In 1993, the government announced that all parents who wanted child care for children between the ages of one and twelve years should have it, and so reform of daycare, both preschool and after-school, have taken place. Costs to parents have increased as well as size of classes.[59] Parents have the option of two types of services: municipally administered daycare service and salaried child-minder services. The first daycare service is usually for children three to twelve and the second for children less than one. Child-minders get fixed monthly salaries and look after a minimum of four children full-time or provide equivalent hours of care for eight to ten children on a part-time basis. Single-parent families have first priority for all services. In 1993, a care allowance of SEK 2000 ($192) per month for parents who wished to care for their children between the ages of one and three at home was introduced.[60]

Future Outcomes and Policy Weakness

The net result of the reforms has been for an increase in social cleavages.[61] Certain sectors, such as immigrants, youth, and single parents, are twice as likely to have problems with income, housing, and employment.[62] There is reluctance on the part of Swedes to dismantle their social welfare policy even further. Polls demonstrate consistently high support among the general populace for publicly funded and provided services. There is not only interest group and popular movements' support for the welfare state but also across-the-classes support. Both working-class and middle-class make demands on the state for provision of social welfare. It appears what has been achieved is a consensus that sacrifices had to be made but that wholesale cuts in benefits and services were and are out of the question. Does this mean future reforms are unlikely? No, more than likely all reform will move toward a welfare pluralist model. The scale of the model will continue to be generous compared to other nations but not as generous as Swedes once envisioned. Circumstances have forced policy makers to face the implications of increased internationalism and competitiveness of post-industrial capitalism.

United States: Uncaring or Prudent Social Services Provider?

American decision makers have always been much more reluctant than their European counterparts to intervene in the general area of social policy. Indeed, it was not until the 1930s that the federal government provided any sort of welfare and social security benefits for the poor and elderly. Even then, the extent and level of coverage were extremely limited. As Table 9.1 shows, this is in sharp contrast to many European governments who had started to provide in this area of policy from the late-eighteenth century.

Why was the United States such a late starter in social policy development? The answer lies in American political culture and the values it advances. There is an emphasis on self-reliance and rugged individualism. These are values that encourage individuals to seek remedies from within themselves rather than from government or society. Such a culture provides a cold ideological climate for welfare policy provision. Poverty was seen as deriving from an individual's faults and not the system's faults. Therefore, in the early part of the twentieth century a punitive approach was taken. Poverty was seen to be degrading, and only a minority of individuals, "the worthy

Table 9.1   Year of Introduction of Various Social Services in Selected Nations

Nation	Old-Age Pension	Unemployment Insurance	Sickness Pay	Medical Services
Germany	1889	1927	1889	1883
Britain	1908	1911	1911	1911
France	1930	1914	1930	1930
Canada	1927	1935*		1947–1966
United States	1935	1935		1965

*An act of 1935 was declared unconstitutional and unemployment insurance was not finally introduced in Canada until 1940.

poor" as the literature of the day refers to them, was suitable to receive assistance. Such policy was conducted solely at the local level, and the federal government remained silent on the matter.

Since the introduction of welfare in the United States in 1935 through implementation of the 1935 Social Security Act, the federal government has tried to develop a rational social welfare system. However, no one has been really happy with their efforts—not the taxpayers who support it, not the bureaucrats who administer it, nor the recipients who live under it. For much of the time since the establishment of large-scale direct federal involvement, welfare policy has remained a central issue in American politics. The debate climaxed in 1995 with the Republican congressional reform to roll back welfare. President Clinton, who opposed the reform in its original form, eventually signed it into law in August 1996. The reform was signed after Democrats and Republicans compromised on changes that were acceptable to both parties, although, when signing the act into law, Clinton said that the bill still had serious flaws in the areas of food stamps and provision of benefits to immigrants. The new reform, many argue, represents an agreement by both political parties to cancel sixty-one years of federal welfare policy as created by the New Deal and transfers control and responsibility of the safety net over to individual states. The United States enters the new century continuing to depart from the argument used in nations such as Germany and Sweden that the responsibility of government is to provide an economic security safety net and an array of social services.

Policy History and Evolution

Social welfare policy arrangement changed with the election of Roosevelt in 1932. The Roosevelt administration's New Deal program establishes the provision of social welfare by the federal government. The Great Depression, which began in 1929, for a time changed American attitudes about poverty, both in terms of who was poor and more importantly why they were poor. It became acceptable, from the 1930s on, that some individuals were poor through no fault of their own and that there were systemic causes that went beyond some individuals' ability to manage. Under Roosevelt the Democratic party became convinced that the federal government had to step in and intervene to address the problems caused by economic crisis.

The centerpiece of the New Deal was the 1935 Social Security Act. The act embodied both the preventive and alleviative approaches to social welfare provision. The former was to be accomplished through a system of social insurance, or income security. Two main mechanisms were established to achieve this: social security and unemployment compensation. Poverty was to be alleviated through transfer payments from the government to a specified population. The major program that fell under this category was Aid to Families with Dependent Children (AFDC), originally called under the 1935 act Aid to Dependent Children.

With the advent of the Second World War and the economic growth of the immediate post-war economy, social welfare was dropped from the institutional agenda. There was a general perception that fewer people needed government help

and the poverty rolls decreased. However, during the Kennedy and Johnson administrations (1960 to 1968), poverty regained its place on the agenda. The Kennedy
administration prepared several programs that were later endorsed and passed as
legislation by the Johnson administration. Most of these programs formed what has
become known as the Great Society and the War on Poverty. Much of the emphasis
of the War on Poverty programs was to further the programs introduced in the
1930s. For example, in 1965 Medicare was introduced as a program for health insurance for the elderly. Also, in the same year, Medicaid, a program of health insurance for the poor, was also established. Other programs passed by Johnson's
administration included housing subsidies, school feeding programs, and special
programs for pregnant women. Medicare, Medicaid, and the remaining programs
were either preventive or alleviative in their approach. The administration, however, also used a curative approach. This can be seen in the 1964 Equal Opportunity Act. Under this legislation the federal government attempted to break the
poverty cycle at an early age by providing a wide range of educational and job training programs, such as Head Start.

When Richard Nixon was elected in 1968, he attempted to change the provision of social welfare by providing programs that could be identified with the Republican party and were inexpensive to fund. Nixon and many Great Society critics
labeled much of the War on Poverty a failure. Many War on Poverty programs were
dismantled or cut back, and President Nixon, influenced by the work of the conservative economist Milton Friedman, pushed for a move away from the alleviative approach. He argued such an approach created disincentives and encouraged welfare
dependency through its promotion of welfarism.[63] What President Nixon achieved
was to change the focus of the social welfare debate away from the issue of poverty
to a debate about how welfare should be provided by government. In the economically uncertain years of the early 1970s, Nixon and his supporters felt welfare was a
luxury the government and the middle-class could not afford. Nixon took an incomes approach and stressed the notion of workfare, that is to say, what Americans
needed was not welfare but work.

With the election of the Democrat Jimmy Carter to the White House in
1976, the United States saw a continuation of focusing on the ills of welfare provision rather than a focus on the causes of poverty. With the election of Ronald
Reagan to the presidency in 1980, hostility to welfare among all sections of the
population was increasing with conservatives advocating extensive government
cutbacks. President Reagan and his supporters argued that welfare provision was a
failure that cost too much and discouraged individuals from working. A rational
individual if given the choice between a low-paying dead-end job with few benefits
and public assistance would choose the latter. Additionally the nation's economic
ill health was because it was overloaded and burdened with the costs of welfare.
Many conservatives argued it was the Great Society and War on Poverty programs
that were directly responsible for much of the economic slowdown and the growth
in the federal budget deficit. This is a return to the philosophy that the individual
and not the system is at fault.[64] Reagan represented an ideological resistance to active

government. During the Reagan years and in his successor's administration, the United States witnessed massive cutbacks that solidified opinion against the notion of welfare. Reagan and his successor George Bush took a punitive approach to welfare provision.

The net result was retrenchment in welfare provision and an increase in poverty levels after 1980. In spite of the growth in poverty and other conditions of social ill health, such as homelessness, by 1992 welfare was seen by many to be the root of America's problems. State after state cut its welfare programs, and the public was united in its desire for federal welfare reform. Presidential candidates of both the major parties stressed their commitment to reform. The successful Democratic candidate Bill Clinton promised "an end to welfare as we know it." The electorate was rewarded some three years later with the reform they so badly wanted.

In 1995, both houses of congress passed resolutions to roll back welfare, and it was eventually signed into law in the summer of 1996 by President Clinton. As Robert Dole, the republican senate leader in 1995 and his party's candidate for the presidency in 1996, argued, "Welfare reform is a story about an America where welfare is no longer a way of life and where people no longer will be able to receive endless federal cash benefits just because they choose not to work." The 1996 Personal Responsibility and Work Opportunity Reconciliation Act ended welfare as the United States had known it since the 1930s.

Policy Structure and Organization

The U.S. government provides welfare in a number of basic ways. Some programs distribute direct cash assistance that recipients may spend as they choose (cash assistance programs). Other programs provide specific goods, such as public housing; or the means to obtain them, such as subsidized rents, vouchers to offset private housing costs, or coupons to purchase food (in-kind assistance programs). Still others provide services or the means to obtain services. Welfare services include health care, childcare, and help coping with drug or alcohol dependency. Goods and services, as opposed to direct cash assistance, are known as in-kind benefits. Other welfare programs create or subsidize jobs for the unemployed. In addition, the government also provides a tax discount to the poor, known as an Earned Income Credit (EIC), which some people consider a welfare program. If calculated as an expenditure—although it is actually money the government does not collect—EIC is one of the more costly U.S. welfare programs.

The 1996 reform dramatically changes welfare policy by requiring recipients to work. The act compels welfare recipients to accept greater responsibility for their own support by requiring "workfare." Workfare requires welfare recipients to perform public service and enroll in job-training programs. Among the highlights of the 1996 legislation are the following provisions: AFDC was eliminated as a nationally-funded federal-state contract that ensured cash payments to families and households supporting children. AFDC has been replaced with Temporary Assistance to

Needy Families (TANF). This is a block grant that provides discretionary funding to individual states. States then provide for families in need with these funds. Thus, the 1996 Act eliminates a national entitlement.

Under TANF, cash support to the needy is limited. Recipients are limited to public assistance for a total of two years with lifetime benefits limited to five years. Control over welfare policy has shifted back to state governments from the federal government, giving state legislatures the flexibility to run their own welfare programs. While at the same time, welfare payments are severely limited. Next, teenage mothers can be denied benefits if they do not live in their parental home and do not attend school. The act also restricts childless adults, ages eighteen to fifty, to three months of food stamps during a three-year period. The policy also requires at least half of all single parents on welfare in any state to work or be in work-related activities by 2002, or the state will lose some of its federal block grants. Finally, the reform denies to legal immigrants most welfare benefits until a lengthy residency period has been fulfilled. Future immigrants are prohibited from receiving Medicaid during their first five years in the country. In 1997, food stamps eligibility for non-citizens was eliminated as were disability payments. The reform can be classified as a punitive approach fused with an incomes approach. As President Clinton stated when he announced his decision to sign the legislation, "Today we have a historic decision to make welfare what it was meant to be—a second chance not a way of life."[65]

Since the 1930s, the delivery of social welfare involves all levels of government. The federal government is involved in policy formulation through deciding types of programs and what social issues will be addressed. It is the responsibility of the federal government to establish minimum benefit levels when policy is adopted. The federal government is also responsible for providing funding to states to support delivery of welfare services—for example, through grants in aid to support unemployment compensation.

Implementation of social welfare is left to the states. This responsibility includes drafting rules and regulations for eligibility. In some cases, individual state governments must supplement federal funding of welfare programs. Additionally states will provide supplementary welfare assistance through their own general assistance programs. Such relief is available for needy individuals who do not qualify for categorical assistance—for example, categories such as the elderly, the blind, the disabled, or recipients of TANF. States also maintain institutions that care for the destitute who need more than financial assistance—for example, facilities for the mentally ill, orphanages, and senior citizen homes. Local government is also actively involved in the administration of various welfare programs. Local welfare officials decide if an individual is eligible to receive benefits and what amount they should receive.

Future Outcomes and Policy Weakness

The real problems in American social welfare policy are not problems of organization, administration, or service delivery. They are problems that revolve around deep-rooted political conflicts over a series of questions. For example, what is the nature and cause of poverty and inequality in America? What should the role of government be? What should the taxpayers' burden be? What is the appropriate strategy for coping with social problems? In sum, American social welfare policy is a continuing struggle over the issues posed by poverty, inequality, and other social problems.

What made such sweeping changes possible in the late 1990s was the widespread dismay with the welfare system that many characterized as symbolic of big government run amok—costing taxpayers money, demeaning beneficiaries, contributing to the breakdown of the American family by encouraging men and women to forget their marital responsibilities, and encouraging illegitimacy.

The United States in this new century is preparing for one of its biggest social experiments since Franklin Delano Roosevelt promised "some measure of protection to the average citizen." Some argue that there will no longer be guarantees that the poor and their children are entitled to federal benefits for as long as they need them, that the safety net has been removed for many of the American poor. In reality, no one knows precisely what the ramifications of the reform will be, for change of this magnitude in welfare provision has never been enacted. However, the questions remain. Will the poor once pushed off the welfare rolls find jobs? Or will more families end up on the streets? Freed from federal mandates, will the states devise innovative new programs? Or will they simply encourage the needy to migrate to states with better programs? What we do know is that the social contract in the twenty-first century between the government and the poor has changed.

Chapter Ten

Health Care: A Right or a Privilege?

Modern societies have consistently been concerned with obtaining citizens' good health, the search for cures to diseases that plaque mankind, and generally caring for their sick. However, health policy, that is to say the involvement of the state in the preoccupation of the above concerns, is a relatively modern phenomenon. As mentioned in the discussion on social welfare policy, health policy is part of a nation's social policy. The development of health care provision by government is linked with the notion of welfare-state growth. Additionally, as scientific medicine has advanced, there has been increased need for regulation of such activities by the state. The link between welfare provision and good health is important to grasp. Good health depends upon individuals receiving or achieving adequate income, satisfactory housing, a safe water supply, an adequate waste disposal system, safe working and living conditions, an unpolluted environment, and adequate nutrition. The objective of health policy is to promote and attain good health; the goals of welfare policy are to provide the adequate or satisfactory conditions that good health requires. In many societies, inadequate welfare policy, that is to say welfare policy that does not adequately provide a safety net for its citizens and where all regardless of status are not guaranteed income or housing or safety, will undermine any type of direct medical provision.

The good health of a population is important for any society to achieve for a very simple reason. Healthy people are more productive than unhealthy people. Productivity is not confined to the workplace, it also includes maintaining living conditions and raising healthy families. In recent years, research has increasingly pointed to the relationship between a population's improving health standards and economic growth. Such research can be classified as one of two types. The first compares a nation's performance over time and gross domestic product (GDP).[1]

The second type looks at economic impact of household health. Such research looks at the relationship between health and productivity and earnings.

A clear link exists between a nation's disease levels and its income.[2] Indications that are key to the demonstration of this relationship are life-expectancy rates, infant-morality rates, birth rates, and climate conditions. Data for fifty-three countries, between 1965 and 1990, demonstrate improvement in adult life expectancy was responsible for eight percent of total growth.[3] Such growth was the result of improvements in productivity attributed to a healthier workforce; less absenteeism; increased incentives for investment in human and physical capital as life expectancy increases; and increase in saving rates, as workers have an incentive to save for retirement.[4] Studies conducted by the Pan American Health organization and the Inter-American Development Bank also support these arguments, pointing to the relationship between health and economic growth. Such studies indicate if male life expectancy is increased by one year, GDP will be increased by an additional one percent after fifteen years.[5] Several studies across nations have shown the correlation between economic performance and birth rate. As a population's health improves, child mortality rates decrease. Over time, this leads to a fall in fertility rates. After birth rates fall, economic growth increases, as the proportion of the population participating in the labor force increases.[6] However, evidence also shows that an increase in the number of young adults does not automatically lead to growth.[7]

In terms of economic input of household health several studies are pointing to a consistent pattern. Sick workers take more sick days than healthy workers, even when they are self-employed. Some dimensions of health clearly affect workers' productivity.[8] The effect of sickness on individual productivity is greater in poorer nations. Overall health will influence earnings.[9] Improving the health of the poorest households is a route out of the poverty trap.

In 2000 the World Health Organization (WHO) published the first-ever analysis of the world's health systems.[10] One hundred and ninety-one nations' health systems were measured against five performance indicators. The indicators were overall level of population health; health inequalities within the population; overall level of health-system responsiveness (a combination of patient satisfaction and how well the system acts); distribution of responsiveness within the population (how well people of varying economic status find that they are served by the health system); and the distribution of the health system's financial burden within the population (who pays the costs).[11]

WHO argues that the health and well-being of individuals depends critically on their health systems. The report finds, as one would expect, wide variation in performance.[12] Performance variation is found even among nations with similar income levels and health expenditures. A key recommendation of the report is that health insurance is extended to as many individuals as possible. WHO refers to the need for prepayments on health care in the form of insurance, taxes, or social security. In particular, nations should provide insurance to as large a percentage of low-income groups as possible. Currently in those nations where this is not the situation the poor pay a higher percentage of their income on health care than the wealthy.[13]

Table 10.1   Health Care Systems by Selected WHO Indicators Rankings

Nation	Performance Overall Rank	Health Level Rank	Responsiveness Level Rank	Fairness in Financial Contribution Rank	Health Expenditure per Capita ($) Rank
Brazil	125	111	130*	189	54
Germany	25	22	5	6	3
Japan	10	1	6	8*	13
Great Britain	18	14	26*	8*	26
Sweden	23	4	10	12*	7
United States	37	24	1	54*	1

*denotes tie with other nations

Source: Adapted from World Health Report 2000, Annex Table 1.

Table 10.1 shows how each of the text's six nations' health systems ranked in terms of overall quality. From the table it is possible to see that only one of the six nations, Japan, was among the top ten and only three others made the top twenty-five. Each individual nation's performance will be highlighted during the discussion of each nation's health care policy.

There are a number of roles the state may play in providing health care. Primarily the state may be a regulator, a funder/purchaser, or a provider/planner. In many nations the state will combine all or most of these roles. We will see that how a nation behaves in each role depends on the scope and extensiveness of government's role in the provision of well-being for their citizens.

Brazil: Unequal and Exclusive Care

Brazil, as a nation, faces a myriad of diseases and health issues that pose serious problems for the health care sector. Infant mortality, although lower overall than in previous years, is still very high. Also, certain sectors, such as urban strata and rural areas, have witnessed increases in infant mortality in the last decade. WHO has calculated healthy life expectancy for children based upon Disability Adjusted Life Expectancy (DALE). DALE summarizes the expected number of years to be lived in full health. Brazil ranked 111th with an average of 59.1 years of healthy life for babies born in 1999. It is one of Cardoso's stated government health care goals for the new century to reduce infant mortality rates. Brazil also faces a huge amount of infection and chronic diseases; tuberculosis is a persistent problem, as is malaria, leprosy, malnutrition, and in the last ten years HIV/AIDS. Brazil starts the new century with the fourth-highest number of HIV/AIDS cases in the world. These all exist in conjunction with other diseases such as cancer and heart trouble.

Policy History and Evolution

Over the years, the Brazilian state has implemented a number of measures that have attempted to answer health needs. Successive governments have realized the health care system is inadequate to deal with the nation's disease and general health burden. For example, in the 1940s, Special Services for Public Health (SESP) was created to provide public health information and preventive medical care for remote populations.[14] From the early 1960s to the mid-1980s, the military dictatorship centralized the entire health care system. This resulted by the 1980s in 76 percent of inpatient care and 38 percent of ambulatory care being government managed.[15] However, the successive military governments were ineffective in both expanding and improving care to all Brazilians.[16]

One reason contributing to the inability of the military government to expand health care provision was their commitment to stimulating economic growth rather than expending state funds on social services. The government supported rapid growth through privatization, which created obstacles to public-sector provision of health care. Privatization reinforced health-care inequalities. Also, under privatization, fraud and waste of public resources in health care provision flourished.[17] Private health providers ordered unnecessary treatments and procedures. It was commonplace for service provider contracts to be awarded on the basis of friendship and personal gain rather than merit or cost-effectiveness. Benefits were distributed disproportionately to the upper and middle classes. The poor and disadvantaged, in particular rural Brazilians, were completely neglected. They received lower-quality amenities, suffered unnecessarily, and for the most part were denied access to basic health care.[18] In return for economic expansion, the Brazilian public health care system was forced to concentrate on offering curative services to those who were ill rather than implementing preventive services aimed at prevention and eradication of illness. An attempt to redress this situation came in 1967 with the establishment of the National Institute of Social Wellness (INPS). INPS provided optional health care to all those employed in the formal sector.[19] Such individuals could opt to pay a premium to INPS for health coverage. The benefit was limited to providing basic care for employees, their pregnant wives, and infants. INPS was a consolidation of the pension, disability, and health care programs. In reality the program did little for those employed in the formal sector and provided no coverage for those in the informal sector.

As the result of the development, in the early 1970s, of a movement supporting reform of public health care, legislation was enacted that attempted to alter government commitment and responsibilities. The reform movement, led by the Brazilian Center of Health Studies (CEBES), placed individuals in key bureaucratic positions, so as to implement and control change that supported the goals of the movement. First, reformists desired to strengthen the public sector so as to ensure proper distribution of benefits, equal rights, and improved access to health care for millions of Brazilians. Next, reformists attempted to shift the emphasis of the health care system from curative treatments and procedures to preventive measures, including vaccinations and improved sanitation. Third, reformists were committed to providing universal access to health care. They publically argued that the amount of money and resources it would take to cover all Brazilians would be minimal compared to the cost of treatments and procedures necessary once illness or disease had set in. Many obstacles confronted reform. Ironically, many of the obstacles that were present in the 1970s are still present today. Thus, any change in health care provision faces obstacles such as insufficient financial resources, private sector mobilization opposing reform, the bureaucracy, and a culture of corrupt practices.

In response to the demand for reform, the government in 1975 introduced a plan for immediate care (PPA). Under the PPA emergency care was provided to anyone, either in facilities run by INPS or in contracted facilities. This represents the first real step toward universalization of health care in Brazil. Also, in 1975 the government redefined health care to include hospitalization as well as preventive treatments.[20] The new definition required that INPS be expanded, and it became the National Institute of Medical Assistance and Social Security (INAMPS). The newly expanded agency was given the responsibility for delivery of all curative medical assistance and hospitalization. By the end of the 1970s, INAMPS was responsible for financing 89 percent of hospital care in Brazil.[21] Preventive health activities, communicable diseases, health centers, public health labs, and sanitariums were to be under the direct auspices of the ministry of health.[22] Some authors argue this division of responsibilities inspired the construction of new models of health care delivery that abandoned the focus on hospitals and shifted it to the populace.[23]

Basically the early 1980s saw centralization of health service delivery through the creation of the Integrated Health Act Program (AIS). By 1987, there were moves to provide universal access to the INAMPS system through further decentralization. For example, all IMAMPS staff and facilities were transferred to the control of municipalities. Additionally each state was requested to develop its own health care systems. State governments were authorized to contract with private providers. IAMPS hospitals were also transferred to state government control while health centers were passed to the municipalities.[24]

The goal of decentralization was to provide a network of geographically organized health services so as to provide adequate coverage for all populations. Policy makers viewed the municipalities as the most appropriate level of government to assess the health needs of citizenry through the provision of targeted services.[25] This new emphasis on increasing equity of access to care, community participation, and decentralization was given the official name of Reforma Sanitaria.

National support was so strong for Reforma Sanitaria that it influenced the drafting of the 1988 constitution. With the constitution's ratification, the Sistema Único de Saúde (SUS) was created. This was a single health system, which represented the merging and unification of the previous health agencies. The social security budget (predominately made up of earmarked taxes and employee and employer contributions) was to be the main source of government subsidized health care. Thus, despite the focus on state and municipal funding, the federal government was to be the primary player in financing health care outlays. The goal was to provide a system which theoretically covered the entire nation. Coverage was extended to those outside the social security system. Under the social security system, individuals receive medical and hospital treatments. The SUS is the foundation of health care provision in Brazil today.

The constitution of 1988 forced health policy to have defined objectives and governmental strategies (see Box 10.1). The fulfillment of services would be controlled and carried out by the municipalities and by the states, minimizing the role of the federal government. SUS integrated the federal health networks and the public state and municipal networks.[26] Currently not all states have absorbed INAMPS networks. Many states argue they have difficulty funding the services to maintain these networks. Similarly only a few municipalities have absorbed the establishment of INAMPS for the same lack of financial resources.

Under the 1990 Organic Health Law much of the constitutional provisions of 1988 were consolidated. The constitution and the 1990 organic law have achieved universalized access to medical care, a unified public health system, decentralization of management, and a structure for health care which encompasses the federal, state, and municipal levels of government.[27] The process of development since 1990 has been slow and hindered greatly by the successive financial crisis of the mid-1990s. However, this should not color judgment of the reforms.

Such health reforms can be classified as comprehensive policy making. They were innovative and introduced radical change by breaking with past patterns of policy delivery. Subsequently, reform has been incremental in nature. This is especially true since 1995. The period from 1995 on has been marked by successive minor ad-

---

Box 10.1   Brazilian Constitutional Health Strategies and Objectives

Objectives:

1. Universalization of Care: The entire public, private, or state-controlled network would now care for the population in a universal manner, without restrictions or clauses of cover;
2. Equality of Care: As well as universal coverage, everyone would have access to the same forms of coverage throughout the entire national territory;
3. Completeness of Actions: Everyone would have access to health as a whole concept, or composed by actions on the individual, the collectivity, and on the environment.

Strategies:

1. Unity of Control: Although decentralized, the system would now have a single control in each sphere of the government, avoiding the former duplication of efforts which existed between the structures of the INAMPS, the Ministry of Health, and the state and municipal bureaus;
2. Social Participation: Society would participate in the management of the system via Health Councils organized in all the spheres of government, which would have functions in the field of planning and supervision of health actions.

justments to administrative organization of health care, to types of services delivered, and further decentralization of control to the municipalities. The most notable new programs in the late 1990s are the Community Health Agents Program (PACS) and the Family Health Program (PSF). Both have caused major changes in the way resources are allocated, health care is paid for, and how services are organized at the local level. Supporting both of these programs was the introduction in 1996 of NOB, the goal of which is the promotion of basic operational norms for SUS so as to reduce corruption and define policy strategies, priorities, and tactics.

Over the last fifty years, the provision of health care to the Brazilian population-has undergone many changes. Reforms since the 1940s have attempted to shift health care delivery from private to public provision through decentralization to the municipal level; to provide more ambulatory care relative to hospital care; and to reallocate resources toward prevention. The success of such reforms is still inconclusive.

Policy Structure and Organization

Today there are clearly two health care systems available to Brazilians—public and private. The public health system oversees basic preventive needs while the private (nonprofit and for-profit) sectors deliver the bulk of medical services that include government-subsidized inpatient care.[28] The Brazilian health care system is organized on four levels: federal, state, municipal, and the private sector. The federal level through the ministry of health is responsible for the provision and regulation of basic health services. This includes endemic diseases as well as maternal/child care and vaccinations. Also under the auspices of the ministry of health is the administration of global disease control, sanitation control, and health technology.

The state level through the operation of community health centers is responsible for some endemic diseases, parental and infant care, as well as vaccinations. As Brazil decentralized health care management and administration, community health centers have expanded their role. This is in spite of a lack of personnel, lack of equipment, and inefficient management. The municipal level is primarily concerned with emergency care. At this level, municipal hospitals and community health centers offer limited preventive services while concentrating mostly on immediate care.

As a result of the rising demand for quality health care, the government has allowed the private sector to enter the health care system.[29] Private-sector health care consists of for-profit institutions, philanthropic institutions (called "Santa Casas" and usually headed by the Catholic Church), health maintenance organizations (which offer prepaid systems), cooperatives (owned and operated by physicians), and medical groups. Approximately 25 percent of Brazilians are covered by private health care plans. Most of those covered are emerging middle-class to wealthy Brazilians. American companies, such as Aetna and Cigna, in recent years have offered more options and choices to Brazilians.

Managed care entered Brazil in the mid-1990s. Managed care is defined as "services provided under the administrative control of large, private organization and with captivated payment mechanisms."[30] Such health care provision has emerged because of the rise of privatization, public sector cuts imposed as conditions for IMF/World Bank loans, globalization (through the elimination of trade barriers as a result of treaties such as GATT and NAFTA), and constitutional arrangements.

Future Outcomes and Policy Weakness

The Brazilian health system is characterized by low-quality care and lack of equipment and technology. In spite of its theoretical objectives, in practice it offers limited coverage. There is a lack of followup and little control and evaluation of care. Regardless of considerable state funding of health care, the direction of funding has created an imbalanced system. Thirty to forty percent of state subsidies are spent on expensive technology only to be used by the most affluent segments of the population, thus negating those most in need. Seventy percent of Brazil's hospital beds and 68 percent of its health care personnel are located in six southern states. Urban residents account for 83 percent of all hospital internments and 93 percent of specialized treatments.[31]

The result of government spending is that basic and preventive services have been neglected. Consequently these services have diminished amongst the entire population. The ramifications arising from the neglect of preventive care are such that therapeutic treatment in hospitals dominates funding at the expense of health promotion and disease prevention programs. For example, hospital-based assistance expanded from 44 percent in 1985 to 77 percent in 1990 of municipal health spending, while expenses from primary care decreased from 35 percent to 3 percent.[32] This represents a significant decrease in primary care. If it is coupled with the fact that HMOs finance and provide health care but limit their coverage to low-cost procedures, the net result is that the burden of treating high-risk individuals is on the publicly-funded health service. There is an overrepresentation of physicians in the southeast; 61.5 of all Brazilian physicians are located in the region. Less well-off Brazilians are unable to afford hospital-based medical care.[33] All of these problems are compounded by the lack of financial resources in relation to the health care need. The Cardoso government, as its predecessors, has responded to pressures to cut health care expenditure.

Indeed the Brazilian government, itself, is a major obstacle to the success of the health care system. Economically the government lacks sufficient funds to properly manage its programs and facilities. Table 10.1 shows how Brazil ranks against the other nations discussed in the text. Brazil ranks low in the financial fairness of the system because most individuals make high out-of-pocket payments for health care.

In spite of the government raising resources through foreign investors, foreign governments, and international loans, as in a $350 million loan from InterAmerican Development Bank, and through taxes, health care expenditures have increased.[34] In 1999, 60 million Brazilians were not covered by health insurance. This caused Brazil to forfeit federal grants because of a 1988 constitutional mandate that "health care was a right of all Brazilians."[35] Additionally, in the same year, IMF and World Bank restrictions forced Brazil to cut its health care budget. As a sign of the system's troubles, by the summer of 1999, 12,000 Brazilian physicians had refused to join health co-ops. This has increased the number of citizens who have to rely on private care.

Further problems are the continued practice of "double door" health care. This is where individuals with private coverage utilize less expensive or free public facilities and programs. Corruption and fraud also often prevent vital funds from reaching their targets and those most in need from receiving services.[36]

Many would argue the Brazilian government's commitment to health care has diminished over the last five years.[37] This is very different from the period immediately following the ending of military rule. From 1985 to 1992, the Brazilian government's commitment to health care was strong. This is evident by their success in eradicating polio, wiping out measles, implementing and funding a vaccine for Hepatitis B and increasing life expectancy from 45 to 65 years of age. Brazil provided more than 6,500 hospitals with as many doctors and physicians as Great Britain in the same period (1.46 per 1,000 people). Why the change in commitment? Simply, by 1992 obstacles to and problems of adequate public provision began taking their toll. Corruption, fraud, and bureaucratic clientelism, as well as physician opposition, forced the government to cut back on health care expenditures.[38] The WHO 2000 Report ranks Brazil 54 out of 191 nations in terms of health expenditure per capita. How Brazil compares to the other discussed nations is shown in Table 10.2. From the table, it is clear that Brazil lags behind in public expenditure per capita. When total health expenditure as a percentage of GDP is focused on Brazil, it is clearly close to Japan, higher than Great Britain, and not far behind Sweden. However, the number of hospital beds per 1,000 is significantly lower than the other five nations.

A further obstacle to successful delivery of health care is prevailing bureaucratic rivalries. These have plagued Brazil since the end of authoritarian rule. Such rivalries have diluted many of the enacted reforms. As a result, much of the progress originally made through the sanitary movement vanished as bureaucracies maneuvered for support, hindered each other's administrations, and took on the needs of the newly emerging private-sector health establishment.

At the same time that government commitment has weakened, the Brazilian health care sector has witnessed foreign private investment. Private investors and companies possess much bargaining power and have effectively molded legislation to ensure that their interests are protected. Many Brazilian health care advocates now argue the only hope for public-sector health care provision is further decentralization so as to cut back even further on national expenditure. It is believed this would weaken the private sector by making inroads into the power of bureaucratic clientelism and increasing support at the local level where the most need falls.

The future challenge is to find more effective funding sources to provide services to the poorer states. Currently funding is often too late or misappropriated. Standardizing health plans to require minimum coverage and abolishing exclusions of care for certain diseases would improve confidence in health care as well as force private companies to "commit" to all Brazilians. Technology must be improved and

Table 10.2   Health Expenditures and Services by Nation, 1990–1998

Nation	Public $1 as % of GDP	Private $2 as % of GDP	Total Health[3] Expenditure as % of GDP	Health Expenditure per capita $	No. of Doctors per 1,000 People	No. of Hospital[4] Beds per 1,000 People
Brazil	3.4	4.0	7.3	359	1.3	3.1
Germany	8.3	2.5	10.7	2,727	3.4	9.6
Great Britain	5.9	1.0	6.8	1,480	1.6	4.5
Japan	5.9	1.4	7.1	2,379	1.8	16.2
Sweden	7.2	1.4	8.6	2,220	3.1	5.6
United States	6.5	7.5	13.9	4,080	2.6	4.0

[1]Public health expenditure consists of recurrent and capital spending from government budgets, external borrowing and grants (including international), and social health insurance funds.

[2]Private health expenditure includes direct household (out-of-pocket) spending, private insurance, charitable donations, and direct service payments by private corporations.

[3]Total health expenditure is the sum of public and private health services not including provision of water and sanitation.

[4]Hospital beds include inpatient beds available in public and private general and specialized hospitals and centers.

Source: Adapted from World Bank Health Statistical Reports 2000.

maintained. Unfortunately, much of Brazil's health care problems centers around money. Pressure from other nations, the IMF, and the World Bank, as well as continued corruption, perpetuates the problem of lack of financial resources.

Germany: Stubbornly Maintaining Established Principles

Using Esping-Andersen's welfare state typology, Germany's health care system corresponds to a corporatist-governed system. Benefit provision is dictated by individuals' membership in regional or occupational sickness funds. The system is based upon a commitment and dedication to values and principles adopted nearly one hundred years ago. The financing and organization are essentially provided through the social insurance scheme established by Bismarck in the 1880s. Such a system is relatively autonomous from the state. Today in Germany, even with the problems of reunification, 90 percent of the population is covered by social insurance for sickness benefits and health care.

Social insurance is employer based, with employers and employees paying equal shares of the insurance contributions. The majority of those not contributing to social insurance are covered by private insurance. It is a widely accepted German belief that "the nation is obligated to offer a network of benefits to all citizens."[39] Germans accept that they are governed by an unwritten social contract that guarantees physicians and health care providers provide adequate services that are accessible to all and conform with the broader public interest.

Policy History and Evolution

German health care began in the late 1800s and was based on the principles of solidarity, subsidiarity, and corporatism. These principles are weaker today than in the past but are still the driving force behind the health care system. *Solidarity* is the commitment by all Germans to the norm that it is their responsibility and duty to take care of each other.[40] More specifically, it is the willingness of the healthy in society to pay for the care of the sick, the wealthy to pay for the poor, and the young to pay for the old. *Subsidiarity* is the belief in shared power, mutual respect, and the commitment to building, securing, and incorporating regional groups and social organizations into the system. It stresses the primary importance of self-help and the caring functions of the family and then voluntary organizations rather than state agencies. Each region develops its own health care provision and is pledged to cooperate with other regions to formulate national policy. *Corporatism,* in Germany, is a system that involves the representation of both elected officials and occupational and professional groups in the governing of health care. For example, employee and employer groups are represented on governing boards of sickness funds. Corporatism enhances effective participation in health policy formulation and implementation and contributes to the political feasibility and social acceptability of health care reforms. This ensures that employers and employees can counter other influential health sector groups, such as physicians and pharmaceutical companies. It also strengthens the government's capacity to formulate and implement policy. The disadvantage of the corporatist principle is it is difficult to change or alter the system. Agreement is necessary from all parties to change rules or procedures.

With these principles as the foundation of health care provision, the modern German health care system was created in 1864 with legislation making it mandatory for all workers to be members of mutual aid societies. Such societies were organized by employers and employees and acknowledged the tradition that employers are obligated to care for their employees. This was the birth of social security. Under the 1883 Health Insurance Act, sickness funds were established. This was the first sign of a national commitment to maintaining the population's health and well-being. It was a policy that nation after nation emulated and adopted over the following decades. The act stipulated that all German workers were to be offered health insurance by sickness benefit societies that they enrolled in. This pacified the trade unions, promoted social stability, and set the stage for the extension of health coverage to other sectors.[41] By 1930, all Germans were covered by health insurance.

The post–Second-World-War settlement established two different types of health care systems through the creation of two Germanies. In East Germany, socialism brought with it a nationalized health care system and the erosion of the private sector. In West Germany, statutory health insurance was maintained, stricter regulation of the medical profession was introduced, and there was a renewed commitment to the principles of the pre-war system. By 1960, total health care expenditures (public and private) was 4.7 percent of GDP. Of the total expenditure, 67.5 percent were public monies coming from sickness insurance funds. However, most medical goods and services, with the exception of a few public hospitals, were provided by private suppliers.[42]

There were attempts to reform the West German health care system, first in the 1950s and then the 1960s, but most were aborted. Health insurance coverage and the minimum range of services offered by the sickness funds were extended in the period. Students, farmers, and disabled individuals were brought into the system, and where necessary their contributions were paid for out of public funds. Birth control, abortion, sterilization, and cancer-screening became compulsory elements of all health funds packages. The 1970s and early 1980s saw the enactment of a number of laws that attempted to deal with the cost explosion in the German health sector. Despite such legislative efforts, costs continued to increase. An example of a cost-containment policy was a 1972 law that shifted the financial burden of new hospital investment from direct taxation to social insurance funds. This led to a sharp increase in health insurance contributions. In 1977, the government passed the Health Cost Containment Law, establishing "Concerted Action" (*Kowzertierteaktion*), which was a federal health finance and budget commission. Its weakness was its lack of power to impose any real cost containment measures. Between 1975 and 1992, thirteen health policy laws were passed that all dealt with cost reduction.

In 1989 and 1992, the government enacted two reforms that introduced elements of "self-responsibility" in health expenditure.[43] The 1989 Health Insurance Structural Reform Law requires sickness fund expenditures to increase no faster than wages. The law also clearly defines what fraction of the German national interest can be spent on health care. The 1992 Health Care Structural Reform Law (GSG) was to be phased in by 1997 and represents a clear break with the incremental reforms of the previous twenty years. Some authors have classified the law as a victory over interest group politics.[44] The GSG introduced a package of structural reforms. For example, hospitals' annual budgets are limited to insurance contribution revenues; greater consumer choice is offered in which sickness fund to be a member of; prioritization of outpatients is to occur rather than inpatient treatment; there are stricter controls on prescription and pharmaceutical pricing; and there is cross-subsidization among the funds so as to help those funds with high risk clients. As a result of the law, differences in sickness funds' membership was equalized in respect to age, gender, income, and the number of covered dependents. Policy makers feel that the new rules do not jeopardize the principles and values behind German health care.[45]

Financially, the GSG established aggregated spending targets and caps, as well as stringent capital spending controls on construction and equipment. The act also changed the manner in which reimbursements were distributed and made some very unpopular decisions involving the hospital sector. Hospitals could no longer receive funds from the private sector. Physicians were instructed to pay back hospitals one-third of their contracted earnings. Hospitals were ordered to create more jobs, in particular in the nursing area. Finally co-payments for inpatient care were increased.

The part of the GSG that caused the most controversy concerned the budgetary process. Built on pre-existing decision making and implementation structures, the GSG forced hospitals and ambulatory care providers to submit regional budgets and, more significantly, reorganized the sickness funds by allowing them to compete for clients. This eliminated the longstanding rule that certain jobs, ages, social classes, and regions could only enroll in funds designated for them.[46] The objective for such a change was the strengthening of payer purchasing power through organizational consolidation.

The GSG is generally considered successful and shares with past reforms a reliance on the corporatist principle. The GSG has also contributed a transfer of power to market-based commercial health care organizations. Additionally it has been blamed for the increasing tension between competing interests. Physicians and specialists, public and private carriers, as well as wholesale and retail pharmacists now compete more intensely for resources, funds, and customers. Prior to the GSG, health care providers and specialists were assured of work and funds and did not have to exert energy in search of customers. Since the act, they now have to sell themselves to new patients and clients. Costs have been helped by an increase in the number of direct payments by patients for certain services; however, annual health budgets have not decreased. By 1995, there was nearly a 10 percent increase in the health budget while total expenditure on inpatients almost doubled.[47]

Reunification has obviously been an easy target to blame for the failure of reform. In the late 1990s, there was much talk of further deregulation of health care although not much agreement on how much further to proceed. In 1996, four additional cost-containment laws were enacted, and currently two more are in the parliamentary process. One of the laws enacted created a new program that allows retired individuals and their families to choose between financial compensation for informal care and payment for residential and other professional care. This replaces means-tested funding.[48]

Policy Structure and Organization

Germany entered the twenty-first century with a restructured health care system that remains committed to its founding principles.[49] As discussed earlier, the German health care model is corporatist and is a decentralized, multi-payer system that disperses authority and control among thousands of private, nonprofit funds, which are governed by consumers and providers. These "sickness" funds are financed through payroll taxes in addition to employer and employee contributions (based on ability to pay). Sickness funds have the status of public-law bodies. Thus, they are key actors in health care decisions. They also implement and administer all decisions and social programs that are set by the state in framework legislation.[50] Sickness funds not only give all Germans a say in health care policy but also ensure that their voice will be taken seriously. The sickness funds act as intermediaries between the government and citizens. They assure that enacted policies and programs are based on "true" national interest. Through "concerted action" the German government acts as an "umpire" that establishes rules and sanctions actors according to agreed upon goals. There is no formal national budget for health care, just strict guidelines.

The German health care system is nearly universal. Access to benefits is based on need and individuals are required to join sickness funds in order to make their contributions as well as receive information and guidance about health-related issues and programs. Health care benefits are comprehensive and include medical, dental, vision, pharmaceuticals, holistic medicine, and hydrotherapy. German health care benefits also include full maternity leave, sickness pay, and payment for rehabilitation.

Hospitals in Germany come under three different categories: *Lander* or state-owned, nonprofit or for-profit. *Lander* hospitals are the most prevalent. These state-owned hospitals house more than 50 percent of the total hospital beds. Nonprofit hospitals are usually owned by religious groups and contribute nearly 35 percent of the total hospital beds. For-profit hospitals are currently the fastest-growing type with 15 percent of the total beds.[51]

Physicians provide care under negotiated "fee for service" payment agreements. Their salaries and fees are paid by sickness funds, and rarely do individuals pay point-of-service fees. Individuals are given a relatively free choice of physicians and hospitals, and since the 1992 GSG can shop around for sickness funds that charge less and provide greater or more convenient services.

The federal government divides up health care responsibility between three levels of government: 11 states, 26 districts and 328 counties. Each level is autonomous and receives input from all areas of society: government, private sector (sickness funds), advisory groups (physicians, health care professionals), and citizens. This "corporatist" model ensures that all opinions, interests, and needs are articulated and incorporated in the policy-making process. Since the federal government has no power of implementation, it is up to these levels of government to work with sickness funds, advisory groups, and hospitals to implement the policies they craft that are sanctioned by the federal government.

Table 10.1 shows the generosity of the German health care system. It ranks third in the WHO 2000 report on health expenditure per capita. In terms of fairness in financial contributions, the German system also ranks highly at number six. This is the highest ranking for any of the nations discussed in this text. Finally, it also ranks highly in terms of responsiveness.

The German health care system is financed through a combination of taxes, government subsidies, and individual contributions. The government contributes about 21 percent of the necessary funds distributed through each level of government. Sickness funds, which make up nearly 60 percent of health care funds, are financed by mandatory payroll deductions from employers and employees. These contributions are based on the individual's ability to pay. Private insurance makes up another 7 percent of the total health care expenditure. This also involves employer contributions and employee co-payments as well as out-of-pocket expenses.[52]

Nine out of ten Germans are enrolled in statutory sickness funds. These funds can be compared to Blue Shield or Blue Cross in the United States. The sickness funds are organized by region, craft, or company. The GSG adoption of a cross-sectional subsidization now allows more enrollment choices. Only about 10 percent of Germans are covered by private insurance. Those covered are primarily self-employed, civil servants, or those higher-paid workers in society. Some sickness fund workers also pay for private insurance to obtain more senior physicians, personal services, and private hospital rooms that sickness funds do not provide. Private insurance is growing but is looked upon as another threat to the solidarity and foundation of German health care.

Future Outcomes and Policy Weakness

Similar to other industrialized nations, Germany has suffered from increased health care costs. In the 1970s, costs for physicians and hospital care rose 25 to 30 percent, and sickness fund payments rose five times the rate of salaries.[53] In addition, pharmaceutical costs became a staggering 16.5 percent of the total health care costs.[54] Prior to the 1990s, attempts to control costs met with little success.[55] Since then, there has been some cost containment.

Many believe Germany has dealt with rising costs more effectively than most other nations. The reason often given is the continued support of the traditions and principles that are the foundation of the system. In recent years, such principles have come under increasing attack, but they are still subscribed to by the majority. After reunification, Germany was faced with building up an East German health care system that was highly ineffective and decades behind in supplies, technology, and equipment. Some authors argue the unification of the two Germanies is "equivalent to the U.S. incorporating Mexico within its health care system."[56] Dismantling the state-run system in East Germany, retraining health care professionals, and replacing the Eastern model with the West German system provided incredible challenges.

Physician frustration has been growing over the years and further weakens policy. Physician salaries and incentives are negotiated and are capped. Even if physicians service more patients, their fees are automatically reduced to keep spending under the negotiated cap. This acts as a disincentive to many doctors. Physician frustration in the new century may lead to increased costs and loss of services.

Trends toward the introduction of market practices have fared in Germany much as they have in all industrialized nations. Attempts to control costs, increase opportunities, and attract funds and investments make such practices attractive, but for most Germans they challenge tradition and their cultural commitment to take care of each other. However, growing numbers of Germans support market practices such as risk selection. Recent calls for sickness fund reform are also evidence of support for market practices. The government claims increased competition will control costs as well as ensure universal coverage.

In spite of changes over the last decade, Germany still remains firmly committed to adhering to and perpetuating the beliefs and values that their health system is built upon. Their commitment is unparalleled in today's world. German health care compared to many other systems is productive and efficient. Table 10.2 shows that they have more physicians than the other discussed nations, and with the exception of Japan provide far more hospital beds. Additionally they utilize more inpatient and outpatient care, and they rely on price controls, which are bargained for and not subject to government control. In fact, German health care provides more care with fewer resources, Germans visit physicians more, and they spend less on outpatient care and pharmaceuticals.[57]

Recent reforms have not seriously damaged the principle of solidarity and equitable access to care. Corporatist governance in the German health care sector appears to be holding strongly, and many argue it will continue to do so for a number of reasons. In essence, it reduces uncertainty and minimizes transition costs. It also corresponds to the tradition of self-administration and fits the major needs of the major political parties as well as the regulative pretenses of the ministerial bureaucracies. Fee-contracting between patients and providers is opposed by corporatism. Additionally the corporatist framework allows unions and employer organizations to provide strong links to sickness funds. Corporatist governance has depoliticized difficult health policy issues, such as cost containment, for it allows policy makers to delegate responsibility for regulation. This means they may avoid blame for unpopular measures.

Great Britain: To Dismantle or Not?

In Britain in the new millennium, serious questions are being raised about the future of national health care provision. Indeed Britain's National Health Service (NHS) is the subject of heated public debate. This is a recurrent theme in British politics. The nature of state intervention in health care has undergone dramatic change during the twentieth century, and it seems that it will continue to do so in the first years of the new century. Britain in the last decade has imposed a market into its state-administered health system. Health reform in Britain has always been part of a wider political agenda and has generated deep controversy among Britain's political parties, governments, and the health establishment. However, in spite of the divisions over the nature of reform or the type of state health intervention devised, there has always been a general societal commitment to providing effective health care as a public service to everyone who needs it. Provision should be in an equitable manner; however, in reality this has not always been the case. The NHS closely corresponds to Esping-Andersen's social democratic model because of the level of tax financing, state provision, and claims to benefits being based on social citizenship.

Policy History and Evolution

The commitment and sense of responsibility to all citizens in the area of health care began in the nineteenth century with the Poor Laws.[58] Such legislation provided health care for individuals committed to state-funded institutions known as workhouses or poorhouses. In spite of such institutions, until 1911 when the Lloyd George government introduced national health insurance, formal health care was practically nonexistent. For the majority of the working class, health care was a last priority and most received rudimentary care. The 1911 National Health Insurance Act gave coverage to all manual workers over sixteen earning below $200 per year for medical, sickness, disablement, maternity, and sanitarium care. Approved societies administered cash benefits, and local insurance committees oversaw medical and sanitarium benefits. Manual workers, both male and female, were required to pay weekly contributions in order to receive coverage. National insurance did not cover the dependents of the insured, higher-income individuals, workers between the ages of fourteen and sixteen, and the self-employed. Medical services were limited and did not cover many areas such as specialist consultation. By 1939, national health insurance covered less than 50 percent of the population, and the only specialist services available to those covered by the system were for venereal disease and TB.[59]

Prior to 1948, health care in Britain was administered mainly through voluntary institutions and limited public facilities. Voluntary hospitals were funded and managed by charitable organizations. Services were offered in exchange for low patient contributions. Government-administered hospitals gave primary care to the elderly and the chronically ill. They were funded through taxes and government grants. Most medicine had to be paid for, except by the poorest individuals. For general medical purposes 45 percent of the population had a doctor assigned to them under national insurance, while children and those considered the poorest qualified for free treatment.[60] Such individuals were tested to prove their eligibility.

By the first years of the Second World War, it was obvious that health care reform was badly needed and some would say was inevitable. Richard Titmuss argues that the war and post-war political situations were directly responsible for the shape of health care reform in the 1940s.[61] The groundwork for such reform was the 1942 Beveridge Report. As discussed in the chapter on British welfare policy, the report was the foundation for radical change in state intervention in the area of social services. Central to the report's recommendations was the establishment of a National Health Service for prevention and cure of disease and disability. Such a service was to be free to the user at the point of delivery. Of all the proposals in the "cradle to grave" provisions of the Beveridge Report, the creation of a national health service was probably one of the most controversial but also the one that was most popular with the public. It eventually became the centerpiece of the British Welfare State.

The Labour Party was elected to office in 1945 with a commitment to a universal, free, and comprehensive health service. In 1946, the National Health Service Act was created, and it became operational in 1948. The act created the National

Health Service (NHS). Under the legislation there would be nationalization of all hospitals; new regional hospital boards; the creation of health centers; redistribution of doctors around the country; and new salary provisions for doctors, including provisions for specialists to treat private patients in NHS hospitals. In order to get compliance and support from Britain's doctors, the Minister of Health, Aneurin Bevan, agreed to allow general practitioners (internists) to retain private patients and allow specialists to have "pay beds" in NHS hospitals to treat private patients.

The NHS was designed to "secure improvement in the . . . health of people."[62] It promised to give equal access to medical care and provide availability of comprehensive preventive and curative care. The NHS would be funded primarily through general taxation and organized in a tiered system that would have centralized administration, regional hospital boards, local health authorities, and executive councils. In addition to the tiered system, the NHS would consist of a tripartite of providers: hospitals, communities, and family practitioner services. Most hospitals were placed under public ownership and placed into administrative regions, with each region possessing at least one teaching facility. Community services were managed by the local authorities and controlled home nursing as well as ambulatory services. Physicians were permitted to have private practice; however, many did not.

In 1974, there was a movement to consolidate and improve the administration of the tripartite components because there seemed to be little communication or interaction among the three tiers. Critics argued this caused the NHS to be ineffective in distributing funds, sharing information, and tracking illnesses. As a result, Regional Health Authorities (RHA) and District Health Authorities (DHA) were established to integrate the tripartite providers as well as provide greater public health planning. Both the RHAs and the DHAs were responsible for managing and providing services for their district.

By 1980, the NHS had undergone significant change. Most of the improvements were made in the areas of professionalism, management, and consumerism. The different sectors of the NHS became more autonomous, and many of its workers became better trained and specialized. Managerially, the NHS still suffered from a lack of integration and communication between districts and levels. The 1974 reorganization improved conditions. This was achieved mostly through downsizing and giving more responsibility to RHAs. Further reorganization occurred in 1982, when RHAs were eliminated, leaving the DHAs with full responsibility and authority. This resulted in centralized policy making under the direction of the health services supervisory board. This board made national strategic decisions as well as creating NHS objectives. In terms of the consumer, activity was increased by, and on behalf of, health care consumers. Private insurance was on the rise, consumer "pressure" groups were forming, and health care institutions, as a result, were being organized.

Many Britons have always suspected that the Conservative party, if given a chance, would destroy and dismantle the NHS. Their chance did eventually come. As the years passed, government became increasingly concerned over the rising costs of the NHS, its inefficiency, and its increasing inequalities. However, when

Margaret Thatcher came to power in 1979, she tried to calm fears by proclaiming, "The National Health Service is safe with us."[63] It was not until her third and final administration that radical reforms of the NHS were set in motion.

In her first and second administrations the Conservatives concentrated on the other aspects of the welfare state that they thought needed eroding; however, some modifications in health policy were introduced. For example, from 1979 private health care was encouraged, and from 1983 health authorities were required to contract out domestic, catering, and laundry services. By 1987, Thatcher's patience with the NHS had run out. NHS costs were skyrocketing, and the Conservatives argued the system was not sensitive enough to individuals' wishes. There was inefficiency and too much variation in local health authorities' performance. Thatcher wanted to see a flourishing private health sector. Just as the overriding thrust of her social welfare reforms was to encourage business enterprise and discourage dependency on state welfare, Thatcher believed that private health care was the only way to reintroduce efficiency and cost containment in health care provision. Publicly much was made of her own choice of private health care treatment. She argued Britain deserved a health care system that was once again among the best in the world. This could only be achieved through privatization. Privatization would bring down costs and expenditures and bring in much-needed funds and competition.

The system Thatcher envisioned was articulated in the Griffith Report of 1983. The report recommended a move to an insurance-based health care system supported by private companies. Thatcher's plan was designed to make the NHS more businesslike, including more competition between levels of health care as well as competition between hospitals, providers, and physicians. Unfortunately for Thatcher, private insurance did not absolve government of responsibility for overall spending. As a result, as the demand for more and better health care increased, so did the need for funds to supply the demand. Thatcher's plan simply backfired, and the consensus built by the British government since 1948 eroded. Fearing the loss of support, Thatcher quickly rescinded her recommendation, claiming:

> The principle that adequate health care should be provided for all, regardless of their ability to pay, must be the foundation for any arrangement for financing health care.[64]

Thatcher's retraction was against the wishes of her economic advisors, Milton Friedman and Friedrich Hayek, but in terms of restoring the confidence and integrity of the British government, it was necessary.

In truth, the late 1970s and 1980s saw the NHS struggling to fund a system that demanded new technology, that was confronted with an aging population, and where there was insufficient government revenue to keep up with rising expectations. By 1989, the NHS was under tremendous pressure from every sector in British society. No one disagreed that it was underfunded or inefficient. The NHS had no budget constraints and was a large and unwieldy state bureaucracy. As a result, the Thatcher government presented a new reform program in a government white paper and introduced the 1990 National Health Service and Community Act.

This legislation sought to make health care more efficient and less costly by encouraging competition within the health care industry. The market redefined the roles and relations among existing health care actors by transforming them into separate purchasers and providers. Labour, since its election in 1997, has retained the basic structure, with some modifications, set up by the 1990 legislation.

Policy Structure and Organization

Britain offers all citizens universal access to health care across a wide range of services. These include hospital services, outpatient services provided by general practitioners and family doctors, and aftercare services provided by local authorities. Approximately 80 percent of the cost of provision is paid through general taxation. The rest is met from individuals through their national health service contribution and from co-payments toward the cost of pharmaceuticals and specialized services. For example, the cost of a prescription currently is $10. Co-payments make up about 10 percent of health care funds. Private insurance makes up nearly another 10 percent of total health coverage, and covers an estimated 15 percent of the population.[65] Co-payments are either reduced or do not apply to children less than sixteen, expectant mothers, women who have had a child in the past year, women aged sixty and over, men aged sixty-five and over, individuals who suffer from chronic illness, disabled veterans and low-income families. Under the Conservative governments of Thatcher and Major co-payments were increased in amount, and more restrictions were placed on eligibility rules for free services. For example, prescription charges were increased more than 40 times the rate of inflation from 1979 to 1997.[66]

Structurally, the NHS operates as an internal market made up of purchasers and providers. The objective of such roles is to produce greater efficiency and cost-effectiveness. Central state control is maintained through the health ministry. For example, all appointments of health authorities' chief executives is the responsibility of the minister of health. Essentially the system is composed of three sectors: the public, the semi-autonomous public, and the private.

The DHAs have the freedom to buy services from NHS or private-sector hospitals, while NHS hospitals may choose to opt out of health authority control and manage their own affairs as self-governing trusts. Large practices of general practitioners can become GP fund holders and receive budgets to use in purchasing diagnostic hospital services and elective surgical procedures. Services can be purchased from either the public or the private sector. The Labour party has announced that it intends to remove formal fund-holding status by 2002 and replace it with integrated care. Under such a scheme, general practitioners will be grouped together into local community groups. Each group is to have the same access to funds to spend. Under this scheme general practitioners will still purchase health care for their patients but will have more control over local health care. Also available is a completely private sector of institutions and purchasers. Box 10.2 outlines the three sectors of provision.

Box 10.2 British Health Care Service Provision		
Public Sector	**Semi-Autonomous Public Sector**	**Private Sector**
• Directly managed units under the control of DHAs	• Trust status hospitals accountable directly to the Ministry of Health	• Private hospitals
• Non-fund holding GPs	• Fund holding GPs	• Sole private doctors or doctors operating in semi-autonomous sector, as well as private
• No at-site service fees for patients. All fees paid out of patient taxes and contribution	• No at-site service fees for patients. All fees paid out of patient taxes and contributions	• Fees paid by private health insurance

In order to improve service and guarantee higher levels of patient care, Patient Charters were started in 1992. The charters list the rights and service standards patients can expect. In particular, they pledge to provide treatment within a specific time span, since long delays for treatment and elective surgery were among the chief complaints about the system. Since 1992, separate charters have been created for the various kinds of health services, such as for dental, mental health, and maternity care. In contrast, emergency care has always gained high approval.

Since Labour's election in 1997, three key themes underpin and guide health policy. They are first a commitment to narrowing the health gap. The government has introduced initiatives such as Health Improvement Programs, Health Action Zones, and Healthy Living Centers. Basically this shifts emphasis from health care to good health. It is hoped to regenerate communities and raise the standards of health. The second theme is a commitment to quality. Mechanisms to achieve this include improved clinical governance and a greater emphasis on evidence-based medicine. The third theme is a greater emphasis on primary care. It is hoped that primary care groups (general practitioners in practice) and Trusts will play a more significant role in the purchasing and delivering of health care at the local level.[67]

Future Outcomes and Policy Weakness

The early 1990s reforms have met with much criticism and the Labour party, since its election in 1997, has laid out an ambitious agenda for modernizing the NHS. Many Britons still argue that the provision of health care is inequitable and that there is a health gap. They constantly lobby for improvement in the quality of health care services and primary care. When Britain is compared to other nations in the WHO 2000 report (see Table 10.1), facts emerge that support and detract from much of the criticism. Britain ranks better than the United States, Germany, and Brazil in terms of the level of health. In terms of the system's responsiveness, they do not rank well against the nations discussed in this text with the exception of Brazil; however, when taken on a worldwide basis, they score well. As for the financial fairness of the system, Britain and Japan score the same and are much higher than the other discussed nations. Interestingly only one nation of our discussed nations, Brazil, ranks lower in terms of health expenditure per capita. However, once again, if taken on a worldwide comparison, Britain is ranked fairly high.

In response to criticism, the Labour government has argued the root of all the system's problems are escalating costs and poor management capacity in the health service. In March of 2000, Tony Blair announced the Labour party's new commitment to health policy by announcing that the NHS had not had its day and that a modernized NHS, not private medical insurance, is the future path Britain would take. Blair's vision is of an NHS where every patient gets the same standard of care wherever they live in Britain. The system introduced in the 1990s is one where competition replaced cooperation, where cash was more important than care, and profits were valued more than patients. One of the main criticisms leveled at the NHS in the last decade was that patients in one geographic area would receive better care than patients in another area.

In the 2000 budget, Labour has authorized a $26 billion cash boost for the NHS. This would bring the nation more in line with Sweden, Germany, and Japan in terms of overall expenditure as a percentage of GDP. In return for this massive infusion of cash, the NHS will undergo radical change over a four-year period. Blair announced that the reforms will come under his own personal guidance as chair of a new cabinet committee overseeing health care reforms.[68] The number-one goal of the reforms is to put to an end the practice of treatment depending on where someone lives rather than clinical need. Next, Labour wishes to see an end to hospitals in some areas offering first-class care while patients in other areas re-

---

Box 10.3   Blair's Challenges to the NHS

The Five Challenges

- **Partnership**
  All parts of the NHS to work together to reduce unnecessary hospital admission, end bed blocking, and provide the right level of beds and services.
- **Performance**
  All units to come up to the standards of the best and root out poor performance.
- **Professions**
  Introduction of more flexible working practices.
- **Patient Care**
  Most serious conditions to be treated quickly and nobody having to wait too long for an operation.
- **Prevention**
  Balance spending on treating illness with tackling the causes of ill health and ensure that those most at risk of certain illnesses are given the advice and help they need.

ceive second-class service. Thus, performance targets will be set. Labour announced that they wish these reforms to be carried out in consultation with all stakeholders in the NHS. Blair publicly threw down five challenges to those working in the health service to improve the care they offered to patients. They involve partnership, performance, professions, patient care, and prevention (see Box 10.3). The future is unclear, but what is clear is that it is impossible for the NHS to continue in its existing form. Whether the Blair 2000 initiative is the right path is questionable. It could be argued that it is a fine-tuning, that it is not radical enough, and that it is simply a Band-aid. Only time will tell. What is certain is that the British public is now truly dissatisfied with the NHS. There can be no significant change until the British policy makers solve a basic problem in health care provision: How do you finance the NHS at the level needed merely to maintain a constant level of provision?

Japan: Healthy Satisfaction

Today the Japanese people are among the healthiest in the world. The WHO 2000 report ranks the nation number one in terms of the population's health. Not only do the Japanese live longer than most other nationalities, but they also have the lowest rate of infant mortality.[69] Once again the WHO 2000 report ranks them first in healthy life expectancy with 74.5 years of age (see Table 10.3). Japanese culture promotes many forms of good health, a healthy diet, a strong commitment to exercise, a strong work ethic, and an enjoyment of one's natural surroundings. As would be expected, Japan provides a comprehensive national health care program for its citizens—a system with which many Japanese are satisfied.[70] Once again, this seems to be evident in the WHO 2000 report. Compared to other nations and, in particular, to the nations discussed in this text, Japan ranks consistently either at the top or near the top (see Table 10.1).

Table 10.3   Health Life Expectancy and Equality of Child Survival

Nation	Total Population at Birth Years in Age	Rank Years in Age	Equality of Child Survival Rank
Brazil	59.1	111	108
Germany	70.4	22	20
Great Britain	71.7	14	2
Japan	74.5	1	3
Sweden	73.0	4	28
United States	70.0	24	32

Source: Adapted from WHO 2000 Report.

Policy History and Evolution

The Japanese health care system has undergone several stages. Pre–Second World War, much of the health care system was shaped by German health care programs.[71] Japanese medical students were trained by German practitioners who also established Western medical practices in Japan. One such practice was to allow Japan's health care system to be run by entrepreneurial physicians. These physicians could charge what they wanted, treat whomever they wanted, and set the foundation for physician ownership of hospitals and clinics that continues today. One backlash to physician control was the enactment of the 1922 Health Insurance Law. Under this legislation, health insurance was offered to all citizens working in mines, fisheries, and factories; approximately two million Japanese received coverage. In 1938, the Ministry of Health and Welfare (*Koseisho*) was established and charged with overseeing health care. In Japan today, the Koseisho is responsible for most health decision making. Thus, the Koseisho is responsible for public health, disability funding, and maintaining all health care facilities. By the outbreak of war, health insurance had been extended to millions more Japanese.

World War II and the subsequent American occupation of Japan not only affected society (as discussed in the chapter on Japan) but also greatly impacted the health care system in order to conform to the imposed constitution and its demands that "all people still have the right to maintain the minimum standards of wholesome and cultured living in all spheres of life . . ."[72] In 1948, the Medical Service Law was enacted. This became the foundation for health care regulations and control of health care facilities in modern Japan. Also, in the same year, the Social Medical Fee Payment Fund was established. This reconstructed the pre-war system of health insurance. Under the system, both public and private employees were covered fairly well. However, all other sectors were not covered by any public health insurance scheme.

A decade later, Japan moved closer to universal health coverage by requiring local governments to provide health insurance to the unemployed. By 1961, every Japanese citizen had health care insurance. It was provided through a variety of avenues, such as employment, trade unions, or local governments. The national government also invested heavily in education and training of medical personnel. This period can be characterized as the "golden era" of Japanese health care. Japan saw not only increased coverage of its citizens but also vast improvements in organization and service. There was universal coverage, increased numbers of hospitals and clinics, increases in the number of physicians, and special needs for certain individuals such as the disabled and mentally ill were addressed. Undoubtedly, this brought social benefit, but it also brought great fiscal costs. By the end of the 1970s, health care costs were at an all-time high. An act providing free medical care for the aged in 1972 contributed to the rise in costs. This legislation was later revised in 1986 so as to transfer part of the health costs of the aged from national health insurance.

The economic miracle of the 1970s and 1980s brought with it both positives and negatives. Among the negatives was the reality that as the nation became wealthier there were large gaps and inequities in health care access and benefits. The less affluent in Japan were paying higher contributions to health insurance and receiving less benefit. As a result, in the mid-1980s, Japan attempted to enact cost control programs and procedures to reduce spending and rectify inequities. Examples of cost control measures were shifting costs to consumers, limiting fee increases to providers, and giving greater responsibility to local, or "prefecture," governments.

Compounding these problems, the economic boom also brought additional social problems, including drugs, suicide, pollution, inadequate housing, and disposal of garbage. Each had their effect on health care. Health care costs were on the rise again, and diseases like cancer, which were almost nonexistent in Japan a decade earlier, were also increasing. Additionally, by the 1980s Japan was rapidly becoming the fastest-aging country in the world with nearly 13 percent of its population over the age of 65 years.[73] The remainder of the 1980s and the subsequent 1990s has been a period for successive Japanese governments to cope with the end of the economic miracle and its ramifications for the health care system.

Policy Structure and Organization

The present-day system is one in which there is universal coverage, where the government devotes one of the lowest proportions of GDP to health care, and subsequently has a less than generous per capita expenditure (see Table 10.2). Japan also possesses the most hospital beds per capita than any other nation (see Table 10.2). They also have a system that utilizes the most sophisticated medical technology.

Universal coverage is provided by the national health insurance program. It evolved out of the 1922 National Health Law and has been expanded and amended several times. The insurance program is funded by payments from both employers and employees as well as national subsidies. Box 10.4 shows the various insurance schemes, who is covered and who insures. From Box 10.4, it is obvious that the Japanese health care system is fragmented and complex. Under this system, with the exception of health services for the aged, all insurance schemes collect contributions which go to the various health funds and pay the health costs to mostly privately run hospitals through a system of fees-for-services. Under most of the insurance schemes, members are required to pay 10 to 80 percent of their medical expenses depending on the type of treatment provided.

Physicians in Japan control the dispensing and prescribing of medication and own and operate the hospitals, clinics, and medical facilities where they practice. In addition, physicians are free to negotiate and consult with health insurance providers, medical associations, and pharmaceutical companies to keep prices down and assure physicians' additional income. Traditionally, physicians in Japan have a higher gross income because of ownership and contracts than do most physicians in other countries. Also, Japanese physicians, unlike other physicians around the world, are revered by their patients and society as a whole.

Box 10.4   Health Care Service Provision in Japan

Public Sector	Semi-Autonomous Public Sector	Private Sector
• Directly managed and united under the control of District Health Authorities • Non-fund-holding GPs • No at-site service fees for patients. All fees paid out of patient taxes and contributions.	• Trust statute hospitals accountable directly to secretary of state • Fund-holding GPs • No at-site service fee for for patients. All fees paid out of patient taxes and contributions.	• Private hospitals • Sole private patients or practitioners operating in semi-autonomous sector as well as private • Fee paid by private health insurance.

The Japanese health care system is made up of four primary mechanisms: public health centers, physicians' offices, clinics, and hospitals. Public health centers are designed to deal primarily with prevention of illness, as well as health maintenance. Physicians' offices are where most health issues are first addressed. These offices are where physicians first see patients and refer to other physicians or facilities. Clinics are distributed throughout communities and deal with inpatient as well as outpatient care. Clinics also perform curative rather than preventive care. Hospitals perform inpatient and outpatient care, utilize high technological procedures and devices, and perform curative rather than preventive care.

Japanese health care is financed through a combination of public and private funds. Japanese citizens account for nearly 20 percent of health care finances through co-payments. Citizens over the age of 70 account for almost 10 percent of private funding.[74] The Social Insurance Medical Fee Fund (SIMF), which has branches in each prefecture, consists of various taxes (general tax revenue, health insurance tax, sales tax), distributes funds to different levels of government, and serves as an intermediary between insurance plans and providers, as well as acting as a source to review insurance claims.

Future Outcomes and Policy Weakness

The main problem today is controlling costs and preventing waste, while maintaining the dedication and commitment to prevention and service. Recently, Japan has attempted to convince hospitals and physicians to distribute more responsibility to clinics and other facilities to take the pressure off hospitals. These alternative institutions are cheaper and can more effectively and efficiently deal with local patients. The problem with this transition is that by transferring care to clinics and other alternative institutions, hospitals, and the physicians who own them, lose revenues and lucrative contracts based on the amount of clients. As a result, funds for alternative institutions are difficult to secure since physicians tremendously influence policy making and implementation of policy.

The rapidly aging population in Japan is also another major problem the Japanese health care system faces. This will require increasing public monies to deal with their long-term health needs. As in so many nations, senior care is expensive, especially as many older Japanese no longer have extended families to aid in the payment of health care expenses. Japan is already one of the most medicated countries in the world (19 percent of health care costs are for medication consumption), and now with the aging population and the rise of chronic illness (cancer, etc.), those expenses will undoubtedly increase.

Because of historical deference to and reverence for physicians, the Japanese health care system has been accused of blindly rewarding funds, services, and resources regardless of the success and efficiency of practice. As a result, many have criticized the health care system as lacking a commitment to modern management. The recent economic woes have brought closer scrutiny and increased criticisms of a system that sees physicians getting richer and services and treatment getting more difficult to obtain.

In April of 2000, the National Long Term Care Insurance Program went into effect.[75] The law allows private companies to tap into Japanese public funding, dispatch home-helpers to needy residents, and bill the Japanese government directly for services rendered. The effects on Japan will be great. Not only will billions of new public dollars be pumped into Japan's long-term care system, but Japan will also open itself up to foreign insurance companies and corporations as never before. Foreign companies will now have the ability to compete in the Japanese health care market, create new jobs, invest in Japan, and offer more health care options for the Japanese. The Koseisho claims that this law constitutes double-billing, since foreign companies will receive payments from the Japanese government in addition to patient fees. They suggest that companies should reimburse part of the government payment, thus limiting the amount of money foreign companies can make in Japan. Regardless of this controversy, Japan is attempting to reform its health care system.

Sweden: Still Committed but for How Long?

As the model for social democracy, one would expect Sweden to have a long history of public commitment to health care provision. Indeed many consider it to be a pioneer in public health promotion and prevention.[76] However, with the crisis of welfare expenditure came a questioning of what Sweden can realistically spend on health care provision. Additionally questions were raised about the system's efficiency. In terms of comparing the Swedish system overall with the five other nations discussed in this text, the WHO 2000 report ranks the Swedish system higher than Brazil, Germany, and the United States but below Japan and Great Britain. This is in spite of having a top-ten health expenditure per capita ranking. Where Sweden does rank impressively is in the overall health of its citizens and in expected life expectancy score (see Table 10.3).

There is little covert political or social struggle around health care issues. This is because the politics of health care is directly incorporated into mainstream politics. All health care politics is carried out within local party political structures. A fundamental principle of the health care system is that it is a public-sector responsibility to provide and finance health services for the entire population. It is a universal system. All residents of the country, whether contributing to the system or not, are entitled to hospital, outpatient, and privacy care. Technically Sweden does not have a national health service akin to that of Great Britain. This is because the majority of services and finances are under local government jurisdiction. Responsibility for these services rests primarily with the county councils, which levy taxes to raise the financial resources required to operate the system. Thus, the local politicians are responsible for health services in Sweden. The system can be characterized as decentralized and socially democratic.

Policy History and Evolution

Sweden's health care system began with the Collegium Medicium in 1660. This system was Sweden's first introduction to publicly-sponsored health care and set the standard for future health care policies.[77] In 1752, the first general hospital was established in Stockholm and gave Swedes medical services paid for by local government. In 1800, King Gustavus Adolphus created "crown" hospitals that were designed to fight syphilis contracted by soldiers during the Thirty Years War. These crown hospitals were funded first by a head tax (1800), then a liquor tax (1864), and finally property and income taxes (1900). The crown hospitals decentralized control of health care to the county level, replacing the parish. The 1866 transition from monarchical rule displayed Swedish commitment to public health care and was manifested in the Public Health Act of 1874. Under the act, health care coverage was further expanded through the creation of local boards for sanitation, sewage, and water. These aided counties in controlling waste and instilling preventive measures.[78]

From the late 1930s on, the Social Democrats began molding government and society so as to perpetuate and ensure public health care. They utilized royal committees and the remiss process to make and pass policy and the county councils to help shape and administer health care policy and reforms.[79] In the late 1940s, there was an attempt to extend Sweden's heath care system further than the British NHS; however, the attempt failed. Among the proposed reforms was placing all physicians on salaries controlled by local authorities. Additionally, there were to be no outpatient or inpatient care costs. The abortive reform was strongly opposed by individual physicians, businesses, and the Swedish Medical Association. Such groups feared that the proposed reform would force physicians to leave public hospitals so they could pursue private practices, and also that it would cost too much, thus hindering growth and technology acquisition.

As the Social Democrats maintained control of government, they continued to attempt to reform and expand health care. In 1955, the National Insurance Law was enacted. This covered the entire population for medical cash benefits (funded by sickness funds, taxes, and government subsidies). The 1960s saw the government challenge what it perceived to be the monopolistic power of Swedish physicians. The result was first to change the role of physicians and second to limit their ability to generate private income. This was achieved through a number of measures. For example, the 1959 Hospital Law eliminated private beds and fees for inpatient care. Next, Austrian physicians were encouraged to immigrate to Sweden through an incentive program. The goal was to create an influx of competing physicians. Finally, it was made mandatory that low-income individuals be treated at fixed rates. By 1969 further reforms eliminated private practice from public hospitals completely, and all physicians were placed on full-time salaries, thus eliminating the fee-for-service system in Sweden.[80] The success of the Social Democrats' health care reforms was in part attributed to their ability to control and mold government to their advantage. Reform was also successful because it caught the Swedish public's imagination.

When the Social Democrats lost power in 1976, their successors did attempt to rescind many of the reforms of the previous years. Most notably, they reinstated the ability of physicians to operate private practices by allowing them to accept fees for services rendered in their spare time. However, the Social Democrats quickly regained power. Under the 1982 Health and Medical Services Act, all people are offered health and medical services on equal terms and access. By 1986, the Dagmar reform had been enacted. This changed the manner in which funds were allocated to individual hospitals. No longer would government subsidies to hospitals be paid per patient visit. Rather, funds would be distributed according to the number of inhabitants. It was hoped this would ensure equal distribution of funding; control the overuse of resources; force physicians to contract with county councils; and allow the county councils to control the private sector, thus ensuring decentralization.

The 1990s has witnessed real efforts by the government to control the rising costs of public health care. Part of this effort has involved a search to eliminate wasted resources. The need was obvious. By 1990, health care services were consuming 10 percent of GNP and employing 10 percent of the work force.[81] There was much criticism of wasted expenditure and overemployment of staff, including physicians. Further criticism pointed at overuses of hospitalization and long waiting lists for procedures. In order to meet much of the criticism the government introduced the Kopparberg Model in 1991. Its objective was further decentralization of the health care system. In this model, fifteen municipal districts or Primary Care Centers (PCC) were designed to form "boards," which determined the needs and preferences of the districts. Funding for this model was based on population and needs. The goal was to reduce the use of hospital outpatient referrals as well as monitor the use of resources by hospital specialists. Kopparberg hoped that hospitals would receive more money for patient care if they attracted PCC referrals.

In 1992, the Stockholm Model examined the process by which hospitals and regions obtained funds and resources. Instead of distributing resources and funds by global budgeting (population, revenues), the Stockholm Model determined distribution by the sale of services to health districts, a form of an internal market. This placed actual "need" and "use" over the population and foreseeable use and need of a particular hospital or region. As a result, health care in Stockholm was able to be more responsive to patients' needs and preferences through more competition and greater choice. In addition, health care was revitalized, became more productive, and waste was diminished.

Policy Structure and Organization

Health care, like social welfare services, is seen as a public-sector responsibility and is supported by the national insurance system. It is a health care system characterized by a decentralized system of publicly-funded county health services. Responsibility for health care, both inpatient and outpatient, is a duty of the county councils and large municipalities. The commitment to health care transcends all levels of care (state, county, municipality) and incorporates the participation of all aspects of health from prevention and education to cure. The success of the universality of the system is attributed to commitment from all sectors of society. It is supported by not only Social Democrats but the opposition and the mass of citizens. For Swedes, health care is a basic human right.[82] Caring for the less well-off, as well as the ill, is a societal responsibility as much as it is a family responsibility.

All residents are covered by national insurance. Many consider Swedish health care benefits to be among the most impressive and most inclusive in the world. For a small fee, Swedes receive primary care outpatient services, hospitalization, and pharmaceuticals. In recent years, the fees have increased so as to reduce costs and discourage overuse or abuse of the system. If an individual is ill or must stay home to care for sick children, he or she receives a taxable daily allowance, 75 to 85 percent of lost income, depending on the length of absence. For those individuals who incur considerable costs for medical treatment and prescriptions there is a ceiling, after which treatment/drugs are free of charge. County councils, together with the health insurance system, pay most of the hospitalization costs and laboratory fees. A large proportion of private physicians' fees for outpatient care is also covered by the national insurance scheme. Swedes also receive subsidized dental care. Adults pay full cost to $800. Above this, health insurance bears a rising proportion of the costs, from 25 percent to 70 percent. In recent years, reforms passed by county councils have given patients the freedom to choose where and from whom they wish to receive medical treatment. Thus, patients may choose the health center and/or doctor and even the hospital they wish to stay in. If their choice is outside their council's geographic jurisdiction, they must receive a referral. Within their own geographic area patients do not require referrals to receive specialist services. Since 1992, patients are subject to care guarantees. Primary care services are offered to patients the same day the patient contacts them, and if a medical consultation is required, it is guaranteed within eight days of primary contact.

Central government, county councils, and local authorities are all active within the Swedish health care policy sector. Each level has the right to finance activities by levying taxes and fees. Central government formulates health policy by laying down basic principles for health services through laws and ordinances. Today central government is more interested in the results and performance of services rather than how they are organized. Central government can exercise control through evaluating implemented health services. The main central government department involved in health care is the Ministry of Health and Social Affairs (*Socialdepartementet*). The Ministry drafts proposed new legislation for parliament, prepares government regulations, and provides commissions with necessary data and information. The central government's main advisory and supervisory health service agency is the National Board of Health and Welfare. It is the responsibility of the board to evaluate whether services being provided correspond to the central government's goals.

The county councils are responsible for providing health services to the general population. This requires that they determine resource allocation and planning for the services to be provided. The county councils own and run hospitals, health centers, and other health facilities. The local authorities also have their own area of responsibility within health care. Mainly the local authorities deal with the care of the elderly or physically challenged in their residences. Since 1992, the responsibility for nursing homes has been transferred to local authorities from county councils. At the same time, the local authorities also assumed the financial obligation of paying for patients who had to remain in a hospital because there was no alternative care facility. From 1995, a similar arrangement has come into force concerning the living arrangements and support for long-term mentally ill individuals.

Swedish health care expenditure in 1999 was around 8.6 percent of GNP.[83] Approximately 90 percent of the costs were spent on care provided or financed by the county councils.[84] Health services account for 85 percent of the operations of county councils.[85] In 1997, 77 percent of these operations were financed by tax revenues. The county councils are allowed to levy a proportional tax on residents' incomes. The tax rate is on average 10.2 percent. Other revenue sources are grants and payments for certain services received by the central government. Patients' fees also contribute to county councils' revenues. Thus, Swedish health care is funded by four interrelated sources: personal income tax, the National Health Insurance System, National Grants, and user fees. Personal income tax accounts for nearly 82 percent of health care funding, and user fees constitute outpatient physician consultations at $9 per visit, inpatient care at $7 per visit, and drug prescriptions at $10.

Traditionally, Sweden distributed health care funds to individual hospitals, facilities, and clinics according to historical patterns of need. Unfortunately, as in other nations, the majority of funds and resources over the years were allocated to larger counties or regions merely because of population and revenue and not necessarily need. This produced much waste and competition between counties and municipalities. Compounding this lack of parity is the reduction in the tax bases of councils and thus diminished council revenues, which has led to cuts in health services. In the early 1990s, most county councils introduced some form of purchaser-provider model, such as the Stockholm model. Purchaser-provider models allow for payment to be made according to results or performance and not fixed annual allocations. In some counties, competition with the private sector has been encouraged.

Future Outcomes and Policy Weakness

One problem with the Swedish health care system is the lack of general practitioners.[86] The 1990s saw the Swedish government fail to achieve targets set for the number of practicing physicians. Part of the reason for the lack of physicians is that Swedish physicians have less opportunity to make additional income outside of their public-sector salary. Physicians often receive training in Sweden and emigrate in order to practice elsewhere, or they opt for the limited private sector in Sweden. Additionally, physicians from other countries choose not to practice in Sweden because of limited opportunities and less flexibility.

Another problem involves health care efficiency and organization. Counties and municipalities are under tremendous pressure to receive funds, attract physicians, properly admit/refer/diagnose patients, and transfer information to other levels of care, as well as adapt to national health care cuts. The Stockholm County Model addressed some of these concerns, and reformists have proposed other recommendations to make the system more efficient and cost-effective.

Sweden's historical commitment to health care has created problems. Costs keep increasing, and Sweden must constantly find ways to justify cuts in services. The government must be perceived to still be committed to providing a health care system that is accountable, accessible, and equitable. Efficiency must not replace the goal of universal affordable access. Privatization has been supported by some critics as a way to make the system more efficient, and it is increasing in Sweden.[87] In the late 1990s, Sweden began converting publicly owned primary care centers into private group practice arrangements. These private group practices contract with local counties and provide additional choices for patients, as well as opportunities for physicians. However, privatization, in the long run, may threaten equity and damage the system's ability to depend on loyalty from broad constituencies. It has already presented problems with demand regulation.

Commitment to universal health care is strong in Sweden. History and tradition ensure its existence, yet the means for achieving this are not clear. Limited resources, rising costs, insufficient staff, waste, and politics produce more and more dissatisfaction with the present system. Some recommend further decentralization, restructuring administrative responsibilities, and giving even more power to counties and municipalities. Others believe a move toward privatization will solve many of the problems. The path to be taken is not clear, but what is certain is that the Swedish health care system will have to be restructured in the coming years.

United States: Big Spending, Low Return

At the start of the new century, health care is a controversial item on the American public agenda. It is, however, unlikely that a major overhaul of the system is on the near horizon. This is in spite of the fact that health expenditures in the United States continue to outpace inflation. Today expenditure is approximately 14 percent of GDP (see Table 10.2). According to the WHO 2000 report, the United States spends a higher proportion of its GDP on health care than any other nation. However, it only ranks 37 out of 191 nations worldwide in terms of overall performance. When compared to the nations discussed in this text, it ranks only above Brazil and is significantly lower than Japan, Britain, Sweden, and Germany (see Table 10.1). Additionally, approximately 18 percent of the U.S. population has no health insurance coverage, while millions more have such limited coverage that they would be put into economic impoverishment if serious illness hit. From the early 1990s, affordability of health care was not solely a working-class family's concern, but it also became a middle-class concern.

The history of health care in America is one of fallen public expectations and of lost chances. Many Americans are deeply ideologically opposed to federal government ownership of health care facilities, employment of health care professionals, and universal coverage. Such a system is viewed as "socialized" medicare and thus "un-American." However, there is general dissatisfaction with the system. Taking such factors into account Esping-Andersen's liberal category may be applied to the American health care system.

Policy History and Evolution

The foundation of the U.S. health care system is entrepreneurial. This is very different from most of the systems discussed in this text. Early government assistance was to "support" individual or group activities aimed at improving health and informing society or assisting the economically or physically disadvantaged. Government was the "safety net" for those who had no other options in health care. In the European nations discussed in this text, government took a different role. From the beginning, European governments attempted to be leaders in the field of health care provision. With the establishment of the U.S. Public Health Service in 1798, a pattern was set. The well-off or the "haves" of society were afforded the very best in health care and services while the "have nots," or the poor and disadvantaged, have had to compete and struggle for limited resources and adequate health care provision and services.

Until the early 1900s, the less well-off in America were left to treat themselves or each other. The first expansion of services and facilities to serve the poor and the destitute occurred in the period prior to World War I. Approximately 4,000 hospitals were established and run by religious groups and communities. Such institutions relied on the patronage of the wealthy and charged patient fees. Over time, these facilities became "workshops" or training grounds for physicians. Expansion of these nonprofit hospitals was achieved in 1946 through the Hill-Burton Hospital and Survey and Construction Act. Under the act, a one-time federal contribution for the construction of rural medical facilities and hospitals was established. The federal contribution amounted to nearly 25 percent of the total costs of construction. The act also served to attract physicians to such newly constructed facilities.

Simultaneous to this facility expansion was the development of a medical insurance industry. Initially, there was support for a national insurance system similar to some European nations; however, by the early 1900s the movement against it was so strong that the idea was removed from the public agenda.[88] Blue Cross was established in 1933 and introduced the first "prepayment" system in the United States. Initiated in the states of California and Michigan, these "Blue Plans" eventually spread to all states in the union. These plans utilized community ratings to calculate premiums that applied equally to all citizens within that community. Unfortunately, as high-risk groups and activities began to stand out, the Blue Plans changed to an experience rating based on individual health status in order to minimize risks and maximize profits.

The 1940s saw tremendous private insurance growth, and by the early 1950s it was estimated that nearly 50 percent of Americans had some form of health care insurance.[89] Such industry development was facilitated by generous tax exemptions. There was some support for a national insurance system proposed by President Harry S Truman in the 1950s, to replace private insurance; however, any congressional activity was defeated by the American Medical Association and the insurance lobby. Supporters of national insurance were pacified by legislation, such as the Kerr Mills Amendment to the 1960 Social Security Act. Under this, grants for insurance to the medically indigent were supported.

The 1960s witnessed a new dialogue on the reform of American health care. Both John F. Kennedy and Lyndon B. Johnson attempted to change and expand health care to certain sectors of the population. The first victory was the extension of health care insurance to those who qualified for social security. A second victory was the passing of the 1962 Migrant Workers Act. This act provided federal funding of health programs for migrant workers for the first time in American history. In addition, the act led to the creation of rural clinics designed to offer care, health care information, and preventive programs. The success of the legislation also led to its expansion to low-income families. Next, community mental health centers were established in 1963. These centers were designed to give mental health assistance. In addition, the War on Poverty program was a direct influence on the numerous amendments to the Social Security Act between the years of 1963 through 1967. These amendments gave states increased funds for activities primarily involving maternal and child care. The Economic Opportunity Act of 1964 and the Comprehensive Health Planning Act of 1966 were both a result of this vision and helped states and localities fund neighborhood health facilities as well as hire personnel and obtain necessary resources.

The real centerpiece of the War on Poverty health care reforms were Medicare and Medicaid. Medicare was designed to provide health insurance to all older Americans and some disabled citizens as well. Medicaid provided federal grants to states for insuring selected lower income citizens. For the most part, Medicaid aided single mothers with dependent children and the elderly. Both were single-payer arrangements for health care provision. The goal of these two programs, ideally, was that they function like private insurance. Physicians and hospitals would be reimbursed for "reasonable and necessary" expenses with little interference by the federal government. Realistically, the rising costs of health care (15 percent rise in costs between the 1960s and 1970s) forced the federal government to become more involved with both Medicare and Medicaid. Frustrations also rose on both sides of the Medicare/Medicaid issue. Physicians and hospitals complained of receiving fewer reimbursements than they deserved, and patients criticized service in addition to limited coverage.

The 1970s saw perhaps one of the most important developments prohibiting a move toward a system similar to that of public health provision in the United Kingdom or Sweden or Germany. That development was the introduction of a managed care system. Such a system was sanctioned under the 1973 Health Maintenance Organization (HMO) Act, in which $375 million was appropriated to subsidize the formation of prepaid insurance groups. HMOs offered comprehensive services, greater efficiency, and improved convenience for consumers. Through tax exemptions and other benefits, the federal government encouraged employers to offer HMOs to employees, thus shifting the burden and responsibility of health care further away from the public sector and more securely into the hands of the private sector. Kaiser Permanente was one of the first companies to introduce a prepaid plan to the West Coast of the United States. Shortly thereafter, other managed care options began to surface. Preferred Provider Organizations (PPOs) and Independent Practice Associations (IPAs) were introduced and boasted more flexibility than HMOs, discounted fees for patients with a designated physician, and the luxury of being preferred by both physicians and hospitals. It seems that physicians and hospitals felt that PPOs and IPAs allowed them to treat insured patients while at the same time maintain a private practice. By 1978, 43 percent of physicians contracted with a PPO, although they claim that only 12 percent of their income was derived from insurance patients.[90]

During this time efforts were being made to establish a Comprehensive Health Plan (CHP). Introduced in the late 1960s, the CHP was believed to be a vehicle to increase local coordination, facilitate planning, and use resources more efficiently. As a result of increased efforts to implement a CHP, regional medical programs were established, linking medical schools and practitioners and increasing communication among all levels of health care. In 1974, Congress passed the National Health Planning and Resource Development Act (NHPRD). This act mandated the implementation of nearly two hundred health planning areas to guide hospital construction, initiate new technology and develop master plans for health services. In addition, the NHPRD controlled hospital bed supply, hospital charges, and the monitoring of physicians and hospitals through peer review boards. As the United States entered the 1980s, an ideological shift took place. Arising at the same time was a drastic increase in health care costs. The Reagan Administration began a period of diminishing health care support and elimination of federal grants. This was part of the Reagan health care privatization agenda.

As in so many other nations, the United States in the late 1970s and early 1980s witnessed escalating health costs and the implementation of cost-containment measures. However, the cost control measures were to no avail. Medicare costs were increasing at alarming rates, physician and hospital costs were rising dramatically, and access was becoming even more limited. At the same time, the uninsured population was expanding rapidly. Some of the attempts to control costs included Diagnosis Related Groups (DRGs). These groups signified America's first major national effort to identify, describe, and specify costs for categories of disease and illness. The goal of the DRGs was to contain hospital costs and achieve better efficiency in the delivery of health care. This was to be accomplished by preestablishing schedule payments for each category of illness (470 total illnesses to begin with). In addition, Resource Based Relative Value Scales (RBRVSs) were introduced to measure and develop consistent fees for physicians' services. As a sign of the times, Congress passed the Catastrophic Coverage Act of 1988. This attempted to solve the problem of individuals spending down any resources accumulated to reach the poverty limit and thus qualify for Medicare or Medicaid assistance. Most of the act was soon repealed, however, because of pressure from seniors' groups.

During the Bush administration it became obvious to all that there was an "emergency" of health care provision in the United States. Costs were escalating, the population of uninsured was growing, and managed care was now seen to put profit above health care. Congress considered a number of plans to introduce some form of national health insurance.[91] All plans, although different in operation, had the same objective. They would entitle everyone in America, regardless of economic or employment status, to selected medical services from physicians, hospitals, and health care providers. All the proposed legislation wanted limited cost sharing by patients, government payments to cover costs to health care providers, and taxation change to finance the plan. It was hoped to replace private insurance premiums with public expenditures through taxes on individual households. Many Republicans, although opposed to national insurance, offered alternative ways of dealing with the "crisis of care." Most of the suggestions used tax credits or vouchers to require everyone to have private insurance coverage.[92]

When Bill Clinton took office in 1992, the time seemed ripe for radical reform. Table 10.4 summarizes the cost dimension of the American health care system from 1960 until Clinton took office. Clinton had two objectives. First, he desired to extend medical coverage to the 15 percent of Americans who were uninsured. Second, he wanted to stop the spiraling cost of medical care. The task of developing the new administration's health care proposal was delegated to Clinton's wife, Hillary, and Ira Magaziner, an industrial policy expert. In 1993, an outline of the plan that the Clinton administration wished congress to consider was released. The proposal was for congress to pass a Health Security Act. Among other things, the act required employers to provide health care coverage, extended coverage to all Americans, created an internal market device called Health Insurances Alliances to purchase coverage and services, and placed price controls on insurance policies. The Clinton plan wanted to achieve managed competition in which access to both

Table 10.4 U.S. Health Expenditures, 1960–1993 by Type of Expenditures (in billions of dollars)

Type of Expenditure	1960	1970	1980	1985	1987	1989	1990	1991	1992	1993
Hospital	$9.3	$28.0	$102.7	$168.2	$194.1	$231.8	$256.5	$282.3	$306.0	$326.6
Physician	5.3	13.6	45.2	83.6	104.1	127.3	140.5	150.3	161.8	171.2
Dental	2.0	4.7	13.3	21.7	25.3	28.6	30.4	31.7	34.7	37.4
Other professional	0.6	1.4	6.4	16.8	22.6	32.2	36.0	40.4	46.4	51.2
Home health care	0.0	0.2	1.9	4.9	5.9	6.1	11.1	13.2	16.8	20.8
Drugs and other medical nondurables	4.2	8.8	21.6	37.4	45.4	54.4	61.2	67.1	70.8	75.0
Vision products and other medical durables	0.8	2.0	4.5	7.1	8.1	9.6	10.5	11.3	12.0	12.6
Nursing home care	1.0	4.9	20.5	34.9	40.6	48.9	54.8	60.6	65.5	69.6
Other personal health care	0.7	1.3	4.0	6.1	7.7	9.5	11.4	13.8	15.8	18.2
Program administration and net cost of private health insurance	1.2	2.8	12.1	25.3	19.4	32.3	38.3	37.0	39.5	48.0
Government public health activities	0.4	1.4	7.2	12.3	14.6	19.0	21.6	22.9	23.7	24.7
Research	0.7	2.0	5.6	7.8	9.1	11.3	12.2	12.9	14.2	14.4
Construction	1.0	3.4	6.2	8.6	9.2	10.8	12.1	11.9	13.2	14.6

Notes: Research and development expenditures of drug companies and other manufacturers and providers of medical equipment and supplies are excluded from research expenditures but are included in the expenditure class in which the product falls.

Source: Adapted from Health Care Financing Administration, Office of the Actuary; data from Office of National Health Statistics.

the sale of health insurance and the purchase of health care at affordable rates would be provided to everyone through the insurance alliances.

Clinton's plan was an attempt to shape market forces within a framework of national health insurance. The plan was formally submitted to congress in October 1993 and never emerged as legislation. Why is an interesting question. Part of the reason for its failure was of course the health industry's opposition and consequently the large amounts of money spent to secure its defeat. The "bootstrap" doctrine that is ingrained in American political culture also contributed to the reform's defeat. For many Americans, national health care is socialism and therefore directly threatens individual rights, responsibilities, and freedom. Much of the reason for the defeat of the plan was the actual nature of the plan itself. The plan was disliked generally by everyone. It seemed to offer more bureaucratization, and there was no evidence it would be cost-effective. Indeed many opponents argued it would simply not cut costs. Many disliked the proposal because they thought it was an attempt to harness state power so as to extend the scope of the state in the direction of universalism.

Both Democrats and Republicans in Congress drew up alternative plans but to no avail. A consensus could not be achieved, and the chance to enact radical health care reform passed. Reforms regulating HMOs have been passed in the later years of the 1990s, but these do nothing to attack the problem of access.

Policy Structure and Organization

The U.S. health care system is considered "the paradox of excess and deprivation."[93] The United States boasts the greatest density of high-tech services, more employees per bed than any other country, and arguably the best medical research and training in the world.[94] At the same time, America also possesses the highest health care costs (twice the average of twenty-four industrialized nations), the largest health care expenditure of any industrialized nation (14 percent of GDP), 18 percent of the population with no insurance, and 50 million citizens who are underinsured.[95] Ironically, one of the world's wealthiest and most powerful nations ranks considerably low in many health-related areas, although it does score well on responsiveness (see Tables 10.1, 10.2, and 10.3). One must question why such a situation exists. For example, why can Great Britain spend approximately seven percent of GDP on health services and yet rank eighteenth overall compared to America's 14 percent of GDP expenditure and overall ranking of thirty-seventh. How can the American system be so responsive and yet be so unequal in terms of financial fairness of the system (see Table 10.1)? Life expectancy and infant mortality also lag behind most other industrialized nations (see Table 10.3). It is no wonder that recent polls have shown that 75 percent of Americans support health care reform as well as some form of a national health system, even if it means higher taxes. There is also great regional variation in the quality and level of health care services, in spite of the requirement that the various states adopt federal guidelines and regulations in order to obtain necessary funds and grants. For the most part, individual states are given broad discretion in determining their own health care policies and systems.

In the United States, the majority of the population receives insurance through the workplace on the basis of a voluntary decision by employers to provide it. Public programs are limited to certain categories of population. Therefore, the American health care system is a market-oriented one. Structurally the system that emerges is three-tiered: those with private insurance coverage who can go to whomever and wherever they want in terms of care; those in the HMOs; and the uninsured. Physicians have traditionally been paid on a fee-for-service basis. However, the rise of managed care has changed the payment method. HMOs use market criteria to price and limit health care provided by physicians and hospitals so as to keep the profit margins at acceptable levels. Today approximately 180 million Americans are served by HMOs. Many physicians are salaried employees of managed care companies.

The American health care system is financed at many different levels. At the government level, the federal government is responsible for around 56 percent of expenditure while the state and local levels pick up the other 44 percent.[96] On the federal level, health care revenues are collected through income and corporate taxes. At the state level, revenues are collected through income and sales taxes, while at the local level health revenues are provided through sales and property taxes. Additionally health care revenues are supplemented by voluntary agencies. National health expenditures in the year 2000 show that approximately just over 50 percent of the total came from private sources, while a little more than one-third came from federal and the remainder from state and local government sources.[97]

Future Outcomes and Policy Weakness

Medicare and Medicaid pose serious problems for policy makers. Since their inception, the two programs have provided health insurance to a very clearly defined population. For Medicare benefits, one must either be sixty-five years of age, permanently disabled, or at the end stage of a fatal disease. For Medicaid, benefits are provided for selected segments of lower-income populations, such as families receiving aid, the elderly, or those disabled. Both Medicare and Medicaid provide a valuable service and yet, as costs have risen and the population ages, the government has raised deductibles, limited coverage, and denied increases in reimbursements. As a result many who theoretically qualify can no longer obtain necessary care. This places a higher burden on hospitals, which are obligated to take care of such individuals; in turn the hospitals pass on the cost to other clients.

What will continue to block the development of public health care provision in the United States is the dominance of a culture that fears "big" government. American culture places emphasis on individualism, self-reliance, and limited government. Under such cultural beliefs, the role of government is to secure the right of the individual to preserve oneself. Direct provision by government of health services means erosion of the individual's rights and choices. This equates to socialism, which to many is much worse than the inequalities of the current system.

Rising costs will continue to prove an obstacle to health care provision. Over the past decade there has been approximately a 12 percent increase in health costs (see Table 10.4). This affects every level and sector. Thus deductibles are higher, and fees for services have increased, as have insurance premiums. Such costs are passed on to others. Prices increase so that businesses can cover insurance benefits; physicians and hospitals increase their fees to cover the costs of new equipment and their malpractice and liability insurance. The consequence has been cutbacks in types of service, for example, emergency rooms, and lack of coverage to high-risk groups or individuals.

The checks-and-balances system, which works elsewhere in American government, does not do so in the health sector. Thus, health care reform has been slow and heavily opposed by the health industry, which spends millions and millions of dollars to ensure that there is not radical reform of health care provision in the United States.

Chapter Eleven
Education Policy: Private or Public?

Education is a field where there is much formal as well as informal institutional activity. The twentieth century has seen a greatly expanded state role in education in all industrialized societies. The pattern is for a mix of family, market, and community involvement integrated with state activity. From nation to nation, the mix and the integration can greatly vary. Education policy is difficult to analyze because there is general support for it but tremendous controversy over the substance of policy. Some individuals believe education policy should encourage greater equality in society through promotion of social mobility.[1] Others believe education should contribute to the well-being of the economy.[2] The more educated the workforce, the more they can contribute to an efficiently run economy. It also provides individuals with skills that allow them to be financially autonomous from the state. The better educated the workforce the more competitive a nation will be in global markets.

As in the case of health policy, the state's role in education policy may be as a regulator, a funder/purchaser, or a provider/planner. A review of the literature suggests that the private sector is comparatively small in most nations.[3] Most common is for states to be funder/providers. However, where nations differ is in the level of administrative centralization of the educational system. In short, who controls education will vary from nation to nation. Educational systems differ in their characteristics. For example, when does compulsory education start and finish, although all education systems are divided along age lines (see Table 11.1). Next, what are the different forms of specialization that are available, and finally, does a system stratify by ability as well age?

Table 11.1 Duration of Compulsory Education

Nation	Duration of Education in Years
Brazil	8
Germany	12
Great Britain	11
Japan	9*
Sweden	9*
United States	10*

*Education system allows other alternatives.

Source: Adapted from World Development Indicators, World Bank Report 2000.

Brazil: Still Exclusive and Not Inclusive

Public provision and regulation of education in Brazil are complex issues because of the nation's size and territorial expansion and its diversified cultural universe. The government has to adapt education to different existing realities. When the present Brazilian educational system is looked at, it is very much the result of the evolution of a historical process of development, within the wider context of Brazilian socio-political and economic development. The educational policy sector is complicated because the different levels of government—federal union, states, and local authorities—all have wide-reaching autonomy in the organization of education. Alongside state-run and -funded educational establishments is a broad range of private schools. Generally speaking, Brazil is considered to have one of the most developed systems of education in Latin America.[4]

Policy History and Evolution

The basis of Brazil's educational system was launched in 1549 with the assistance of Jesuit priests. For the next two hundred years, the Jesuits were the only real educators in Brazil. They concentrated their attention on secondary schooling. It was not until 1834 that the state became active in educational policy with the enactment of the Additional Act. This legislation delegated provisional governments the prerogative of developing legislation regarding elementary education. In sum, the national government was freeing itself of the responsibility of elementary education and set in motion a process of decentralization of basic education.

It was not until the 1920s that the national government began to take a strategic position in formulation and coordination of policy. The change was forced upon the government by the economic, cultural, and political changes brought about by World War I. Major reform of the elementary school system took place, and state governments were granted authority to legislate in the area of education. The reform movement culminated in 1932 with the publication of the Manifest of Pioneers. This document summarized an outline of how education should be delivered to the masses and redefined the role of the state in the educational process. It was during this period that the first Brazilian universities were established. The 1934 constitution incorporated many of the demands of the reform movement and attempted to guarantee a provision of public education to all children. However, with the establishment of the *Estado Novo* ("New State") in 1937 and the granting of a new constitution, the commitment to public education for all was rescinded.

With the fall of the *Estado Novo* in 1945, public provision of education returned to the policy agenda. In 1948, the government sent to congress a draft of the Law of Directives and Basis of National Education. The law attempted to establish compulsory age limits for public provision of education. The law was not approved until 1961. However, in spite of the delay in formal legislation, the Brazilian educational system underwent significant change in the period from 1948 to 1961. Much of the change was fostered upon the system by the action of CAPES (Coordination of Improvement of Higher Learning Personnel) and a campaign by the left to fight adult illiteracy and expand elementary- and university-level schooling to the less well-off. From the mid-1950s to the enactment of the 1961 legislation, societal support for free public universal schooling grew. The 1961 legislation provided such a schooling system in principle. In practice, its delivery was left to state and local government, and this resulted in great regional disparities.

In 1969 and 1971, further laws were passed by congress that introduced significant changes in the structure of elementary and secondary schooling and higher education. The goal was to enroll more children aged seven and older in public schools and provide them with a basic education of eight years with a common core of studies.

The 1988 constitution and its commitment to redemocratization has, as part of its core pledges, a commitment to universality of fundamental schooling and the eradication of illiteracy in Brazil. The constitution also outlined the provision of when education was to start. In 1993, the government published a ten-year educational plan for all and redefined it in the political strategic plan of the Ministry of Education and Sport from 1995 to 1998. The plan's goals were to make elementary schooling universal; the reduction of attrition with an 80 percent elementary school graduation rate; the restructuring of secondary education; a curriculum reform of elementary teacher training programs; and expenditure to reach 5.5 percent of GNP. As a result of the plan, the Cardoso government put into operation several initiatives, such as distance learning, decentralization of federal funding, and curriculum reform.

In 1996 Congress approved a constitutional amendment sponsored by the Cardoso administration that will channel most public funds earmarked for education to primary schools. States and municipalities are expected to spend at least 25 percent of their total revenues on education. The 1996 law provides for only 10 percent of these funds to be spent directly by local governments by the year 2008.

The remaining 15 percent goes into a revenue-sharing fund that provides grants to the municipalities in proportion to the number of students enrolled in elementary school. At least 60 percent of all grant monies must be spent on improving teacher salaries.

Policy Structure and Organization

The system's objective is compulsory education for all children between ages seven and fourteen. The educational system is organized on five levels. The first level covers voluntary infant education (subdivided into creches, preschools, and kindergartens). Infant education is conceived as a preliminary step to formal schooling and provides services for children who are newly born to six years of age. It is thought to complement family care. Creches and day nurseries are for children up to three years of age, kindergarten schools are for children aged four to six. It is only after the 1988 constitution that infant education became a municipality responsibility. The nongovernmental sector is strong in this area and the Ministry of Education has encouraged greater participation and collaboration between public provision and community participation. However, infantile education is still quite restricted. The government estimates only 17.5 percent of the zero to six age span is enrolled in any program at this level.[5] The second level is compulsory elementary education starting at seven. Elementary schooling is also known as first-degree schooling. Children seven to fourteen are offered a common and a diversified curriculum. That is to say each student is expected to follow a core mandatory curriculum and then they also study their individual regional societies, cultures and economies. The Ministry of Education's 1999 data estimate 95.4 percent of the seven to fourteen population have access to elementary schooling.[6] This means about one million children aged seven to fourteen are still not in school. The third level in the system is secondary education which lasts three years starting after a student has graduated elementary school. This is commonly referred to as second-degree schooling. Students fifteen to nineteen follow a common mandatory curriculum and then a specialization depending on the educational system the school is a part of. Students may opt to attend a technical school rather than a secondary school. Such schools offer occupational education. Also included as a technical school is the normal school, which is responsible for educating elementary school teachers for first through fourth grade. Current data shows 33.4 percent of the fifteen to seventeen population enrolled in a second-degree school.[7] The fourth and fifth levels are higher education and post-graduate education. The higher-learning system is made up of public and private institutions. There are 894 institutions of which 222 are public. Of the 894 institutes, 127 are universities, 68 of which are public. The remainder are various vocational institutions. The higher-learning system is fairly restricted, and only 10 percent of the relevant age span is enrolled in higher learning.[8]

The Ministry of Education calculates there are currently 54.2 million students enrolled in the whole educational system. Of this number 86 percent are enrolled in public-sector institutions.[9] Where the private sector draws most enrollment is higher education. The private sector is responsible for 62 percent of all enrollments in institutions of higher learning.[10]

When administration is focused on, data indicates infant and elementary education is administered by local authorities (municipalities), while the states offer secondary schooling, and in some states, universities. The federal government is in charge of higher education. It is also responsible for providing technical assistance and funds to state and local authorities, so that they ensure the provision of compulsory schooling to all Brazilian children aged seven and older. The objective is to correct for regional differences. Southern Brazil has illiteracy rates and schooling levels close to many developed nations whereas Northern Brazil has rates similar to the poorest nations in the world.[11] One way the federal government attempts to correct regional variations is by distributing textbooks and funding school meals. Additionally, they fund construction and repair of schools. The federal government's goal is to provide at least the minimum conditions to increase student access and maintain enrollments.

Each level of education has a regulating organization and is managed by a central executive organization. For example, at the federal level, the regulating organization is the National Council of Education, and the managing organization is the Ministry of Education. In each state, the regulating organization is the State Education Council, and the managing organization is the State Secretarial for Education. At the municipality level, the Municipal Councils of Education regulate while the cities' secretarial or departments of education manage. Each system is autonomous for the purposes of hiring as well as for resource management.

Control of the education budget has been transferred from the federal government to state and municipal governments. The federal government does provide funds to diminish regional variations. The bulk of federal government expenditure is on higher education. Federal universities account for only 22 percent of overall university enrollment but receive 80 percent of all federal spending on education.[12] A 1995 World Bank Study indicated the poorest 20 percent of the population was allotted 16 percent of total spending on education, where as the wealthiest 20 percent received 24 percent.[13] Overall elementary and secondary schooling is a low priority.

Future Outcomes and Policy Weakness

Despite provisions in the 1988 constitution decreeing federal expenditures for education, public-sector provision remains underfunded, and considerable variations exist in opportunity between urban and rural populations, among the nation's regions, and among social classes. Funding and resources remain scarce, and the problems Brazil faces are many. Advances have been made over the past ten years but as Minister of Education Parrlo Renato put it, "We still have a long way to go, to get where we want."[14]

The main obstacle to public provision of education is the health of the economy. If the economy falters even more, then education will be reduced as a priority on the national agenda. Part of debt consolidation is retrenchment in social services, and education will be hit heavily. Decentralization is a further weakness. The educational problems Brazil faces need centralized planning and administration. There is a high dropout rate, large numbers of students repeat grades, and teachers are poor in quality. Illiteracy rates have decreased, but in absolute numbers, 15.2 million Brazilians are illiterate.[15] The rate is particularly high (83 percent) among the 30 and older population. Female participation in secondary education is at 57 percent, while it is at 42 percent for males.[16] Illiteracy rates vary regionally and between rural and urban areas. Illiteracy is highest (40 percent) in the Northeast, which has a high proportion of rural poor.[17]

In the area of education, the government relies on a partnership with nongovernmental organizations and the community. This is commonly referred to as the "third sector." If economic recovery does not take place at the anticipated rate, the third sector will be hit heavily, and demand will exceed the sector's ability to participate in the partnership.

Improving the rate of education must go hand-in-hand with diminishing the levels of poverty in Brazil. The dropout rate is fueled by the need of children to help with their family resources. Many Brazilian children work from the age of ten. A study conducted in the mid-1990s shows 30 to 40 percent of elementary and secondary students worked full-time jobs.[18] The poor in Brazil are still poor even if they are no longer impoverished by spiraling inflation. If new priorities for social spending do not occur, the educational system will find itself once again in trouble. The gap between rich and poor must be closed even further.

Germany: A Crisis Waiting to Happen

Generally Germany is characterized as having one of the best and most extensive educational systems in the world.[19] However, there are of course shortcomings. As in other policy areas, unification has brought structural and substantive problems to public provision of education. The "new" Germany has had to integrate two very different educational systems. The systems were not only different in terms of levels of institutional provisions but were also based on entirely different philosophical foundations. Today, policy makers face a series of challenges in attempting to impose the same standards and norms across Germany. The historical evolution of educational policy will be traced from 1945 and the separation of Germany into two district states.

Policy History and Evolution

The rebuilding of Germany's education system in the immediate years after the nation's defeat in 1945 was heavily influenced by each of the occupying powers' political interests and educational philosophies. Thus, two very different systems evolved. Each system's political, ideological, and cultural objectives were reflected in a curriculum that endorsed the two very different socioeconomic and ideological environments existing in the two halves of Germany from 1945 to 1989. In the Western zone, the United States insisted on an educational system that "reeducated" German children and adolescents in the ways and values of democratic society. The education system in West Germany was shaped by the core democratic values of federalism, individualism, range of choices and opportunities, and the involvement of a mix of public and private institutions. While in the East, the system was shaped by Marxist-Leninist ideology and an emphasis on socialist values. The system was modeled upon the Soviet model with a commitment to centralized control of provision and content with the government, through the communist-controlled Socialist Unity Party (SED), retaining a monopoly over education and rigid control of all aspects of the system. Each system moved quickly to ensure that all students received instruction from teachers who could be entrusted to educate pupils according to the values of each system's dominant ideology. In both Germanies, there was a range of teachers who held Nazi sympathies and views. In the West, thousands of teachers were dismissed and replaced with instructors who could show their commitment to democratic values, while in the East those individuals appointed as teachers had to show that they had opposed fascism and supported Marxist-Leninist ideology.

West Germany policy makers soon implemented a reform program that regenerated the education system. Part of this effort was achieved through a massive reconstruction program of educational facilities. By the early 1950s, provision of education was standardized throughout West Germany. Each state was given the responsibility of operating its own educational system; however, there was little variation in the type of system.[20] Education was to be mandatory and the structure of schooling the same. According to the Basic Law of 1949 all citizens should be able to choose the type of education they want and have access to their preferred vocation. Education was free and mostly coeducational. The Dusseldorf treaty of 1955 made school attendance mandatory for a minium of nine years, starting at six years of age.[21]

By the 1960s, the system consisted of four levels: (1) voluntary elementary education; (2) primary education; (3) secondary education; and (4) further education. The early 1970s saw further reforms reorganizing secondary education, increasing the number of students eligible for further education, and establishing comprehensive schools (*gesamtschule*) in some states. The move to comprehensive schools, as elsewhere in Europe, was motivated by a desire to diminish elitist bias in secondary education.[22] Reforms were also passed expanding adult education. The reform program was hindered by the effects of the mid-1970s recession, thus only some of the goals of the program were achieved.

By 1951, East Germany had undertaken a program of reform that centralized and politicized education. Public education was made free and expanded through the establishment of preschools and kindergartens. Because of the vast majority of women participating in the workforce, enrollment at these schools was extremely high. Admission standards to higher-education establishments were reduced so as to make a university place accessible to all. All children attended a uniform ten-grade polytechnic, which emphasized technical education. Upon graduation, approximately 85 percent of students entered two-year vocational schools while the remaining attended special classes to prepare for university. A proportion of these students prepared in secondary schools for two years, while the rest attended vocational school for three years of preparation. All students were required to spend one day per week in the workforce, at a factory, office, or farm. The whole system had a strong emphasis on vocations. This was to ensure that all East Germans realized the importance of labor.

By the 1980s, there were six general universities, a technical university, and several dozen specialized institutions of higher education. Enrollment in higher education initially favored the children of workers, but by the 1970s, it favored mostly the children of the state's intelligentsia—white-collar workers and professionals. One of the criteria for attending was demonstration of loyalty and commitment to Marxist-Leninist ideology. In some respects, the system was extremely successful: Literacy was more than 95 percent by 1989, and the proportion of unskilled workers was around 13 percent compared to 70 percent in 1955.[23]

The events of 1989 and the abrupt halt to the Socialist party's dominance led to a radical transformation of the political and philosophical foundations of the system. The East German educational leadership was removed from power and the bureaucratic educational infrastructure was dismantled. However, regardless of the fact that West and East had structurally divergent systems, both nations regarded education in the same manner. It was a constitutional right and a public responsibility, and both systems emphasized similar student achievement goals.[24] Thus, when agreement came to unite the two Germanies, education was an immediate target for policy makers.

In May 1990, it was agreed that each state should develop its own educational strategies. The August unification treaty specified that by June 1991, all states should have complied and new laws would be passed confirming individual states' arrangements. All Eastern states replaced the general polytechnic school system with the West German system.[25] There are differences in name and organization, but education in the Eastern states resembles closely that of the old West German model. The old East German higher-education structure was also revamped, new institutions were built so as to improve geographic access to further education, the faculty was cut, and the Western states made large subsidies to higher-education institutions situated in the East.[26] What remains to be seen is how quickly the values and preferences of the old East German system will be eroded. Some authors argue the Marxist-Leninist influence on education will take many years to overcome.[27]

Policy Structure and Organization

As stated earlier, the "new" Germany's educational system is a multi-level one that provides free education to all children in coeducational institutions. Elementary education (*kindergartner*) is the first level and is for children aged three to five. Attendance is voluntary. By 1995, 80 percent of German children were attending kindergartners. Starting in 1996, all children were guaranteed a kindergarten place.

This has been made possible through the integration of the former extensive East German kindergarten system.

Primary education is the second level and consists of basic school (*grundschule*) for children aged six to ten. At the age of eight, all children are evaluated and placed according to their aptitude and skill level in one of three tracks. Each track leads to a different secondary school option for children. Secondary school is divided into intermediate secondary for students aged ten to sixteen and senior secondary for those aged sixteen to eighteen. Intermediate school places students in one of three types of school based on their track placement in primary school. Those students who are less academically gifted with a high level of practical skills are placed in *hauptschule,* so as to prepare them to be laborers and unskilled workers; *realschule* enrolls students with technical abilities and prepares them for trade and industrial careers; the gymnasium is for academically gifted students who are prepared for higher education. All secondary schools strongly emphasize future career choices. On graduating, intermediate secondary school students receive an intermediate school certificate. Almost one-third of the school-age population attend each of the three intermediate secondary schools. A large number of *hauptschule* graduates become apprentices in shops and factories. They are also required to enroll in compulsory part-time educational courses. The remaining *hauptschule* graduates enroll in some type of full-time vocational school until the age of 18. *Realschule* graduates more or less follow the same curriculum as *hauptschule,* except they also take additional foreign languages, shorthand, processing, bookkeeping, and computer skills. On graduating *realschule* graduates enter senior secondary schools that are technical schools (*Fachoberschule*) or specialized grammar schools (*Fachgymnasuim*). A few transfer over to the gymnasium, but it's rare. For those graduating the gymnasium, they may continue senior secondary school at the same gymnasium and prepare for entrance into a university at the age of eighteen. They also may transfer into the comprehensive *gesamschules.* *Gesamshcules* are alternatives to gymnasiums.[28] They provide a broader range of educational opportunities than traditional gymnasiums. However, such schools' popularity is mixed and has been resisted by many conservative geographic areas. For example, by the late 1990s there were only a few *gesamschules* in conservative Bavaria. Even in more perceived progressive states their presence is insignificant compared with the traditional gymnasium.

By the late 1990s, there were about 314 institutions of higher learning with around 2 million students.[29] Approximately 80 percent of the institutions are located in the old West Germany. All students have to take a qualifying exam (the *Abitur*) to attend. Until the 1980s, everyone who passed the *Abitur* had access to a higher-education institution. Since then there have been selection criteria put into place because the demand for places is now much greater than the supply. Tuition is nominal. The fee includes extensive rights to health care and other social benefits. Students have to meet their own living expenses. To do so, there is an extensive federal and state loan program. Students from lower-income families receive interest-free loans. Half of the loan must be repaid within five years of graduating. Other students receive loans at relatively low levels. Students graduating in the top third of their class or within a shorter time than usual (five years) have portions of the loan forgiven. Loans are also made available to those enrolled in vocational training.

Private education exists at all levels, but today only approximately five percent of the school-age population attends. The numbers of students attending private establishments have increased in the 1990s. A handful of private universities exists. The state does not involve itself in private-sector educational provision. They do not inspect, regulate, or fund in any way such institutions.

The Basic Law of 1949 clearly gives the states responsibility for education.[30] This includes financing education, maintaining schools, teacher training, educational standards, and standardized curricula. Higher education is a shared responsibility with the federal government. The role of the federal government is to oversee vocational education, to finance educational stipends and allowances, and promote research at universities through fellowships. The federal government also passes laws on the general principles governing higher education; however, they have no power to reform higher education. That power remains the states' prerogative. In short, higher education is a shared responsibility and works because of cooperative federalism. The federal government and the states cooperate extensively with regards to higher education matters, including financing.

Overall then, the German education system is decentralized. To counterbalance such decentralization, a number of nationwide joint permanent advisory bodies help develop and implement educational policy. Educational planning is more important since unification, so the federal government ensures that it plays a role through such advisory bodies. Their role in implementation is guaranteed by having implemented and administrated the Federal and Land Commission on Education Planning and the Promotion of Research.

Education is the second-largest item of public spending in Germany.[31] The first is social security and welfare. Education spending in 1998 amounted to five percent of GNP. All spending on education is paid out of general revenues. At the elementary, primary and secondary education levels, the states bear the major burden. Local governments are responsible for maintaining and operating school facilities. At the higher-education level, the states remain the major funding source, although the federal government provides some funding. In the 1990s, the states paid approximately 74 percent of total education costs, local governments about 16 percent, and the federal government about 10 percent.[32]

Future Outcomes and Policy Weakness

The future is one of consolidating the integration of the two systems. The current education system is heavily regulated by the state government bureaucracies. Such structures have in the past resisted innovation and experimentation in new curricula. The major problem facing policy makers is the length of the school day. Approximately 96 percent of German children attend schools that end at 1:00 P.M. five days a week.[33] This presents a problem for many families where both parents must work or where there is single parent as head of household. Some Germans believe that this has led to more children attending private schools that stay in session all day.

In the immediate future, policy makers will have to attempt to ensure that standards are the same in all states and that qualifications are mutually reorganized across the country. Higher education also presents another problem: There are not enough institutions or faculty. Additionally, more money must be spent in order to bring the overall quality of Eastern state institutions up to Western ones.

There is not yet a crisis in education because attention is still focused on structural integration. However, as time passes and parity does not occur, then it will be inevitable that the social state finds itself in crisis with its education policy.

Great Britain: The Withering Away of Public Education

Education has always dominated the policy agenda and been a highly divisive political issue in Britain. The history of British education policy is one of deficiency, in spite of having one of the highest literacy rates in the world at more than 99 percent.[34] A survey conducted by the Organization for Economic Cooperation and Development (OECD) found in a study of its twenty-four member-countries that Britain spends less of its GDP on education than most of the other member nations.[35] In addition the nation had one of the highest teacher-pupil ratios, was an extremely poor provider of preschool, and had one of the lowest proportions of young people entering tertiary education. Study after study has found that since the late-nineteenth century, Britain lags behind its industrial competitors in educational provision.[36] The problems that plagued Britain over the last fifty years have become more acute as the nation enters the twenty-first century. Poor economic performance has exacerbated Britain's education problems. All new governments, regardless of their partisan affiliation, have had as one of their central goals the raising of educational standards. Left and right agree that this is a priority; however, they disagree on the means by which to achieve it. Thus, the highly politicized nature of educational policy in Britain.

Policy History and Evolution

Public education came late to Great Britain. The first real provision of public education was by the church in the early nineteenth century.[37] In this era, education was predominantly for the children of the aristocracy and landed gentry. The first state instrument in education came in 1856 with the creation of the government's education department. Inspired by the provision of mass compulsory education in Bismark's Germany, Britain's first education act was passed in 1870. Under this legislation, the government provided state-financed primary education. Provision was through newly created school boards. Such boards were given responsibility for providing schools in those areas where there were none. In order to carry out their responsibility the boards were given the power to levy local taxes to build primary schools. All other education was privately funded or offered by churches. Higher education was clearly not the prerogative of the masses.

All students in public-governed schools had to pay fees. Such fees were abolished in the Education Act of 1891. Church schools were pressured to also comply. As an inducement, the government offered grants to any church school to subsidize their costs if they stopped charging pupil fees. This led to partisan division in the school boards and created financial problems for many of them. To eliminate such problems the government enacted the Education Act of 1902. This established Local Education Authorities (LEAs). Such authorities were regionally based and given responsibility for providing schools and education in their locality. The legislation also authorized the LEAs to use public funds for church-affiliated schools, to inspect all schools, to veto the appointment and dismissal of teachers in church schools, and established scholarships for secondary education. The policy was highly criticized for its use of state taxes to support private church schools. By the start of the 1900s, public schools had become the popular choice for education.[38] Modifications continued after the end of World War I with the 1918 Fisher Act. This act required all elementary schools to provide some form of post-elementary education at the end of primary school. In 1936, the government raised the school-leaving age from fourteen to fifteen; however, it was never implemented because of the outbreak of the Second World War in 1939.

The first major move to universal public provision of education came with the publication of the Beveridge Report in 1942. Earlier chapters on British welfare and health policy have discussed the significance of the report. Alongside the "giants" of want and disease was the "giant" of ignorance. This proved to be a more difficult area to reach agreement over. The left represented by the Labour party wanted universal provision by the state, while the right led by the Conservative party wanted selective provision of education, with individuals being free to choose how and where their children would be educated.

Britain's educational system by the 1940s was fragmented and divisive. It reflected Britain's class system. Thus, academic success was for a select few, though, of course, there were some exceptions to this. Only a very small percentage of the school population stayed on at school until they were eighteen. Only four thousand students entered a university in 1938; of those only 1 in everyone 150 came from elementary schools—the rest were privately educated.[39] If the United States is compared with Britain, for the same year, 1 in 125 attended university while only 1 in 1,000 did in Britain.

Major reform came in 1944 with the passing of the Butler Act. Under this legislation, a universal education system was introduced in Britain. The system provided free and compulsory secondary education up to age fifteen, and this was increased to age sixteen in 1973. Overall control of education was in the hands of the newly created Ministry of Education, and day-to-day administration was to be by the LEAs. All elementary schools were abolished and education divided into three stages, primary (five to eleven), secondary (eleven to eighteen) and further education (college and university). At eleven years of age, students took an examination, the "eleven plus," and according to their aptitude and intelligence scores on this exam were placed in one of three types of secondary school: grammar schools for the academically minded, technical schools for those interested in applied science and technology, and secondary modern schools for the practical rather than academic pupils. All children placed in secondary moderns would be reviewed at age thirteen for possible transfer to grammar and technical schools. Approximately 20 percent attended grammar and technical schools while the remaining 80 percent went to secondary moderns. Attendance at a secondary modern was seen to be failure on the "eleven plus."

The Butler Act also provided for means-tested grants for any student who wished to pursue further education. Those students at grammar and technical schools who took General Certificate Examinations (GSEs) and attained certain grades could stay on at secondary school until eighteen. They could apply for a grant or their parents could pay for their tuition from fifteen to eighteen. Finally, nursery education should be available for all children aged three to five. The act was passed by the coalition government, but implementation was left to the Labour government after 1945. Much of the economic difficulties faced by the government in the late 1940s meant that many of the proposed Butler programs were dropped before they had even been started. Thus, many of the critical parts of the Butler Act were never put in place.[40] To compound this, there was a lack of suitable buildings to house all the new students and a drastic shortage of trained teachers.[41]

By the 1960s, the implementation of the Butler Act was generally recognized as both flawed and damaging to the interests of most children. The "eleven plus" theoretically placed children according to their aptitude and ability, and all schools were to have parity of esteem; the "eleven plus" was not supposed to be viewed as an examination to be passed or failed. In reality, it was seen as such an examination. It led to only two possibilities: One was for students to go on to grammar and technical schools and take examinations which could lead to a university place, while the other led to no qualifications and leaving school at fifteen.

The overall objective of the Butler Act was to provide academic opportunities to the working-class through the provision of free secondary education. In the 1950s and early 1960s under the Conservatives, spending on schools was increased greatly and many new schools at all three levels were built. Also, new examinations were introduced, called Certificates of Secondary Education (CSEs) for those attending secondary moderns. This was aimed at restoring parity of esteem. It also provided the possibility for those who did extremely well on the CSEs to transfer to grammar and technical schools to study for GSEs for a possible place at a university. In terms of higher education, the period also saw more than 10 new universities being created so as to expand higher education possibilities.

The late 1950s and early 1960s saw the publication of a number of reports looking at educational provision.[42] Such reports supported growing societal criticism of secondary education and the selective system it was based on. It led to demands for a new system of comprehensive schools to replace grammar, technical, and secondary moderns. Rather than an area having three secondary schools (local grammar, local technical, and local secondary modern) it would have comprehensive schools, where pupils would be placed in streams according to their ability and aptitude. Each stream would then follow common curriculums but at different development levels.

When Labour took office in 1964, Educational Secretary of State Tony Crosland declared, "If it's the last thing I do all secondary education will be comprehensive."[43] In 1965, all LEAs were asked under circular 10/65 to produce plans to detail change to a comprehensive school system. However, Labour was not united on this policy; many have argued that the Labour leadership, including Prime Minister Harold Wilson, were loath to get rid of grammar schools, as they were grammar school products. Thus, the policy was implemented whereby LEAs were requested to comply with changing over to comprehensives rather than being demanded to change. By 1970, 32 percent of secondary students were enrolled in comprehensive schools, and only eight percent of LEAs had not drawn up plans to dismantle the old system and replace it with a comprehensive system.[44]

When Labour was replaced by the Conservatives in 1970, Prime Minister Ted Heath appointed Margaret Thatcher as Secretary of Education. Under Thatcher, the Crosland 10/65 circular was canceled; however, the number of children attending comprehensives by 1974 was 62 percent. During Thatcher's term in office, the school-leaving age was raised to sixteen, and she pledged to bring about nursery places for everyone.

The comprehensive program was completed by the newly elected Labour government in 1974. However, eight Conservative-controlled LEAs fought to preserve grammar schools and 150 remained open during their time in office. At the same time that the restructuring of secondary schools was taking place, there was also a debate over standards. This was referred to in 1976 by Labour Prime Minister Jim Callaghan, in a speech at Ruskin College, Oxford University, as the "Great Education Debate." Callaghan raised questions about levels of literacy and numeracy, the purpose of the curriculum, and the needs of industry. He also expressed concerns over teaching methods. Callaghan called for the involvement of teachers, professional bodies, higher education, parents, both sides of industry, and the government to be involved in the debate. This led to legislation enacted in 1978. Critics have labeled the legislation as weak because it failed to deal with the crisis outlined in the "Great Education Debate." Mainly, it failed to address centralization of control through a national curriculum and testing. Rather the legislation created parent governors, established parental rights to information in school files, and promoted parental choice in school selection.

What this act accomplished was the groundwork for the Conservative education agenda. Once elected to office in 1979, Prime Minister Margaret Thatcher's education minister Keith Joseph became the first minister to control a spending department. By 1981, Joseph promoted cuts in education funding, advocating that the quality of education is not affected by the amount of money spent on it. The early 1980s saw reforms implementing an Assisted Places Scheme, which provided subsidies for modest-income families to send their children to private schools. This was an early pilot scheme for a national educational voucher system under which parents could buy education for their child from the school of their choice.

The intent of Thatcher and Joseph was to introduce market forces into education. The voucher system was seen as one way to make education more responsive to market forces. The British right from 1981 to 1988 wanted a market-led system in education where schools competed with each other for "customers." They believed the competition would lead to a general rise in standards. However, in order for this to be achieved, the "producer" monopoly had to be curtailed. This could be arrived at by reducing the influence of teachers and LEAs. Through legislation passed in 1986 and 1988 the government delegated more financial and managerial responsibilities to individual schools, thus taking such responsibilities away from LEAs. This was achieved through introducing local management of schools (LMS). The main purpose of LMS was to ensure individual schools were effectively managed and responsive to customer needs. The scheme encouraged greater parental and community involvement in every school. Any school could "opt out" from local authority control to become a grant-maintained school, receiving central government grants and thus be removed completely from LEA control.

Similar moves away from local authority to market economy funding were instituted for colleges of further education and polytechnics, which on doing so became full universities. All curricular changes were put in the hands of government-appointed quangos. This allowed for the establishment of a national curriculum until the age of sixteen to be operated by government and not teachers.[45] All children were to be tested at ages seven, eleven, fourteen, and sixteen so as to set national standards.

The 1990s saw conservative education policies develop along similar lines to those set in the 1980s. The market was extended into primary schools with the publication of league tables of performance and the introduction of a voucher system for nursery school places. Further measures were taken to encourage more schools to "opt out" from local authority control. The 1994 reform provided simplification of the national curriculum.

Since the election of Labour in 1997 Britain has seen more of the same. In spite of Tony Blair's pledge in the Labour manifesto of 1997 to make education its "number-one priority" with "zero tolerance of underperformance" in schools, Labour has more or less continued Conservative education policy with a few refinements. Soon after taking office, Labour published a white paper, "Excellence in Schools," which proposed, among other things, more pupil testing with a baseline assessment for all children when they start school; new English and math tests for nine-year-olds; targets of attainment for all schools to be monitored by local authorities; more parent governors; and inspection of all schools every six years rather than four. Within the paper, Labour also proposed a back-to-basics approach with more devotion in primary schools to literacy and numeracy. They also proposed compulsory home/school contracts in which parents agreed to be responsible for their children's school behavior, attendance, and completion of homework. Labour promised to cut class size and abolish the assisted places scheme.

Box 11.1   Labour Government Educational Successes

- improvements in literacy and numeracy standards; risen from 58 percent to 70 percent expected standard in English and from 54 to 69 percent in math
- nursery places for all four-year-olds and well over a third of three-year-olds; 100,000 places established in 1999–2000
- 70,000 new childcare places in 1998–1999 with 350,000 planned for 2003
- 300,000 fewer five- to seven-year-olds in classes over thirty in size, with none by September 2001
- new Sure State programs to support parents and children in deprived areas
- agreements to achieve a total of 800 specialist schools and 250 beacon schools approved to date
- 62 percent of primary schools and 93 percent of secondaries connected to the Internet
- reform of teaching methods
- a National College for School Leadership, and a General Teaching Council in preparation.

In Labour's first budget, Chancellor Gordon Brown made $1¾ billion of extra spending available to schools from reserve funds to reduce class sizes and purchase resources. Additionally he made $2 billion from the windfall tax available for capital projects, such as refurbishment of old schools. In 1998, Labour moved away from its commitment to free education for all by passing legislation that introduced tuition fees for universities and abolished the old maintenance grants system. Such grants were provided by LEAs to each student to cover their living costs while attending institutions of higher learning. From 1998, students were eligible for means-tested government loans to be repaid by the students once they were working and earning more than $15,000 per annum. Labour argues the less well-off will not suffer under this change. However, the changes are symbolic of how far the Beveridge ideal of universal provision has been sacrificed for market forces.

By the summer of 2000, the Labour government declared it had made strides in implementing changes that were bringing about a more efficient and cost-effective system. Box 11.1 highlights their self articulated successes while Box 11.2 shows the tangible progress made for post-sixteen learning.

Policy Structure and Organization

The British system today provides free compulsory education for all children aged five to sixteen years old. It is organized on four levels: the nursery (three to four years of age); primary (five to eleven); secondary (eleven to eighteen); and post-secondary education (college and university, eighteen and older). There are regional differences for England, Scotland, Wales, and Northern Ireland. Private schools, receiving no public grant support, educate about five percent of Britain's school-age population. All other schools either are publicly maintained completely or receive public grant support. More than 85 percent of students in publicly maintained secondary schools in England and Wales attend comprehensive schools. The

---

Box 11.2   Changes in British Post-Sixteen Learning

- a new right to timeoff for study for sixteen- to seventeen-year-olds
- improvements to Work-Based Training for Young People; Reform of apprenticeships
- the Connexions strategy to attract more young people to further education and training
- the Connexions service, a new youth support service to advise young people, piloted in 2000 and national from April 2001
- pilots of education maintenance allowances to help young people to afford to continue learning
- a new standards fund for further education and the first fifteen beacon colleges
- 25 percent of eighteen- to twenty-one-year-olds in higher education in year 2000 and thirty-five percent by 2002
- the launch of the University for Industry, and sixty-eight learn direct development centers running in local communities
- expansion of family literacy and numeracy initiatives, reaching twelve thousand parents in 2000.

---

remaining 15 percent attend grammar or specialist schools. Comprehensives are non-selective while grammar and specialist schools are selective. That is to say non-selective schools enroll students without reference to ability and aptitude. Scottish secondary schools are almost completely non-selective while in Northern Ireland they are almost completely selective.

Almost half of Britons aged three to four years old attend state nursery schools; 35 percent of children stay on after sixteen at schools for a further year; and 25 percent enter further education institutions, half of them part-time. Less than 20 percent remain in school for two years after age sixteen.

Power is balanced between central government, which sets the legislative framework and controls the majority of resources and local government, which has a certain amount of discretion over structure and organization and some influence over spending levels. Since the late 1980s and early 1990s, the balance has shifted toward central government with the drive to establish market forces in education. There has been a greater role for local authorities since Labour's 1997 electoral victory. However, central government stills holds the upper hand. Central government now controls the curriculum. In England and Wales, a national curriculum of core courses is utilized for students five to sixteen years old, and all schools are inspected by the Office for Standards in Education. National testing takes place at seven, eleven, and fourteen to assess students' progress.

Local government fiscal control has also been eroded by the "opt out" policy. The departments of education in England, Wales, Scotland, and Northern Ireland, led by the secretary of state for education, are responsible for overseeing all education in Britain. The office for standards reports directly to the state department. The nation is divided into nine geographic areas, and each area is divided into several districts; district inspectors are in charge of each district. All districts report to the office for standards. Each county or city has a chief education officer or director of education. Under such officials, administrative officers act as links between the LEAs and the individual schools. All primary schools have a board of managers, and all secondary schools have a board of governors.

More than 80 percent of funding for education is provided by the national government. The remainder is contributed by local authorities, private endowments, and parents. International comparisons indicate that Great Britain spends less on each pupil than many other nations.[46]

Future Outcomes and Policy Weakness

Education in Britain is a mass system with a strong bias toward superior provision for a small number of individuals. However, the new millennium brings fresh challenges that make extra demands on national resources. The main obstacle to public provision of education is the link between educational standards and the economy's performance. The educational infrastructure has been undermined by years of reform and financial neglect. If a modern and effective education system is to survive, it must have the funding. Social exclusion will continue to be a problem as long as there are regional disparities in wealth and resources. The biggest challenge lies in the ability of the government to modernize the system. This does not mean simply up-to-date buildings and facilities; teaching approaches and techniques also need to be addressed.

What lays ahead is an uncertain picture for Britain's educational system. Future success will be determined by the system's ability to fulfill four strategic goals in the first years of the new century. First, policy must develop learning and increase achievement at all ages in order for citizens to be able to handle the demands of the knowledge-driven economy. Next, the cycle of deprivation must be broken so as to create a more inclusive society. Third, more resources must be spent on information and communications technology. And finally, the way policy is developed and implemented as well as the services being provided must be streamlined and made more efficient through modernization of facilities and teaching pedagogy.

Japan: Only the Best

The educational system of Japan is generally considered to be one of the best in the world. The adult literacy rate exceeds 99 percent, and Japan ranks among the top-ten nations in the world in educational attainment.[47] High enrollment and retention rates are chief characteristics of the system. Culturally, education is held in high esteem, and academic success is vital for societal and career success. Such esteem has led to excessive competitiveness and extreme pressures on children to study and to do well academically. Indeed some authors argue that the determinants of societal success are solely determined by where an individual goes to school.[48] Driving the whole process is a person's educational record (*gakureki*). In Japan, *gakureki* is a selection system that rewards an individual in all societal strategic areas. It is based solely on the rank of the university that someone attends. The level of degree attained is not important; what *is* important is where you got the degree.

Some might argue that it is no different in nations such as the United States with its Ivy League universities or Great Britain with Oxford and Cambridge; however, it is different. In such nations, of course, attending the elite institutions of higher learning undoubtedly gives an individual an advantage, but success in later life cannot always be predicted by where someone went to school. A study released in 2000 by Alan Krueger, a Princeton economist, and Stacy Berg Dale, a researcher with the Andrew W. Mellon Foundation, found that students with exceptional abilities earned virtually the same incomes twenty years after graduation, whether they went to Harvard or to the University of Houston. There are other paths and opportunities that exist. In Japan, such alternative routes to success are practically nonexistent. Study after study show that more than 60 percent of top elected officials and corporate leaders are all recruited from the top-ranked university in Japan, the University of Tokyo.[49] Such overwhelming bias is not shared by the elite institutions in other nations. There is much criticism internally of *gakureki,* and many Japanese would like to see its demise; however, there is not an acceptable alternative so the contemporary Japanese system is still very much dominated by it.

Finally, when considering Japanese education, the role of character education and discipline must be recognized as a central element and concern in education policy making.[50] Japanese schools are run according to strict rules, and reflect the Japanese educational system's priority of moral child development. The primary goal of education in Japan is to create a workforce that has the skills and creativity to contribute to a knowledge-based economy and maintain the nation's global economic competitiveness. A secondary goal is to facilitate a society that is harmonious and cooperative. A strict disciplined-based educational system is geared toward producing such harmony and cooperativeness.

Policy History and Evolution

When the modernization process was started in the late nineteenth century, education was seen by policy makers to be fundamental in its establishment. Much of the system was copied from Western nations. The early educational system was decentralized, with high degrees of teacher autonomy. It was soon realized that such a system was incompatible with Japanese culture, for it did not reflect Japanese values. In the late 1890s, there was a move to reorient the educational system with Japanese traditional conservative values. These ideals were embodied in the 1890 Imperial Rescript on Education. The system that emerged from this edict remained until the end of World War II.

The new national education system stressed service to the state, the pursuit of learning, and morality. By 1900, school enrollment was approximately 90 percent of the school-age population.[51] The system was highly centralized, with the national government controlling all aspects of it from funding to curriculum. Education was egalitarian and almost universal at the primary level while at the secondary and higher levels it was elitist and highly selective, emphasizing different levels of aptitude and abilities. College education was limited to a few national universities and was dominated by males in both faculty and student body.[52] The 1930s saw a growing preoccupation with militaristic and nationalistic influences on school curriculums.

The Second World War devastated the educational system and discredited the pre-war educational philosophy. With American occupation and the move to democratization came an overhaul of the educational system. Indeed, what the occupation policy makers and the U.S. Education Mission set up in 1946 in Japan was a structure imitating the American educational system. Kindergarten was followed by six years of elementary school, three years of lower secondary (junior high), and three years of upper secondary (senior high). Education was to be compulsory for nine years. All upper-secondary schools were comprehensive (nonselective); curriculum and textbooks were revised; courses emphasizing nationalistic morals were replaced with social studies; school boards were elected; and teacher unions established. It was a move to decentralize the educational system and place more control in the hands of teachers, parents, and the community. Simply, the system was somewhat alien to Japanese values and culture.[53] At the same time, the higher-education system was also opened up with an increase in the number of institutions.

With the ending of formal occupation in 1952, policy makers undertook modification of the education system with its overall structure kept intact. Education was among the most important issues on the public agenda. The desire was to go back to a more centralized system with an emphasis on control of curriculum and content. All the modifications reflected Japanese educational philosophy in terms of instruction and administration. The ministry of education was given complete responsibility. This reflected a move back to centralization; school boards were no longer elected but appointed, morals as an instructional course was put back into the curriculum, and the ministry selected texts that conformed to acceptable content standards. Such modifications were expensive.

By the 1960s, there were demands to open up and expand higher education. With fulfillment of such demands came turbulence. The 1960s in Japan, as elsewhere, witnessed student mobilization and riots. The government responded with reform in 1969 and in the early 1970s of both higher learning and the public school system. Reform included curriculum revision, government subsidization of private educational institutions, and standardized university entrance examinations for public national universities.

Despite such changes, by the early 1980s the educational system was seen by many to be too rigid and in need of reform. The system was also blamed for much of Japan's newly emerging social problems. Additionally, as economic growth started to falter, concern grew that Japanese education was not responsive to the new conditions dictated by global changes. The reform movement of the 1980s wanted changes that would produce a more flexible, creative, and internationalized curriculum. Such a curriculum would stress individuality and diversity—values that went against traditional Japanese precepts. A series of reports published between 1985 and 1987 by the National Council on Educational Reform outlined the new directions that Japanese education should pursue.[54] By the late 1980s and early 1990s, the government moved to implement changes in most of the areas outlined in the report. One of the focal points of the change was university reform. Other changes saw the 1994 introduction of comprehensive high schools. Such schools are selective but are designed to give students more choices in subject matter and scheduling. The reform was designed to create more individualism and creativity.

In spite of the above changes, the system that emerged in the late 1990s still reflected long-standing Japanese cultural and philosophical ideals and values. Education is still esteemed, and character development is still integral to the curriculum. The system is controlled by the central government through the ministry of education.[55] There is still demand for reform. In June 1996, the ministry issued a report recommending reforms that were appropriate for the new millennium. As yet, the reforms have not been implemented, but they reflect a move toward adapting non-traditional methods and ideas.

Policy Structure and Organization

The system of public education is free and compulsory from elementary school until the end of junior high school. However, 97 percent of Japanese go on to complete senior high even though it's not compulsory.[56] There is no state provision for preschool; that function is provided in most cases by corporations and family. The state provides kindergarten for children aged five, elementary schools for grades one through six, junior high for grades seven through nine, and senior high grades ten through twelve. Approximately one-third of senior high school graduates continue on to higher education.[57]

Private-sector provision does exist at every level within the system.[58] There are a high number of private kindergartens because children are accepted at an earlier age than for public ones. One percent of elementary schools, five percent of junior high, nearly 25 percent of senior high schools, and 72 percent of universities are private. Whether public or private, all high schools are informally ranked according to their success in placing students at the ten to fifteen elite universities. Most high schools are selective, and students enter through passing examinations. In addition to regular schooling, approximately 50 percent of students attend private after-hours schools (*Juku*).[59] Such schools supplement regular schooling and are held every day after school, including Saturday afternoons. The regular school week is all day Monday through Friday and Saturday mornings. University enrollment is highly selective and competitive.[60] All students preparing for university entrance examinations attend special private after-hours schools (*Yobiko*).

Table 11.2 shows that Japan spent less of its GDP on education in the late 1990s than any of the other nations discussed in this text, which, given the importance of education, is surprising. All nations have witnessed a decrease in expenditure,

Table 11.2   Public Expenditure on Education

Nation	% of GNP 1980	% of GNP 1997
Brazil	3.6	5.1
Germany	*	4.8
Great Britain	5.6	5.3
Japan	5.8	3.6
Sweden	9.0	8.3
United States	6.7	5.4

*Not available

Source: Adapted from World Development Indicators, World Bank Report 2000.

but Japan has experienced the largest. This is undoubtedly because of the economic crisis of the early 1990s. As in the policy areas of health and welfare, the central government bureaucracy is the prime actor in the planning and implementation of education policy. The majority of policy making is carried out by the ministry of education with the ministry of finance playing a central role through the budget-making process. The role of local bodies is limited to purely administrative tasks because public education is overseen and subsidized by national government.

Future Outcomes and Policy Weakness

Commitment to funding public provision of education and the primacy of education on the public agenda is not in question now or in the foreseeable future. The problems faced by Japan in this policy area are the possible restructuring of the principles and philosophy behind the educational system. If Japan is to continue as an economic superpower then it must reinvent its educational system so as to break with the tradition of rigidity, non-creativity, and social conformity. In many ways, these were all conducive to helping Japan attain its stature economically in the rebuilding of the economy after World War II. However, today many Japanese see such characteristics as obstacles to progress and economic stability in the new millennium. Perhaps the criticism can be judged as too harsh at the elementary to high school level where scale and quality of provision is among the best in the world. However, the mode of instruction and curriculum does lead many to question whether Japanese youth are drilled in memorization exercises rather than intellectual thought processes. The biggest challenge will be to challenge the elitist position of the top universities, with so few Japanese attending them; the vast majority of students in higher education attend private institutions, only a few of which are highly ranked. With economic recession and downsizing, many of the graduates of such institutions are no longer able to acquire white-collar jobs in the corporate world. Such individuals could become a growing class of discontented voters as time passes.

Sweden: Equal Access Guaranteed

Sweden's long history of social democracy has established an exceptionally generous and comprehensive welfare state. As part of that welfare state, there have been
considerable achievements in education. Part of these achievements came through
education reforms implemented in the 1960s. Today many critics argue that the reform activity of the 1960s should be viewed as an example of policy failure through
state interventionism or the implementation of social invasive policy.[61] However,
what cannot be criticized are the fundamental principles on which the Swedish education system is built. All children and adolescents have equal access to public-
sector education, regardless of circumstance or location. All schools, irrespective of
location, offer equivalent education. The Swedes planned the system during the late
1940s, tested it in the 1950s, implemented it across the board in the 1960s and
1970s, refined it in the 1980s, and modified it in the 1990s. Such a policy plan en-
tailed enormous organizational efforts at the implementation stage and large-scale
funding. Refinement and modification can be seen directly as a result of economic
recession rather than as the result of detailed policy evaluation. And perhaps this
has led to the critique of education policy being a failure.

  Education is undoubtedly a policy area that possesses symbolic value every-
where, yet nowhere is political weight conferred, regardless of outcomes, so heavily
as in Sweden. The Social Democrats invested a large amount of their political prestige in education policy, and it was a central component of their post–Second-
World-War platform. An indication of this lies in the prominence of many of the
party's leading figures in the design and implementation of education policy.[62] To
understand the evolution of Swedish education policy is to comprehend the role of
the Social Democratic party in articulation of social policy aims and objectives. Not
only were the Social Democrats the domineering party of government and parliament, but they also held the policy initiative through controlling the societal debate.[63] Thus, they managed to control and dictate the type of compromises and
agreements that were reached.

Policy History and Evolution

Provision of compulsory elementary school was introduced in 1842. From that period until the end of World War II, an organizationally diverse system of primary
and secondary education developed. Students completed six years of compulsory
primary school, and for those who continued on there were no less than nineteen
different types of schools that could be attended.[64] Such a system was seen to mir-
ror the class structure, for each of the different schools recruited students from
fairly specific social strata. Public education was the source of hostility and conflict
among and between social groups. There was much debate and demand for reform
to introduce a universal basic education system.

  The groundwork for reform was laid in the Social Democrats' 1944 post-war
program. The objective of post-war education policy was the dismantling of the old

system and its replacement with new single comprehensive schools that would provide nine or ten years of compulsory education. This would also open up secondary education to everyone. Previously secondary enrollment had been based on the financial ability of families to pay for their children's education. Thus, the overall goal was social equality. This placed education policy firmly on the Social Democrats' agenda for social change, and education was to be an instrument for change. Such an agenda dictated that there would be state intervention to ensure the erosion of inequalities in individuals' conditions and prospects. The Social Democrats believed that with a comprehensive school policy, individuals would be socialized into accepting the demise of the bourgeois character of the capitalist state.[65]

The proposed reforms were put forward in the public inquiry of 1948 and then taken to the parliament in 1950. Responsibility for carrying out the reform was delegated to a large number of semi-independent national boards and agencies such as the National School Board. This allowed for modification of formulators' original goals and intentions. Sweden legislated by 1962 that all children attend nine years of compulsory comprehensive education. All children between the ages of seven and sixteen had to attend a public-sector school or an independent school approved by the state for compulsory schooling. Attendance at compulsory schools is free at the point of service, the child's municipality of residence pays for it even if a child chooses to attend a public-sector school in another locality or an independent school. Municipalities are obliged to provide upper-secondary school for sixteen- to nineteen-year-olds. Upper-secondary schools integrated theoretical and vocational study programs.

Further reforms took place in the 1970s. They were mostly aimed at upper-secondary education. For example, in 1970 all existing academic and vocational education upper-secondary schools were amalgamated into one type of school, the upper-secondary school (*gymnasieskola*). The remaining reforms were aimed at secondary education so as to match it to the needs of the labor market. In 1977 the government incorporated all post-secondary education (university and professional training colleges) into a single system. With the election of the conservative Bourgeois government in the late 1970s, further reform of the whole system in the early 1980s was inevitable. Basically the conservatives wanted to move the system toward decentralization. For example, the responsibility for many local schools was transferred to consumers. All schools were given greater flexibility and freedom in managing their resources. A new national curriculum was introduced with an emphasis on Christian morality. Schools were encouraged to create income—for example, through charging for previously free items such as school lunches. However, as unemployment grew in the 1980s, any plans the government had to further reduce education expenditure had to be shelved. The themes of the 1980s were decentralization and deregulation. For example, the central government abandoned its control of post-secondary curriculums for all general-study programs.

With the election in 1991 of a coalition government of center-right parties, a new wave of education reforms was set off. As of 1991, any parent wishing to enroll his or her child in comprehensive school at the age of six could do so subject to municipal consent. As of 1997, municipalities are now obliged to accept all six-year-olds. A system of school vouchers was approved in June 1992. Under this scheme, municipalities are required to distribute at least 85 percent of the average cost per student in the public-sector municipal schools to an independent school if a family chooses to send its child there. Many argue that this has led to an increase in the number of independent schools as more children opt out of the public sector.[66] In 1993, similar reforms were made for upper-secondary schools and comprehensive schools for the physically disabled. Higher-education administration and financing were also reformed in the mid-1990s. Market forces were introduced and higher-education institutions were given more autonomy and their funding was linked to output indicators. The reform was crystallized in the 1993 Higher Education Act. Under this, all allocation of grants and monies to institutions from the central government was tied to number of students enrolled and the achievement of each institution.

By 1995 to 1996 new curriculum was introduced for secondary schools. However, even though demands in the same year were levied at government to remove the voucher system and other reforms of the early 1990s, the Social Democrats have not complied. However, they did reduce the school voucher to 75 percent. They have also commissioned studies to report on how municipalities can have more control of independent schools. Presently the discussion is centered around forbidding independent schools that collect vouchers to also charge fees. There is also discussion of reducing the size of independent school classes below the public-sector's class size in order for them to receive approved status. In 1998, the government established a new type of school, for preschoolers. Municipal authorities are now mandated to provide preschool; however, participation is optional. Preschool must comprise 525 hours and is offered to all five- to six-year-olds for free.

Policy Structure and Organization

The present system is a structurally uniform system from elementary level to upper secondary to further education. All schools are comprehensive and coeducational. The curriculum at the elementary and secondary levels is uniform. All public education is totally or partially financed by the public budget. Tuition is free of charge in all public institutions, and various financial assistance schemes are provided for upper secondary, adult, and higher education. Students opting out and attending independent schools receive vouchers that supplement the school's fees.

Elementary or compulsive schools can be national, municipal, or private (independent). Approximately 98 percent of all children attend municipal compulsory schools.[67] Only two percent of compulsory school graduates choose not to go on to upper-secondary school.[68] Upper-secondary schools offer both vocational and academic programs for sixteen- to nineteen-year-olds and offer curricula with specific goals for each type of school. Higher education comprises universities and professional training colleges and institutes. The number enrolled in higher education has increased since 1991 by 50 percent.[69] Today slightly more than 30 percent of adults attend institutes of higher learning.[70] All students graduating from upper-secondary school have the basic qualifications to enter higher education. However, if demand exceeds the number of places then selection criteria are put into place based on level of attainment. Students receive grants to study at both upper-secondary schools and higher-education institutions. At the upper-secondary level, the grant is automatic. At the higher-education level, students must fulfill certain requirements to qualify for assistance. To receive assistance students must declare their own income, and the greater the income the less assistance. No account is taken of the student's family economic situation or, if married, of their spouse's situation. Assistance is limited to those under the age of forty-five and is granted for a maximum of six years. Exceptions can be made for graduate students. All continuation of assistance is based on academic performance. Assistance takes the form of a non-repayable grant and a repayable loan. The non-repayable grant is approximately 30 percent of the total amount. Both grants and loans are inflation indexed. The loan repayment rate is low and begins six months after the final receipt of assistance. Repayment is expected at a rate of four percent of annual income.

Responsibility for education policy lies with the government and parliament. With the exception of agriculture and employment training, the Ministry of Education has full jurisdiction over all public education. Independent of the ministry are central administrative authorities that work in accordance with government-issued instructions.[71] Such agencies carry central administrative authority over education. The trend in education policy is for decentralization of responsibility and decision-making powers. Thus, more responsibility has been shifted from the central government to municipal levels of government. The objective is for parliament and central government to control education through defining national goals and guidelines. Parliament and government share general policy decisions on the objectives, activities, and finances of the education system. Parliament legislates on the appropriation of funds, and the government issues the ordinances and guidelines that apply to the various levels of the system and decides on the distribution of appropriations. The government also lays down curricula for the whole system.

The local level is responsible for ensuring that the system is organized and administered according to national goals. Within this framework, the local level has a considerable amount of autonomy in deciding how to implement policy and how to distribute funds. Usually responsibility is divided up among different municipal agencies for each level of education. It is the responsibility of municipalities to tend to all facilities, to build new ones, to coordinate all school and preschool activities, pay teachers' salaries, fund all schools, and pay the vouchers to those families opting out and selecting independent schools. Every municipality lays out its objectives in a school plan. Each plan has to be reviewed and assessed to see if there is compliance. The Vocational Agency for Higher Education (*Högskoleverket*) deals with questions concerning higher-education institutions.

All municipalities are given single general grants by the state. From such monies they are obliged to provide education services. State grants supplement each municipality's taxation revenue. The grant monies attempt to equalize differences between municipalities in terms of fiscal base. The monies are "no strings" attached grants. Thus, no municipality is obliged to spend the money according to state dictates. However, if a municipality is considered to be not performing its obligations then the government can intervene and force the municipality to spend the money a certain way. In addition to the single grant there are also special state grants for research and development and in-service training. All independent schools must be compensated for students who enroll in this type of school by the municipalities. The majority of higher-education bodies are state-owned and -funded.[72]

Future Outcomes and Policy Weakness

Similar to other nations, such as England, Sweden has introduced more choice and market forces into the educational system. Increased choice, decentralization, and parity among independent and municipal schools have been the goals set by successive Swedish governments since the 1980s. The impact of the implementation of such goals in the upcoming years could be far-reaching. Improving the effectiveness and efficiency of education could be achieved through market forces playing a role in production and consumption of education. However, it could also result in increased educational costs, a rise in enrollment in private education, increase in disparities, and social tension. Also important to the success of the system is input and buy-in from teachers and parents. Much of the literature points to the debate and decision-making process being dominated by politicians.[73] Any policy that is so completely left in the implementation stage to bureaucratic agencies is subject to that agency's level of commitment. Charles Bullock argues that any policy, even if conditions are favorable, will be sabotaged if an agency is not committed to it.[74] It is still too early to predict the level of commitment by the Swedish education-implementing agencies. However, it is important to understand the impact of decentralization upon the implementation process.

   If anything can be learned from the Swedish experience in education policy, it is that reform takes a long time to achieve. In Sweden, reform took nearly three decades to take hold, and for much of the time the same government was in power, which meant consistency is planning and implementation.

United States: A State of Flux

Of all the basic provisions of an advanced welfare state, education is the only one offered as a right of American citizenship. However, because education is a state and local responsibility rather than a national one, it is a right that is not always equally extended to or received by citizens. Education policy is highly decentralized and overseen by fifty different state education boards and at least fifteen thousand local school boards.[75] This makes any attempt to implement a coordinated provision of public education futile. Over the last decade, education has resurfaced as a heated issue on the public agenda. Much of the controversy has been stimulated by what many critics refer to as America's falling education standards. In short, that American students have fewer skills, abilities, and aptitudes than students in other industrialized nations. This has led to growing concern about how competitive the American economy can be in future years with workers who are ill-prepared. As in the other discussed nations, there has been growing interest in the introduction of market forces. As the United States enters the new millennium a clear consensus is formed that the nation's education system is underperforming and failing to educate American children and adolescents to be fully functioning efficient workers in a global economy.

Policy History and Evolution

Publicly financed education can first be seen in the United States in the 1830s. It was provided at the elementary level and was part of a reform movement that advocated "common school." Led by leaders such as Horace Mann, the movement argued children should be prepared to be good citizens through providing a basic education.[76] Part of being a good citizen was having a decent standard of living and being able to compete equally with others; Mann advocated education was the route to such social equilibrium. By the 1860s, more than 50 percent of children were enrolled in elementary schools financed by property taxes levied by local authorities who were delegated authority and responsibility for education by state governments. The 1870s saw expansion of high school education through the 1874 Supreme Court decision validating the use of taxes for public high schools. Up to this point, high school was available only to those of the elite class. The expansion of higher education also came in this period, as the need for more teachers grew.

Stimulated by the influx of large numbers of immigrants and the needs of a rapidly expanding industrializing economy, a mass-based secondary education system was in place by the mid-nineteenth century. With such developments came heated debate over what students should be learning; in particular, whether secondary school should be responsible for academic and/or vocational training. In 1918, congress attempted to resolve the debate by providing federal funding for vocational education programs. It was hoped that industry demands, as well as immigrant children, would be addressed by such training. This orientation to public education was laid out in a report by the National Commission on the reorganization of secondary education, and was known as "The Cardinal Principles."[77] The principles advocated a utilitarian approach to educating the masses. They should be educated for the workforce. As secondary education developed in this period, it became a two-track system, one track for a small elite who was prepared to enter into higher education, and the other track for the masses who would enter the workforce and perform menial but vital labor in a variety of areas.

The Great Depression (1929 to 1941) made it very clear that public education was underperforming. The absence of jobs and the belief that the road to future employment was through education resulted in increased secondary school enrollments.[78] Re-industrialization during World War II led to reform emphasizing the need for comprehensive curriculum providing academic and practical skills. Students should be prepared for the real world. Such policy continued well into the 1950s, until the complacency it created was confronted by two events that forced policy makers to rethink both the structure and the substance of education in the United States.

The first event was the Supreme Court's 1954 ruling in *Brown v. Board of Education of Topeka*. The Brown decision very simply stated that separate but equal education for African Americans as created by *Plessey v. Ferguson* violated the equal protection provisions of the Fourteenth Amendment. Simply put, segregation was unconstitutional. The federal government was forced by the Brown decision to look at the need for federal assistance to minority and low-income groups. Additionally, even though desegregation was stalled for years until the 1964 Civil Rights Act, local authorities were forced to look at reform of public education. The second event was the 1957 Soviet launch of the Sputnik satellite into space. This development was seen to be symbolic of the USSR's technological superiority and American vulnerability to attack from communist superior military strength. As a response, congress almost immediately passed the 1957 National Defense Education Act. This act provided millions of federal dollars for math, science, and foreign language education programs.[79] This resulted in the design and implementation of new curricula, increases in the numbers of teachers being trained, and a reorientation in focus to academic excellence rather than real-world skills.

The 1960s and 1970s saw a preoccupation with the pursuit of equity in national education policy. The period was a turbulent one with demonstrations and public protests punctuating American society. As part of Lyndon Johnson's Great Society and War on Poverty program, two laws were enacted that were the first serious attempts by government to remedy past societal inequities. These laws also attacked the role of the federal government in education policy. The 1965 Elementary and Secondary Act targeted $1.5 billion in federal aid for remedial course work, research, and instructional materials in the nation's poorest schools. In the same year, the Equal Opportunity Act was also passed. This established the Head Start Program, which was designed to provide cultural enrichment to preschool children from poor families. The program was appropriated with less than $200 million but took off almost immediately, and by 1966 Head Start served 733,000 poor, mostly minority children.[80] Interestingly enough, this annual enrollment was not exceeded until after 1990.

Critics have argued the legacy of the 1960s was permissive education. In order to strengthen equal opportunity, a number of strategies were implemented. For example, graduation requirements were eased, access to education for minorities, women, and foreign loan students was increased and protected by federal and state laws, and there was a general move away from a structured, disciplined learning environment to more open and free-wheeling classrooms. Authors, such as Thomas Toch, describe the 1960s and 1970s as a period when public education was in a shambles.[81] Other authors, such as James Coleman, argue permissive education resulted in an exodus of city whites fleeing to the suburbs in search of good old-fashioned education. Effectively, segregation was in place once again.[82] By the late 1970s, many believed that public schools were inferior to private, parochial schools.[83] In response to such criticism, there was a move back to academic rigor and opposition to equity through civil rights and anti-poverty measures. Local authorities responded by implementing minimum skill levels and demanding that standardized test scores and other performance indicators improve. The efforts to raise performance, however, were hindered by financial impediments. The tax revolt led by California Proposition 13 and Massachusetts Proposition 2½ led to tax limits being adopted in seventeen states. Property taxes were capped; thus revenues for public schools were limited. The revolt was fueled by voters' discontent with government, and part of this discontent was dissatisfaction with public schools.[84]

The net effect of the 1970s was to ensure that the 1980s was to be a decade of crisis for local school authorities with few guarantees of federal assistance. Ronald Reagan made it very clear in 1981 that his presidential administration would make it a priority to eliminate the federal department of education. Reagan led a conservative backlash against what he and supporters described as liberal equity policies that weakened curriculums, limited parental choice, rewarded participation not achievement, and generally educated American children and adolescents poorly in basic skills as well as the sciences. The backlash led to support for the introduction of market forces through mechanisms such as vouchers, which allow parents to use tax dollars to pay for private education over public education for their children. The demand for reform led to increased graduation requirements, enhanced standards for teacher certification, and, in some areas, teachers' salaries being tied to their students' performances. In 1983, a report published by the National Commission on Excellence in Education declared American education to be in a state of crisis. They concluded the only way to restore quality was to react vigorously.[85] The report found American workers to be ill-prepared for the new global competitive marketplace, and their performance was below that of the past generation. By 1986, thirty-five states moved to adopt legislation reforming educational processes and structures. Further reports also highlighted the failure of American higher education to produce quality graduates.[86] It was argued that most graduates could not perform simple tasks such as giving change, writing letters, or understanding an article from the newspaper. In short, Americans were functionally illiterate.

By the late 1980s, more individuals were advocating revamping education so as to place the focus on equality of performance not equality of access. They also argued for further decentralized decision making, the reform of school administration, stricter accountability, and restructuring of the curriculum. Underlying these demands was the objective of making education responsive to market needs. Such re-invention was experimented with in a number of states and cities. At the federal level Reagan and his successor George Bush fostered a "New Federalism" approach to education policy. Simply put this meant turning responsibility and funding for education over to the state governments. An example of this approach is the America 2000 program launched in 1991 by the Bush administration. The program was a national plan for school reform. It advocated national standards of student performance, evaluating local schools through public report cards, and upgrading teacher preparation. The program also called for the development of a New American Schools Development Corporation responsible for redesigning public education. Each congressional district was to designate one school that would act as a million-dollar model school and parents were to have freedom of choice between public and private schools. In order not to force federal expectations on state and local governments, states and localities were requested to conform their schools to the national plan. If they did, then they would be designated America 2000 communities. There was quick compliance, and within a year thirty-two states and hundreds of local communities had subscribed to the plan. The Development Corporation raised more than $50 million to design model schools.[87]

America 2000 seemed doomed once Bush failed to win reelection to office in 1992. However, Bill Clinton maintained America 2000 as part of his education policy by revamping it as Goals 2000: The Educate America Act. Clinton's reform package endorsed national performance standards and eight specific objectives that American schools should achieve by the year 2000.[88] To support Goals 2000, a number of panels and councils were created as well as three research and development centers. Clinton also articulated when signing Goals 2000 in April 1994 that $700 billion would be provided for education for 1995. The act, however, said little about higher-education reform. It is too early to predict the outcome of this reform. The barriers and obstacles facing the goals of the act are many. Only time will tell whether the United States can continue to have such a highly decentralized education system. In short, whether Goals 2000 can be achieved by the present infrastructure or not is still to be seen. Conservative opposition has already forced reconsideration of many of the objectives and in particular of national standards.

Policy Structure and Organization

The U.S. basic structure of educational provision is that of school districts based on population. Thus, the number of districts per county or state varies greatly. Each district is autonomous and is loosely guided by state boards. The national government does not operate the educational system. Therefore, its role in education is secondary to state and local governments. This, then, negates the ability of the federal government to initiate policy. In recent years, legislation such as Goals 2000 and America 2000 represent efforts by the federal government to circumvent the norm that policy cannot be directly mandated at the national level. By offering instruments such as grants to the states, local communities, and schools that adopt federal models, the federal government is taking control of education policy guidelines and overall objectives. However, the state and local governments still have tremendous authority in terms of formulation and implementation of policy.

The American education system consists of three levels: elementary, secondary and higher education. It is provided free of charge to all students. However, fees are charged for special items such as laboratories and lunches. At publicly-funded higher-education institutions, students pay tuition, which represents a small proportion of the real costs of their education. The remainder is subsidized by state governments. In recent years, the trend for state legislatures is to mandate public higher-education institutions to think of themselves as state-assisted and not state-funded. For example, California State University, which is the largest publicly-funded comprehensive system in the United States, has been mandated to raise 10 percent of its budget through other sources of revenue. The majority of students work or receive loans to cover their living costs and supplement tuition. All universities receive public funds in some way. Private institutions benefit from federal student grants and loans and indirect costs billed to government through contracts.

Elementary school can start at four years of age with preschool or Head Start (partially state-supported). There is no provision of public preschool. All children enroll in kindergarten in their fifth year and attend five days a week for three hours per day. Children go to school full-time beginning in the first grade at age six and graduate in the sixth grade at age eleven. In some districts, elementary school ends in fifth grade. On graduation from elementary school, students are placed in middle school or junior high until the age of thirteen when they enter senior high until eighteen years of age. High schools are comprehensive, and students are not separated by academic ability.

University or junior college enrollment is based on attaining certain scores on SAT exams. For those not bound for higher education there is no vocational training which guarantees a job upon successful completion of school. Private institutions of higher learning tend to be ranked among the best and are highly expensive. To attend one of the private-ranked top-fifty national universities, students and their families in the year 2000 must have approximately $25,000 for tuition and books and a further $15,000 to $25,000 for living expenses. Hence, many claim that the nation's elite universities are biased against students from lower economic strata. The response to this charge has always been that all students may apply for loans and scholarships. However, loans to cover such costs eventually may prove prohibitive. Also, many in the middle class believe the system discriminates against them, for their children do not qualify for the necessary loan amounts based on family income.

The option to go outside of the public system at all levels has always been there. The only prohibition is cost. The United States has the largest number of private elementary, secondary schools, and universities in the world. Fourteen percent of all elementary school children are enrolled in private schools, while nine percent of all secondary school students do, as do 28 percent of all university and college students.[89] Part of the current school voucher debate centers around the opening up of private schools to more children from families who otherwise could not afford it. This is part of the free-market model of education. The rationale behind vouchers is they would foster increased consumer choices, which, in turn, would force public schools to offer a better "product" in their competition for students. There is no data that proves this. Also, many fear the poor would still have no choice because the amount given is insufficient to subsidize lower-income families' tuition costs. Quite simply, the cost would still be out of their reach. Thus, those who would leave public schools for private are still the more affluent families. Public education would become the sole province of the lower-economic strata and, as one cannot divorce any discussion of poverty from race in America, of certain racial groupings. It would be starved of resources, and thus the opportunity of social mobility through education would be denied for so many in the nation.

Future Outcomes and Policy Weakness

Many individuals point to American elementary and secondary education falling behind other nations. Such arguments rest on educational outputs as measured by standardized achievement tests. Things will not change unless the federal government makes education policy a major part of its national policy agenda. Up until now education policy is symbolic policy making. The problems with public education are many and are present at every level. For example, dropout rates are high (20 to 30 percent), and minorities are clearly disadvantaged when higher-education enrollments and graduating rates are looked at. Incremental policy making will not fix these problems. Better off states will always do better. There needs to be some coordination or centralization of education policy.

The major problem with American education like so many other nations is funding. In particular, American decentralization of education has played a significant role in defining access to educational services. The viability and efficiency of public education regionally has been affected by states being delegated the funding responsibility for public education. It has led to disparity in spending levels, with some states spending considerably more per student in public schools than other states. There are real cost differentials even accounting for differences in cost of living, salaries, and materials. In the early to mid-1990s, some states were spending one-third less than other states to educate a comparable population of children. In short, the decentralization of education underscores socioeconomic and cultural differences from state to state. To compensate for this inequity, the federal government does retain the right to intervene whenever state education decisions or policies are deemed to benefit outside interests and not the public interest. One of the system's positives according to Heidenheimer, Heclo, and Adams is that American education policy makers are more accessible and susceptible to pressure.[90]

Chapter Twelve
Environmental Policy: To Regulate or Not?

So far the policies discussed provide specific benefits or services to citizens, and regulation of behavior is not particularly salient. Environmental policy is characterized by regulation of behavior of individuals and organizations without producing immediate tangible services and benefits. However, to include environmental policy with the discussion of social welfare, education, and health policy is appropriate, for environmental policy making interacts and contributes in many ways to each of the other policy sectors, and quality of "life in general." As a policy sector, environment is relatively new; however, the issue, or some aspects of it, has been on many governmental agendas for many years.[1] What is endemic to recent environmental policy is the acquiescence that environmental problems are the result of many activities of modern industrial society. Indeed these are activities that are vital to growth and economic well-being. When looking at the environment in industrialized nations, it has to be viewed in the context of population growth and levels of consumption.[2] Environmental policy making is a curbing of activities that in many ways benefit society. Hence, in some economically weak nations environmental policy making is a luxury they perceive to be only available to developed nations. Authors such as McCormick argue environmental policy is a post-materialist political concern.[3]

The environmental agenda differs from nation to nation. All nations are interested in the long run in developing policy about global risk; however, all nations also have to formulate policy that deals with quite specific and focused issues. It is these issues which interact with other social policy sectors. Increasingly many nations are building on the basis of sustainable development which promotes social and economic progress to be inseparable from environmental sustainability and technological strengthening.

A precise definition of sustainable development is difficult to achieve and may mean different things to different nations. The most commonly cited definition is the

1987 Brundtland Commission Report which argues it is "development that meets the needs of the present without compromising the ability of future generations to meet their own needs." Additionally the report goes on to argue that sustainable development should meet the needs of the poor in the world, and economies should take into consideration the impact of human activity on the surrounding environment. Quite simply for many nations, including the six discussed in this text, sustainable development is development that encourages long-term production and consumption patterns that do not degrade the human or natural environment.[4]

What then is environmental policy? It is a governmental action taken to solve the problem of society's relationship to its physical environment, which includes elements of air, water and soil. Environmental problems refer to the result of human and societal actions that are perceived as undesirable and harmful to the physical environment and citizens' physical well-being.

Brazil: Affordable Environmental Consciousness

Brazil has often been characterized as having generally poor ecological development, and in particular, poor development of the Amazon rainforest. Vivid pictures of the extensive burnings of Brazilian rainforests were cited as prime examples of disastrous economic development and total disregard for the environment. For many individuals, Brazil was guilty of contributing to the threat of global warming. When Brazilian development projects of the late 1960s, 1970s, and early 1980s in the Amazon region are looked at, there is indeed environmental disregard. Federal policy of subsidization of agricultural production or cattle ranching in the Amazon region also caused environmental waste as the rainforest was cleared and burned for occupation. If such problems are added to Brazil's sheer geographic size, her natural and human resources, the diversified industrial base, and size of the economy, it can be clearly seen why policy makers at the federal, state, and local levels of government were forced to formulate and implement laws and regulations protecting Brazil's environment.

Sustainable development is a high priority on the Brazilian public agenda and today there is a new environmental consciousness in the nation. Such consciousness was undoubtedly helped by the holding of the first Earth Summit in Rio de Janeiro in 1992. The domestic Brazilian environmental agenda, depending on the region, includes urban development and planning, basic sanitation, pollution abatement, waste and toxic materials' disposal, transportation, energy-efficiency promotion, ozone-depleting substances substitution, sustainable land-use, development of agro-biodiversity and phylogenetic resources, desertification, climate change and El Niño effects research, sustainable use of freshwater resources, water basin management, protection of humid ecosystems, coastal management, oceanographic research, development of non-predatory fisheries, institutional building, ecological zoning and monitoring, and green accounting, as well as the enforcement of environmental law over large territories. A good part of Brazil's ecological problems stem directly from the "pollution by poverty" and lack of sustainable development opportunities.

Policy History and Evolution

Concern with the environment and formulation of policy really evolved with the transition to democracy. From the 1980s on, there has been an abandonment of *desenvolvimentismo* policy. Such policy gave priority to economic growth and infrastructure building over all else. Indeed social and environmental factors were totally negated under such a policy. In 1981, the National Environment Policy was enacted.[5] This details the goals and mechanisms of formulating and implementing environmental regulations and programs. Under the legislation the federal government was granted the power to plan, coordinate and monitor the implementation of environmental policy. Box 12.1 outlines the main elements of the 1981 law.

The 1981 law also established the National Council for the Environment (CONAMA) and the National System for the Environment (SISNAMA). The former was to be responsible for environmental policy formulation while the latter was to manage implementation of such policy. As a result of the National Environment Policy, the 1988 constitution includes a specific section on the environment. In this section, the environment is dealt with as a communal asset of the people that is essential to providing a healthy quality of living. Public power and society are charged with preserving and protecting the environment for the benefit of present and future generations. In 1989, the government successfully passed a revision of the 1981 Environment Policy Act. The revision incorporates ecological crime. Any individual found guilty of activities that are potentially hazardous to human, animal, or plant life is liable to suffer detention penalties.

As a consequence of the United Nations conference on the Environment and Development (Rio de Janeiro, 1992) and its Agenda 21 report, the Brazilian government enacted, in June 1994, Decree n°1.160, which created the Inter-ministerial Commission for Sustainable Development (CIDES). This is a national-level body

---

Box 12.1   The 1981 Brazilian National Environment Policy

1. Governmental action to secure ecological balance, holding the environment as public patrimony worthy of protection and safekeeping for collective use
2. Judicious use of the soil, the subsoil, water, and air
3. Planning and survey of the use of environmental resources
4. Protection of eco-systems, with the preservation of representative areas
5. Zoning and control of activities deemed potentially or actually environment polluting
6. Encouragements to study technological research directed to the rational use and the protection of environmental resources
7. Follow-up of environmental quality
8. Restoration of spoiled areas
9. Protection of areas risking ecological damage
10. Environmental education at all schooling levels, including community education, in order to make for active participation in the defense of the environment.

linked to the Ministry of Planning and Budget. CIDES' main goals are to advance the Agenda 21 goals and objectives where possible. The commission also acts as environmental counsel to the president of the republic on any decisions pertaining to policies and strategies necessary for sustainable development.

In Cardoso's campaign manifesto and inauguration speech, the goals of sustainable development, the protection of the environment, pursuit of global accords on the environment, as well as the strengthening of science and technology are identified. Thus, in the first Cardoso administration a series of domestic policy actions dealing with the environment were passed. All such measures had an additional goal of decentralizing the environment's management and establishing partnerships with interested stakeholders. The federal government adopted a series of measures leading to the partial or total transfer of the planning and implementation of environmental policies to the states, municipalities, nongovernmental organizations (NGOs) and other public and private entities. In his second year in office, Cardoso created the National Fund for the Environment. This was created to provide funding opportunities for NGOs and municipalities in a completely decentralized manner.

An example of Cardoso's willingness to cooperate globally was the 1996 signing of a new bilateral agreement for cooperation in space emphasizing the use of technology for research and analysis on the environment.[6] The Cardoso administration made it clear in its first term in office that cooperation with the United States on environmental matters was a course of action that it would pursue. Hence, agreements have been signed between the two nations for cooperative practices in protecting the rainforest.

Among the federal laws and decrees enacted were those regulating forestry activities, protection of fauna, promotion of fisheries, establishment and management of conservation units, the use of pesticides in agriculture, and pollution control. There are federal standards for water quality, water management, air quality, emissions from automotive vehicles, and pollution of the marine environment. In essence, the Brazilians established a "green protocol," which makes the environmental variable a relevant criterion in decisions pertaining to government subsidies and credits by official development promotion agencies. Additionally, Brazil launched the "green credit card" to fund environmental projects furthered by NGOs and the National Executive Environmental Agency (IBAMA). In terms of decentralizing environmental management by 1996 the Cardoso administration had established new environmental initiatives, such as the integrated national policy for legal Amazonia. This is in partnership with local state governments and the region's community. Additionally, the federal government has required all state and local governments to reactivate their environmental and economic zoning.

Cardoso's second term has not been as productive in terms of environmental policy making because of economic difficulties. However, the federal government continues its emphasis on decentralization. For example, the administration continues to lend support to the National Fund for the Environment (FNMA). FNMA channels 80 percent of its resources to NGOs and local authorities of towns with populations less than 120,000 for specific projects. Additionally, the government continues to give 20 percent of the total funding for the National Plan for the Environment with the remainder of monies being supplied by international agencies. Another program highlighting the partnership between the federal government and the states is the Decentralized Executive Program. Under this program the states select indicative projects of sustainable development that are financed by the Ministry. The basic idea of the program is that these states qualify for funding by developing infrastructures oriented in the direction of environmental management. Eleven federal states have already been admitted.

Policy Structure and Organization

Four main components of Brazilian environmental policy may be identified: (1) conservation and sustainable use of natural resources; (2) pollution control and licensing of polluting activities; (3) urban environmental quality; and (4) the global environmental agenda. Brazilian conservation policy is based on economic and ecological zoning. Such zoning allows for the sustainable use of natural resources. The Amazon was the first ecological zoning project with other regions being zoned at regular intervals. The goal of conservation is the maintenance and protection of ecological processes and ecosystems. Pollution control has been necessary since the economic growth of the 1950s. Such growth was based on the combination of large-scale energy intensive production, cheap natural resources, and a highly mobile labor force. A number of environmental impacts developed as the automotive industry, petrochemical and steel industries, and the agribusiness sector also developed. Only since the late 1980s onward has the industrial sector incorporated environmental management strategies into their operational procedures. Partly the industries have been forced to incorporate these strategies by legal requirements. However, compliance is also because of corporations becoming interested stakeholders. Prevention of environmental damage is more cost-effective than attempts to control pollution and environmental degradation.

The government has also encouraged changes in the energy infrastructure that includes both renewable and non-renewable sources. By the mid-1990s, 60 percent of Brazil's total energy comes from renewable sources, mainly from hydroelectric and sugarcane alcohol. Ethanol has been widely championed as a fuel substitute for gasoline. Indeed Brazil was a pioneer in this area. Hydroelectric energy accounts for 35 percent of total consumption, while petroleum products represent a 30 percent share.

The urban environmental quality element of Brazilian environmental policy covers basic sanitation, waste management and disposal, and recovery of contaminated sites. Heavy urbanization has forced Brazil to face a number of environmental problems. This area lags far behind the others. Urban infrastructures and services do not meet assessed needs adequately. Some progress has been made, but improvement is still required on basic sanitation, sewage treatment systems, and the water supply. While the other nations in this text have dealt with recycling and which model to implement, Brazil still has to deal with how to collect and dispose of its trash. Many urban towns still do not have regular trash collection services. Most of Brazil's collected waste, including hazardous waste, still goes to large open-area landfills. There has been some experimentation with recycling in a few medium-size cities, but this is not common.

Air quality remains a serious problem. Several Brazilian states launched sanitation and cleanup initiatives, most of which are being financed by multilateral financial institutes.[7] However, they are still either in the contracting phase or are so newly installed that it is too early to determine whether they will be successful or not. In terms of the global environment, Brazil has become a party to a series of international agreements adopted in recent years to protect the global environment.[8] As a developing nation, Brazil has been granted preferential and differential treatment under such agreements; however, such participation is still a considerable burden to the Brazilian economy.

Environmental policy-making goals and strategies are clearly federally defined, but formulated and implemented through a series of cooperative relationships between the federal government, state governments, the municipalities, and NGOs. Thus, decentralization is a key characteristic of Brazilian environmental policy making. CONAMA is responsible for formulating policy nationally. It's a collective decision-making body, chaired by the Minister of the Environment, Minister of Natural Resources and the Legal Amazonian Region (MMA); other members include representatives of other relevant ministries, state governments, the federal district, and trade unions' representatives. Implementation is carried out by SISNAMA, which is made up of entities of the union, state governments, the federal district, municipalities, and government foundations. SISNAMA answers to the National Council for the Environment. There is an attempt to include all the vital stakeholders in both formulation and implementation. Environmental policy making is the pursuit of a consensus through negotiation and agreement between industry and government. In this framework, the federal government's responsibility is to stimulate and direct the adoption of policy through promoting shared responsibilities and partnerships. The emphasis is on dialogue, persuasion, and societal consciousness building. The goal is to produce optimal management of natural resources. Conservation and sustainable development responsibilities are gradually being taken up by Brazilian corporations.

Much of the financing for implementation of environmental projects in Brazil is through funding opportunities from multilateral and bilateral agreements. The World Bank finances 70 percent of Brazil's National Environment Program. By 1995 Brazil had more than $5 billion in loans from multilateral agencies for ongoing environmental projects. Internally the Brazilian National Development Bank has authorized more than one billion dollars to environmentally friendly initiatives by the private sector.

Future Outcomes and Policy Weakness

Without doubt, Brazil is a newly industrialized nation that is environmentally conscious. The pursuit of sustainable development is genuine; however, the pressures to be part of the global environmental partnership could prove to undermine the effort. Progress has been made. Figure 12.1 shows the progress made in deforestation rates. Brazil, despite its industrial sector's stature, is still a developing country that suffers from serious social problems and where democracy is still relatively new. Environmental management cannot be dissociated from social policies; if it is, then projects that are detrimental to the environment but generate employment would be considered valuable and pursued. This is the struggle for any developing nation to come to terms with.

Environmental policy making is expensive. Flexible fiscal mechanisms have been put in place that allow for substantial foreign investments for environmentally sound projects. However, in the twenty-first century, Brazil's environmental policy must be put into the context of Brazilian society and its social problems. If the choice for government expenditure is between building schools and hospitals or clean air and there are few external sources of financing at terms that are affordable for the Brazilian economy, the choice is clear. If sustainable development hinders economic growth, then it will become increasingly difficult for legislators at all levels to vote for legislation that, while protecting Brazil's environmental quality, would mean fewer jobs. Further challenges to national environmental laws and institutions will be generated by managerial problems created by increasingly unclear lines of environmental jurisdiction between state and federal levels of government, overlapping responsibilities between sectional and environmental institutions, and a lack of technical training and qualified human resources to carry out environmental management as international demands grow stronger.

million hectares a year

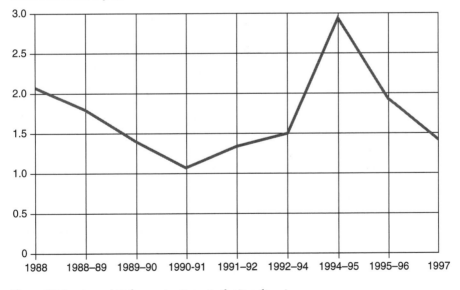

Figure 12.1   Annual Deforestation Rates in the Brazilian Amazon
Source: Adapted from INPE/IBAMA 1998.

Notes: Data for 1993 and 1994 are estimates based on the mean rate of deforestation during 1992–94. The 1997 rate is estimated from an analysis of 47 Landsat images.

Germany: How Much and for What Cost?

In a nation aggressively developing its industrial sector, the pursuit of environmental goals while simultaneously attempting to keep industry's costs to a minimum is a major challenge for policy makers. The debate in Germany has been centered around the costs and benefits of environmental policy to the nation's international competitiveness. As in numerous other nations, the solution that has been focused on is sustainable development. As Europe's largest and most successful industrial nation, Germany may provide lessons about how efforts to implement sustainable development affect policy choices that are sensitive to the needs of industry.

Policy History and Evolution

Environmental policy in Germany until the 1920s took the form of laws dealing with air and water hygiene. From the 1920s, air pollution started to become a problem in certain regions, in particular the industrial region around the Ruhr Valley. A number of measures were demanded to protect the environment; however, it was not until the 1950s that clear air initiatives were enacted by the state legislatures governing the Ruhr Valley. Much of the subsequent legislation developed for the Ruhr Valley in the 1960s, and the environmental research it stimulated, became the foundation of federal policy enacted in the 1970s as the Federal Clean Air Act. Additionally the creation of a special environmental protection division in the Federal Ministry of the Interior in the late 1960s helped to establish the environmental policy sector in Germany.

The 1970s saw a rapid increase in German environmental policy development. Much of this can be attributed to the adoption of the first federal environmental program and the creation of the Council of Environmental Advisors (SRU). The task of the Council was to report on the environment's condition and identify undesirable developments. It was also hoped that the Council would pinpoint ways in which such developments could be avoided in the future. In 1974, the government established the Federal Environmental Agency (UBA). The agency was answerable to the federal ministry of the interior and was to supply advisory support on environmental issues and scientific expertise.

The major environmental problems faced by Germany in the 1970s were high levels of localized and regional air pollution and contaminated water. To meet such problems, a number of measures were introduced dealing with the problem at the source. For example, new regulations were enacted that heightened chimneys on coal-burning power stations and industrial plants. However, success at the local level simply meant shifting the problem. While local air quality improved, there was wide dispersion of airborne pollutants that affected areas previously without environmental damage. In essence, German environmental policy in the 1970s was short-sighted and focused on specific and localized problems without seeing the effects on the total environment in the long run.

By the 1980s, the long-run effects of dealing with localized air pollution had brought a further environmental problem for Germany in the form of forest damage caused by acid deposition leading to forest decline (*Waldsterben*). This became a major issue on the environmental policy agenda and the government enforced new regulations that demanded that industry comply with installation of end-of-pipe pollution control technologies in all fossil-fueled power plants. Measures to reduce automobile exhaust emissions were also introduced in the late 1980s. By the end of the decade, Germany witnessed a large reduction in pollution.[9] In 1985, an amendment to the federal Clean Air Act was passed, which gave the state governments and local authorities expanded authority to deal with pollution and environmental protection. One year later, the federal government created the Federal Ministry for the Environment, Nature Protection and Reactor Safety (BMU). The creation of the new ministry was partly in response to public anxiety over the Chernobyl nuclear incident in the USSR. One of the first pieces of environmental legislation enacted by the ministry was the 1986 administrative regulation governing Technical Instructions on Air Quality Control (TALUFT). This set standards for ambient air quality, deposition, and emissions. The priority of environmental protection in Germany can be seen in public opinion polls of the period.[10] The permanence of the environmental issue on the public agenda and politics is reflected by the rise of the Green Party and its electoral prominence in the mid-1980s.

By the start of the 1990s, environmental protection was a given priority for policy makers whose attention had expanded from air pollution problems to other environmental problems, such as waste disposal, depletion of the ozone layer, and the greenhouse effect. Reunification compounded the number of new problems that policy makers faced. By the late 1980s, East Germany had reached extremely high levels of pollution. These new problems, plus the failure of previous policy focusing on localized problems, led the environment ministry to conclude that all future policy was to be cross-sectoral, preventive, and focused on sustainable development. This required a rethinking of environmental policy design so as to formulate future policy that integrated environmental policy with economic policy, energy policy, and resources and transportation.

As the debate grew on how to implement this new model of environmental policy, economic recession started to take hold. Industry, facing falling profits and layoffs, started to complain loudly of the costs of aggressive environmental regulations. Indeed, industry's expenditure on environmental protection had almost doubled between 1980 and 1987. The BDI estimated that in 1991 the combined private and public sectors' environmental protection expenditure in Germany was approximately 1.74 percent of GDP.[11] This compares to approximately 1.36 percent in the United States and 1.02 percent in Japan. The BDI called for a moratorium on new environmental regulations. At the same time, the environmental ministry was being advised by the environmental agency that future costs to industry to comply with environmental regulations would increase. These two pressures forced the environmental ministry to seek greater cooperation and input from industry and to begin a dialogue on future regulation. Eventually, it led to the adoption of the "closed-cycles economy."

The closed-cycles economy was a plan for cross-sectoral policy, focusing on conservation and waste reduction, leading to sustainable development. As part of this plan, the Avoidance of Packaging Waste Ordinance was passed in 1991. Under this law, all manufacturers and distributers are responsible for collecting, processing, and recycling any packages or containers sold with their product, with higher collection and sorting requirements being staged in. A more aggressive regulation conforming to the plan was the 1994 Waste Framework Law.[12] The legislation underwent lengthy legislative discussion and many amendments so it could comply with EU directives on waste. The framework established a preferential hierarchy for the disposal of materials used in products. The hierarchy, in order of preference, was avoiding waste so materials could be reused; the burning of recycled products and waste to produce energy; and disposing of waste in landfills after incineration to reduce the volume of waste. In the last years of the 1990s, subsequent laws have been passed identifying what percentages of products should be reused, recycled, or disposed of.

The German government entered the twenty-first century very clearly committed to the goal of environmental modernization. It is committed to protecting natural resources while promoting employment and sustainable economic growth. Part of this goal is to be achieved by ecological tax reform. Such tax reform effectively went into operation in April 1999, with the introduction of a new electricity tax and an increase in the petroleum tax. It is a graduated tax that will increase each year until 2003. Financial incentives will be offered for energy conservation and the harnessing of new renewable energy sources. Electricity that is generated using renewable energy sources—wind power, solar energy, geothermal heat, water power, landfill gas, and biomass—is not subject to the new electricity tax. Additionally companies in the manufacturing, agricultural, and forestry sectors will qualify for lower environmental tax rates, as will local public transportation and natural-gas-propelled vehicles. It was felt exemptions had to be made so as not to impair the competitiveness of German industry.

The goal of ecological tax reform is to achieve conservation by the gradual increase of energy and raw materials. Any revenues generated will be used to lower non-wage labor costs. It is hoped the introduction of such a tax will accelerate structural changes in German industry, encourage investment aimed at energy conservation and lead to the introduction of environmentally sound production processes. Finally it is hoped to significantly reduce carbon dioxide emissions by the year 2005.[13] This was not innovative policy making by the German government; other nations, such as Sweden, introduced their own ecological tax reforms in the early 1990s. Great Britain has also automatically raised the fuel tax by six percent every year since 1993—on an open-ended basis. However, the late summer of 2000 witnessed widespread public opposition to government fuel taxes in Germany, and in particular in Great Britain. The British government has consistently refused to back down on the amount of tax levied on petroleum.

The most recent example of environmental protection in Germany went into effect in April 2000. Such legislation has as its objective the doubling of renewable energy sources, from 5 to 10 percent by year 2010, as a proportion of the total amount of energy generated. Such legislation included the "Act as Granting Priority to Renewable Energy Sources" and amendments to the "Energy Industry Act" and the "Law on Excise Tax on Oil and Oil Products." The newly implemented legislation provides price supports to enable electricity generation from renewable energy sources on an economically viable basis. It also expands the list of renewable energy sources by adding methane. It is hoped the support will also stimulate demand for renewable energy technologies, which will encourage technological innovation, job creation and new export opportunities. The new act builds on existing legislation and provides considerable incentives to ensure greater use of renewable energy sources through extending financial assistance to groups and organizations that comply.[14]

Policy Structure and Organization

Formulation of environmental legislation is divided up among the three levels of government in the following manner. The federal government is responsible for all framework legislation concerning waste management, air pollution, federal waterways, and industrial pollution. The state governments provide regulations for nature conservation, landscape management, and water pollution protection. The local environment is the responsibility of local authorities, in as far as it's affected by urban development planning.

Implementation and enforcement of all legislation affecting the environment are totally in the hands of the states and local authorities. The exception to this is nuclear safety, which is the responsibility of the federal government. Such a division of formulation and implementation responsibilities requires a good deal of cooperation between the federal government and the states.

All legislation is proposed and formulated within the ministries of the environment with input from the environmental agency, the Federal Office for Nature Conservation (BFN), the economics ministry that is responsible for industry, and the finance ministry that control appropriations. As in all other policy areas, the policy that often emerges is the product of a consensus reached through compromise, or it is policy that is not coordinated because it is the result of interest group politics. Up until the late 1980s and early 1990s, there was a lack of communication at the federal level between the environmental ministry and industry. Since then, the closed-cycles economy plan has fostered a new, more open relationship with voluntary actions by industry forming a much more informal approach to environmental issues. Policy formulation is a mix today of regulatory instruments, persuasive tactics, increased consumer awareness and economic instruments. An example of how this relationship fosters policy can be seen with the 1994 proposal from the German automobile industry for a voluntary used-car recovery scheme. The proposal envisioned manufacturers setting up collection and recovery schemes and charging a small fee to dispose of a vehicle and recycling as much of it as was practical.

Financing of German environmental policy is a mix of private and public monies. State and local taxes supplemented by federal payments to the states to cover the cost of administering federal law cover the burden of environmental policy implementation. It is hoped the new ecological tax will generate significant new revenues. The new revenues will be used to cover implementation costs but mostly will be used to finance reductions in payroll contributions divided between employers and employees, thus decreasing some economic burden on industry that will cover costs of complying with environment regulations.

Future Outcomes and Policy Weakness

The core of Germany's environmental policy in the first years of the new century is the creation of a sustainable economy. This will be dependent on the ability of policy makers to identify the best mechanisms for achieving the goals of its legislation of the last ten years. What is needed for viable sustainable growth is a cooperative relationship between state and industry at every stage of the policy process. The progress that has been made between government and industry over the last few years must be maintained. Many have argued that the large number of exceptions in the ecological tax legislation is incompatible with the tax's environmental goals.[15] However, a different perspective is to argue that it is symbolic of policy makers' desire to have industry as a willing partner in sustainable growth rather than a resentful servant.

Great Britain: To "Green" or Not?

As in other nations, Great Britain's environment has suffered as it became more populated and technologically advanced. Environmental protection is an important issue in Great Britain and has led to much heated debate. It has led to the presence of a green party and to what some call the "greening" of British politics.[16] Britain's post-war consensus was built on the assumption that economic growth would provide the needed extra resources for welfare state expansion. Commonly referred to as the "age of affluence," it was also the start of the modern British environmental debate. While Conservative Prime Minister Harold Macmillan told voters, "You've never had it so good," many environmentalists now believe that the price to pay for economic growth and its emphasis on industrialism and the consumption of non-renewable natural resources was damage to Britain's environment.

Policy History and Evolution

As the world's first industrialized society, Britain has had to deal with environmental problems from its earliest days as a modern society. Prior to World War I, the British government dealt fairly successfully with sewage contamination and impure water supplies. However, there was no real environmental policy, although much legislation did contain elements that were concerned with aspects of the environment. The first piece of legislation that dealt solely with the environment was the 1956 Clean Air Act. The act was passed to deal with the problem of severe urban smog. In the next decade, a further clean air act was passed, and by the 1970s industrial pollution was reduced significantly.[17] For most of the 1960s, the government's environmental efforts were aimed at policy that promoted the substitution of gas and electricity for coal. Legislation was also passed that severely restricted urban and suburban development in certain areas and regulated the disposal of radioactive waste.

Environmental concern truly started to increase in Britain in the 1970s. The decade saw a number of enacted laws dealing with pollution and environmental damage. The centerpiece of the legislation was the 1974 Control of Pollution Act. This transferred a large amount of responsibility for environmental matters to local government authorities and specified disposal standards and penalties for polluting Britain's cities and countryside. In 1981, the Wildlife and Countryside Act dealt largely with rural environmental issues. Because British central government is organized into self-contained policy sectors, much of the debate around environmental policy centered not on the substance of policy but on who should carry it out.[18] British environmental policy was sparse because of the absence of a central unified coordinating ministry of the environment. The first move in this direction came with the creation of the Department of the Environment in the early 1970s. It was a cabinet-level department and according to British Prime Minister Edward Heath, it was to integrate environmental and economic decision making.[19] However, the new department was limited because key environmental issues were not put under its control but left to other departments, such as energy and agriculture. The election of Margaret Thatcher's Conservative government in 1979 did not bode well for environmental legislation. Thatcher's emphasis on market forces and deregulation directly conflicted with the regulatory nature of most environmental legislation.

By the 1980s, as Britain's environmental problems grew and there was an absence of clear legislation, the demands from environmental groups for an integration of functions of a number of departments dealing with policy sectors impaired by environmental issues grew. It led to the creation of important new agencies to deal with the environment, such as Her Majesty's Inspectorate of Pollution (HMIP), the National Rivers Authority (NRA), and the Waste Regulatory Authorities (WRA). HMIP was formed in 1987 and was to be responsible for issuing administrative edicts in the area of air pollution, radio-chemical waste, hazardous waste, and water pollution. The NRA was set up in 1989 by the Water Act, which privatized the various public water authorities. The responsibility of the NRA was pollution control, flood defense, control of water reserves, controls of fishing, and navigation and recreational use of waterways and coastal waters. Each agency promulgated administrative ordinances that regulated the environment in the areas of pollution, waste control, and disposal of toxic substances. By 1988, Margaret Thatcher had publicly displayed a commitment to environmental protection and raised its position on the public agenda. However, the Conservatives found it difficult to define a distinct environmental program. They were torn between their desire to deregulate and the desire to punish those who broke laws such as anti-pollution legislation.

The first-ever comprehensive statement on British environmental policy was published in the 1990 white paper, "This Common Inheritance."[20] It laid out the environmental issues facing Britain; however, it did not present a coherent strategy for policy action. It did lead to the 1990 Environmental Protection Act, which deals with the collection and disposal of waste, both domestic and industrial. The legislation contained 120 clauses and was more far-reaching in its coverage of environmental issues than any previous legislation. The 1990 act required that all local authorities devise strategies for regulating waste, with a target set for 2000 of 25 percent recycled waste. One year later in his first speech on the environment, Prime Minister John Major announced the creation of a new agency to deal with environmental protection and enhancement. Details of the new agency were published in "Improving Environmental Quality," a government consultation paper. However, it soon became clear that this was not an environmental agency that would coordinate policy across the land but rather a pollution-control body. The agency came into being in 1996 after the 1995 Environment Act was passed. The principal functions of the agency are flood defenses, water resource management, pollution control, fisheries, navigation of waterways, recreational use of water and land, and conservation. These functions are to be carried out through the environmental agency's supervision of HMIP and NRA.

In January 1994 the Conservative government reacted to criticisms from various environmental groups that it was not responding to the demands set out by the 1992 Rio Earth Summit by issuing "Sustainable Development: The U.K. Strategy." The document mostly rehashed existing policies. However, it did list a number of initiatives to promote sustainable growth. These included a panel on sustainable development made up of five prominent experts; a roundtable on sustainable development consisting of thirty members from a combination of business, local government, environmental groups and academia; and a program "going for green," which would publicize the sustainable development message to local communities and individuals. The Conservative government introduced additional measures in 1996 that brought them some success and praise.[21] For example, a bio-diversity action plan was launched in May, while in August air-quality targets were announced for eight key pollutants; included in these was the recognition that traffic was a chief source of air pollution.

Labour stressed in their campaign for office in 1997 that if elected they would reorganize government so as to have a cross-departmental approach to environmental protection. Such a departmental approach would be backed by a parliamentary environmental audit committee. They pledged to reduce carbon dioxide emissions by 20 percent by 2010, to have cleaner and more efficient use of energy, to develop renewable energy sources and programs for home energy efficiency, to form an under-25 environmental task force for the unemployed, to promote environmental technology industries, and to create employment and regulation of economic growth to protect environmental quality. In short, Labour pledged itself to sustainable growth.

Following the 1997 election, the departments of environment and transport were merged to become the Department of the Environment, Transport and the Regions (DETR). Labour announced that the merger would lead to a more integrated approach to policy making in the areas of the environment and transportation. Under the leadership of the Deputy Prime Minister John Prescott, DETR is responsible for a range of interrelated policies and actions (see Box 12.2).

Box 12.2   DETR Responsibilities

Sustainable development: promoting sustainable development across government, throughout the United Kingdom and abroad.

Environment protection: protecting and improving the environment—air, water, or land—including energy efficiency, inland waterways, and waste reduction and recycling.

Countryside and wildlife: improving the quality of life in rural areas, conservation and enhancement of the countryside and its wildlife, and participation in international work to preserve global biodiversity.

Integrated transport: promoting integration across all the modes of transport at local and national levels for economic growth, better environment and a more inclusive and healthy society, while maintaining and improving safety standards across all modes through regulation.

English regions: including the establishment of the regional development agencies.

Regeneration: improving quality of life in economically deprived areas, whether inner-cities, new towns, or rural communities, to combat social exclusion.

Local government: setting the structure and finance of local authorities.

Housing: promoting a decent home for all, whether provided by registered social landlords and local authorities, the privately rented sector, or through home ownership and tackling homelessness.

Construction: industry sponsorship and building regulations.

Labour's vision of sustainable development was published in "A Better Quality of Life" in May 1999. Sustainable development for Britain is about improving access to services, tackling social exclusion, and reducing harm to health caused by poverty, poor housing, unemployment, and pollution. It means international cooperation to combat global environmental threats. It means acting to protect people from hazards such as poor air quality and toxic chemicals. And it means safeguarding wildlife, landscapes, and historic buildings, all of which are highly valued by the British public. If such issues are tackled, and at the same time the government attempts to deliver schools and hospitals, decent housing, jobs, and improved living standards for all, then economic growth remains vital. Such growth, the Labour government argues, must contribute to a better quality of life. The British notion of sustainable development recognizes that the environment, economy, and society are interdependent. In short, sustainable economic development should result in social progress that recognizes the needs of everyone, effectively protects the environment, uses national resources prudently, and leads to high and stable levels of economic growth and employment. The government announced 150 core and headline indicators of sustainable development that will be used to monitor progress.[22] Various bodies were created to evaluate sustainable development efforts and a commission will begin work in July 2000 to renew the efforts and create agreements and action to be taken by all sectors. To achieve sustainable development newly appointed "Green Ministers" were delegated specific responsibilities governing environmental protection.

In 1999, the government spent approximately $500 million on environmental protection and energy efficiency, $200 million on the countryside, and $250 million on health and safety.[23] Most of the money is channeled through the department's agencies and sponsored bodies, and through capital allocations to local authorities. The first major piece of environmental legislation from the new government was the 1999 Pollution, Prevention and Control Act. The act aims to reduce industrial pollution and extends the number of processes covered from 2,000 to 7,000. Emissions standards for some industrial processes are also tightened. It also incorporates energy efficiency as the basis for negotiating discounts in a climate change levy to be introduced in 2001.

The British record is uneven in terms of actual legislation; however, the commitment is clear. Great Britain's commitment to environmental protection can be seen by its active involvement in global efforts to protect the environment. Such activity is mainly through financial contributions and expertise. The British communities have also been among the EU's leaders on the environmental agenda.

Policy Structure and Organization

The current Labour government's environment policy goals are summarized in Box 12.3. The majority of environmental activity takes place at the local level, with the national government providing leadership, vision and goals. The direction of environmental policy for Great Britain is through the secretary of state for the environment and junior green ministers. At the national level, there is a unified pollution regulating body, the Environmental Agency. The agency integrates the national government's functions on pollution control. It is only responsible for industrial processes' emissions. Non-scheduled process emissions are the responsibility of local district councils.[24]

Local governments also play an important role in waste regulation. Prior to the 1990 Environmental Protection Act, local authorities were responsible for regulation of waste. Since the 1990 act, responsibility for the collection of household and some commercial and industrial waste is divided up between different tiers of government, with local authorities, mostly county councils, being required to contract out such services to private companies through a competitive bidding process for disposal. Such a process became known as compulsory competitive tendering. The Local Government Act, which came into force in April 2000, replaced compulsory competitive tendering with a duty on local authorities to achieve best value. The act also removed crude and universal capping, and introduced new reserve powers. Responsibility for waste regulation lies with the counties. In certain metropolitan areas the responsibility for both disposal and regulation is held by the local authority.

Many local authorities have become involved in promoting environmental initiatives that give them more active involvement in environmental policy leadership.

Box 12.3   Labour Government Environmental Policy Goals

- To protect and improve the environment, and to integrate environmental policy with other policies across government and the international arena
- To enhance opportunity in rural areas, improve enjoyment of the countryside, and conserve and manage wildlife resources
- To create a fair and efficient land-use planning system that respects regional differences and promotes development that is high quality and sustainable
- To enhance economic development and social cohesion throughout England through effective regional action and integrated local regeneration programs
- To improve health and safety by reducing risks from work activity, travel, and the environment.

For example, many local authorities pledged to fulfill the 1992 Earth Summit's Agenda 21 through strategic plans. Subsequently Tony Blair insisted that all local authorities develop such plans by 2000. Many authorities have issued environmental vision statements, while some have undertaken thorough reviews of their activities and established environmental performance indicators. The real problem for most local governments is their lack of resources and what they perceive as lack of enforcing powers. Until they possess sufficient resources and such powers, they will not be able to do anything beyond carrying out their statutory duties in the environmental policy sector.

Labour has attempted to increase local government funding resources.[25] In January 2000, an overall increase of 5.8 percent in national support for local governments was introduced. Additional increases in funds for local councils were promised for the next three years. Labour is also promising an extra $50 million in grants to aid all local authorities to deliver better services. With the addition of these new monies, the Labour government since taking office has increased grants to local authorities by $10 billion, which represents an increase of 7.8 percent.

Future Outcomes and Policy Weakness

The British response to environmental problems has improved since the early 1990s, and there is more support for it to be on the British public policy agenda. However, it is still restrictively defined and poorly understood. Sustainable development, conservation, energy sources, and pollution will continue to be issues of high priority on the public agenda in the first decade of the new century. However, success at dealing with them will be hard to achieve for any national government unless they devote time and money to developing an infrastructure that supports environmental protection. Environmental policies in Britain tend to reflect the interaction of the various institutions of environmental management and environmental interest groups rather than coherent political policy by government. Thus, those who are the subject of environmental regulation often have undue influence on the design and implementation of regulations.

Japan: Friendly Protection

Japan has a long history of environmental degradation because of its push to industrialize in the late-nineteenth century and then again post-1945 with the effort to rebuild the economy. Environmental crisis occurred in the late-nineteenth century, early-twentieth century, and the late-twentieth century.[26] In the first of these crises, river and rice fields were contaminated by heavy copper mining effluents, and large numbers of Japanese were made seriously ill. In the early-twentieth century crisis, cadmium poisoning caused an outbreak of itai-itai disease, a painful bone complaint. In the late-twentieth century, mercury contamination in fishing waters led to hundreds dying of Minamata, a disease that affects the central nervous system. By the 1970s, many Japanese were experiencing health complaints caused by smog, arsenic, and polychlorobiphenyl poisoning from industrial processes. It is not surprising, then, that Japan has enacted strict legislation governing environmental protection. Indeed today many know Japan as a world leader in environmental awareness and cleanup.[27] In spite of this action, significant problems still remain: pollution of waters, acid rain and air pollution, smog, and waste disposal.

Policy History and Evolution

The critical juncture for environmental policy making in Japan was the 1960s. Both government and industry as well as the general public started to acknowledge that there was a detrimental link between industrial activity and the environment, which could have consequences for citizens' well-being. The first response was to implement environmental impact assessments (EIAAS). Any application for a large-scale industrial project to either national or local government was appraised on the project's abilities to meet national environmental standards. The early 1960s also saw clean air and water legislation, which were not strictly imposed by the national government, but which prompted local government to impose stricter conditions on new industrial developments. This was not through official promulgation, which is forbidden under the constitution unless there is national legislation authorizing it; rather it was through unofficial communications to corporations and business planning applicants.

In 1967, Japan's first coordinated piece of environmental legislation, the Basic Law for Environmental Pollution Control, which was followed the next year with further air and noise pollution laws, was passed. The 1967 basic law laid down the fundamental principles, responsibilities, and regulating spheres of governmental environmental policy, all of which had to be operationalized by ordinances, administrative regulations, or specific laws. Under the basic law, the national government is given the authority to establish environmental quality standards for air, water, soil, and noise, and the power to enforce them. The standards were to vary from region to region. Additionally the basic law set the tone for the relationship between governmental agencies, local authorities, and industry. The law states that protection of the living environment is to be pursued in "harmony" with social economic development. This led to a number of instances when strict environmental measures were "killed" because they would hurt economic growth and well-being.

Many criticized the 1968 laws that stemmed from the basic law as inadequate, weak, and difficult to implement. To meet such criticism and to monitor public concern, the government, in consultation with industry, set the nation's short-term goals for improving environmental quality and the necessary strategies to reach the goals. The main emphasis was on clean air measures and toxic substances. Because of the nature of the relationship between government, industry, and bureaucracy, many of these measures were implemented consistently. It also led to the enactment and enforcement of stricter environmental laws. In a special session, parliament passed a package of fourteen environmental laws and regulations in 1970, and in 1971 created the environmental agency. Until its establishment, the responsibility for controlling environmental pollution was mainly taken care of by the ministry of welfare. In addition to coordinating policy, the agency was to provide general advisory council to government and to develop national standards. The agency's jurisdiction was limited to items specified in the Basic Law for Environmental Pollution Control, and thus it could not deal with other issues of environmental importance such as sewage contamination. The agency cannot implement or enforce legislation in certain areas. However, it can supervise environmental efforts. One of the most important effects of the agency's establishment was it stimulated the development of special environmental agencies at the prefecture and municipal levels.

The regulatory laws passed in the 1970s represent a period of policy innovation and include the Area-Wide Total Pollution Load Control System for air pollutants and effluents, an environmental chemicals law, and a cost-apportionment scheme for companies involving preventive and remedial measures. At the national or local level, strict standards for environmental quality and emissions, and a compensation system for health impairments due to environmental pollution was imposed. Additionally, legislation such as the Nature Conservation Law was also enacted during this period so as to halt the destruction of the natural environment. These laws were fairly successful in addressing the environmental problems they focused on; however, they were insufficient to deal with growing urban pollution and the degradation of forests and farmlands.

The 1980s saw more legislation enacted to enhance conservation and protect the quality of air and water. In 1980 Japan joined the Ramsar Convention for the preservation of wetlands and waterfowl habitats. Much of the impetus for action in the 1980s was the 1983 Environmental Agency Report on environmental quality. In the report the agency called for a more integrated approach to environmental politics and a broader consideration of the ecosystem's needs. The Ozonosphere Protection Law was passed in 1988. This law restricted the manufacture of chlorofluorocarbons and introduced acceptable substitution materials. In the same year, a fundamental revision of the compensation law took effect. From this time on, no new individuals suffering from air pollution would be certified as pollution victims.

The period also saw measures that addressed the problems of noise, waste, disposal, ground subsistence, odor, soil pollution, and agricultural chemicals. There was also a significant increase in the number of antipollution agreements at the local level. In 1969, there were 37, five years later there were 1,113 and by 1984, there were 8,187 such agreements.[28] Japan also started dialogue with its neighbors on the problem of acid rain.

As a response to the 1992 Rio Earth Summit's Agenda 21, the Japanese government revised almost completely the 1967 Basic Law for Environmental Pollution Control and in 1993 parliament passed the New Basic Environment Law. This is intended to form the basic foundation for Japanese environmental laws and policies in the twenty-first century. At the heart of the new basic law is a commitment to sustainable development and international cooperation to meet global environmental demands. This new basic law outlines the environmental responsibilities for all levels of government, industry, and citizens and prescribes the necessary policy instruments to protect the domestic and global environment of Japan. Additionally, a new national requirement for environmental impact assessment is contained in the law, and it outlines a framework for volunteering agreements on pollution reduction. This builds on the 1992 air pollution regulation which attempts to reduce pollution levels by restricting the types of vehicles registered in two major urban areas, Tokyo and Osaka. The new basic law also requests that all corporations comply with mandated standards on pollution reduction and waste disposal. The compliance is voluntary, but large numbers of companies had submitted plans for pollution reduction and waste disposal by 1999. As part of the 1993 legislation, a basic environmental plan was to be produced by 1994. The plan describes the direction of Japan's long-term environmental policy. Basically, the plan calls for the operationalizing of the 1993 basic environment law in statutes and legislation. Thus, within the plan, improvements to social infrastructures, such as sewage and transportation, are detailed. Also, the plan promotes the role of nongovernmental actors, including NGOs, in environmental protection. Finally, it calls for education and wide distribution of information. The plan obliges local authorities in those areas with serious pollution problems to draw up environmental pollution control programs to be approved by the prime minister.

Environmental Impact Assessment (EIA) became law in June 1997; however, its enforcement did not have to occur until 1999. Essentially assessment is self-assessment carried out by the project's operating agency. All assessment is limited to the execution stage of a project and is not carried out in the planning stage as in Britain, Germany, and Sweden. Once projects are in operation they must be reexamined regularly.

The last years of the twentieth century were consumed with the debate over the introduction of a carbon tax. Such a tax is authorized by the new basic law's section on possible economic instruments that could achieve environmental goals. Industry heavily opposes such a tax, arguing it would drive up costs and cause many companies to relocate to areas that are less energy efficient.

Policy Structure and Organization

Local authorities bear the responsibility for much of Japan's environmental policy and in doing so have dictated national policy content. National environmental policy is shaped by local initiatives and often national standards will lag behind local. The chief actor at the national level is the bureaucracy. Bureaucrats both formulate and implement environmental policy in Japan through the Environment Agency. At one time, there was discussion of converting the agency to a ministry; however, this did not materialize because of the demise of the liberal democratic government and the political reforms that resulted.[29] The environmental agency over the years since its creation has developed a good working relationship with industry. As part of the relationship, there is constant dialogue and exchange of information between all relevant public and private institutions and representative bodies. An example of information exchange is the numerous private technical hearings that are held by the agency. In such hearings, industry shares its technical knowledge with the agency. As a result policy is formulated and implemented, often with industry's input. In essence, this process allows environmental targets, such as emission standards, to be viewed as technical problems to be solved by industry and then the solution is backed by agency regulations at agreed appropriate times. Hearings are held almost continuously, so standards and environmental targets are constantly being revised. In sum, an initial hearing means that all relevant information is shared prior to policy formulation and subsequent hearings ensure that implementation is carried out in a workable time frame.

The considerable autonomy of prefectures and metropolitan authorities (local government) in environmental policy has given rise to a flexible regulatory framework with industry playing a prominent part in environmental protection. Prefectures are responsible for ensuring that industries comply with national regulations. In those areas where national regulations are insufficient—the most heavily industrialized areas—prefectures have been given authority to apply their own standards through local ordinances. Additionally local government augments statutory regulations with persuasion and formal contracts. This ensures a good dialogue between policy makers, administrators, and industry.

Local regulation in environmental standard setting is three-tiered. This reflects the dynamics of the relationship between industry and local government. The first tier is recommendations or administrative guidance (*Gyosei Shido*). Such recommendations or guidelines are published as targets. National agencies may also issue these. Information is also circulated that will allow target compliance. The incentive to comply with the target is that there will not be further regulation. In instances where there is not compliance, the second tier of regulation will occur—the local ordinance. Such ordinances have force of law and are promulgated and enforced by the local authorities. The third tier of local authority, environmental regulation, is the contractual agreement. It's a type of voluntary agreement between local authorities and specific corporations or companies involved in large scale developments. Under such agreements, the business agrees to meet environmental standards specifically set for the development. There are often exchanges between local authorities on the type and success of such agreements, which leads to continuity across regions.

The local government regulatory structure is supported by an institutional infrastructure and information collection process at both the local and national levels. Thus, there is a series of environmental advisory bodies, consisting of academics, local bureaucrats, and representatives from national agencies, such as the ministry of finance and the environmental agency. Such bodies advise policy makers through recommendations.

The new basic plan of 1993 has not really affected the powers of local authorities to set local environmental standards. However, there has been one change and that is local efforts now have to conform to the basic environmental plan. There are now national standards which meet global requirements.

Future Outcomes and Policy Weakness

Many argue that Japanese antipollution regulations, especially at the local level, are stricter than equivalent regulations in other nations. It is also argued that Japanese investment in environmental protection is extremely high in comparison to other nations and that negative impacts on economic growth are slight. However, what seems to have occurred in the last decade is structural economic modernization without systematic ecological innovation. In short, the urgency of environmental protection for policy makers is dissipating as Japan battles an increasingly competitive global market. The good fortune for environmental policy makers is that Japanese industry has voluntarily undertaken an active role in environmental protection. Industry understands the ramifications of environmental degradation and has responded quite innovatively. Perhaps industry has been so responsive because they know they cannot escape responsibility; however, their response is truly centered around the knowledge that policies take into account their needs and capacities and thus the costs are manageable. The question is: As global markets become increasingly more competitive and Japan experiences economic downs for long periods of time, how will industry renew its environmental obligations? In short, how long will industry-led voluntary actions be a sufficient basis for a coherent long-term national strategy on the environment?

Sweden: Societal Protection

As would be expected in the "model" welfare state, there has been a strong concern with environmental issues on the part of the Swedish state. This has been accompanied by a strong societal environmental consciousness ensuring that environmentalism is a significant political force. Authors such as Gustafsson and Jamison divide Swedish environmentalism into distinct chronological phases.[30] In each phase, environmental perspectives have evolved and interacted with other societal issues to produce regulatory environmental policy instruments and specific environmental programs. As the new century opens, Sweden clearly sees itself in the forefront of sustainable economic growth.

Policy History and Evolution

In the early part of the twentieth century, traditional interest in the state of natural resources and their preservation can clearly be seen. In the first years of the 1900s, a number of state agencies were established to deal with issues pertaining to the environment. What legislation that existed prior to the 1950s dealt mainly with conservation and public health measures. By the 1950s, it became clear to many Swedes, including policy makers, that industrial emissions were having a damaging effect on the Swedish environment. A number of ordinances were enacted to deal with the curtailment of industrial emissions.

By the start of the 1960s, the national government formed several royal commissions to investigate Sweden's environmental issues, to define the problems facing Sweden, and to recommend possible strategies that could be adopted to meet such problems. The commissions comprised members from all relevant affected interests, political parties, bureaucratic organizations, and scientific communities. This is a classic way of formulating policy in Sweden. By 1963, the government publicly announced its plan to formulate an overall environmental policy once all the commissions had delivered their reports and findings. Thus, in 1965 the Environmental Policy Bill was introduced into parliament by the government. Several commissions had produced their reports prior to the bill's introduction. What is significant about the introduction of the bill is that it preceded any visible public opinion on environmental problems. The Swedish government anticipated future public demands.

The 1965 bill was simply a statement of intent of environmental protection, rather than specific guidelines of regulatory control. The bill acted as a catalyst for Swedish political parties to focus their attention on the environment. From the mid-1960s, all parties adopted environmental platforms and sponsored environmental bills.[31] In 1967, it led to the establishment of the Environmental Protection Board (EPB) within the department of agriculture. With the EPB's creation the entire pollution control administration was reformed. All air and water pollution authorities established in the early 1960s were to be answerable to the EPB, as was the National Conservation Authority. Thus, in one body all of the state agencies and organizations that had previously dealt with environmental problems were brought together. The EPB was the first state environmental agency of its kind in the world. Soon after the EPB's establishment parliament passed the Environmental Protection Law that was conceived by many to be the most vigorous legislation to be found anywhere at the time.[32] The law went into effect in 1969 and stipulated that anyone who intended to engage in activities that would pollute had to take protective measures, which, to the best of their abilities, were technically and economically reasonable. There is no explicit mention of air quality standards or references to public health. The act specifies several types of industries that must obtain permits from either the Franchise Board for Environment Protection or a permit exemption from the National Environmental Protection Board. In both cases, the government is laying out the conditions under which polluting activities can be carried on, as well as the protective measures to be taken. In 1970 source emissions standards were promulgated for the specified industries in the Environmental Protection Act. This allowed the technical and economic feasibility requirements to be determined.

Sustainability was first introduced as a defining concept within Swedish environmental policy in the early 1970s with the enactment of the 1972 National Land-Use Planning Act (FRP). The act dwelt extensively on environmental issues and ecological care. The FRP is not a law in the strictest sense. Rather, it's a set of ecological guidelines for planning authorities in their construction and supervision of housing and building. A year later, Sweden passed its first hazardous products control legislation and set in motion a whole series of local government ordinances governing waste materials. Nuclear power also became a topic of environmental concern as did energy in the late 1970s and early 1980s. Other issues that became part of the environmental agenda in the 1980s were the ozone layer, sustainability, and ecocycles. All such issues were publicized and dealt with by government in a similar manner to the other nations discussed in the text.

The legislation that deals most succinctly with the issue of sustainable development is the 1987 National Resources Act. This act delineates the basic requirements for ecologically, socially and economically sustainable development of the Swedish physical environment. Within the legislation, land and water areas important to certain activities are prescribed, as are certain geographical locations which are considered to have natural and/or cultural values of national interest. Basically the act prescribes the use of land and water in such a way as to support an ecologically, socially and publicly sound economy. Protection of designated areas is delegated to local authorities. Additional demands are made on local authorities by government bill 1990/91 environmental policy. This bill requires all municipalities to include environmental concerns in all of their activities. Subsequent acts and regulations determine more precise tasks for local authorities in the environmental arena. The laws are considered frameworks, and thus municipalities are left to interpret and translate national policy into local decisions. Municipalities are also required to make plans for local energy needs and handling of waste.[33] Since 1991, all municipalities must produce environmental impact assessments (MKB) to accompany their energy and waste management plans. Such plans are intended to aid the national government in achieving environmental goals, such as promoting recycling, decreasing the quantity of waste, and reduction of hazards associated with waste.

To formalize government goals parliament enacted government bill 1992/93, No. 180 dealing with ecocyclical development. With this bill, the government introduced the German model of producer responsibility that covers products even when they are no longer in use. The legislation also sets levels of recycling and targets for reuse of various packaging materials to be reduced by January 1997. With ecological sustainable development clearly accepted as Sweden's overall objective, parliament introduced new environmental quality goals in 1998. All goals are to be achieved by 2020 to 2025 and are framed as general targets. In order to achieve the targets, each public sector's central authorities, county administrative boards, and local authorities must present detailed goals and strategies to fulfill the general targets within their own field of activity by the end of 2000. To help facilitate this process, a new environmental code came into effect in January 1999. The basic premises of the code are that energy and other natural resources are to be used more efficiently; materials are to be reused or recycled; social, economic, and technical development is to be directed toward low-resource products and methods; pollution emissions are to be no greater than people or nature can tolerate; biological diversity is to be safeguarded; harmful substances alien to nature will have no place in the environment; and valuable cultural environments are to be preserved. Over the next five years, specific actions to meet these goals will be determined by all the responsible authorities. The new code replaces fifteen separate environmental laws. The government argued that the existing laws were poorly implemented because in many instances laws conflicted with each other. The new code applies to the total environment and its related activities, regardless of whether or not a permit is required. In the event of environmental damage being caused, it's up to the individual who caused it to actually prove that due consideration was shown in accordance with environmental rules. This represents a major change as previously there was no burden of proof.

Policy Structure and Organization

Sweden's environmental policy has certain principles enshrined in law. First, there is the "polluter pays principle." Thus, whoever causes environmental damage is responsible for remedying the problem. Next, reusable energy sources are the nation's first priority, and all materials, if possible, are to be reused or recycled. Third, if environmental quality standards are needed, they may be introduced whenever the government feels the time is right. If standards are in force, all local authority environmental plans must meet them. Fourth, environmental impact assessment must be carried out prior to the execution of large-scale projects. Permission will only be granted if such assessment is carried out and proves to have no impact on health and natural resources. Where government owns land that contains an ecosystem or type of landscape that should be preserved, then the government may designate such areas as national parks. Additionally local authorities may designate certain areas as natural reserves. All coasts, rivers, and lakes have shoreline regulations. No development of any kind is permitted within three hundred meters of the waterline. Next, all processes that have emissions are defined as environmentally hazardous, and permits must be obtained for the processes to occur.

Waste management is now under the control of local authorities. Each authority has complete autonomy to manage waste as they see fit. However, each authority must have a plan outlining the amounts and types of waste and what's being done to reduce the flow. Any waste that is the legal responsibility of the producer must be taken care of by that producer. Finally, permissions to perform certain tasks or activities are subject to permit or license. Such licensing is for limited periods of time and subject to review. The environmental code also has strict penalties for breach of any environmental regulation. Previously those found guilty of gross negligence had charges and penalties imposed against them. Now it is possible to punish those guilty of negligence. Any manufacturer who disregards procedures, license agreements, or permit rules is required to pay an environmental sanction charge. This can be in addition to other penalties. Victims of environmental damage may seek damages from those who produced or caused the damage. New insurance policies must be taken by those in environmentally hazardous activities to cover the possible damage, claims and cleanup costs.

Economic incentives/disincentives have been part of Swedish environmental policy since the 1970s. Thus, a number of new taxes and charges have been introduced in the last few years. For example, taxes on sulphur, nitrogen oxide, fuel and petrol, pesticides, deposits on bottles and batteries, and from 2000 a new tax on waste have been imposed. Data shows that most of these economic incentives/disincentives have had the desired effect.[34] Revenues from such charges are used to finance environmental and nature conservancy measures.

In Swedish environmental policy, three governmental levels are involved in planning. The central government and its agencies draw up national goals and then formulate legislative and administrative measures to achieve such goals. The second level is county administration, which has the task of coordinating and initiating regional efforts. Additionally they encourage and review all local efforts. Municipalities are the third level of government and also the most important unit for public environmental planning. Since the late 1980s through several new legislative and national policy directives, Swedish municipals have been delegated increased responsibility for environmental policy implementation.[35]

Decentralization and sectionalization are important features of Swedish environmental policy administration and organization. There are differences between geographical areas in the way environmental issues are handled by governing municipalities. For example, in large municipalities environmental issues are usually administered by a separate section for environment and health while in smaller municipalities environmental issues are handled by a section that handles other matters. Often there will be cooperation between municipalities that border each other. This is especially true in air and water quality management, nature conservation, and waste management. Cooperation may take many forms. The most common is partnership between companies dealing with collection and treatment of waste. Because environmental issues impact a large number of policy sectors, many municipalities have developed specific units to coordinate environmental matters cross-sectionally. In sum, local authorities have supervisory powers in many areas of the environment and are responsible for developing and pursuing national environmental quality goals.

At the national level of government, the ministry of environment is the main unit responsible for environmental issues. The ministry is responsible for environment protection, nature conservancy, air and water quality, biological diversity, ecocycle programs, waste management, building and physical planning, chemicals control, nuclear power safety programs and radiation protection. The ministry can administer financial incentives in the environmental policy field. The central administrative agency for environmental protection is the Swedish Environmental Protection Agency. Under the agency's supervision national and international environmental efforts are coordinated. All environmental knowledge and information are compiled and disseminated by the agency. Additionally, they propose new targets, strategies, and controls for policy programs. In the last decade, the agency is also responsible for evaluating existing programs and monitoring the state of the environment. Finally, the agency implements government and parliamentary policy decisions through collaboration with other agencies, local authorities, industry and business, and voluntary organizations.

The national government currently allocates $100 million on environmental improvements. Most local government expenditure is raised through revenues from taxes and charges on environmental activities. The majority of the national government expenditures are on adapting national programs to environmental requirements. The bulk of local government expenditure is on waste management and recycling.

Future Outcomes and Policy Weakness

On the whole, Swedish environmental policy has been successful in achieving its goals and objectives. For example, measures to curb industrial emissions have been successful. The challenge in the upcoming years is to socialize consumers into more ecological social lifestyles. Consumption constantly grows, and thus waste grows. Such waste will soon prove harmful to soil and water. Increased traffic flow and large cars devour the profits from better exhaust emission control and cleaner fuel. There is also growing dependence on energy as a result of increased automation. Control of industrial damage to the environment is under control. Now it's time to better regulate societal damage. Only then will sustainability be achieved in a timely fashion.

United States: How Much Government Intervention?

Environmental issues are one of the items at the forefront of the American policy agenda. Opinion polls regularly demonstrate that the majority of citizens are concerned over degradation of the environment and that government needs to be more responsive to environmental protection.[36] Compounding these feelings is constant media exposure of urgent environmental problems. The dilemma for policy makers and the American public is that environmental protection requires regulation of behavior—more government intervention and interference in people's daily lives. How that dilemma plays out determines how American environmental policy is formulated and implemented.

Policy History and Evolution

Concern with the environment in the United States is not a late twentieth-century phenomenon. Indeed, conservation and problems caused by regional urbanization were matters of public concern by the late 1800s. However, the first real government commitment to environmental activities did not occur until the depression; the Roosevelt administration established new federal agencies to oversee specific resources.[37]

Environmental policy making prior to the mid-1960s was fragmented and characterized by limited numbers of participants and incremental bargaining and compromise. There was no consistent presidential commitment, and policy formulation was the prerogative of a few congressmen. All of this changed in 1963 after the first real piece of legislation was enacted in the environmental policy arena. The Clean Air Act of 1963 was supported and passed by John F. Kennedy and the Democrat-controlled Congress. The Act was strongly opposed by corporate lobbies and was generally a weak piece of legislation. The enforcement procedure was too complicated, in that it required state action to initiate lawsuits against polluters. Further acts passed in the 1960s which attempted to protect the environment were, for example, the 1965 Water Quality Act, the 1966 Endangered Species Conservation Act, and the 1967 Air Quality Act. Such acts established standards and made federal grants available to states that wished to comply.

The end of the 1960s and the beginning of the 1970s saw the launching of a national environmental policy with the passing in 1969 and enactment in 1970 of the National Environmental Policy Act (NEPA). This legislation provides the foundation for future policy action and activity in environmental policy. One of the main provisions within the act is the requirement that all major federal construction must complete Environmental Impact Statements (EIS). Such statements must show a government project to not significantly impact the environment. If the EIS shows to the contrary, and if damage is done, procedures and mechanisms are in place to correct that damage. Why such a flurry of environmental policy activity in the mid- and late-1960s? The answer lies in the growth of environmental interest groups, renewed congressional interest, and environmental crises such as offshore oil spills in California.

The 1970s began with the creation of the Environmental Protection Agency (EPA) in 1970. The agency was created by Richard Nixon through executive order and given the job of coordinating and enforcing all environmental laws. Prior to its establishment, several agencies across several federal departments were responsible for monitoring and regulating the environment. Nixon's action was surprising to many considering he had originally been opposed to activist environmental legislation. However, his "new" interest sparked congressional interest and the result was the passing of a series of laws in the early 1970s. The first was the 1970 Clean Air Act, which set national standards for ambient air quality through NAAQS (National Standards Ambient Air Quality). Each state was to develop plans to meet NAAQS requirements, which the EPA was to approve. If any state plan did not meet federal requirements, the EPA was authorized to prepare and enforce a plan for the state.

Additionally, the EPA was mandated to set exhaust emission standards for the auto industry and develop plans for the introduction of catalytic converters and fuels with reduced lead levels. Other acts, such as the Federal Environmental Pesticide Control Act of 1972, the Federal Water Pollutants Control Act Amendments of 1972, the Resource Conservation and Recovery Act of 1976, and the Toxic Substances Control Act of 1976 soon followed. The magnitude and scope of such legislation are impressive, and each provided in some way federal support of environmental protection. For example, the 1972 Water Pollution Control Act sets targets for the amount of discharged pollutants in navigable waters to be achieved by 1985. It also provides $23 billion in grants to local governments to construct water treatment plants and install best available technologies by 1983. Through other legislation such as the 1976 Resource Conservation and Recovery Act, the regulation of hazardous waste storage is mandated, and the EPA is given authority to establish hazardous waste disposal standards. However, many of these acts were weakened by the requirement that state and local government compliance had to be sought by the EPA. The EPA simply did not have the resources, including manpower, to enforce compliance.

The net result of the 1970s frenzy of environmental legislation is it gave rise to a strong industry and business coalition opposing pro-environmentalism. Many critics argued environmental protection was helping to increase costs and inflation and thus was responsible for slowing economic growth. The burden on business was too large. Compliance to strict environmental regulations increased costs and thereby damaged profits. Subsequent strong presidential involvement in the formulation of environmental policy can also be attributed to Nixon's creation of the EPA. During Jimmy Carter's tenure in office, superficial legislation was adopted in 1980 which set aside approximately $1.6 billion in emergency funds to deal with environmental spills or dumping. It also allowed the EPA to shift its emphasis from conventional pollutants and increased the agency's budget by 25 percent.

By the time Ronald Reagan was elected to the White House, it was clear that business complaints about excessive environmentalism had been heard. Reagan argued that there was no need for additional legislation. He argued for "reasonable" environmentalism and that bureaucrats had gone crazy and exceeded their authority. In essence too much government, too much regulation, was anti-business and anti-growth. Thus, Reagan's policy agenda focused on reducing government regulation and reversing the federal government's role in environmental protection. The Reagan years meant reduced budgets for implementating environmental policy, repeal of legislation pertaining to the environment passed in the previous administration, and the appointment of policy makers who were anti-environment.[38] This led to hundreds of dismissals of EPA staff, many of whom were environmental law attorneys. Additionally, the entire staff of the President's Council on Environmental Quality was fired.

The key way in which the Reagan administration planned to foil environmental protection was through the introduction of cost-benefit analysis in environmental policy design. Any new EPA regulation had to submit to a cost-benefit analysis. Publicly the government claimed that it was attempting to ensure that any money spent on proposed regulation would result in increased benefits rather than increased costs to taxpayers. The problem is there are many issues, and environmental protection is one of them, where the dollar costs will always seem to be higher than the benefits, because a dollar amount cannot be assigned to the benefits of environmental esthetics or increased life span for both endangered species and humans. Most new environmental regulation failed the cost-benefit test and thus Reagan achieved his objective of promoting industrial growth through reduced regulation of the environment.

By 1988, public concern was strongly in favor of environmental protection and environmental interest groups had become quite militant. This forced or, let us say, encouraged George Bush to make environmental policy a key issue in his 1988 campaign for the presidency. He told voters he wanted to be known as the "environmental president." He delivered somewhat on his promise, although it can hardly be argued that he can be characterized as an activist environmental president. In terms of legislation, two major pieces of legislation were passed: the 1990 Clean Air Act Amendments and the 1992 Energy Policy Act. Bush originally proposed clean air legislation; however, it was much weaker than what congress wanted. The act that was passed in 1990 and signed by Bush was closer to congressional desires and thus had much stricter and costly regulations imposed on industry. The act mandates that air quality throughout the United States meets certain standards. This was to be achieved by reducing emissions from industrial processes and cars, including those pollutants that cause acid rain. Finally, the act also introduced standards for phasing out chemicals that attack the ozone layer. Additionally Bush approved an increase in the EPA's budget and supported areas of America's coastline being declared off-limits for oil exploration. However, his refusal to at first support an environmental treaty produced at the 1992 Rio Earth Summit until its provisions aimed at slowing global warming were modified and weakened and his refusal to sign a treaty protecting endangered species created much opposition to him by environmental groups.

The 1992 presidential election pitted Bush against two Democrats he labeled as "environmental crazies." Clinton and his vice-presidential candidate, Al Gore, perceived there was general dissatisfaction with Bush on the environment and criticized the president for not being committed to controlling environmental damage and allocating minimal funds to environmental cleanup and protection. Bill Clinton promised to reverse the record on environmental protection while Al Gore promised that being tough on environmental protection did not mean being tough on business.[39]

Clinton and Gore did attempt to balance the demands of economic growth while protecting the environment from increased damage. Many would argue that this has meant being too generous to business and not producing tougher environmental legislation.[40] The Clinton administration focused its environmental policy efforts mostly on more generous funding of environmental mandates and making the system less bureaucratically rigid. Additionally, major change in the leadership of all the main environmental agencies involved in formulating and implementing policy was completed by Clinton's first year in office. A number of measures have been implemented that have toughened standards; however, for the most part Clinton's environmental policy agenda was frustrated by a Republican-controlled congress determined to reduce federal government regulation. The one major piece of legislation that the Clinton administration managed to enact was the 1996 law introducing stronger protection for infants and children against pesticide contamination.

The last years of Clinton's second administration pushed the idea of cost-effective environmental reform. The success of the Clinton administration was to shift the focus of environmental initiation from congress to the White House. This was symbolized by his replacement of the council of environmental quality with the White House office on environmental policy and support of cabinet status for the EPA as a department of the environment.

Policy Organization and Administration

American environmental policy making has been predominantly incremental and adaptive because of the necessity of majority building in the American policy process. With the creation of the EPA in 1970, the federal government committed itself to be the prime level of environmental regulation. For many years congress was the major institution responsible for formulating policy within the environmental arena; however, the last decade has witnessed decreased congressional leadership in formulation. Kraft argues this is understandable given congressional "gridlock" and lack of progressive sentiments generally on Capital Hill.[41] Authors such as Switzer argue congress simply failed to lead the environmental agenda-setting process and thus lost the initiative in formulating policy.[42] She cites, among the reasons for such failure, the fragmented committee system, congressional members being cross-pressured from pro-business and pro-environment lobbies, insufficient resources such as time and expertise, and finally a concern with the "local" rather than the "national."[43] The states have increasingly become policy initiators and formulators and have taken much of this function away from the federal government.[44] The response of particular state governments to environmental issues is dictated by factors such as severity of environmental damage, urbanization levels, fiscal resource base, who controls the state legislature, and the prevalence of professional legislators and administrators.[45] Additionally, the level of an individual state's environmental interest groups and strength of industry will affect state government responses.

In terms of implementation, federal and state governments share responsibility, often with state governments having to comply with federal regulations. Implementation by the federal government is usually through the EPA. Generally local governments play a minor role in implementing current regulations. The exception to this would be in areas where the environmental movement is visibly strong, such as the Western states.[46] In such areas many times local policy makers are pressured into implementing stricter rules than required by the state or federal policy makers.

Future Outcomes and Policy Weakness

The United States has pioneered environmental policy development, first through command-and-control measures and later through voluntary and market-based approaches. The United States has been one of the most active nations in developing and complying with global environmental agreements. Thus, the United States is a nation with extensive experience in the environmental policy sector. Policies are not always successful, but compared to many other nations, America has a strong record of commitment. Part of the reason for this record is that the United States has a set of well-developed institutions responsible for implementing environmental policies. What allows one policy to be successful and another environmental policy to be a failure is not exactly clear. However, future success is more likely to be achieved by policies that are based in a sound socioeconomic and ecological context. Such policies should understand their ramifications over time, their interactions across geographical areas, and the interests of the various stakeholders, from community to business. It appears that in all likelihood the United States will continue to deal with the environment through policy that takes into account cost-effectiveness, voluntary action, and consensus building. Such policy will allow for flexibility and more public-private partnerships. Public-private partnerships are crucial to the American perception of sustainable development. It seems more than likely that sustainable development principally will be responsible for creating objectives, targets, and strategies for environmental policy.

The costs of environmental protection and its role in government budget deficits will continue to emphasize the notion that government must be accountable through cost-effective measures. The need for new types of environmental policy will continue, and policies that were passed in the last years of the twentieth century will more than likely be the path taken in the first decade of the new century. There will be more tax incentives to phase out environmentally damaging activities, such as ozone-deflecting substances, business will more than likely be asked to publicly articulate its activities that harm the environment, and there will be increased emphasis on performance reporting and subsidization to various sectors, such as agriculture, to create incentives to comply with environmental consciousness.

Suggested Further Readings

S.J. Anderson, "The Policy Process and Social Policy in Japan," *Political Science and Politics,* vol. 25, Mar. 1992, pp. 36–49.

R.J. Berry, *Environmental Dilemmas* (New York: Chapman & Hill, 1993).

S. Bowles and H. Gintes, *Schooling in Capitalist America* (New York: Basic Books, 1976).

J.K. Bracs, "Welfare Reform and the Race to the Bottom: Theory and Endure," *Southern Economic Journal,* vol. 66, no. 3, 2000, pp. 505–512.

P.M. Burnes and I.G. Barnes, *Environmental Policy in the European Union* (Cheltenham: Edward Elgar, 1999).

H. Cavanna, *Challenges to the Welfare State* (Cheltenham: Edward Elgar, 1998).

J.E. Chubb and T.M. Moe, *Politics, Markets, and American Schools* (Washington: Brookings Institution, 1990).

L. Darling-Hammond, "Best Schools for Student Success," *Daedalus,* vol. 124 (4), Fall 1995, p. 153.

A. Deacon, "The Green Paper on Welfare Reform: A Case for Enlightened Self Interests," *Political Quarterly*, vol. 69, July/Sept. 1998, pp. 306–320.

G. Esping-Andersen (ed.), *The Welfare State in Transition* (London: Sage, 1996).

G. Esping-Andersen, *The Three Worlds of Welfare Capitalism* (Cambridge: Policy Press, 1990).

V.E. Faria, L.S. Graham, and R.H. Wilson, *Policymaking in a Redemocratized Brazil*, vols. 1 & 2 (Austin: University of Texas Press, 1997).

H. Flippo, *The German Way* (Berlin: Passport Books, 1997).

F.C. Fowler, "What They Don't Tell Us About European Schools," *The Clearing House*, vol. 70, p. 13, September 1996.

R.B. Freeman, B. Swendentors, and R. Topel, *The Welfare State in Transition* (Chicago: University of Chicago Press, 1997).

N. Ginshing, *Divisions of Welfare* (Newly Park: Sage, 1992).

A. Gould, *Comparative Welfare Systems: A Comparative Analysis of Japan, Britain, Sweden* (New York: Addison-Wesley, 1994).

T. Gray (ed.), *UK Environmental Policy in the 1990's* (London: Macmillan, 1995).

R.B. Helms (ed.), *Health Care Policy and Politics: Lessons From Four Countries* (Washington: AEI Press, 1993).

A. Hicks and D. Swank, "Politics, Institutions, and Welfare Spending in Industrialized Democracies, 1900–1982," *ASPR* 86, (3) 1999, pp. 658–674.

A. Jameson, R. Eyerman, and J. Craner, *The Making of the New Environmental Con* (Edinburgh: Edinburgh University Press, 1990).

D. John, "Environmental Policy and Policy Reforms," *International Political Science Association*, Proceedings, Seoul, 17–21 August, 1997.

H.D. Klingemann, R.I. Hofferbert, and I. Bridge, *Parties, Policies and Democracy* (Boulder: Western, 1994).

J. Miles and J. Quadagno, "Envisioning a Third Way: The Welfare State in the Twenty-First Century," *Contemporary Sociology*, vol. 29, no. 1, Jan. 2000, pp. 156–170.

E. Overlye, "Convergence in Policy Outcomes: Social Security System in Perspective," *Journal of Public Policy*, 14 (2), 1994, pp. 127–174.

S.J. Pharr and R.D. Putman (eds.), *Disaffected Democracies* (Princeton: Princeton University Press, 2000).

P. Pierson, "Fragmented Welfare States: Federal Institutions and the Development of Social Policy," *Governance*, 8 (4), pp. 449–478, 1995.

F. Powell and A.F. Wessen, *Health Care Systems in Transition: An International Perspective* (London: Sage, 1999).

D. Seedhouse, *Reforming Health Care: The Philosophy and Practice of International Health Reform* (New York: Wiley & Sons, 1995).

S. Steinmo, "Why is Government So Small in Arena?" *Governance*, 8 (3), pp. 303–334, 1995.

S. Tsuru, *The Political Economy of the Environment* (London: Athlone Press, 1999).

PART IV

PUTTING THE PIECES TOGETHER: SIMILARITIES AND DIFFERENCES ACROSS NATIONS

Chapter Thirteen
Are Nations Similar or Not?

In this chapter, the education, environment, health, and social welfare policy sectors are compared across the six discussed nations. It is clear from a cursory examination of the comparative policy literature that nations face similar problems which differ in severity. The feasibility of chosen policy solutions also differs from nation to nation. Authors such as Martin Harrop acknowledge growing interdependence between nations and increasingly how nations suffer common or similar problems.[1] However, the same authors argue that there is not necessarily a convergence of policy solutions.[2] National policy makers formulate and implement solutions that respond to their individual electoral pressures. From the discussion of education, environment, health, and social welfare in Japan, Germany, Britain, Brazil, Sweden, and the United States, it is possible to conclude that each nation shares common problems and have supported similar policy instruments to deal with them. Admittedly, although solutions are broadly similar, they do vary in substance.

What all the nations discussed in this text share is that the approach taken by policy makers depends on cultural attitudes and values. Additionally, policy in one area is affected by policy in another area. What seems to occur is nations develop solutions that are very similar but differ in the role government plays in defining the services provided, the amount spent, and the priority given to a particular policy solution. Each policy sector will now be discussed individually so similarities and differences may be identified.

Social Welfare Policy and the Six Nations

Analysis shows that all six nations have implemented similar general social welfare systems with a diversity of welfare outcomes and variance in the stability of arrangements under increasing pressures. All share similar pressures, such as economic recession and inadequate sources of revenue to reform existing practices. Government responses to social problems can be categorized as one of three types. The first is to retreat from meeting the needs of citizens, in particular the needs of the less well-off and disadvantaged. In doing so the state redirects social responsibility to the market or family or community. All six nations have experienced periods of sudden redirection. In the United States and Britain, the retreat has been much stronger than in the rest.

The second type of response is government is seen to be the last resort. Here, before government plays a role in provision, the resources of family, local community, and the private sector should be exhausted or be shown to be inadequate. Abrahamson refers to this as a "welfare triangle" model.[3] State, market, and civil society are the three principal providers of welfare. Such a response can also be seen in all six nations depending upon the time period. However, what occurs is that different nations drift toward different corners of the triangle in emphasis. For example, in Britain, Germany, and the United States, the market and state have been emphasized; in Sweden, state and market; in Japan, society is first and the state the last resort, although a willing one. In Brazil the order is society, state, and market. From the analysis, it is clear that as the importance of civil society declines the shift will be toward the market in social welfare provision. Some authors argue this is an inevitable part of modernization.[4]

The third type of response is investment in physical and information technology infrastructures. This can be found in all the nations with the exception of Brazil in the latter part of the 1990s. It is perceived that such investment will improve the effectiveness of the welfare image and bring out a general improvement in people's quality of life through creating and stimulating economic growth, employment opportunities and new markets internally and externally. Such investment requires welfare investment in training and employment opportunities. Esping-Andersen argues manufacturing can no longer provide mass employment. At the same time, high-quality service jobs such as banking, teaching, and middle management are diminishing in quantity. The choice, Esping-Andersen argues, is for private-sector junk jobs, requiring little skill or employment in state-led social service sector expansion.[5]

When each response is utilized by a government, its supporters always justify it on the grounds of the impact of state activity on economic performance. However, the literature offers no compelling evidence to suggest that one response is better than another.[6] What it does show is that each of the six nations mixes the three types of response in different proportions in different policy regulations.[7]

The six nations in this text offer contrasts between different political tendencies, levels of economic development and success, labor market orientations, higher and lower levels of social protection and welfare spending, and between a Bismarckian or

Beveridgean approach to welfare policy. The nations also represent different political traditions and orientations. When the nations are looked at in terms of levels of welfare spending, Sweden and Germany spend substantially more than the others, with Britain and Japan following and then the United States and Brazil.[8] Sweden and Britain follow the Beveridgean approach while Germany, Japan, and the United States follow the Bismarckian. Brazil at present has tendencies to integrate both the Bismarckian and Beveridgean approaches, perhaps due to its economic uncertainties.

All nations have had periods of right-wing governments committed to a minimalist state with a limited range of responsibilities. Of course, the notion of "right wing" varies from nation to nation. In Brazil, the right has been represented by authoritarian governments for long periods of time committed to preserving the status quo and repressing social equality. In Germany and Sweden, center-right coalitions in the 1980s and 1990s remained strongly committed to state welfare and its system of social protection and argued for the system to be more cost-effective through the introduction of market forces. In Britain and the United States, radical neo-conservative governments ruled in the 1980s and massive welfare-state retrenchment occurred. In the 1990s, although left of center parties have been elected in both nations, they have chosen centrist welfare policies committed to the market's role in welfare provision and investment in technology and education to bring employment opportunities rather than welfare dependency. In Japan, general societal acceptance of family and community responsibility have allowed for less than generous welfare provision.

All six nations have similar challenges in the new century. They face demographic changes, including the aging of their populations; labor market changes, which could cause unemployment and sub-employment, which both increase the need for social benefits and question the Bismarckian model of social insurance through employment; economic shifts from the pressures of national competitiveness in global markets; pressures on national budgets from recession, increases in interest rates, and high national debts; changes in family infrastructures, such as high teenage pregnancy rates, increases in single-parent families, the shrinking of the nuclear family; and finally social changes stemming from the continuing problems of past modern society. These challenges manifest themselves differently and at different levels in each of the six nations. However, in one way or another they all face them.

Sweden has low levels of debt, unemployment and poverty, very high proportions of elderly, and large numbers of one-parent families. The nation provides benefits at higher levels than the other five nations, thus the burden will be immense in future decades. The resources of the 1980s and the 1990s have shown Swedes that they are no longer assured of economic security. Uncertainty about the "Swedish Social Democratic model" will continue as the new century progresses.

Germany has experienced rising levels of unemployment and poverty, although not high if compared to Brazil. There are large numbers of one-parent families and an increasing aging population. Reunification has caused fiscal pressures and strong economic burdens. Providing for the needs of those not integrated into full-time employment will become more taxing as the twenty-first century progresses.

In Great Britain, demographic pressures are decreasing but are still very strong. Unemployment rates were once very high but are now declining and are average compared to other European nations. The number of single-parent families is extremely high, and many of them live under the poverty line. Fiscal pressures are moderate compared to the 1980s but are still prevalent. The shifts established in the early 1990s and consolidated by "new Labour" in the latter years of the decade have made for more compassionate social welfare provision, and this has reduced fiscal burdens. Britain's social welfare is no longer state-funded but state-assisted.

Brazil has an extremely high poverty rate, a high proportion of single-parent families, and extraordinary numbers of groups eligible and in need of entitlements and provisions. The demographic position is still favorable, but the birth rate is high, as is unemployment. The government carries a large burden of debt. Without doubt the Brazilian welfare system will experience the most challenges and the most difficulties in providing adequate provision unless major change and reform is initiated.

The United States faces growing numbers of elderly, low unemployment rates, high numbers of single parents, increasing numbers of poor, and moderate fiscal pressures. Japan faces an extremely high proportion of elderly, rising unemployment rates, severe fiscal pressures, a low number of single-parent families, and low debt.

In terms of policy responses and outcomes, common trends can be seen among the six nations. All nations have experienced cuts in benefits and cost containment. All have attempted to decentralize responsibility and reform the managerial infrastructure of welfare provision. Market-oriented reforms have also been introduced, in particular in Sweden and Britain. Also common is increasing privatization in certain areas of social benefits. All nations have converged in the promotion of pension schemes over state pensions. However, only in two nations has there been a regime shift in welfare philosophy: Britain and the United States. However, Sweden in the late 1990s also shifted the basis of its pension scheme. In Britain the move has been toward welfare minimalism. The United States, which has always provided a minimal provision of welfare, has abandoned the welfare safety net, which represents a radical departure from New Deal and Great Society social welfare philosophy.

For the most part, the discussion of social welfare provision reflects a convergence in state responses. However, it is too early to determine whether the six nations will continue to converge on the same path. Individual economic stability will determine this. The discussion shows that politics does matter in determining policy outcomes. In all nations with the exception of Brazil, right-wing conservative ideology and government has become more prevalent. Policy outcomes over the last two decades in the social welfare sector may be understood as a market-oriented restructuring of the welfare system in response to growing conservative ideological viewpoints amongst policy makers, elected officials and voters. In Brazil, the changes in social welfare provision are also determined by politics. Here the drive has been to offer Brazilians entitlements that are due to all individuals living in a democracy. So the evidence points to politics having an impact and thus making a difference. Perhaps what we should now argue is that policy convergence has been brought about by ideological convergence and not purely economic factors. Social welfare policy in the six nations displays a pattern of retrenchment and restriction of welfare in the face of the challenges posed to each nation over the last twenty years.

Health Policy and the Six Nations

From the discussion of the six nations there is obviously variation in the type of involvement by government in health care provision. Governmental intervention ranges from minimal responsibility in the case of the United States and Brazil to complete responsibility in the case of Sweden and Great Britain. The discussion shows that each nation's health policy outcomes are a result of its institutional economic status. As Roemer argues, no health system is static.[9] From the discussion, the role of political ideology as a determinant of a health care system outcome can also be seen. The United States can be judged to be a pluralistic health care model with no universal coverage. Germany, Japan, Sweden, and Brazil are examples of nationalized health insurance models. Such schemes have universal coverage, but it is a fee-for-service system in which doctors remain independent professionals with all fees covered by national insurance. The ownership of hospitals is both private and public; the level and type of insurance funding vary in each nation. Britain falls into a national health service model which, for the most part, is a state-owned system of hospitals where specialists are salaried and primary care physicians are contracted for and paid on a per capita basis for each patient.

All nations discussed are searching for growth of markets in health care provision. They all share a similar reason for the search: the increasingly high costs of health care provision. A common theme among all the nations is that no matter the cost-containment strategy the level of governmental involvement in the provision of health care is affected. As costs escalate the move in all nations, with the exceptions of Sweden and Germany, is to make health care more a private than a public good.

Using a typology designed by Roemer the United States can be classified as an entrepreneurial and permissive health system; Germany, Japan, and Brazil can be classified as welfare health systems, and Sweden and Great Britain as universal and comprehensive systems.[10] The classification is based on the assumption that political ideologies and economic levels are the major determinants of a health care system.

Each nation's government has played a role in varying degrees of involvement in health care policy making. Sweden's health care supervisory authority, the National Board of Health and Welfare (NBHW), is one extreme where the national government is involved at every level of policy making. The NBHW oversees all health service personnel, evaluates health care quality and has the authority to force changes in physician and hospital procedures. In Japan, the ministry of health, the

Koseisho, controls all health care decisions and policy making. Similar to the Swedish NBHW, it has the power to dictate and enforce all policies. Germany, much like Great Britain and the United States, possesses a policy-making process by committee. Rather than the complete responsibility of developing health care policy falling on the government's shoulders, a multitude of actors join the process, including the medical professionals, hospital professionals, insurance companies, pharmaceutical companies, advisory groups, and unions. This is not to say that in Sweden and Japan nongovernmental groups are not influential; they are, but not to the extent that such groups are in Germany, Britain, and the United States.

The trend in all nations is to allow more group involvement in the health policy-making process. Every nation is confronted with rising costs, diminishing resources, aging populations, and frustrated health care professionals. Attempts to solve the problems of funding and less than sufficient care has led to the incorporation of all groups in society. Again, the role of such groups varies from nation to nation. In Sweden, Japan, and Germany, the role is advisory; in Great Britain, it's influential; while in the United States and Brazil, the role is dominating. Indeed in Brazil, the involvement of "other" actors has led to widespread corruption and fraud. Many individuals are concerned about the power of insurance companies in the United States and the intentional deflection of health care policy from the federal government to the individual states. It is argued that this has created serious problems such as accountability for health care service provision.

It may not be a coincidence that the nations with the strongest commitment to health care and the longest tradition in providing care to citizens have systems structured in a manner in which the state possesses much control. In Germany, Sweden, and Japan, the health care infrastructure is overseen by a governmental agency. The German health care system, which has remained virtually intact since its inception in the late-nineteenth century, is divided into different levels, each with their own responsibilities and level of autonomy. The heavy influence of the German national government is shown by the enactment of the Structural Reform Act of 1993. This legislation reaffirmed Germany's commitment and dedication to providing the most effective and productive delivery of health care as well as emphasizing the state's authority. Great Britain's National Health Service (NHS) has, over the last decades, increasingly become more influenced by political as well as economic actors. However, it has maintained its authority despite restructuring in the 1970s and 1980s. Such reforms were attempts to improve delivery, efficiency, and communication between the different levels of health care providers.

Health care organization in Japan, Sweden, Germany, and Great Britain is administered on various levels to maximize efficiency, productivity and to add a sense of "community" to the system. In the United States, health care provision is also on many levels, but unlike the other nations, the national government delegates great authority to individual states and entrusts responsibility to private companies. Brazil, also, has attempted to delegate the state's health care responsibilities. However, the system has been engulfed with a wave of corruption and fraud that has destroyed the level of trust Brazilians have in the health care process.

All of these nations finance their health care system similarly. In fact, each nation relies on a combination of public and private funds to finance health care provision. Taxes (income, social security, property, corporate and sales), subsidies, and grants predominate public financing, whereas private revenues are gathered through individuals' contributions including deductibles and payment fees for pharmaceuticals and other services. Government expenditures depend greatly on tradition but more importantly on economic stability. The difference between these nations lies in the amount of GDP allocated for health care and the percentage of private versus public contribution.[11] The United States, which possesses the least commitment to public health care, spends the greatest amount of its GDP on providing health care to its citizens. However, 60 percent of total health care expenditures are provided by private revenues. In Germany, only 7 percent of total health expenditures come from private contributions and nearly 60 percent of health care is financed through payroll deductions administered by the sickness funds. In Japan, only 20 percent of expenditures are from private contributions. The trend in health care financing is to move to an "American" model which relies more heavily on private contributions and emphasizes less taxes and government subsidies.

The pressure on government to provide and fund health care increases as costs rise, as new technology and procedures become essential to maintaining care and expertise, and the demand for better treatment grows. Since the 1970s, each nation has begun to experience such problems. Great Britain, Sweden, Germany, Japan and Brazil have all started to incorporate private insurance into the system. It has become crucial for nations such as Brazil to embrace privatization in the health care sector so costs may be controlled and competition stimulated. In the traditional public health systems of Germany, Sweden, Japan, and Great Britain, problems have arisen when privatization occurs. Many argue that privatization will force public provision to be "better" as it competes with the private sector.

The future outlook for public health care provision in the six nations does not look "healthy." In each nation, the obstacles and pressures in maintaining an educated, modern, sufficiently funded, and efficient health care system has become greater and more difficult to overcome. Each nation has its own particular difficulty in raising funds as well as controlling costs. The move toward privatization means less control by government and more influence by the private sector, which functions by placing focus on the bottom line, profits. The question remains at what cost will this be to the general good health of citizens.

Education Policy and the Six Nations

From the discussion of education policy in the six nations, it is obvious that some nations are doing better than others, but that all nations are facing similar problems in the delivery and quality of education provided by the public sector. It seems apparent that in those nations such as the United States where funding is highly decentralized, there are undoubtedly regional inequalities. All nations pay lip service to holding education in high esteem, but fail to appropriate sufficient funding. Most of the nations, with the exception of the United States, provide vocational training for adolescents who are not bound for higher education. All nations have flirted with introducing market forces, indeed some more than others—for example, Great Britain. The pattern is clear: When there are public expenditure crises, rising economic difficulties, and rising unemployment, the move is toward education expenditure being concentrated on subjects of clear economic relevance and the delivery of it in the most cost-efficient and competitive manner. Britain and Sweden have introduced voucher systems whereby the state makes up the extra costs of sending children to private schools. Other nations, such as the United States, have experimented with the idea in specific geographical locations.

Public provision of education, public subsidy, and public control dominate in all nations. Overall, the private sector is comparatively small with the exception of the United States. In all nations, the state is both funder and provider; however, the nations differ on which level of government is the funder and provider.

In all nations, education is a strongly supported public agenda item. Additionally, in all nations the level of public satisfaction is declining. This has led to widespread societal debate in all nations about the goals of educational policies and their linkage to a nation's economic success and competitiveness in global markets.

Environmental Policy and the Six Nations

From the discussion, it appears all nations' political concerns about the environment have passed through similar stages of development. In certain nations the process has been longer and more painful than in others. For example, in Japan and Brazil the pursuit of industrial policy and economic development has had far more serious effects of environmental degradation, destruction of natural resources and risk to human life than in the other four nations. From an analysis by Antony Downs of the environmental issue in the United States, a model for policy making may be extrapolated and used to explain policy formulation and adoption in the nations under discussion.[12]

Downs argues that political concern in the United States about the environment went through a five-stage process from initial public concern to governmental response.[13] Stage one is the pre-problem stage. In this stage, the problem exists and may be severe, but there is low public awareness, little if any media interest, and it is marked by high interest-group alarm. Stage two is alarmed discovery and euphoric enthusiasm. The problem is articulated through a visible event, the public becomes alarmed and demands action, and government responds with policy promises. Stage three is the realization of the cost of significant progress. The high costs of taking policy action are articulated and weighed in terms of the sacrifices they require. Stage four is gradual decline of public interest. The reasons are issue boredom or rejection of the scale of changes needed or decline of public interest due to the involved costs. Stage five is the post-problem stage. The issue is not high on the public's mind, but the original problem still exists, and institutions remain in place to deal with the problem but with severely reduced funding. In other words there are peaks and valleys.

This process can clearly be seen in all the nations discussed in this text. In each nation, stages very similar to the Downs model have taken place. From 1965 to 1973, the problem of environmental quality developed into an issue of public concern in all six nations. In a short span of time, it produced a number and variety of policies, programs, and organizational changes. In short, in all six nations environmental problems were politically perceived, politically observed, and symbolically tackled by government. Basically in the 1960s and early 1970s there was a convergence of events and factors that led to similar agendization of environmental problems in each of the six selected nations. In each, and especially among the poorest or less stellar economic performers, the demand for natural resources to achieve socioeconomic goals made society's relationship to the physical environment more problematic. Additionally as each nation grew technologically sophisticated, it became increasingly easier to assess the environmental effects of economic and social activity. All nations have suffered depreciated factors in the environment, and, as each nation started to reach a critical level, increased perceptions of environmental problems have been triggered. As each nation experienced some sort of environmental crisis, public apprehension increased, and new environmental groups and coalitions that cut across established political cleavages were formed.

Similarly each nation since the 1970s has passed and enforced stricter environmental policy instruments. All six nations have introduced conventional regulatory approaches, such as regulations dealing with emissions and performance standards. Economic instruments are also common to all of the nations. In some nations, environmental taxes are used, whereas in others, such as Germany, permits are the mode of economic instrument. Common to all six nations is a desire to achieve more voluntary agreements in which business and industry cooperates voluntarily rather than being legally mandated to perform. The Japanese have promoted this type of environmental protection policy longer than any of the other nations, but all the other five have started to see that voluntary agreements can support and back regulating policy. Each nation discussed in this text has at certain points needed to use regulatory instruments solely to achieve environmental goals. For some it is earlier than for others. Regulatory instruments have been implemented through either legislation or administrative regulatory processes.

In all six nations, environmental policy reflects the tension between protecting industry on one side and protecting the citizen on the other. At what cost to industry does policy protect the physical well-being of citizens? All nations have faced societal debates about the negative impact of imposing environmental regulation on industry. Only one nation, the United States, during Reagan's presidential administration, has seriously attempted to persuade citizens that industries have been attacked and regulated too much and that there should be a rollback of environmental policy. However, in Germany the debate did produce a moratorium on environmental policy in the 1980s.

All countries are committed to sustainable development and each is working toward it in a manner that reflects their individual political, cultural and policy processes. In each nation, there has been a trend toward the funding of independent environmental ministries, departments or agencies. In some of the nations, special environmental agencies also occur at the state and local levels. Also common to all nations is environmental impact assessment, although it is implemented differently.

Finally all environmental policy was preceded by and responsive to growing environmental awareness and the growth of environmental groups. In each nation, environmental protection became increasingly important at the start of the 1970s. Environmental groups range from grass roots initiatives to environmental interest groups to the development of "green" political parties in Germany, Sweden, Britain, and Japan.

Chapter Fourteen
Discernable Patterns

This text provides an overview of four policy sectors and their evolution and organization in six industrialized nations. The text is exploratory and descriptive and does not offer prescriptive analysis. What is clear from the discussion of the policy process in each nation is that policy making is political and influenced by culture, historical development and economic conditions. The context in which policy is formulated will affect implementation. From the discussion it is obvious that nations do share similar experiences and reactions in the four policy sectors. What now remains is to ascertain whether there are any discernable patterns.

From the discussion it is clear that certain patterns exist. First, the debate among policy makers in the areas of education, environment, health, and social welfare is not about whether the state should have such policy but about who bears major responsibility for it. In each of the six nations, the debate centers around two alternative providers, state or market. The state as a provider has come to be perceived as noncompetitive, inefficient, cumbersome and anti-choice, whereas market processes are seen to be competitive, to provide choice, to be cost-efficient and rational. Each nation has experimented with the introduction of market processes into the policy sectors with differing degrees of intensity and success. In the first decade of the twenty-first century, it will be seen whether the changes and the restructuring of policy responses meet existing conditions and new demands.

The second pattern is that in each nation the policy agenda and policy formulation are heavily influenced by the relationship of the individual nation to the global context. No nation is an island; the growing interdependence of nations and the impact of the international context on a nation's domestic policy agenda is clearly established. Each nation has been affected by crisis in other nations. Additionally a nation's policy makers will be affected by international organizations. For example, the effect of the European Union on Sweden, Germany, and Great Britain when they formulate and adopt new policies is significant. In these three nations, national policy making must conform to the European Union's rules and regulations.

Items on the policy agenda also seem to cross national borders. In each of the four policy sectors, the nations have experienced similar problems and have responded by considering implementation of similar solutions. One such example of this is the move to introduce market forces in public education through vouchers. Thus, there is a convergence in the ways nations handle similar problems. However, nations differ in policy outcomes and the degree of commitment to the policy solution by the administrative apparatus.

The relationship of a nation's economic well-being with its policy agenda is the fourth pattern. All nations are generous with policy formulation when their economy is in a period of growth; however, as soon as economic decline takes hold, the natural inclination for policy makers is to be more selective in the use of state resources and to "cut back." Economic decline has produced political strain in each of the nations and each nation has fallen back to retrenchment of public provision in such periods.

The fifth pattern is the mix of actors and the arenas in which policy making occurs in each nation determine policy substance and style. This is the one dimension in which nations show increased variations. Finally, policy makers in all the discussed nations face similar constraints. At different times certain constraints will be more prevalent in certain nations than in others.

The first constraint is insufficient financial resources. All policy makers, be they Brazilians, Germans or Americans, must operate within the available financial resources. This, of course, is a function of the nation's economic health in a given period of time. Crucial here is the willingness of budgetary decision makers to make appropriate provisions of funding. A second common constraint on policy makers is the level of political support for any policy solution. Support is necessary for policy endorsement and successful passage through the formulation and adoption stages of the policy process. However, political support is still necessary once a policy is adopted. If implementing agencies do not support a policy then its likelihood of success will be compromised. Often in each nation the policy adopted is not the best in terms of solving the problem but is the one that got the most support. The next common constraint is competence of policy initiators. Those who design and push policy solutions must be skillful in maneuvering the policy environment. Timing is the fourth constraint on policy makers. Policy makers must decide if and when the time is right to introduce policy measures. A final constraint is policy networks. In each nation policy networks exist and have their own characteristics. Networks can also be referred to as policy communities. In each of the six nations the layout of the policy community will influence the network and type of policy that is eventually implemented. Depending on the nation and the particular issue the policy community can be cohesive or fragmented. For example, environmental policy in each of the nations is an area in which the power of the policy community is sharply defined, and this has clearly affected policy outcomes.

The discussion ends with a question for the reader to ponder. Can governments truly provide solutions to problems, or is their job merely to respond in such a way so as to control problems and provide a stimulus to other actors who will provide the essential solution? In essence: Is the true goal of policy makers in the modern state to tend and comfort and not to lead society?

Endnotes Part One

Chapter 1

1. Aristotle, *Politics* (translated by Benjamin Jowett) (New York: Oxford University Press, 1921).
2. E. Feldman, "Comparative Public Policy: Field or Method," *Comparative Politics*, 10 (1978), pp. 278–305.
3. M. Harrop, *Power and Policy in Liberal Democracies* (Cambridge: Cambridge University Press, 1992), p. 2.
4. Ibid., pp. 3–5.
5. A. Przeworski and H. Teune, *Logic of Comparative Social Inquiry* (New York: Wiley, 1970), pp. 27–35.
6. Harrop, p. 6.
7. G. Rimlinger, *Welfare Policy and Industrialization in Europe, America, and Russia* (New York: Wiley, 1971); A. King, "Ideas, Institutions and the Politics of Governments: A Comparative Analysis," *British Journal of Political Science*, 3 (July/Oct.), pp. 293–313, 409–423; P.R. Calm, *Comparative Social Policy and Social Security* (London: Martin Robertsons, 1973).
8. H. Wilensky, *The New Corporatism, Centralization and the Welfare State* (Beverly Hills: Sage, 1976).
9. M. Weir, A. Orloff, and T. Skocpol (eds.), *The Politics of Social Policy in the United States* (Princeton: Princeton University Press, 1988), pp. 61–63.
10. I. Gough, *The Political Economy of the Welfare State* (London: Macmillan, 1979); C. Offe, *Structural Problems of the Capitalist State* (London: Macmillan, 1982).
11. M. Lipset, *Political Man* (London: Heinemann, 1960), pp. 61–65.
12. Ibid., pp. 404–406.
13. H. Wilensky, *Comparative Social Policy: Theories, Methods and Findings* (Berkeley: University of California Institute of International Studies, 1983); H. Wilensky, *The Welfare State and Equality* (Berkeley: University of California Press, 1975); H.L.K. Tingsten, "Stability and Viability in Swedish Democracy," *The Political Quarterly*, vol. 26, pp. 140–151; J.H. Goldthorpe, "The Development of Industrial Society," *Sociological Review Monograph*, no. 8, 1964; and F. Parkin, *Class Inequality and Political Order* (London: McGibbon and Kee, 1971).
14. H. Marcuse, *One-Dimensional Man* (London: Routledge & Kegan Paul, 1964), pp. 10–12.
15. H.L. Wilensky, *The Welfare State and Equality*.
16. F. Castles (ed.), *The Comparative History of Public Policy* (Oxford: Oxford University Press, 1989); F. Castles, *The Social Democratic Image of Society* (London: Routledge and Kegan Paul, 1978); and F. Castles, *Comparative Public Policy: Pattern of Post War Transformation* (Cheltenham: Edward Elgar, 1998).
17. D. Hibbs, "Political Parties and Macro Economic Policy," *American Political Science Review*, 71, pp. 1467–1487.
18. Gough, *The Political Economy of the Welfare State*, pp. 79–91.

Chapter 2

1. A. Przeworski and H. Teune, *Logic of Comparative Social Inquiry* (New York: Wiley, 1970), p. 30.
2. G. Sartori, "Comparing and Miscomparing," *Journal of Theoretical Politics*, 3 (April), pp. 243–257.
3. J.L. Linz and A. Stepan, *Problems of Democratic Transition and Consolidation: Southern Europe, South America, and Post-Communist Europe* (Baltimore: Johns Hopkins University Press, 1996), pp. 7–11.
4. M. Dogen and D. Pelassy, *How to Compare Nations: Strategies in Comparative Politics* (Chatham: Chatham House, 1984), p. 3.
5. Castles, *Comparative Public Policy: Patterns of Post-War Transformation*, p. 27.

Endnotes Part Two

Chapter 3

1. IBGE, *Annuá Estatístico do Brasil 2000* (Rio de Janeiro: IBGE, 2000), p. 19.
2. T.G. Goertzel, *Ferdinand Henriquez Cardoso: Reinventing Democracy in Brazil* (Boulder: Lynne Reinner, 1999), pp. 3–5.
3. L.A. Payne, *Brazilian Industrialists and Democratic Change* (Baltimore: Johns Hopkins University Press, 1994); K. Sikkink, *Ideas and Institutions: Development in Brazil and Argentina* (Ithaca: Cornell University Press, 1991); P.R. Kingstone and T.J. Power (eds.), *Democratic Brazil: Actors, Institutions and Processes* (Pittsburgh: University of Pittsburgh, 1999).
4. IBGE, *Annuário Estatístico do Brasil 1991* (Rio de Janeiro: IBGE, 1991), p. 37.
5. Along with Mexico, South Africa, Greece and Portugal.
6. A.P. Montero, "Getting Real About the Brazilian Real Plan," *Hemisphere* (Feb. 1997).
7. Ibid.
8. IBGE, *Annuário Estatístico do Brasil 1998, 1999, 2000* (Rio de Janeiro: IBGE, 1998, 1999, 2000).
9. R.M. Levine, *Father of the Poor. Vargas and His Era* (New York: Cambridge University Press, 1998), pp. 8–9.
10. R. Berins Collier and D. Collier, *Shaping the Political Arena: Critical Junctures, the Labor Movement and Regime Dynamics in Latin America* (Princeton: Princeton University Press, 1991), pp. 165–195.
11. Levine, *Father of the Poor. Vargas and His Era*, pp. 8–15.
12. T.E. Skidmore, *Politics in Brazil, 1930–1964: An Experiment in Democracy* (New York: Oxford University Press, 1971).
13. G. O'Donnell, *Modernization & Bureaucratic Authoritarianism: Studies in South American Politics* (Berkeley: Institute of International Studies, University of California, 1973).
14. T.E. Skidmore, *The Politics of Military Rule in Brazil, 1964–85* (New York: Oxford University Press, 1988), p. 49.
15. Payne, *Brazilian Industrialists & Democratic Change,* chapter 4.
16. The process was referred to in Brazil as ABERTURA.
17. This was Brazil's first civilian president since 1964.
18. IBGE, *Annuário Estatístico do Brasil 1998* (Rio de Janeiro, 1998), p. 11.
19. K. Wayland, *Democracy Without Equity: Failure of Reform in Brazil* (Pittsburgh: University of Pittsburgh Press, 1996).
20. Previously was five years. Changed to four-year terms in a June 1994 constitutional amendment.
21. T.J. Power, "Politicized Democracy: Competition, Institutions, and 'Civic Fatigue' in Brazil," *Journal of Interamerican Studies and World Affairs, 33,* no. 3 (Fall 1991).
22. Ibid.
23. A. Montero, "Brazil" in Mark Kesselman et al. (eds.), *Introduction to Comparative Politics,* 2nd Ed. (Boston: Houghton Mifflin, 1999), p. 350.
24. The Debureaucratization Ministry.
25. S. Mainwaring, "Brazilian Party Underdevelopment on Comparative Perspective," *Political Science Quarterly* 107, no. 6, 1993, p. 692.
26. Ibid., p. 692.
27. S. Mainwaring, "Brazil: Weak Parties, Feckless Democracy" in S. Mainwaring and R. Scully (eds.), *Building Democratic Institutions: Party Systems in Latin America* (Stanford: Stanford University Press, 1995), pp. 370–380.
28. S. Mainwaring, "Politicians, Parties, and Electoral System: Brazil in Comparative Perspective," *Comparative Politics,* 24: 1 (Oct. 1991), pp. 33–38.
29. IBGE, *Annuário Estatístico do Brasil 1998* (Rio de Janeiro: IBGE, 1998), pp. 23–27.
30. Ibid., 1980, p. 5 and 1992, p. 3.
31. Power, "Politicized Democracy: Competitions, Institutes and 'Civic Fatigue' in Brazil."
32. B. Ross Schneider, *Politics Within the State: Elite Bureaucrats and Industrial Policy in Authoritarian Brazil* (Pittsburgh: University of Pittsburgh Press, 1991).
33. Montero, "Brazil."

Chapter 4

1. D.P. Conradt, *The German Polity,* 6th Ed. (New York: Longman, 1996), pp. 35–43.
2. R. Rose and C. Page, "German Responses to Regime Change: Culture, Class, Economy or Context," *West European Politics,* 19 (Jan. 1996), pp. 1–27.
3. Allied Powers were Britain, which occupied northwest Germany; France, which occupied the southwest; the United States, which occupied the south; and the Soviet Union, which occupied the east.
4. Territories east of the Oder and Neisse Rivers to Poland and the Soviet Union; the Saar region to France.
5. Similar Soviet moves in Poland and Hungary intensified the Western allies' fears.
6. Conradt, p. 16.
7. Conradt, p. 16.
8. West German democracy was based on a document that would serve as a constitution for West Germany until a more formal document could be drafted for the whole of Germany. The temporary document was entitled the Basic Law and set down the democratic parameters of the New Federal Republic of Germany.
9. Large numbers of East Germans tried to flee East Germany while socialists and communist parties in West Germany maintained healthy support levels.
10. Kiesinger was supported by a coalition of CDU-SPD.
11. Social Democrats were the major party in the coalition government that emerged in 1969.
12. Koll formed a coalition with the Free Democratic party to form a center right government.
13. R.G. Livingston, "Relinquishment of East Germany," in F. Starr (ed.), *East Central Europe and the USSR* (New York: St Martin's Press, 1991), pp. 81–85.
14. Conradt, *The German Polity,* p. 22.
15. Ibid., pp. 22–23.
16. Ibid., p. 22.
17. Perestroika, the democratization of the Soviet Union, and the abandonment of communism.
18. Such as Hungary, which dismantled its borders with Austria in May 1989.
19. P. Merkl, *German Unification in the European Context* (University Park: The Pennsylvania State University Press, 1993, chapter 1.
20. Five new states are formed in the territory of the former East Germany. These become the eastern states of the Federal Republic of Germany.
21. First free all-German elections since 1932.
22. In spite of original caution and lack of enthusiasm by British Prime Minister Margaret Thatcher and French President François Mitterrand.
23. West Germany since the 1960s witnessed a large-scale influx of guest workers from Southern Europe and Northern Africa. The 1990s saw a large influx of illegal aliens and asylum seekers from former communist states.
24. Reduced unemployment and sick pay benefits.
25. Went into operation in January 1999.
26. The communist party maintained strong support in East Germany, winning over 20 percent of the votes. This gave it over five percent of the total German vote.
27. GDR became part of the Federal Republic of Germany under article 23 of the Basic Law.
28. Article 8.1 Basic Law and 28.1.
29. Ibid., Article 8.1.
30. Article 20.1 Basic Law.
31. This indicates the largest source of revenue, income and corporation taxes.
32. Article 79.3 Basic Law.
33. Used only twice in 1972 (unsuccessfully) and successfully in 1982.
34. Conradt, *The German Polity,* pp 192–194; U. Thaysen, *The Bundesrat, the Lander and German Federalism* (Washington, D.C.: Johns Hopkins University Press, 1994), p. 9.
35. Such as the decline of the Free Democrats, shifting party loyalties, and protest voting, such as right-wing republicans.
36. T. Skocpol, "Bringing the State Back In," in P. Evans, D. Ruesdsemeyer, and T. Skocpol (eds.), *Bringing the State Back In* (Cambridge: Cambridge University Press, 1985), pp. 3–43.

37. Cases may be appealed only if a plaintiff can demonstrate a similar case involving the service and that federal law has been interpreted differently by the high courts of other states.
38. N. Johnson, "The Federal Constitutional Court: Facing up to the Strains of Law & Politics in the New Germany," *German Politics,* vol. 2, no. 3 (1994), pp. 131–148, p. 138; and N. Johnson, "The Interdependence of Law and Politics: Judges and the Constitution in West Germany," *West European Politics,* vol. 5, no. 3 (1982), pp. 136–252, p. 237.
39. R. Katz and P. Mair, "Changing Models of Party Organization and Party Democracy: The Emergence of the Cartel Party," *Party Politics,* vol. 1 (Jan. 1995), pp. 5–27.
40. G. Smith, W. Paterson, and S. Padgett, *Developments in German Politics* (London: Macmillan, 1996), p. 239.
41. P. Kratzenstein, *Policy and Politics in West Germany: The Growth of a Semi Sovereign State* (Philadelphia: Temple University Press, 1987).
42. J. Richardson, G. Gustafsson, and G. Jordan, "The Concept of Policy Style," in J. Richardson (ed.), *Policy Styles in Western Europe* (London: Allen & Unwin, 1982), pp. 1–16.
43. Conradt, *The German Polity,* p. 138.
44. Ibid., p. 139.

Chapter 5

1. B. Coxall and L. Robins, *Contemporary British Politics,* 3rd Ed. (London: Macmillan, 1998), p. 19.
2. Britain was still the world's third economic and military power in 1945.
3. Commonwealth is the name given to colonies, former colonies, and protectorates that accepted the British monarch as their head of state.
4. The main welfare state measures were as follows: 1945 Family Allowance Act; 1946 National Insurance Act; 1946 National Insurance (Industrial Injuries) Act; 1948 National Assistance Act; 1946 National Health Service Act; 1944 Education Act. For a detailed discussion of each of these see Chapter 10, The United Kingdom, this text; also Coxall and Robins, *Contemporary British Politics.*
5. Churchill resigned in April 1955 as Conservative prime minister, and Attlee in December 1955 as Labour leader.
6. Although by 1962 Britain completely depended on the United States for supply of nuclear weapons.
7. This follows two unsuccessful applications in 1961 and 1967.
8. Coxall and Robins, *Contemporary British Politics,* pp. 24–28.
9. The right urged a move to monetarism while the left an alternative economic strategy revolving around import controls.
10. Five percent pay norm literally meant the maximum anyone was allowed to receive as a pay raise was five percent.
11. M.J. Smith and S. Ludham (eds.), *Contemporary British Conservatism* (London: Macmillan, 1996), chapter 5.
12. Thatcher publicly articulated this as getting our money back. Claiming Britain was paying too much in return for what they received in subsidies and grants. She eventually got two-thirds of the sum paid in the previous decade back.
13. Coxall and Robins, *Contemporary British Politics,* p. 29.
14. For example, public transportation, refuse collection and public utilities all "sold off" to private enterprises or mixtures of public and private agencies.
15. I. Crewe, "1977 to 1996," in A. Seldon (ed.), *How Tory Governments Fall* (London: Harper-Collins, 1996).
16. With the exception of a few Middle Eastern Kingdoms, it's the only country in the world that doesn't incorporate its major constitutional rules into a single document.
17. P. Madgurck and D. Woodhouse, *The Law and Politics of the Constitution of the United Kingdom* (London: Harvest Wheats Leaf, 1995), see pp. 11–81.
18. England, Scotland, Northern Ireland, Wales.
19. No other branch of government can make or overturn any law or parliament; thus they cannot restrict or rescind parliamentary action.

20. V. Bogdanor, *Constitutions in Democratic Politics* (Aldershot: Gower, 1988), p. 55.
21. G. Peele, "The Law and the Constitution," in P. Dunleavy, A. Gamble, I. Holiday, and G. Peele (eds.), *Developments in British Politics 6* (New York: St. Martin's, 2000), pp. 69–89.
22. D. Kavanagh, "Prime Ministerial Power Revisited," *Social Studies Review,* 6: 4, March 1991.
23. M. Burch and I. Holliday, *The British Cabinet System* (London: Harvest Wheatsheaf, 1996), pp. 30–45.
24. From time to time, this notion of collective responsibility has been broken.
25. R. Crossman, "Introduction," in W. Bagehot, *The English Constitution* (London: Fontana, 1964); T. Benn, "The Case for a Constitutional Premiership," *Parliamentary Affairs,* XXXIII: 1, Winter 1980; M. Foley, *The Rise of the British Presidency* (Manchester: Manchester University Press, 1993).
26. A. Seldon, "Policy Making and Cabinet," in D. Kavanagh and A. Seldon (eds.), *The Major Effect* (London: Macmillan, 1994); Burch and Holiday, *The British Cabinet System,* pp. 1–9.
27. The House of Lords has the power to introduce bills, although bills dealing with financial matters can only originate in the House of Commons. The Lords can also offer amendments to bills passed by the House of Commons, and Commons is obligated to consider these amendments before passing a bill into law. The Lords have the right to delay legislation and may delay bills for up to about a year. Financial bills, however, may only be delayed for a month, and they become law in 30 days whether or not the House of Lords approves of them. The terms of the Parliament Acts of 1911 and 1949 forbid the Lords from disapproving nonfinancial bills if the House of Commons has passed them in two successive sessions. The only exception is a bill to lengthen the life of a Parliament past five years, which requires the assent of both chambers.
28. These are Lords Temporal who are hereditary or appointed for life duration; Lords Spiritual who are the archbishops and senior bishops of the Church of England; and the Law Lords.
29. Each MP is elected by single-member electoral constituencies by simple majority.
30. 1970–1980 saw a strain in party discipline.
31. Each cabinet department has an opposition MP who acts as the opposition's party spokesman in that particular area.
32. A. Adonis, *Parliament Today,* 2nd Ed. (Manchester: Manchester University Press, 1993), chapter 1.
33. Principles derived from British law include the right to trial by jury; the right to due process; freedom from unlawful imprisonment (writ of *habeas corpus*); the trial system of prosecution and defense; and the presumption that a person is innocent until proven guilty.
34. In the 1984–1985 coal miners dispute, the courts interpreting the 1982 Employment Act froze the entire assets of the miners' union.
35. C. Hood and O. James, "The Central Executive," in P. Dunleavy, A. Gamble, I. Holiday, and G. Peele (eds.), *Developments in British Politics 5* (London: Macmillan, 1997), pp. 177–202.
36. P. John, "Local Governance," in Dunleavy, Gamble, Holliday, and Peele, *Developments in British Politics 5,* pp. 253–274.
37. W. Hall and S. Weir, *The Untouchables: Power and Accountability in the Quango State* (London: The Democratic Audit/Scarman Trust, 1996), pp. 19–41.
38. John, p. 275.
39. For example, by restoring London with its own elected local governance body. An election was held in May 2000 and won by Ken Livingstone, who became mayor as an independent.
40. G. Peele, "Political Parties," in P. Dunleavy, A. Gamble, I. Holliday, and G. Peele (eds.), *Developments in British Politics 5,* pp. 89–109; J. Fisher, *British Political Parties* (London: Harvest Wheatsheaf, 1996), chapter 1.
41. Ibid., pp. 89–91.
42. Peele, "Political Parties," p. 108.
43. R. Baggott, *Pressure Groups Today* (Manchester: Manchester University Press, 1995), pp. 72–76.
44. W. Grant, *Pressure Groups, Politics and Democracy,* 2nd Ed. (Hemel Hempstead: Prentice Hall/Harvest Wheatsheaf, 1995), pp. 27–28.
45. M.J. Smith, *Pressure Politics* (Manchester: Baseline Books, 1995); D. March and R. Rhodes, *Government and Pressure Groups* (Oxford: Oxford University Press, 1992).

46. Grant, *Pressure Groups, Politics and Democracy*, pp. 13–18; Baggott, *Pressure Groups Today*, p. 9.
47. J. Greenaway, S. Smith, and J. Street, *Deciding Factors in British Politics: A Case-Studies Approach* (London: Routledge, 1992), p. 27.
48. Smith, *Pressure Politics*, pp. 7–9; March and Rhodes, *Government and Pressure Groups*, p. 79.

Chapter 6

1. Second only to the United States in the world.
2. In pre–World-War-II Japan, there were flirtations with democratic government which led to the Japanese accepting the ideas and practice of democracy.
3. E.O. Reischauer and M.B. Jansen, *The Japanese Today: Change and Continuity* (Cambridge, MA: Belknap Press of Harvard University Press, 1995), p. 19.
4. M. Weber, *From Max Weber: Essays in Sociology*, edited by H.H. Gerth and C. Wright Mills (New York: Oxford University Press, 1946).
5. The Shogun Military clans.
6. M. Gayn, "Drafting the Japanese Constitution," in J. Livingston, J. Moore, and F. Oldfather, *Postwar Japan: 1945 to Present* (New York: Pantheon, 1973), pp. 19–24.
7. Ibid.
8. By the end of 1996 about 40 percent of Japan's industrial force was unionized.
9. A legal Japanese Communist party emerged; it was hoped that it would play a role in promoting strong democratic opposition.
10. Kishimoto, *Politics in Modern Japan;* T.J. Pempel, *Policy and Politics in Japan: Creative Conservatism* (Philadelphia: Temple University Press, 1982).
11. Hundreds of thousands of protestors led by Socialist legislators, union leaders, and student leaders marched against the treaty.
12. Anti-Americanism was so strong President Eisenhower's scheduled visit was cancelled.
13. Predominant party system is a multi-party political system in which one party maintains a predominant position in parliament and the control of government for a long period of time.
14. Japan's manufacturing sector was stimulated by the supply of military goods and repair of equipment.
15. Large corporations guaranteed workers lifetime employment, wage and salary increases based on seniority, and corporate welfare benefits.
16. Oil shocks came in 1973 with OPEC price increases and the 1979 Iran revolution.
17. Former Prime Minister Tanaka was arrested for taking bribes from Lockheed. As the case came to court, it became clear Lockheed had paid at least $10 million in bribes and fees to Japanese politicians and industrialists since the 1950s.
18. Under Nakasone the LDP won its largest electoral victory in 1986.
19. Defeat came first in legislative elections then in the general election.
20. H. Fukui and S.N. Fukui, "The End of the Miracle: Japanese Politics in the Post–Cold War Era," in M.J. Berges and D.A. Borer (eds.), *The Rise of East Asia: Critical Visions of the Pacific Century* (New York: Routledge, 1997), pp. 37–60.
21. T. Hoye, *Japanese Politics: Fixed and Floating Worlds* (Upper Saddle River: Prentice Hall, 1999) pp. 95–107.
22. R.J. Hrebenar, *The Japanese Party System: From One Party Rule to Coalition Government* (Boulder: Westview, 1986); and H. Itake, "Forces for Political Reform: The Liberal Democratic Party's Young Reformers," *Journal of Japanese Studies* 1996, 22 (Summer), pp. 269–294.
23. Hoye, *Japanese Politics: Fixed and Floating Worlds*, pp. 58–59.
24. K. Hayao, *The Japanese Prime Minister and Public Policy* (Pittsburgh: University of Pittsburgh Press, 1973), pp. 3–27; C. Johnson, *Japan: Who Governs* (New York: Norton, 1995), pp. 10–14.
25. Kishimoto, *Politics in Modern Japan*, chapter on Japanese judiciary.
26. T.J. Pempel, *Policy and Politics in Japan: Creative Conservatism*, p. 153.
27. S.R. Reed, *Japanese Prefectures and Policymaking* (Pittsburgh: University of Pittsburgh Press, 1986), pp. 22–43.
28. C. Johnson, *Miti and the Japanese Miracle: The Growth of Industrial Policy, 1925–1975* (Stanford: Stanford University Press, 1982).
29. B.C. Koh, *Japan's Administrative Elite* (Berkeley: University of California Press, 1989), p. 71.

30. Hyung-ki Kin, M. Muramatsu, T.J. Pempel, and Kozo Yanamvra, *The Japanese Civil Service and Economic Development* (Oxford: Clarendon Press, 1995), pp. 55–59.
31. Ibid.
32. Ibid.
33. Reed, *Japanese Prefectures and Policymaking,* p. 27.
34. Ibid., pp. 39–41.
35. LDP, JSP, Clean Government Party (CEP), DSP, and Japanese Communist Party (JCP).
36. D.E. Groth, "Media and Political Protest: The Bullet Train Movements," in S.J. Pharr and E.S. Krauss (eds.), *Media and Politics in Japan* (Honolulu: University of Hawaii Press, 1996).
37. T. Shinoda, "Japan's Decision Making Under Coalition Government," *Asian Survey,* 38: 7 (July 1998), pp. 703–723.
38. C. Everett Ladd, "Japan and America: Two Different Nations Draw Closer," *The Public Perspective: A Roper Center Review of Public Opinion and Policy,* 1995, no. 6, pp. 18–36.
39. J. Woronoft, *Politics the Japanese Way* (Tokyo: Lotus Press, 1986); G. Curtis, *The Japanese Way of Politics* (New York: Colombia University Press, 1988); and K. Kishimoto, *Politics in Modern Japan: Development and Organization* (Tokyo: Japan Echo Inc., 1998).

Chapter 7

1. It is the fourth-largest country in Europe.
2. Statistiska Centralbyrän, *Statistisk Årsbok för Sverige* (Stockholm, 1999), p. 215.
3. Statistiska Centralbyrän, *Statistisk Årsbok för Sverige* (Stockholm, 1997), pp. 28–32.
4. Anonymous, "Welcome Back," *The Economist,* September 27, 1998.
5. The Social Democrats held power alone or in coalition during the periods 1932–1976, 1982–1991, and 1994–present day. Nonsocialist parties were in government 1976–1982 and 1991–1994.
6. F. Castles, *The Social Democratic Image of Society: A Study of the Achievements and Origins of Scandinavian Social Democracy in Comparative Perspective* (London: Routledge & Kegan Paul, 1978), chapters 2 and 3; and T. Tilton, "The Origins of Liberal Democracy: The Swedish Case," *American Political Science Review,* vol. 68, no. 2 (June, 1974), pp. 561–571.
7. P. Vindé and G. Petri, *Swedish Government Administration,* 2nd Rev. Ed. (Stockholm: Swedish Institute, 1978), p. 93; and A. Gustafsson, *Local Government in Sweden* (Stockholm: Swedish Institute, 1983), p. 115.
8. M. Ruggie, *The State and Working Women: A Comparative Study of Britain and Sweden* (Princeton: Princeton University Press, 1984), chapter 2.
9. M.D. Hancock, "Sweden," in M.D. Hancock, P. Conradt, B. Guy Peters, W. Safron, and R. Zanski, *Politics in Western Europe* (Chatham: Chatham House, 1993), pp. 393–410.
10. Did not enter into government with any other party, thus not forming a coalition government.
11. In May 1996 the European Parliament recommended Sweden for membership in the European Union (EU). Membership was approved by Swedish voters in a November 1994 referendum, and after approval by the Riksdag, Sweden entered the EU on January 1, 1995.
12. Hancock, "Sweden," pp. 404–405.
13. Ministers without portfolio operate as an equivalent to British junior ministers. Ministers without portfolio have specific duties within a specific ministry.
14. There are seventy administrative agencies, including the national tax board and the national police board. There are seven commercial agencies, such as the post office and the state railways.
15. Commercial agencies differ from administrative agencies in that the fees they charge for goods and services cover their expenditures.
16. Constitutional reforms ratified in 1968–1969 and implemented in 1970 established the unicameral system. Previously, it was a bicameral system.
17. This has only been allowed since 1970. To date, no votes of no confidence have been held.
18. National referenda have been held on five policy issue areas since 1922. They range from prohibition in 1922 to European Union membership in the late 1990s. The Riksdag can still implement a policy if the referendum finds against it.
19. In practice, the positions are distributed among one major party represented in the Riksdag.

20. The four areas of jurisdiction are business, consumer affairs, equal opportunities, and state administration.
21. W. Childs, *Sweden: The Middle Way on Trial* (New Haven: Yale University Press, 1980); E. Einhorn and J. Logue, *Modern Welfare States: Politics and Policies in Social Democratic Scandinavia* (New York: Praeger, 1989); H. Heclo and H. Madsen, *Policy & Politics in Sweden: Principled Pragmatism* (Philadelphia: Temple University Press, 1987).
22. Hancock, "Sweden," pp. 408–409; and J. Pontusson, "Sweden," in Mark Kesselman et al., *European Politics in Transition* (Lexington: D.C. Heath, 1992), pp. 492–494.
23. Pontusson, p. 492.

Chapter 8

1. 300,000 Americans had lost their lives in battle and the U.S. government spent $300 billion on the war effort.
2. The 80th Congress of 1946 was the first to have both houses controlled by Republicans since 1928.
3. Through the Federal Highway Act of 1956.
4. Between 1940 and 1960, the percentage of college-age Americans who attended college almost doubled.
5. M. Harrington, *The Other America: Poverty in the United States* (London: Macmillian, 1962).
6. When Governor Faubus of Arkansas tried to stop the enrollment of African American students to Little Rock High School, Eisenhower sent federal troops to desegregate the school.
7. The programs also created the job corps to train youth for the employment market.
8. A. Schlesinger, Jr., *The Imperial Presidency* (New York: Houghton Mifflin, 1973).
9. Such a condition became known as stagflation.
10. Supply-side economics posits tax cuts to spur economic growth, which increases government revenues.
11. The Monica Lewinsky extramarital affair.
12. See the introduction to the United States Constitution.
13. Some of the most important of the eleventh through twenty-seventh amendments are the fourteenth, fifteenth, seventeenth, nineteenth, twenty-second, and twenty-sixth. The fourteenth establishes due process and extends protection of Bill of Rights to individual residents of the states. The fifteenth, nineteenth, twenty-sixth, respectively, gave African Americans, women, and eighteen-year-olds the right to vote. The seventeenth gave people the right to elect U.S. Senators; the twenty-second restricted the number of terms a president can serve to two.
14. Are voted in by the electoral colleges, which is an indirect mechanism whereby all eligible citizens vote for a slate of electors (equal to the size of the state's congressional delegation) who then cast their votes for the president and vice president.
15. Schlesinger, Jr., *The Imperial Presidency*. The buildup of power is a twentieth-century phenomena; most date it with the creation of the modern presidency and the election of F.D. Roosevelt in 1932.
16. Number has been fixed since 1910.
17. All government spending must begin with an appropriate bill in the House of Representatives. Congressional oversight is also legtimized by the necessary and proper clause.
18. J.Q. Wilson, *American Government: Brief Version* (Boston: Houghton Mifflin, 2000), Congress chapter.
19. Power of chairs was much stronger pre-1970s because of seniority rule, which specified the individual with the longest uninterrupted tenure on the committee from the majority party would chair the committee. This put power in the hands of elderly, conservative, long-serving congressmen, who often blocked legislation supported by a majority from reaching the floor of the House.
20. L.C. Dodd and B.I. Oppenheimer, *Congress Reconsidered,* 6th Ed. (Washington: Congressional Quarterly Books, 1997), pp. 111–115.
21. Thirteen district courts and three circuit courts.
22. Wilson, *American Government,* Congress chapter.
23. A. Downs quoted in D. McKay, "Industrial Policy and Non-Policy in the U.S.," *Journal of Public Policy,* 3, 1983, p. 45.

24. R. Salsibury, "The Paradox of Interest Groups in Washington," in A. King (ed.), *The New American Political System* (Washington, D.C.: American Enterprise Institute, 1990).
25. B. Guy Peters, *American Public Policy: Promise and Performance* (New York: Chatham House, 1999), p. 21.
26. Ibid.
27. P.H. Stone, "Tobacco's Road," *National Journal,* 1 January, 1994, pp. 1–23.

Endnotes Part Three

Chapter 9

1. G. Esping-Andersen, *The Three Worlds of Welfare Capitalism* (Cambridge: Polity Press, 1990), pp. 26–30.
2. I. Gough, *The Political Economy of the Welfare State* (Basingstoke: Macmillan, 1979).
3. R. Mishra, *The Welfare State in Capitalist Society* (Hemel Hempstead: Harvester Wheatsheaf, 1990).
4. F. Fox Piven and R.A. Cloward, *Regulating the Poor: The Functions of Public Welfare* (New York: Vintage Books, 1971).
5. Ibid.
6. A.C. Medici, *The Welfare State in Brazil* (Austin: University of Texas LANIC Institute, 1998), pp. 1–3.
7. Ibid.
8. J.A. Page, *The Brazilians* (Reading: Addison-Wesley, 1995), pp. 121–153.
9. Ibid.
10. K. Maxwell, "The Two Brazils," in *Latin America,* 9th Ed. (Guilford: Duskin/McGraw-Hill, 2000), pp. 171–176.
11. Ibid.
12. D.J. Schemo, "The ABC's of Business in Brazil," *New York Times,* July 16, 1998, B1, p. 7.
13. Ibid., p. 7.
14. Ibid.
15. S. Kuhnle, "Political Reconstruction of the European Welfare State," in H. Cavanna, *Challenges to the Welfare State* (Cheltenham: Edward Elgar, 1998), p. 64.
16. Esping-Andersen, *The Three Worlds of Welfare,* pp. 53–59.
17. D. Patton, "Social Conditions, Political Strategies, and German Unification, 1990–1993," *West European Politics,* vol. 16, no. 4, pp. 470–491, 1993.
18. S. Mangen, "Social Policy: One State, Two-Tier Welfare," in G. Smith (ed.), *Social Policy in Germany* (Hemel Hempstead: Harvester Wheatsheaf, 1992).
19. Bismarck was the first chancellor in the nineteenth century to establish a nationwide compulsory insurance scheme. Additionally other laws passed, such as the 1870 Poor Law, not only fought poverty but provided regulation of labor markets, protection for workers, and expansion of benefits to workers' families.
20. R. Freeman and J. Clasen, "The German Social State," in J. Clasen and R. Freeman (eds.), *Social Policy in Germany* (London: Harvester Wheatsheaf, 1994).
21. M. Evans, "Exploring Statistics and National Rules on Social Security," in L. Hantrais and S. Mangen (eds.), *Cross National Research Methods in the Social Sciences* (London: Pinter, 1996).
22. M. Wilson, "The German Welfare State: A Conservative Regime in Crisis," in A. Cochrane and J. Clarke (eds.), *Comparing Welfare States: Britain in the International Context* (London: Sage, 1993).
23. For example, April 1996, the government proposed cuts in public expenditure of approximately DM 50 billion. They also proposed cuts in benefits such as sickness wage compensation, increase in pension age for women (60–63), and limitations on preretirement sickness benefits. Such proposals drew public protests from citizens.
24. M. Ferrera, *EC Citizens and Social Protection. Main Results from a Eurbarometer Study* (Brussels: EC Commission, Division V/E/2, 1993). See Introduction.
25. *The Guardian,* 8 May 1996. The newspaper is the leading intellectual newspaper of the British media.

26. Coxall and Robins, *Contemporary British Politics,* pp. 464–468.
27. R.M. Page and R. Silburn, *British Social Welfare in the Twentieth Century* (London: Macmillan, 1998), pp. 13–32.
28. Ibid., p. 43.
29. M. Dean, "Beveridge 50 Years On," *Lancet,* vol. 340, no. 8824, 10 Oct. 1992, p. 900.
30. J. Lewis, "Welfare State or Mixed Economy of Welfare," *History Today,* vol. 45, no. 2, Feb. 1995, p. 4.
31. Ibid.
32. H.M. Treasury, *Public Expenditure Analyses to 1995/96,* Cm 2219 (London: HMS0, 1993), Table 2.4.
33. Welfare services accounted for one-fifth of public spending in 1980.
34. S. Savage and L. Robins, "Welfare Policy in the Thatcher Years," in S. Savage and L. Robins (eds.), *Public Policy Under Thatcher* (London: Macmillan, 1990).
35. C. Jones Finer, "Social Policy," in D. Dunleary et al. (eds.), *Developments in British Politics 5* (Basingstoke: Macmillan, 1997), pp. 305–308.
36. J. Warden, "Britain's New Welfare System Emphasises Self Reliance," *British Medical Journal,* vol. 136, no. 7137, 4 April 1998, p. 1040.
37. Sections of major cities such as London, Liverpool, and Doncaster with long-term joblessness.
38. Page and Silburn, *British Social Welfare in the Twentieth Century,* pp. 33–52.
39. H. Kyung Lee, "The Japanese Welfare State In Transition," in R. Friedman, N. Gilbert, and M. Sheare (eds.), *Modern Welfare States: A Comparative View of Trends and Prospects* (Brighton: Wheatsheaf Books, 1987), pp. 243–263.
40. R. Goodman, "The Japanese-Style Welfare State and the Delivery of Personal Social Services," in R. Goodman, Gordon White, and Huck-Jukwon, *The East Asian Welfare Model* (London: Routledge, 1998) pp. 139–152.
41. Ibid.
42. E. Hobsbawn and T. Roger, *The Invention of Tradition* (Cambridge: Cambridge University Press, 1983), pp. 7–12.
43. Goodman, "The Japanese-Style Welfare State and the Delivery of Social Services."
44. This is provided for by the 1950 Livelihood Protection Law.
45. Japan Institute for Social and Economic Affairs, *Japan 1998–1999: An International Comparison* (Tokyo: JISEA, 1999), pp. 23–25.
46. Benefits provided for under the 1947 Employment Security Law and various companion laws 1947–1948.
47. Ibid.
48. R. Tomasson, *Sweden: Prototype of Modern Society* (New York: Random House, 1970).
49. Esping-Andersen, *The Three Worlds of Welfare,* pp. 26–30.
50. S. Valocchi, "The Origins of the Swedish Welfare State: A Class Analysis of the State and Welfare Politics," *Social Problems,* vol. 39, no. 2, May 1992.
51. Ibid.
52. N. Ginsburg, *Divisions of Welfare: A Critical Introduction to Comparative Social Policy* (Newbury Park: Sage, 1993), pp. 30–66.
53. R. Morris, *Testing the Limits of Social Welfare* (Boston: Brandeis University Press, 1988); and S. Olsson, "Decentralization and Privatization in Sweden," in Morris, *Testing the Limits of Social Welfare.*
54. A. Gould, "The Swedish Welfare State in Crisis," in C. Jones (ed.), *New Perspectives on the Welfare State in Europe* (London: Routledge, 1993), pp. 79–82.
55. Kuhnle, "Political Reconstruction of European Welfare States," pp. 66–67.
56. Ibid.
57. Ibid.
58. J. Palme, "Recent Developments in Income Transfer Systems in Sweden," in N. Ploug and D. Kvist (eds.), *Recent Trends in Cash Benefits in Europe* (Copenhagen: Danish National Institute of Social Research, 1994), pp. 39–60.
59. Ibid.
60. Kuhnle, "Political Reconstruction of the European Welfare States," pp. 65–67.

61. A. Gould, "Sweden: The Last Bastion of Social Democracy," in V. George and P. Taylor-Cooly (eds.), *European Welfare Policy* (London: Macmillian, 1996), pp. 72–94.
62. Ibid.
63. Welfarism is the notion that the state takes responsibility for the financial security of those in society who are unable to manage their own resources.
64. Much of the conservative argument about the effects of welfare on individuals and the economy in general is based on the work of the following authors: M. Anderson, *Welfare: The Political Economy of Welfare Reform in the United States* (Stanford: Hoover Institute, 1978); G. Gildor, *Wealth and Poverty* (New York: Basic Books, 1981); T.R. Marmor, J.L. Mashaw, and P.L. Harvey, *America's Misunderstood Welfare State: Persistent Myths* (New York: Basic Books, 1990); and C. Murray, *Losing Ground: American Social Policy 1950–1980* (New York: Basic Books, 1984).
65. As reported in *New York Times*, August 25, 1996, p. 1, Section 1.

Chapter 10

1. Using mortality rates and fertility rates.
2. World Health Organization, *The World Health Report, 1999: Making a Difference* (Geneva: WHO, 1999), p. 1.
3. D.T. Jamison, L.J. Lau, and J. Wang, "Health's Contribution to Economic Growth, 1965–90," in WHO Director-general Transition Team, *Health Policy and Economic Outcomes, 1998* (Geneva: WHO, 1998).
4. Ibid.
5. *World Health Report, 1999*, pp. 5–9.
6. Ibid.
7. D.E. Bloom and J.G. Williamson, "Demographic Transitions and Economic Miracles in Asia," *The World Bank Economic Review*, 1998, 12(3): pp. 419–455.
8. J. Strauss and D. Thomas, "Health, Nutrition and Economic Development," *Journal of Economic Literature*, vol. XXXXVI (June 1998), pp. 776–817.
9. Ibid.
10. World Health Organization, *The World Health Report 2000—Health Systems: Improving Performance* (Geneva: WHO, 2000).
11. Ibid., chapter 1.
12. Ibid., p. 3.
13. Ibid., p. 5.
14. World Bank, *The Organization, Delivering and Finance of Health Care in Brazil. Agenda for the 1990s* (New York: World Bank, 30 June 1994), p. 20.
15. M. Lewis and A. Medici, *Health Care Reform in Brazil: Phasing Change* (New York: World Bank, 1996), pp. 32–33.
16. K. Weyland, "Social Movement and the State: The Politics of Health Reform in Brazil," *World Development*, vol. 23, no. 10, p. 1700.
17. J.A. Page, *The Brazilians* (Washington: Library of Congress, 1993), pp. 177–179.
18. Ibid.
19. World Bank, *The Organization, Delivery and Finance of Health Care in Brazil*, pp. 20–21.
20. Ibid., p. 20.
21. Ibid., p. 12.
22. A. Haynes, "Health Care in Brazil," *The British Medical Journal*, vol. 306 (20 Feb. 1993), pp. 503–506.
23. A. Haynes, "Brazil: Progress in Decentralizing Health Care," *The Lancet*, 341 (29 May 1993), pp. 1400–1420.
24. World Bank, *The Organization, Delivery and Finance of Health Care in Brazil*, p. 23.
25. Haines, "Brazil: Progress in Decentralizing Health Care," p. 1403.
26. University hospitals were to remain under the Ministry of Education. All medical care of armed forces was not integrated into the SUS.
27. Ronald M. Schneider, *Brazil, Culture and Politics in a New Industrial Powerhouse* (Boulder: Westview, 1996), p. 140. Between 1985 and 1990 the proportion of program funds managed by municipalities increased from 10 to 15 percent and by states from 23 to 33 percent.

28. Federal Research Division, *Brazil: A Country Study* (Washington, D.C.: U.S. Government Printing Office, 1998), p. 152. Private facilities owned 71 percent of hospital beds designated for government-funded health care in 1993. This publicly focused, privately provided health system continues to intensify its focus on high-cost curative care, driving costs up 70 percent during the 1980s. Ibid., p. 115. Percentage of total central government spending in 1990 was 6.7 percent. As a share of GDP (1990) from 2.1 percent to 3.1 percent, close to half of all total health expenditures out of a total of 5.8 percent.

29. As of 1961.

30. K. Stocker, H. Waitzkin, and C. Iriart, "The Exportation of Managed Care to Latin America," *New England Journal of Medicine,* vol. 340, no. 1131, 8 April 1999.

31. Schneider, *Brazil, Culture and Politics in a New Industrial Powerhouse,* p. 142. The distribution of hospitals and out-patient facilities favors the south and the southeast at levels two to four times higher per capita than those in the north and the northeast where health conditions are more precarious and needs greater.

32. Federal Research Division, *Brazil: A Country Study,* p. 141.

33. Ibid., p. 142.

34. E.L. Nascimento, "Sick & Tired," Online, *http:/www.brazil.com/cvapr96.htm.*

35. Anonymous, "Sick System," *The Economist,* 11, Sept. 1999, p. 17.

36. S. Hensley, "Brazilian Healthcare at a Crossroads," *Modern Healthcare,* 17 May 1999, p. 49.

37. Nascimento, "Sick & Tired."

38. Ibid.

39. M.L. Lassey, H.R. Lassey, and N. Jinks (eds.), "Germany," in *Health Care Systems Around the World* (Upper Saddle River, New Jersey: Prentice Hall, 1997).

40. C. Altenstetter, "From Solidarity to Market Competition? Values, Structure and Structure and Strategy in German Health Policy, 1883–1997," in Francis Powell and Albert F. Wessen, eds., *Health Care Systems in Transition: An International Perspective* (London: Sage Productions, 1999).

41. Coverage soon extended to civil servants, coal miners and other employee groups.

42. J. Alber, "Germany," in P. Flora (ed.), *Growth to Limits* (Berlin: DeGruyter, 1988).

43. Lassey, Lassey, and Jinks, *Germany.*

44. B. Blanke and C. Perschke-Hartmann, "The 1992 Health Reforms Victory Over Pressure Group Politics," *German Politics,* 3 (2), Aug. 1994, pp. 233–248.

45. Ibid.

46. Ibid.

47. Altenstetter, "From Solidarity to Market Competition."

48. Ibid.

49. B. Ebbinghaus and A. Hassel, "Striking Deals: Concentration in the Reform of Continental European Welfare States," *Journal of European Public Policy,* 7(1), pp. 44–62.

50. Altenstetter, "From Solidarity to Market Competition."

51. S. Giaimo and P. Manow, "Adapting the Welfare State: The Case of Healthcare Reform in Britain, Germany & the U.S.," *Comparative Political Studies,* December 1999, pp. 967–995.

52. P.F. Cooper and B.S. Schone, "More Offers, Fewer Takers for Employment-based Health Insurance," *Health Affairs,* 16(6), 1997, pp 142–149.

53. R. Lawson, "Germany: Maintaining the Middle Way," in V. George and P. Taylor-Goody, *European Welfare Policy* (London: Macmillan, 1996), pp. 45–46.

54. Ibid.

55. Ibid.

56. A.C. Enthoven, "The History and Principles of Managed Competition," *Health Affairs,* 12 (suppl.), 1993, pp. 23–48.

57. *World Health Report 2000,* pp. 15–17.

58. 1834 Poor Law Amendment Act, 1870 Expansion of 1834 Poor Law.

59. Men paid 4d (approximately 7 cents per week) while women paid 3d (approximately 6 cents).

60. R.M. Titmus, *Problems of Social Policy* (London: HMOs, 1950), p. 13.

61. Ibid., pp. 13–15.

62. K.O. Morgan, *Labour in Power, 1945–1951* (Oxford: Oxford University Press, 1984), p. 157.
63. S. Harrison, "Great Britain," in *The International Handbook of Health Care System,* ed. by Robert B. Saltman (New York: Glenwood Press, 1988), pp. 156–211.
64. P.D. Klein and R. Klein, "Britain's Health Care Experiment," in F.D. Powell and Albert F. Wessen (eds.), *Health Care Systems in Transition: An International Perspective* (London: Sage Publications, 1999).
65. A. Maynard, "Lessons from the United Kingdom," *Health Care Policy and Politics: Lessons from Four Countries* (Washington, DC: The AEI Press, 1993).
66. Coxall and Robins, *Contemporary British Politics,* p. 458.
67. Under Labour since 1997 general practitioners do not have formal fund-holding status, health care agreements have replaced formal contracts and elected local authority representatives sit on trust hospital boards.
68. House of Commons speech, March 22, 2000.
69. Japanese women's life expectancy is 82.8 years, for men it's 76.4. Infant mortality is 4.3 deaths per 1,000 live births.
70. A poll concluded in 1995 by the ministry of health and welfare showed overall satisfaction with the system was high.
71. T. Hoye, *Japanese Politics* (Upper Saddle River: Prentice Hall, 1999), pp. 140–142.
72. Japanese Constitution Article 25.
73. Hoye, p. 141.
74. Japan's Ministry of Health Statistical Report, 1999, p. 26.
75. A. Saphir, "Japan Breaks From Tradition: A New National Insurance Program Will Change Long-Term Care, Create Business Opportunities," *Modern Health care,* 15, Nov. 1999, pp. 11–17.
76. B.L. Kirkman-Liff, "Health care Reform in the Netherlands, Israel, Germany, England and Sweden," *Generations,* Summer 1996, pp. 65–79.
77. Ellen Immergut, "Historical and Institutional Foundations of the Swedish Health Care System," in Francis D. Powell and Albert F. Wessen (eds.), *Health Care Systems in Transition: An International Perspective* (London: Sage Productions, 1999).
78. Ibid.
79. Remiss is a procedure whereby written comments are made by interested parties on committee proposals.
80. These reforms became known as the Seven Crowns Reform.
81. J. Clasen and A. Gould, "Stability and Change in Welfare States: Germany and Sweden in the 1990s," *Policy & Politics* 23(3), 1995, pp. 189–201.
82. Ibid.
83. *World Health Report 2000,* p. 23.
84. Swedish Statistical Reports 2000 (Stockholm), p. 79.
85. Ibid.
86. F. Diderichsen, E. Varde, and M. Whitehead, "Resource Allocation to Health Authorities: The Quest for an Equitable Formula in Britain and Sweden," *eBMJ,* Online, *http://www.bmj.com. cgi.content/full/315/7112/875?ijkey=/1f8u7.iAs4Yo.*
87. Ibid.
88. First facility to care for low-income and destitute citizens was the Pennsylvania General Hospital established in 1752. Treatment was limited and resources scarce, but local needy were afforded some sort of health care.
89. The birth of insurance in the United States began in 1847 with the Massachusetts Health Insurance Company. The company was the first company in the United States to offer sickness insurance to employed workers. Ironically, at this point in U.S. history support for a national insurance system was great as even President Theodore Roosevelt supported legislation to implement a system. It is important to mention that the American Medical Association joined Roosevelt in support for a national insurance system but later joined the growing movement (business, health care workers, insurance companies) to oppose such legislation.
90. A.S. Relman, "Physicians Have Contributed to a Health Care Crisis," in D. Bender and B. Leone (eds.), *Health Care in America* (San Diego: Greenhaven, 1994), pp. 65–69.

91. Among the Bush-era plans considered by Congress were the Comprehensive Health Care for All Americans Act, the National Health Insurance Act, the Mediplan Health Care Act of 1991, and the Universal Health Care Act of 1991.
92. Examples of such plans are the Affordable Health Insurance Act of 1991, the Comprehensive Health Care Access Improvement and Cost Containment Act of 1991, the Health Equity and Access Improvement Act of 1992, and the Comprehensive American Health Care Act.
93. K.J. Mueller, *Health Care Policy in the United States* (Lincoln: University of Nebraska Press, 1993), p. 77.
94. Ibid.
95. Health Care Financing Administrations, (HCFA) Office of the Actuary, Office of National Health Statistics 2000.
96. Ibid.
97. Ibid.

Chapter 11

1. A. Green, *Education and State Formation* (Basingstoke: MacMillan, 1990), chapter 1.
2. F. Hirsh, *Social Limits to Growth* (Cambridge, MA: Harvard University Press, 1976).
3. Green, *Education and State Formation,* chapter 3.
4. R. Schneider, "Brazil: Culture and Politics in a New Industrial Powerhouse," *The Economist,* October 18, 1997, vol. 345, no. 8039, pp. 17–18.
5. *IBGE, Annuario Estatistico do Brasil 2000* (Rio de Janeiro, 2000), p. 3.
6. Ibid., p. 11.
7. Ibid., p. 9.
8. Ibid., p. 8.
9. Ibid.
10. Ibid., p. 15.
11. *World Bank Statistical Indicators 1999.*
12. Ibid., pp. 1–7.
13. World Bank, *Brazil: A Poverty Assessment* (Washington, D.C.: World Bank, 1995), pp. 27–29.
14. As quoted in Nation Roundup, *The Economist,* July 1999, p. 7.
15. *World Bank 1999,* p. 3.
16. Ibid., p. 5.
17. *Annuario Estatistico 2000,* p. 10.
18. R. Schneider, "Brazil: Culture and Politics in a New Industrial Powerhouse."
19. R.K. Kolstad, D.R. Coker, and R.A. Kolstad, "Examining the Excellence of German Schools," *Education,* vol. 117, Dec. 1996.
20. Ibid.
21. In some states it's ten years.
22. F.C. Fowler, "What They Don't Tell Us About European Schools," *The Clearing House,* vol. 70, Sept. 1996, pp. 111–121.
23. P. Bauer-Kaase, "German Unification," in W. Hancock and H. Welsh (eds.), *German Unification Processes and Outcomes* (Boulder: Westview, 1994), p. 57.
24. V.D. Rust and D. Rust, "The Unification of German Education," in J. Clasen and R. Freeman (eds.), *Social Policy in Germany* (London: Harvester Wheatsheaf, 1994), pp. 73–79.
25. Ibid.
26. P. Bauer-Kaase, "German Unification," p. 58.
27. Rust and Rust, "The Unification of German Education."
28. Children with special-education needs attend secondary schools called *sonderschule.*
29. H. Flippo, *The German Way* (New York: Passport Books, 1997), p. 93.
30. See Article 30 of the Basic Law. In this article, the autonomy of the states in most educational and cultural matters is clearly established.
31. Flippo, *The German Way,* p. 71.
32. Ibid., p. 90.
33. The afternoon is devoted to extra homework.

34. *World Bank Statistical Indicators 1999.*
35. Ibid.
36. B. Coxall and L. Robins, *Contemporary British Politics* (London: MacMillan, 1998), p. 452.
37. In 1810, the Protestant non-conformists founded the Royal Lancastrian Association later known as the British and Foreign Society. In 1817, the Anglicans founded the National Society for the Education of the Poor in the principles of the established church.
38. P. Alcocks, *Social Policy in Britain: Themes and Issues* (London: MacMillan, 1996), p. 29.
39. Ibid., p. 93.
40. Nursery education was postponed until circumstances were right, universal provision of such education still being talked about today; many technical schools were never created because it was left to the direction of LEAs, the majority of which could not afford to develop them.
41. Both because of the Second World War.
42. Robbins Report of 1954, Crowther Report of 1959, and the Newsom Report of 1963.
43. Coxall and Robins, *British Politics Since the War,* p. 469.
44. Ibid., p. 471.
45. Core curriculum included English, math, science, and seven basic subjects covering history, geography, technology, art, music, physical education, and foreign languages.
46. *World Bank Statistical Indicators 1999,* p. 13.
47. J. Fallows, *Looking at the Sun: The Rise of the New Asian Economic and Political System* (New York: Pantheon, 1994); D. Lee Stevenson and D.P. Baker, "Shadow Education and Allocation in Formal Schooling," *American Journal of Sociology,* vol. 97, 1992, pp. 1639–1657.
48. E. Fowler, *Say 'Ya Blues: Laboring Life in Contemporary Tokyo* (Ithaca, NY: Cornell University Press, 1996); H. Ishida, *Social Mobility in Contemporary Japan* (Palo Alto: Stanford University Press, 1993).
49. H.R. Kepbo and J. McKinstry, *Who Rules Japan: The Inner Circles of Economic and Political Power* (Westport, CT: Greenwood/Praeger, 1995); C. Johnson, *Japan: Who Governs* (New York: Norton, 1995).
50. M. White, *The Japanese Educational System* (New York: Free Press, 1987) and *The Maternal Child Coming of Age in Japan & America* (New York: Free Press, 1993).
51. Ibid.
52. Three of the Imperial universities did admit women, and there were a number of women-only colleges; generally, however, women had few opportunities to enter higher education.
53. R.P. Dore argues such changes were radical; see R.P. Dore, "Textbook in Japan," in J. Livingstone, J. Moore, and F. Oldfather (eds.), *Postwar Japan: 1945 to the Present* (New York: Pantheon), p. 530.
54. The council suggested that eight specific subjects be considered: designing education for the twenty-first century; organizing a system of lifelong learning and reducing the emphasis on the educational background of individuals; improving and diversifying higher education; enriching and diversifying elementary and secondary education; improving the quality of teachers; adapting to internationalization; adapting to the information age; and conducting a review of the administration and finance of education. These subjects reflected both educational and social aspects of the reform, in keeping with the Japanese view about the relationship of education to society.
55. In 1996, the LDP pledged to work for an end to ministry of education selection of texts; however, on the eve of the 1996 October election the party had to withdraw its pledge due to conservative pressure.
56. Japanese Ministry of Education Statistical Brief (JMESB) (Tokyo, 1999).
57. Ibid.
58. Japan Institute for Social and Economic Affairs, *Japan, 1995, An International Comparison* (Tokyo: JISEA, 1995), p. 92.
59. Ibid.
60. Once enrolled, Japanese universities are not academically intense, curricula is not very demanding, and few go on to graduate school.
61. G. Miron, *Choice and Use of Market Forces: Swedish Education Reform for the 1990s* (Stockholm: Institute of International Education, 1993); T. Husen, "The Swedish School Reforms: Trends

and Issues," in A. Tjeldvoll (ed.), *Education and the Scandinavian Welfare State in the Year 2000* (New York: Garland, 1998).

62. For example Prime Minister Tage Erlander, Olof Palme, Ingvar Carlsson, and Alva Myrdal.
63. G. Richardson, *Drommen om en ny skola* (Stockholm: Liber, 1983), pp. 401–410.
64. S. Marklund, *The School System 1950–1975* (Stockholm: Liber, 1980), pp. 32–36.
65. G. Therbom, *What Does the Ruling Class Do When It Rules* (London: NLB, 1980), pp. 33–34; E.O. Wright, *Class Crisis and the State* (London: NLB, 1978), p. 123.
66. L. Alfredeon, "212 Fria Skolor i höst," *Dagens Nyheter,* 18 August 1993, p. 17.
67. Statistiska Centralbyrän (SC) (Stockholm: Statistisk årsolk, 1999), pp. 19–24.
68. Ibid.
69. Ibid.
70. Ibid.
71. Such as the National Agency for Education (Skolverket), the National Agency for Special Education, the county councils, and the municipals.
72. Although in 1997/98, two universities were put under non-state ownership (private foundations).
73. Miron, *Choice and Use of Market Forces;* and Husen, "The Swedish School Reforms."
74. C. Bullock, "Implementation of Equal Education Opportunity programs: A comparative analysis," in D.A. Mazmaman and P.A. Sabatier (eds.), *Effective Policy Implementation* (Lexington, MA: Lexington Books, 1981).
75. L. Bierlein, *Controversial Issues in Educational Policy* (Newbury Park, CA: Sage, 1993), p. 152.
76. Ibid., p. 147.
77. M.W. Kirst, *Who Controls Our Schools? American Values in Conflict* (New York: Freeman, 1984), pp. 30–35.
78. The number of high school students grew from 7 million in 1930 to over 16.5 million in 1941.
79. Bierlein, *Controversial Issues in Educational Policy,* p. 9.
80. Committee on Ways and Means, U.S. House of Representatives, *Overview of Entitlement Programs* (Washington, D.C.: USGPO, 1993), p. 1690.
81. Thomas Toch, *In the Name of Excellence* (New York: Oxford University Press, 1991).
82. Diane Ravatch, "The Coleman Reports and American Education," in A. Sovensen and S. Spilerman, *Social Theory and Societal Policy* (Westport, CT: Praeger, 1993), pp. 129–141.
83. Ibid.
84. J.W. Guth, W.I. Garms, and L.C. Pierce, *School Finance and Education Policy* (Englewood Cliffs, NJ: Prentice-Hall, 1988), pp. 89–93.
85. The report was *A Nation at Risk: The Imperative for Educational Reform.*
86. The Wingspread Group on Higher Education, *An American Imperative: Higher Expectations for Higher Education* (Racine, WI: The Johnson Foundation, 1993), p. 15.
87. Bierlein, *Controversial Issues,* p. 111.
88. Figures for 1998 projected from statistical abstract 1997, no. 233, p. 153.
89. For example, in 1992 New Jersey spent $10,562 per pupil, Arkansas $9,551, Utah $3,128, Mississippi $3,521.
90. A. Heidenheimer, H. Heclo, C. Adams, *Comparative Public Policy* (New York: St. Martin's Press, 1990), p. 31.

Chapter 12

1. A. Heidenheimer, H. Heclo, and C. Adams, *Comparative Public Policy,* p. 308.
2. OCED, 1991, p. 294.
3. H. McCormick, *The Global Environmental Movement* (London: Bellhaven Press, 1989), Introduction.
4. V. Bhaskar and A. Glyn, *The North The South: Ecological Constraints and the Global Economy* (Tokyo: United Nations Press, 1995), chapter 2.
5. Law no. 6. 938 passed August 31, 1981. Prior to this, pollution control and abatement were dealt with as early as the mid 1960s.
6. S. Kaufman Purcell and R. Roett (eds.), *Brazil Under Cardoso* (Boulder: Lynne Rienes, 1997), p. 73.

7. The states of São Paulo and Rio de Janeiro are already in the contracting phase of the multi-year Tietê River and Guanabana Bay cleanup projects, which will involve the purchase and installation of wastewater and sewage treatment systems for the two largest urban and industrial concentrations in Brazil, budgeted at 2.6 billion dollars and 800 million dollars respectively. The Tietê-Paraná waterway project, running through the most important grain-producing region and the largest industrial development area in Brazil (with a GDP of 250 billion dollars) has an environmental component of 200 million dollars, and an energy generation component, focusing on "alternative" sources, estimated at $4.2 billion. The states of Rio Grande do Sul, Bahia, Pernambuco, Paraná and Santa Catarina are also building sewage cleaning plants and installing or expanding sewage collection networks, with a total estimated budget of $700 million, financed primarily by the IDB. The states of Ceará, Pará and Amazonas have proposed sanitation projects for their capital cities to IDB, with a cost of about 300 million dollars.
8. The Basel Convention on Transboundary Movements of Hazardous Wastes, the Montreal Protocol on the Protection of the Ozone Layer, the Biodiversity and the Climate Change Conventions. The protocol and the conventions establish a number of obligations for state parties, ranging from a careful assessment of their internal situations in the specific problem areas addressed by each agreement—for instance, inventories of greenhouse gas emissions, or of CFC production and consumption—to the adoption of a series of measures for correcting problems where they exist.
9. In particular, in sulphur dioxide pollution.
10. Poll after poll ranked environmental protection with unemployment as top priorities for the German government to deal with.
11. It went into force in January 1993.
12. It went into force in 1996.
13. The target is to reduce by 25 percent from 1990 levels.
14. The new legislation on renewable energy builds on the "Act on the Sale of Electricity to the Grid" passed by all parties in the Bundestag in 1990. That law obliged operators of high-voltage grids to buy electricity generated from renewable sources of energy at a minimum price. Under the new legislation, grid operators will continue to be obliged to buy electricity from producers employing renewable energy sources, but, in contrast to past practice established in 1990, the minimum price will no longer be calculated as a percentage of the average electricity price. There will, instead, be set, cost-oriented rates that differentiate among energy sources. The new legislation also does away with the so-called five percent ceiling on support for renewable energy sources. The 1990 Act on the Sale of Electricity to the Grid stipulated that the special minimum price would no longer apply once renewable sources of energy accounted for more than five percent of total energy production.
15. Editorials, June 19, *Sued Deutsche,* p. 3.
16. M. Roberson, *The Greening of British Party Politics* (Manchester: Manchester University Press, 1992).
17. Clean Air Act of 1968.
18. A.C. Flynn and P. Lowe, "The Greening of the Tories: The Conservative Party and the Environment," in W. Rudig (ed.), *Green Politics Two* (Edinburgh: Edinburgh University Press, 1992).
19. Ibid.
20. CM 1200, *This Common Inheritance* (London: HMSO, 1990).
21. Tony Blair praised Conservative Environmental Minister John Gummer at the 1997 UN Earth Summit as one of the few conservatives to understand environmental issues.
22. *Quality of Life Counts: Indicators for a Strategy of Sustainable Development for the UK: A Baseline Assessment* (London: HMOS, Dec. 1999).
23. *Department of Environment Annual Report 2000* (London: HMOS, 2000).
24. Local authorities' emissions of smoke, dust, grit, odor, and noise.
25. *Department of Environment Annual Report 2000.*
26. N. Hiddle, M. Reich, N. Stiskin, *Island of Dreams: Environmental Crisis in Japan* (New York: Antom Press, 1975), pp. 7–11.

27. J. Gresser, J. Fujikura, and A. Morishma, *Environmental Law in Japan* (Cambridge: MIT Press, 1981), p. 5; M. Hashimoto, "The Japanese Experience of Tackling Pollution," *Japan Review of International Affairs,* vol. 7, no. 1, winter 1993.
28. S. Sano, "The Garbage Superpower," *Japan Echo,* 21 (Spring), pp. 19–25.
29. The debate was very vocal in 1993.
30. M. Gustafson, *From Biocides to Sustain Ability: Swedish Environmentalism 1962–1992* (Center for Housing and Urban Research, University of Örebro, Örebro, 1993); A. Jamison, "The Making of the New Environmentalism in Sweden," in A. Jamison, R. Eyerman, and J. Cramer (eds.), *The Making of the New Environmental Consciousness: A Comparative Study of the Environmental Movements in Sweden, Denmark and the Netherlands* (Edinburgh: Edinburgh University Press, 1990).
31. L.J. Lundquist, *Environmentalism and the Political Structure* (Lund: Prisma/Verdandidebatt, 1971), pp. 105 and 110.
32. A. Jamison, "How Sweden Tackles Pollution," *New Scientist,* Feb. 24, 1972, pp. 424–427.
33. Waste management plans were made compulsory in 1990, energy plans in 1991.
34. L. Lundquist, "Environmental Policy in Sweden: Organization, Instruments, Networks," in K. Hanf and A.-I. Jansen (eds.), *Comparative Research on Environmental Administration and Policy Making in Europe* (Lund: Prisma, 1998).
35. Ibid.
36. D. Rapp, "Special Report," *Congressional Quarterly Weekly Report* (Jan. 20, 1990).
37. For example, the 1933 Tennessee Valley Authority, the 1937 Social Conservative Service, and the Civilian Conservation Corps.
38. Such as Gorsuch Burford as the head of the EPA and James Watts as Secretary of the Interior. Bolter was openly hostile to a strong federal government role in the environment.
39. A. Gore, *Earth in the Balance: Ecology and the Human Spirit* (Boston: Houghton Mifflin, 1992).
40. J. Switzer, *Environmental Politics: Domestic and Global* (New York: St. Martin's Press, 1974), pp. 40–65.
41. M. Kraft, "Environmental Gridlock: Secondary for Consensus in Congress," in N.S. Vig and M.E. Kraft (eds.), *Environmental Policy in the 1990s* (Washington Quarterly Press, 1990).
42. Switzer, *Environmental Politics,* pp. 40–65.
43. Ibid.
44. E. Laverty, "Legacy of the 1980s in State Environmental Administration," in M.S. Hamilton (ed.), *Regulatory Federalism, National Resources, and Environmental Management* (Washington: American Society for Public Administration, 1990).
45. J.P. Lester, "A New Federalism," in N.J. Vig and M.E. Kraft (eds.), *Environmental Policy in the 1990s* (Washington Quarterly Press, 1990).
46. J.P. Hays, "The New Environmental West," *Journal of Policy History,* vol. 3, no. 3, 1991, pp. 223–248.

Endnotes Part Four

Chapter 13

1. M. Harrop, *Power and Policy in Liberal Democracies* (Cambridge: Cambridge University Press, 1992).
2. Ibid.
3. P. Abrahamson, "Welfare and Poverty in the Europe of the 1990s," *International Journal of Health Science,* 1991, vol. 21, no. 2, pp. 1113–1125.
4. F. Fukuyama, "The End of History," *The National Interest,* 1989, no. 16, pp. 3–19.
5. G. Esping-Andersen, "Regulation and Context, Reconsidering the Correlates of Unemployment," in G. Esping-Andersen (ed.), *Why Deregulate Labor Markets* (Oxford: Oxford University Press, 2000).
6. A. Pfaller, I. Gough, and G. Therbom, *Can the Welfare State Compete* (London: Macmillan, 1991); P. Saunders, "Public Expenditure and Economic Performance in GECD Countries," *Journal of Public Policy,* 1985, vol. 5, no. 1, pp. 1–21; G. Esping-Andersen, "Welfare States and

the Economy," in N. Smedser and R. Swedberg (eds.), *The Handbook of Economic Sociology* (Princeton: Princeton University Press, 1994).

7. Ibid.
8. G. Esping-Andersen, *Welfare States in Transition: National Adaptations in Global Economics* (Newbury Park: Sage, 1996), pp. 215–217.
9. M.I. Roemer, "The Countries," in *National Health Systems of the World,* vol. 1 (New York: Oxford University Press, 1991), p. 640.
10. Ibid.
11. *World Health Report 2000.*
12. A. Downs, *Political Theory and Public Choice* (Glasgow: Edward Elgar, 1998), essay #6.
13. Ibid.

Index